T0192743

Advanced Data Structures

Advanced Data Structures presents a comprehensive look at the ideas, analysis, and implementation details of data structures as a specialized topic in applied algorithms. This book examines efficient ways to realize query and update operations on sets of numbers, intervals, or strings by various data structures, including search trees, structures for sets of intervals or piecewise constant functions, orthogonal range search structures, heaps, union-find structures, dynamization and persistence of structures, structures for strings, and hash tables. Instead of relegating data structures to trivial material used to illustrate object-oriented programming methodology, this is the first volume to show data structures as a crucial algorithmic topic. Numerous code examples in C and more than 500 references make *Advanced Data Structures* an indispensable text.

PETER BRASS received a Ph.D. in mathematics at the Technical University of Braunschweig, Germany. He is an associate professor at the City College of New York in the Department of Computer Science and a former Heisenberg Research Fellow of the Free University of Berlin.

Advanced Data Structures

PETER BRASS

City College of New York

CAMBRIDGE
UNIVERSITY PRESS

CAMBRIDGE
UNIVERSITY PRESS

University Printing House, Cambridge CB2 8BS, United Kingdom

One Liberty Plaza, 20th Floor, New York, NY 10006, USA

477 Williamstown Road, Port Melbourne, VIC 3207, Australia

314-321, 3rd Floor, Plot 3, Splendor Forum, Jasola District Centre, New Delhi - 110025, India

79 Anson Road, #06-04/06, Singapore 079906

Cambridge University Press is part of the University of Cambridge.

It furthers the University's mission by disseminating knowledge in the pursuit of education, learning and research at the highest international levels of excellence.

www.cambridge.org
Information on this title: www.cambridge.org/9781108735513

First published 2008
First paperback edition 2019

A catalogue record for this publication is available from the British Library

Library of Congress Cataloging in Publication data
Brass, Peter.
Advanced data structures / Peter Brass.
p. cm.
Includes bibliographical references and index.
ISBN 978-0-521-88037-4 (hardback)
1. Computer algorithms. I. Title.
QA76.9.A43B73 2008
005.1–dc22 2008021408

ISBN 978-0-521-88037-4 Hardback
ISBN 978-1-108-73551-3 Paperback

Dedicated to my parents,
Gisela and Helmut Brass

Contents

Preface

This book is a graduate-level textbook on data structures. A data structure is a method[1] to realize a set of operations on some data. The classical example is to keep track of a set of items, the items identified by key values, so that we can insert and delete (key, item) pairs into the set and find the item with a given key value. A structure supporting these operations is called a dictionary. Dictionaries can be realized in many different ways, with different complexity bounds and various additional operations supported, and indeed many kinds of dictionaries have been proposed and analyzed in literature, and some will be studied in this book.

In general, a data structure is a kind of higher-level instruction in a virtual machine: when an algorithm needs to execute some operations many times, it is reasonable to identify what exactly the needed operations are and how they can be realized in the most efficient way. This is the basic question of data structures: given a set of operations whose intended behavior is known, how should we realize that behavior?

There is no lack of books carrying the words "data structures" in the title, but they merely scratch the surface of the topic, providing only the trivial structures stack and queue, and then some balanced search tree with a large amount of handwaving. Data structures started receiving serious interest in the 1970s, and, in the first half of the 1980s, almost every issue of the *Communications of the ACM* contained a data structure paper. They were considered a central topic, received their own classification in the *Computing Subject Classification*,[2]

---

[1] This is not a book on object-oriented programming. I use the words "method" and "object" in their normal sense.

[2] Classification code: E.1 data structures. Unfortunately, the *Computing Subject Classification* is too rough to be useful.

and became a standard part of computer science curricula.[3] Wirth titled a book *Data Structures + Algorithms = Programs*, and *Algorithms and Data Structures* became a generic textbook title. But the only monograph on an algorithmic aspect of data structures is the book by Overmars (1983) (which is still in print, a kind of record for an LNCS series book). Data structures received attention in a number of application areas, foremost as index structures in databases. In this context, structures for geometric data have been studied in the monographs of Samet (1990, 2006); the same structures were studied in the computer graphics context in Langetepe and Zachmann (2006). Recently, motivated by bioinformatics applications, string data structures have been much studied. There is a steady stream of publications on data structure theory as part of computational geometry or combinatorial optimization. But in the numerous textbooks, data structures are only viewed as an example application of object-oriented programming, excluding the algorithmic questions of how to really do something nontrivial, with bounds on the worst-case complexity. It is the aim of this book to bring the focus back to data structures as a fundamental subtopic of algorithms. The recently published *Handbook of Data Structures* (Mehta and Sahni 2005) is a step in the same direction.

This book contains real code for many of the data structures we discuss and enough information to implement most of the data structures where we do not provide an implementation. Many textbooks avoid the details, which is one reason that the structures are not used in the places where they should be used. The selection of structures treated in this book is therefore restricted almost everywhere to such structures that work in the pointer-machine model, with the exception of hash tables, which are included for their practical importance. The code is intended as illustration, not as ready-to-use plug-in code; there is certainly no guarantee of correctness. Most of it is available with a minimal testing environment on my homepage.

This book started out as notes for a course I gave in the 2000 winter semester at the Free University Berlin; I thank Christian Knauer, who was my assistant for that course: we both learned a lot. I offered this course again in the fall semesters of 2004–7 as a graduate course at the City College of New York and used it as a base for a summer school on data structures at the Korean Advanced Institute of Science and Technology in July 2006. I finished this book in November 2007.

---

[3] ABET still lists them as one of five core topics: algorithms, data structures, software design, programming languages, and computer architecture.

I thank Emily Voytek and Günter Rote for finding errors in my code examples, Otfried Cheong for organizing the summer school at KAIST, and the summer school's participants for finding further errors. I thank Christian Knauer and Helmut Brass for literature from excellent mathematical libraries at the Free University Berlin and Technical University Braunschweig, and János Pach for access to the online journals subscribed by the Courant Institute. A project like this book would not have been possible without access to good libraries, and I tried to cite only those papers that I have seen.

This book project has not been supported by any grant-giving agency.

Basic Concepts

A data structure models some abstract object. It implements a number of operations on this object, which usually can be classified into

– creation and deletion operations,
– update operations, and
– query operations.

In the case of the dictionary, we want to create or delete the set itself, update the set by inserting or deleting elements, and query for the existence of an element in the set.

Once it has been created, the object is changed by the update operations. The query operations do not change the abstract object, although they might change the representation of the object in the data structure: this is called an adaptive data structure – it adapts to the query to answer future similar queries faster.

Data structures that allow updates and queries are called dynamic data structures. There are also simpler structures that are created just once for some given object and allow queries but no updates; these are called static data structures. Dynamic data structures are preferable because they are more general, but we also need to discuss static structures because they are useful as building blocks for dynamic structures, and, for some of the more complex objects we encounter, no dynamic structure is known.

We want to find data structures that realize a given abstract object and are fast. The size of structures is another quality measure, but it is usually of less importance. To express speed, we need a measure of comparison; this is the size of the underlying object, not our representation of that object. Notice that a long sequence of update operations can still result in a small object. Our usual complexity measure is the worst-case complexity; so an operation in a specific data structure has a complexity $O(f(n))$ if, for any state of the data structure reached by a sequence of update operations that produced an object of size n, this operation takes at most time $Cf(n)$ for some C. An alternative but weaker measure is the amortized complexity; an update operation has amortized complexity $O(f(n))$ if there is some function $g(n)$ such that any sequence of m of these operations, during which the size of the underlying object is never larger than n, takes at most time $g(n) + mCf(n)$, so in the average over a long sequence of operations the complexity is bounded by $Cf(n)$.

Some structures are randomized, so the data structure makes some random choices, and the same object and sequence of operations do not always lead to the same steps of the data structure. In that case we analyze the expected complexity of an operation. This expectation is over the random choices of the data structure; the complexity is still the worst case of that expectation over all objects of that size and possible operations.

In some situations, we cannot expect a nontrivial complexity bound of type $O(f(n))$ because the operation might give a large answer. The size of the answer is the output complexity of the operation, and, for operations that sometimes have a large output complexity, we are interested in output-sensitive methods, which are fast when the output is small. An operation has output-sensitive complexity $O(f(n) + k)$ if, on an object of size n that requires an output of size k, the operation takes at most time $C(f(n) + k)$.

For dynamic data structures, the time to create the structure for an empty object is usually constant, so we are mainly interested in the update and query times. The time to delete a structure of size n is almost always $O(n)$. For static data structures we already create an object of size n, so there we are interested in the creation time, known as preprocessing time, and the query time.

In this book, $\log_a n$ denotes the logarithm to base a; if no base is specified, we use base 2.

We use the Bourbaki-style notation for closed, half-open, and open intervals, where $[a, b]$ is the closed interval from a to b, $]a, b[$ is the open interval, and the half-open intervals are $]a, b]$, missing the first point, and $[a, b[$, missing the last point.

Similar to the $O(\cdot)$-notation for upper bounds mentioned earlier, we also use the $\Omega(\cdot)$ for lower bounds and $\Theta(\cdot)$ for simultaneous upper and lower bounds. A nonnegative function f is $O(g(n))$, or $\Omega(g(n))$, if for some positive C and all sufficiently large n holds $f(n) \leq Cg(n)$, or $f(n) \geq Cg(n)$, respectively. And f is $\Theta(g(n))$ if it is simultaneously $O(g(n))$ and $\Omega(g(n))$. Here "sufficiently large" means that $g(n)$ needs to be defined and positive.

Code Examples

The code examples in this book are given in standard C. For the readers used to some other imperative programming language, most constructs are self-explanatory.

In the code examples, = denotes the assignment and == the equality test. Outside the code examples, we will continue to use = in the normal way.

The Boolean operators for "not," "and," "or" are !, &&, | |, respectively, and % denotes the modulo operator.

Pointers are dereferenced with *, so if pt is a pointer to a memory location (usually a variable), then *pt is that memory location. Pointers have a type to determine how the content of that memory location should be interpreted. To declare a pointer, one declares the type of the memory location it points to, so "int *pt;" declares pt to be a pointer to an int. Pointers are themselves variables; they can be assigned, and it is also possible to add integers to a pointer (pointer arithmetic). If pt points to a memory object of a certain type, then pt+1 points to the next memory location for an object of that type; this is equivalent to treating the memory as a big array of objects of that type. NULL is a pointer that does not point to any valid memory object, so it can be used as a special mark in comparisons.

Structures are user-defined data types that have several components. The components themselves have a type and a name, and they can be of any type, including other structures. The structure cannot have itself as a type of a component, because that would generate an unbounded recursion. But it can have a pointer to an object of its own type as component; indeed, such structures are the main tool of data structure theory. A variable whose type is a structure can be assigned and used like any other variable. If z is a variable of type C, and we define this type by

```
typedef struct { float x; float y; } C,
```

then the components of z are z.x and z.y, which are two variables of type float. If zpt is declared as pointer to an object of type C (by C *zpt;), then the components of the object that zpt points to are (*zpt).x and (*zpt).y. Because this is a frequently used combination, dereferencing a pointer and selecting a component, there is an alternative notation zpt->x and zpt->y. This is equivalent, but preferable, because it avoids the operator priority problem: dereferencing has lower priority than component selection, so (*zpt).x is not the same as *zpt.x.

We avoid writing the functions recursively, although in some cases this might simplify the code. But the overhead of a recursive function call is significant and thus conflicts with the general aim of highest efficiency in data structures. We do not practice any similar restrictions for nonrecursive functions; a good compiler will expand them as inline functions, avoiding the function call, or they could be written as macro functions.

In the text we will also frequently use the name of a pointer for the object to which it points.

1

Elementary Structures

Elementary data structures usually treated in the "Programming 2" class are the *stack* and the *queue*. They have a common generalization, the *double-ended queue*, which is also occasionally mentioned, although it has far fewer applications. Stack and queue are very fundamental structures, so they will be discussed in detail and used to illustrate several points in data structure implementation.

1.1 Stack

The stack is the simplest of all structures, with an obvious interpretation: putting objects on the stack and taking them off again, with access possible only to the top item. For this reason they are sometimes also described as LIFO storage: last in, first out. Stacks occur in programming wherever we have nested blocks, local variables, recursive definitions, or backtracking. Typical programming exercises that involve a stack are the evaluation of arithmetic expressions with parentheses and operator priorities, or search in a labyrinth with backtracking.

The stack should support at least the following operations:

– push (obj) : Put obj on the stack, making it the top item.
– pop () : Return the top object from the stack and remove it from the stack.
– stack_empty () : Test whether the stack is empty.

Also, the realization of the stack has, of course, to give the right values, so we need to specify the correct behavior of a stack. One method would be an algebraic specification of what correct sequences of operations and return values are. This has been done for simple structures like the stack, but even then the specification is not very helpful in understanding the structure. Instead, we can describe a canonical implementation on an idealized machine, which gives the correct answer for all correct sequences of operations (no pop on an

1

empty stack, no memory problems caused by bounded arrays). Assuming that the elements we want to store on the stack are of type item_t, this could look as follows:

```
int i=0;
item_t stack[∞];

int stack_empty(void)
{   return( i == 0 );
}

void push( item_t x)
{   stack[i++] = x ;
}

item_t pop(void)
{   return( stack[ --i] );
}
```

This describes the correct working of the stack, but we have the problem of assuming both an infinite array and that any sequence of operations will be correct. A more realistic version might be the following:

```
int i=0;
item_t stack[MAXSIZE];

int stack_empty(void)
{   return( i == 0 );
}

int push( item_t x)
{   if ( i < MAXSIZE )
    {   stack[i++] = x ;   return( 0 );
    }
    else
        return( -1 );
}

item_t pop(void)
{   return( stack[ --i] );
}
```

This now limits the correct behavior of the stack by limiting the maximum number of items on the stack at one time, so it is not really the correct stack we want, but at least it does specify an error message in the return value if the stack overflow is reached by one push too many. This is a fundamental defect of array-based realizations of data structures: they are of fixed size, the size needs to be decided in advance, and the structure needs the full size no matter how many items are really in the structure. There is a systematic way to overcome these problems for array-based structures, which we will see in Section 1.5, but usually a solution with dynamically allocated memory is preferable.

We specified an error value only for the stack overflow condition, but not for the stack underflow, because the stack overflow is an error generated by the structure, which would not be present in an ideal implementation, whereas a stack underflow is an error in the use of the structure and so a result in the program that uses the stack as a black box. Also, this allows us to keep the return value of pop as the top object from the stack; if we wanted to catch stack underflow errors in the stack implementation, we would need to return the object and the error status. A final consideration in our first stack version is that we might need multiple stacks in the same program, so we want to create the stacks dynamically. For this we need additional operations to create and remove a stack, and each stack operation needs to specify which stack it operates on. One possible implementation could be the following:

```
typedef struct {item_t *base; item_t *top;
                int size;} stack_t;

stack_t *create_stack(int size)
{   stack_t *st;
    st = (stack_t *) malloc( sizeof(stack_t) );
    st->base = (item_t *) malloc( size *
                sizeof(item_t) );
    st->size = size;
    st->top = st->base;
    return( st );
}

int stack_empty(stack_t *st)
{   return( st->base == st->top );
}
```

```
int push( item_t x,  stack_t *st)
{   if ( st->top < st->base + st->size )
    { *(st->top) = x; st->top += 1; return( 0 );
    }
    else
        return( -1 );
}


item_t pop(stack_t *st)
{   st->top -= 1;
    return( *(st->top) );
}


item_t top_element(stack_t *st)
{   return( *(st->top -1) );
}


void remove_stack(stack_t *st)
{   free( st->base );
    free( st );
}
```

Again, we include some security checks and leave out others. Our policy in general is to include those security checks that test for errors introduced by the limitations of this implementation as opposed to an ideal stack, but to assume both that the use of the stack is correct and that the underlying operating system never runs out of memory. We included another operation that is frequently useful, which just returns the value of the top element without taking it from the stack.

Frequently, the preferable implementation of the stack is a dynamically allocated structure using a linked list, where we insert and delete in front of the list. This has the advantage that the structure is not of fixed size; therefore, we need not be prepared for stack overflow errors if we can assume that the memory of the computer is unbounded, and so we can always get a new node. It is as simple as the array-based structure if we already have the get_node and return_node functions, whose correct implementation we discuss in Section 1.4.

```
typedef struct st_t { item_t       item;
                      struct st_t *next; } stack_t;
```

```
stack_t *create_stack(void)
{    stack_t *st;
     st = get_node();
     st->next = NULL;
     return( st );
}

int stack_empty(stack_t *st)
{    return( st->next == NULL );
}

void push( item_t x, stack_t *st)
{    stack_t *tmp;
     tmp = get_node();
     tmp->item = x;
     tmp->next = st->next;
     st->next = tmp;
}

item_t pop(stack_t *st)
{    stack_t *tmp; item_t tmp_item;
     tmp = st->next;
     st->next = tmp->next;
     tmp_item = tmp->item;
     return_node( tmp );
     return( tmp_item );
}

item_t top_element(stack_t *st)
{    return( st->next->item );
}

void remove_stack(stack_t *st)
{    stack_t *tmp;
     do
     {  tmp = st->next;
        return_node(st);
        st = tmp;
     }
     while ( tmp != NULL );
}
```

Notice that we have a placeholder node in front of the linked list; even an empty stack is represented by a list with one node, and the top of the stack is only the second node of the list. This is necessary as the stack identifier returned by `create_stack` and used in all stack operations should not be changed by the stack operations. So we cannot just use a pointer to the start of the linked list as a stack identifier. Because the components of a node will be invalid after it is returned, we need temporary copies of the necessary values in `pop` and `remove_stack`. The operation `remove_stack` should return all the remaining nodes; there is no reason to assume that only empty stacks will be removed, and we will suffer a memory leak if we fail to return the remaining nodes.

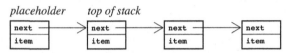

STACK REALIZED AS LIST, WITH THREE ITEMS

The implementation as a dynamically allocated structure always has the advantage of greater elegance; it avoids stack overflow conditions and needs just the memory proportional to the actually used items, not a big array of a size estimated by the programmer as upper bound to the maximum use expected to occur. One disadvantage is a possible decrease in speed: dereferencing a pointer does not take longer than incrementing an index, but the memory location accessed by the pointer might be anywhere in memory, whereas the next component of the array will be near the previous component. Thus, array-based structures usually work very well with the cache, whereas dynamically allocated structures might generate many cache misses. So if we are quite certain about the maximum possible size of the stack, for example, because its size is only logarithmic in the size of the input, we will prefer an array-based version.

If one wants to combine these advantages, one could use a linked list of blocks, each block containing an array, but when the array becomes full, we just link it to a new node with a new array. Such an implementation could look as follows:

```
typedef struct st_t { item_t *base;
                      item_t  *top;
                      int      size;
                      struct st_t *previous;} stack_t;

stack_t *create_stack(int size)
{   stack_t *st;
    st = (stack_t *) malloc( sizeof(stack_t) );
    st->base = (item_t *) malloc( size *
               sizeof(item_t) );
    st->size = size;
    st->top = st->base;
```

```
        st->previous = NULL;
        return( st );
}

int stack_empty(stack_t *st)
{   return( st->base == st->top &&
            st->previous == NULL);
}

void push( item_t x, stack_t *st)
{   if ( st->top < st->base + st->size )
    {   *(st->top) = x; st->top += 1;
    }
    else
    {   stack_t *new;
        new = (stack_t *) malloc( sizeof(stack_t) );
        new->base = st->base;
        new->top = st->top;
        new->size = st->size;
        new->previous = st->previous;
        st->previous = new;
        st->base = (item_t *) malloc( st->size *
                    sizeof(item_t) );
        st->top = st->base+1;
        *(st->base) = x;
    }
}

item_t pop(stack_t *st)
{   if( st->top == st->base )
    {   stack_t *old;
        old = st->previous;
        st->previous = old->previous;
        free( st->base );
        st->base = old->base;
        st->top = old->top;
        st->size = old->size;
        free( old );
    }
    st->top -= 1;
    return( *(st->top) );
}

item_t top_element(stack_t *st)
{   if( st->top == st->base )
        return( *(st->previous->top -1) );
```

```
        else
           return( *(st->top -1) );
    }

    void remove_stack(stack_t *st)
    {    stack_t *tmp;
         do
         {  tmp = st->previous;
            free( st->base );
            free( st );
            st = tmp;
         }
         while( st != NULL );
    }
```

In our classification, push and pop are update operations and stack_empty and top_element are query operations. In the array-based implementation, it is obvious that we can do all the operations in constant time as they involve only a constant number of elementary operations. For the linked-list implementation, the operations involve the external get_node and return_node functions, which occur in both push and pop once, so the implementation works only in constant time if we can assume these functions to be constant-time operations. We will discuss the implementation of this dynamic node allocation in Section 1.4, but we can assume here (and in all later structures) that this works in constant time. For the block list we allocate large parts of memory for which we used here the standard memory management operations malloc and free instead of building an intermediate layer, as described in Section 1.4. It is traditional to assume that memory allocation and deallocation are constant-time operations, but especially with the free there are nontrivial problems with a constant-time implementation, so one should avoid using it frequently. This could happen in the block list variant if there are many push/pop pairs that just go over a block boundary. So the small advantage of the block list is probably not worth the additional problems.

The create_stack operation involves only one such memory allocation, and so that should be constant time in each implementation; but the remove_stack operation is clearly not constant time, because it has to destroy a potentially large structure. If the stack still contains n elements, the remove_stack operation will take time $O(n)$.

1.2 Queue

The queue is a structure almost as simple as the stack; it also stores items, but it differs from the stack in that it returns those items first that have been entered first, so it is FIFO storage (first in, first out). Queues are useful if there are tasks that have to be processed cyclically. Also, they are a central structure in breadth-first search; breadth-first search (BFS) and depth-first search (DFS) really differ only in that BFS uses a queue and DFS uses a stack to store the node that will be explored next.

The queue should support at least the following operations:

– enqueue (obj) : Insert obj at the end of the queue, making it the last item.
– dequeue () : Return the first object from the queue and remove it from the queue.
– queue_empty () : Test whether the queue is empty.

The difference between queue and stack that makes the queue slightly more difficult is that the changes occur at both ends: at one end, there are inserts; at the other, deletes. If we choose an array-based implementation for the queue, then the part of the array that is in use moves through the array. If we had an infinite array, this would present no problem. We could write it as follows:

```
int lower=0; int upper=0;
item_t queue[∞];

int queue_empty(void)
{   return( lower == upper );
}

void enqueue( item_t x)
{   queue[upper++] = x ;
}

item_t dequeue(void)
{   return( queue[ lower++] );
}
```

A real implementation with a finite array has to wrap this around, using index calculation modulo the length of the array. It could look as follows:

```
typedef struct {item_t *base;
                int     front;
                int     rear;
                int     size;} queue_t;
```

```
queue_t *create_queue(int size)
{   queue_t *qu;
    qu = (queue_t *) malloc( sizeof(queue_t) );
    qu->base = (item_t *) malloc( size *
                sizeof(item_t) );
    qu->size = size;
    qu->front = qu->rear = 0;
    return( qu );
}


int queue_empty(queue_t *qu)
{   return( qu->front == qu->rear );
}


int enqueue( item_t x, queue_t *qu)
{   if ( qu->front != ((qu->rear +2)% qu->size) )
    {   qu->base[qu->rear] = x;
        qu->rear = ((qu->rear+1)%qu->size);
        return( 0 );
    }
    else
        return( -1 );
}


item_t dequeue(queue_t *qu)
{   int tmp;
    tmp = qu->front;
    qu->front = ((qu->front +1)%qu->size);
    return( qu->base[tmp] );
}


item_t front_element(queue_t *qu)
{   return( qu->base[qu->front] );
}


void remove_queue(queue_t *qu)
{   free( qu->base );
    free( qu );
}
```

Again this has the fundamental disadvantage of any array-based structure –
that it is of fixed size. So it possibly generates overflow errors and does not
implement the structure correctly as it limits it this way. In addition, it always
reserves this expected maximum size for the array, even if it never needs it. The
preferred alternative is a dynamically allocated structure, with a linked list. The
obvious solution is the following:

```
typedef struct qu_n_t {item_t     item;
                   struct qu_n_t *next; } qu_node_t;
typedef struct {qu_node_t *remove;
                   qu_node_t *insert; } queue_t;

queue_t *create_queue()
{    queue_t *qu;
     qu = (queue_t *) malloc( sizeof(queue_t) );
     qu->remove = qu->insert = NULL;
     return( qu );
}

int queue_empty(queue_t *qu)
{    return( qu->insert ==NULL );
}

void enqueue( item_t x, queue_t *qu)
{    qu_node_t *tmp;
     tmp = get_node();
     tmp->item = x;
     tmp->next = NULL; /* end marker */
     if ( qu->insert != NULL ) /* queue nonempty */
     {    qu->insert->next = tmp;
          qu->insert = tmp;
     }
     else /* insert in empty queue */
     {    qu->remove = qu->insert = tmp;
     }
}

item_t dequeue(queue_t *qu)
{    qu_node_t *tmp; item_t tmp_item;
     tmp = qu->remove; tmp_item = tmp->item;
     qu->remove = tmp->next;
     if( qu->remove == NULL ) /* reached end */
          qu->insert = NULL; /* make queue empty */
     return_node(tmp);
```

```
        return( tmp_item );
    }

    item_t front_element(queue_t *qu)
    {   return( qu->remove->item );
    }

    void remove_queue(queue_t *qu)
    {   qu_node_t *tmp;
        while( qu->remove != NULL)
        { tmp = qu->remove;
          qu->remove = tmp->next;
          return_node(tmp);
        }
        free( qu );
    }
```

Again we assume, as in all dynamically allocated structures, that the operations get_node and return_node are available, which always work correctly and in constant time. Because we want to remove items from the front of the queue, the pointers in the linked list are oriented from the front to the end, where we insert items. There are two aesthetical disadvantages of this obvious implementation: we need a special entry point structure, which is different from the list nodes, and we always need to treat the operations involving an empty queue differently. For insertions into an empty queue and removal of the last element of the queue, we need to change both insertion and removal pointers; for all other operations we change only one of them.

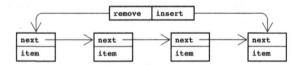

QUEUE REALIZED AS LIST, WITH FOUR ITEMS

The first disadvantage can be avoided by joining the list together to make it a cyclic list, with the last pointer from the end of the queue pointing again to the beginning. We can then do without a removal pointer, because the insertion point's next component points to the removal point. By this, the entry point to the queue needs only one pointer, so it is of the same type as the queue nodes.

The second disadvantage can be overcome by inserting a placeholder node in that cyclic list, between the insertion end and the removal end of the cyclic list. The entry point still points to the insertion end or, in the case of an empty list, to that placeholder node. Then, at least for the insert, the empty list is no longer a special case. So a cyclic list version is the following:

```
typedef struct qu_t { item_t   item;
                      struct qu_t *next; } queue_t;

queue_t *create_queue()
{   queue_t *entrypoint, *placeholder;
    entrypoint = (queue_t *) malloc( sizeof(queue_t) );
    placeholder = (queue_t *) malloc( sizeof(queue_t) );
    entrypoint->next = placeholder;
    placeholder->next = placeholder;
    return( entrypoint );
}

int queue_empty(queue_t *qu)
{   return( qu->next == qu->next->next );
}

void enqueue( item_t x, queue_t *qu)
{   queue_t *tmp, *new;
    new = get_node(); new->item = x;
    tmp = qu->next; qu->next = new;
    new->next = tmp->next; tmp->next = new;
}

item_t dequeue(queue_t *qu)
{   queue_t     *tmp;
    item_t  tmp_item;
    tmp = qu->next->next->next;
    qu->next->next->next = tmp->next;
    if( tmp == qu->next )
       qu->next = tmp->next;
    tmp_item = tmp->item;
    return_node( tmp );
    return( tmp_item );
}

item_t front_element(queue_t *qu)
{   return( qu->next->next->next->item );
}

void remove_queue(queue_t *qu)
{   queue_t *tmp;
    tmp = qu->next->next;
    while( tmp != qu->next )
    { qu->next->next = tmp->next;
      return_node( tmp );
```

```
        tmp = qu->next->next;
    }
    return_node( qu->next );
    return_node( qu );
}
```

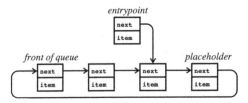

QUEUE REALIZED AS CYCLIC LIST, WITH THREE ITEMS

Or one could implement the queue as a doubly linked list, which requires no case distinctions at all but needs two pointers per node. Minimizing the number of pointers is an aesthetic criterion more justified by the amount of work that has to be done in each step to keep the structure consistent than by the amount of memory necessary for the structure. Here is a doubly linked list implementation:

```
typedef struct qu_t { item_t       item;
                  struct qu_t    *next;
                  struct qu_t *previous; } queue_t;

queue_t *create_queue()
{   queue_t *entrypoint;
    entrypoint = (queue_t *) malloc( sizeof(queue_t) );
    entrypoint->next = entrypoint;
    entrypoint->previous = entrypoint;
    return( entrypoint );
}

int queue_empty(queue_t *qu)
{   return( qu->next == qu );
}

void enqueue( item_t x, queue_t *qu)
{   queue_t *new;
    new = get_node(); new->item = x;
    new->next = qu->next; qu->next = new;
    new->next->previous = new; new->previous = qu;
}

item_t dequeue(queue_t *qu)
{   queue_t *tmp; item_t tmp_item;
    tmp = qu->previous; tmp_item = tmp->item;
```

```
    tmp->previous->next = qu;
    qu->previous = tmp->previous;
    return_node( tmp );
    return( tmp_item );
}

item_t front_element(queue_t *qu)
{   return( qu->previous->item );
}

void remove_queue(queue_t *qu)
{   queue_t *tmp;
    qu->previous->next = NULL;
    do
    { tmp = qu->next;
      return_node( qu );
      qu = tmp;
    }
    while ( qu != NULL );

}
```

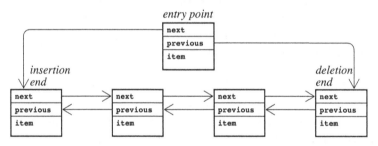

QUEUE REALIZED AS DOUBLY LINKED LIST, WITH FOUR ITEMS

Which of the list-based implementations one prefers is really a matter of taste; they are all slightly more complicated than the stack, although the two structures look similar.

Like the stack, the queue is a dynamic data structure that has the update operations enqueue and dequeue and the query operations queue_empty and front_element, all of which are constant-time operations, and the operations create_queue and delete_queue, which are subject to the same restrictions as the similar operations for the stack: creating an array-based queue requires getting a big block of memory from the underlying system memory management, whereas creating a list-based queue should require only some get_node operations; and deleting an array-based queue just involves returning that memory block to the system, whereas deleting a list-based queue requires returning every individual node still contained in it, so it will take $O(n)$ time to delete a list-based queue that still contains n items.

1.3 Double-Ended Queue

The double-ended queue is the obvious common generalization of stack and queue: a queue in which one can insert and delete at either end. Its implementation can be done as an array, or as a doubly linked list, just like a queue; because it does not present any new problems, no code will be given here. The double-ended queue does not have many applications, but at least a "one-and-a-half ended queue" sometimes is useful, as in the minqueue discussed in Section 5.11.

1.4 Dynamical Allocation of Nodes

In the previous sections we used the operations `get_node` and `return_node` to dynamically create and delete nodes, that is, constant-sized memory objects, as opposed to the generic operations `malloc` and `free` provided by the standard operating-system interface, which we used only for memory objects of arbitrary, usually large, size. The reason for this distinction is that although the operating-system memory allocation is ultimately the only way to get memory, it is a complicated process, and it is not even immediately obvious that it is a constant-time operation. In any efficient implementation of a dynamically allocated structure, where we permanently get and return nodes, we cannot afford to access this operating-system-level memory management in each operation. Instead, we introduce an intermediate layer, which only occasionally has to access the operating-system memory management to get a large memory block, which it then gives out and receives back in small, constant-sized pieces, the nodes.

The efficiency of these `get_node` and `return_node` operations is really crucial for any dynamically allocated structure, but luckily we do not have to create a full memory management system; there are two essential simplifications. We deal only with objects of one size, as opposed to the `malloc` interface, which should provide memory blocks of any size, and we do not return any memory from the intermediate level to the system before the program ends. This is reasonable: the amount of memory taken by the intermediate layer from the system is the maximum amount taken by the data structure up to that moment, so we do not overestimate the total memory requirement; we only fail to free it earlier for other coexisting programs or structures.

This allows us to use the *free list* as a structure for our dynamical allocation of nodes. The free list contains all the nodes not currently in use; whenever a return_node is executed, the node is just added to the free list. For the get_node, the situation is slightly more complicated; if the free list is not empty, we may just take a node from there. If it is empty and the current memory block is not used up, we take a new node from that memory block. Otherwise, we have to get a new memory block with malloc and create the node from there.

An implementation could look as follows:

```
typedef struct nd_t { struct nd_t *next;
                /*and other components*/  } node_t;
#define BLOCKSIZE 256
node_t *currentblock = NULL;
int    size_left;
node_t *free_list = NULL;

node_t *get_node()
{ node_t *tmp;
  if( free_list != NULL )
  {  tmp = free_list;
     free_list = free_list -> next;
  }
  else
  {  if( currentblock == NULL || size_left == 0)
     {  currentblock =
                (node_t *) malloc( BLOCKSIZE *
                            sizeof(node_t) );
        size_left = BLOCKSIZE;
     }
     tmp = currentblock++;
     size_left -= 1;
  }
  return( tmp );
}

void return_node(node_t *node)
{  node->next = free_list;
   free_list = node;
}
```

Dynamical memory allocation is traditionally a source of many programming errors and is hard to debug. A simple additional precaution to avoid some common errors is to add to the node another component, int valid, and fill it with different values, depending on whether it has just been received back by return_node or is given out by get_node. Then we can check that a pointer does indeed point to a valid node and that anything received by return_node has indeed been a valid node up to that moment.

1.5 Shadow Copies of Array-Based Structures

There is a systematic way to avoid the maximum-size problem of array-based structures at the expense of the simplicity of these structures. We simultaneously maintain two copies of the structure, the currently active copy and a larger-sized structure which is under construction. We have to schedule the construction of the larger structure in such a way that it is finished and ready for use before the active copy reaches its maximum size. For this, we copy in each operation on the old structure a fixed number of items from the old to the new structure. When the content of the old structure is completely copied into the new, larger structure, the old structure is removed and the new structure taken as the active structure and, when necessary, construction of an even larger copy is begun. This sounds very simple and introduces only a constant overhead to convert a fixed-size structure into an unlimited structure. There are, however, some problems in the details: the structure that is being copied changes while the copying is in progress, and these changes must be correctly done in the still incomplete larger copy. To demonstrate the principle, here is the code for the array-based stack:

```
typedef struct { item_t  *base;
                 int       size;
                 int   max_size;
                 item_t  *copy;
                 int copy_size; }    stack_t;

stack_t *create_stack(int size)
{   stack_t *st;
    st = (stack_t *) malloc( sizeof(stack_t) );
    st->base = (item_t *) malloc( size *
            sizeof(item_t) );
    st->max_size = size;
    st->size = 0; st->copy = NULL; st->copy_size = 0;
    return( st );
}
```

```
int stack_empty(stack_t *st)
{   return( st->size == 0);
}

void push( item_t x, stack_t *st)
{   *(st->base + st->size) = x;
    st->size += 1;
    if ( st->copy != NULL ||
    st->size >= 0.75*st->max_size )
    { /* have to continue or start copying */
        int additional_copies = 4;
        if( st->copy == NULL )
        /* start copying: allocate space */
        { st->copy =
          (item_t *) malloc( 2 * st->max_size *
           sizeof(item_t) );
        }
        /* continue copying: at most 4 items
           per push operation */
        while( additional_copies > 0 &&
                st->copy_size < st->size )
        { *(st->copy + st->copy_size) =
                        *(st->base + st->copy_size);
            st->copy_size += 1; additional_copies -= 1;
        }
        if( st->copy_size == st->size)
        /* copy complete */
        { free( st->base );
            st->base = st-> copy;
            st->max_size *= 2;
            st->copy = NULL;
            st->copy_size = 0;
        }
    }
}

item_t pop(stack_t *st)
{   item_t tmp_item;
    st->size -= 1;
    tmp_item = *(st->base + st->size);
    if( st->copy_size == st->size) /* copy complete */
    { free( st->base );
        st->base = st-> copy;
        st->max_size *= 2;
        st->copy = NULL;
        st->copy_size = 0;
    }
```

```
        return( tmp_item );
}

item_t top_element(stack_t *st)
{    return( *(st->base + st->size - 1) );
}

void remove_stack(stack_t *st)
{    free( st->base );
     if( st->copy != NULL )
         free( st->copy );
     free( st );
}
```

For the stack, the situation is especially easy because we can just copy from the base until we reach the current top; in between, nothing changes. The threshold when to start copying (here, at 0.75*size), the size of the new structure (here, twice the previous size), and the number of items copied in each step (here, four items) must, of course, be chosen in such a way that copying is complete before the old structure overflows. Note that we can reach the situation when the copying is finished in two ways: by actual copying in the push and by deleting uncopied items in the pop.

In general, the connection between copying threshold size, new maximum size, and number of items copied is as follows:

– if the current structure has maximum size s_{max},
– and we begin copying as soon as its actual size has reached αs_{max} (with $\alpha \geq \frac{1}{2}$),
– the new structure has maximum size $2s_{max}$, and
– each operation increases the actual size by at most 1,

then there are at least $(1 - \alpha)s_{max}$ steps left to complete the copying of at most s_{max} elements from the smaller structure to the new structure. So we need to copy $\lceil \frac{1}{1-\alpha} \rceil$ elements in each operation to finish the copying before the smaller structure overflows. We doubled the maximum size when creating the new structure, but we could have chosen any size βs_{max}, $\beta > 1$, as long as $\alpha\beta > 1$. Otherwise, we would have to start copying again before the previous copying process was finished.

In principle, this technique is quite general and not restricted to array-based structures. We will use it again in Sections 3.6 and 7.1. We can always try to overcome the size limitation of a fixed-size structure by copying its content to a larger structure. But it is not always clear how to break this copying into many small steps that can be executed simultaneously with the normal operations on the structure, as in our example. Instead, we have to copy the entire structure in one step, so we cannot get a worst-case time bound, but only an amortized bound.

A final example of this technique and its difficulties is the realization of an extendible array. Normal arrays need to be declared of a fixed size, they are allocated somewhere in memory, and the space that is reserved there cannot be increased as it might conflict with space allocated for other variables. Access to an array element is very fast; it is just one address computation. But some systems also support a different type of array, which can be made larger; for these, accessing an element is more complicated and it is really an operation of a nontrivial data structure. This structure needs to support the following operations:

- create_array creates an array of a given size,
- set_value assigns the array element at a given index a value,
- get_value returns the value of the array element at a given index,
- extend_array increases the length of the array.

To implement that structure, we use the same technique of building shadow copies. There is, however, an additional problem here, because the structure we want to model does not just grow by a single item in each operation; the extend_array operation can make it much larger a single operation. Still, we can easily achieve an amortized constant time per operation.

When an array of size s is created, we allocate space for it, but more than requested. We maintain that the size of the arrays we actually allocate is always a power of 2, so we initially allocate an array of size $2^{\lceil \log s \rceil}$ and store the start position of that array, as well as the current and the maximum size, in a structure that identifies the array. Any access to an array element first has to look up that start position of the current array. Each time an extend_array operation is performed, we first check whether the current maximum size is larger than the requested size; in that case we can just increase the current size. Else, we have to allocate a new array whose size is the next number 2^k larger than the requested size, and copy every item from the old array to the new array. Thus, accessing an array element is always done in $O(1)$ time; it is just one in the direction of the pointer; but extending the array can take linear time in the size of the array. But the amortized complexity is not that bad; if the ultimate size of the array is $2^{\lceil \log k \rceil}$, then we have at worst copied arrays of size $1, 2, 4, \ldots, 2^{\lceil \log k \rceil - 1}$, so we spent in total time $O(1 + 2 + \cdots + 2^{\lceil \log k \rceil - 1}) = O(k)$ with those extend_array operations that did copy the array, and $O(1)$

with each `extend_array` operation that did not copy the array. Thus, we have the following complexity:

Theorem. An extendible array structure with shadow copies performs any sequence of n `set_value`, `get_value`, and `extend_array` operations on an array whose final size is k in time $O(n + k)$.

If we assume that each element of the array we request is also accessed at least once, so that the final size is at most the number of element access operations, this gives an amortized $O(1)$ complexity per operation.

It would be natural to distribute the copying of the elements again over the later access operations, but we have no control over the `extend_array` operations. It is possible that the next extension is requested before the copying of the current array is complete, so our previous method does not work for this structure. Another conceptual problem with extendible arrays is that pointers to array elements are different from normal pointers because the position of the array can change. Thus, in general, extendible arrays should be avoided even if the language supports them. A different way to implement extendible arrays was discussed in Challab (1991).

2

Search Trees

A search tree is a structure that stores objects, each object identified by a key value, in a tree structure. The key values of the objects are from a linearly ordered set (typically integers); two keys can be compared in constant time and these comparisons are used to guide the access to a specific object by its key. The tree has a root, where any search starts, and then contains in each node some key value for comparison with the query key, so one can go to different next nodes depending on whether the query key is smaller or larger than the key in the node until one finds a node that contains the right key.

This type of tree structure is fundamental to most data structures; it allows many variations and is also a building block for most more complex data structures. For this reason we will discuss it in great detail.

Search trees are one method to implement the abstract structure called dictionary. A dictionary is a structure that stores objects, identified by keys, and supports the operations find, insert, and delete. A search tree usually supports at least these operations of a dictionary, but there are also other ways to implement a dictionary, and there are applications of search trees that are not primarily dictionaries.

2.1 Two Models of Search Trees

In the outline just given, we supressed an important point that at first seems trivial, but indeed it leads to two different models of search trees, either of which can be combined with much of the following material, but one of which is strongly preferable.

If we compare in each node the query key with the key contained in the node and follow the left branch if the query key is smaller and the right branch

if the query key is larger, then what happens if they are equal? The two models
of search trees are as follows:

1. Take left branch if query key is smaller than node key; otherwise take the
   right branch, until you reach a leaf of the tree. The keys in the interior node
   of the tree are only for comparison; all the objects are in the leaves.
2. Take left branch if query key is smaller than node key; take the right branch
   if the query key is larger than the node key; and take the object contained
   in the node if they are equal.

This minor point has a number of consequences:

– In model 1, the underlying tree is a binary tree, whereas in model 2, each
  tree node is really a ternary node with a special middle neighbor.
– In model 1, each interior node has a left and a right subtree (each possibly a
  leaf node of the tree), whereas in model 2, we have to allow incomplete
  nodes, where left or right subtree might be missing, and only the
  comparison object and key are guaranteed to exist.

So the structure of a search tree of model 1 is more regular than that of a tree
of model 2; this is, at least for the implementation, a clear advantage.

– In model 1, traversing an interior node requires only one comparison,
  whereas in model 2, we need two comparisons to check the three
  possibilities.

Indeed, trees of the same height in models 1 and 2 contain at most approximately
the same number of objects, but one needs twice as many comparisons in model
2 to reach the deepest objects of the tree. Of course, in model 2, there are also
some objects that are reached much earlier; the object in the root is found
with only two comparisons, but almost all objects are on or near the deepest
level.

Theorem. A tree of height h and model 1 contains at most 2^h objects.
    A tree of height h and model 2 contains at most $2^{h+1} - 1$ objects.

This is easily seen because the tree of height h has as left and right subtrees a
tree of height at most $h - 1$ each, and in model 2 one additional object between
them.

– In model 1, keys in interior nodes serve only for comparisons and may
  reappear in the leaves for the identification of the objects. In model 2, each
  key appears only once, together with its object.

It is even possible in model 1 that there are keys used for comparison that do not belong to any object, for example, if the object has been deleted. By conceptually separating these functions of comparison and identification, this is not surprising, and in later structures we might even need to define artificial tests not corresponding to any object, just to get a good division of the search space. All keys used for comparison are necessarily distinct because in a model 1 tree, each interior node has nonempty left and right subtrees. So each key occurs at most twice, once as comparison key and once as identification key in the leaf.

Model 2 became the preferred textbook version because in most textbooks the distinction between object and its key is not made: the key is the object. Then it becomes unnatural to duplicate the key in the tree structure. But in all real applications, the distinction between key and object is quite important. One almost never wishes to keep track of just a set of numbers; the numbers are normally associated with some further information, which is often much larger than the key itself.

In some literature, where this distinction is made, trees of model 1 are called leaf trees and trees of model 2 are called node trees (Nievergelt and Wong 1973). Our preferred model of search tree is model 1, and we will use it for all structures but the splay tree (which necessarily follows model 2).

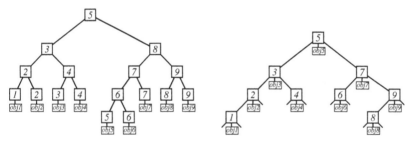

SEARCH TREES OF MODEL 1 AND MODEL 2

A tree of model 1 consists of nodes of the following structure:

```
typedef struct tr_n_t {key_t        key;
                struct tr_n_t   *left;
                struct tr_n_t   *right;
        /* possibly additional information */
                } tree_node_t;
```

We will usually need some additional balancing information, which will be discussed in Chapter 3. So this is just an outline.

From nodes of this type, we will construct a tree essentially by the following recursive definition: each tree is either empty, or a leaf, or it contains a special root node that points to two nonempty trees, with all keys in the left subtree being smaller than the key in the root and all keys in the right subtree being larger than or equal to the key in the root. This still needs some details; especially we have to specify how to recognize leaves. We will follow here the following convention:

– A node *n is a leaf if n->right = NULL. Then n->left points to the object stored in that leaf and n->key contains the object's key.

We also need some conventions for the root, especially to deal with empty trees. Each tree has a special node *root.

– If root->left = NULL, then the tree is empty.
– If root->left ≠ NULL and root->right = NULL, then root is a leaf and the tree contains only one object.
– If root->left ≠ NULL and root->right ≠ NULL, then root->right and root->left point to the roots of the right and left subtrees. For each node *left_node in the left subtree, we have left_node->key < root->key, and for each node *right_node in the right subtree, we have right_node->key ≥ root->key.

Any structure with these properties is a correct search tree for the objects and key values in the leaves.

With these conventions we can now create an empty tree.

```
tree_node_t *create_tree(void)
{   tree_node_t *tmp_node;
    tmp_node = get_node();
    tmp_node->left = NULL;
    return( tmp_node );
}
```

2.2 General Properties and Transformations

In a correct search tree, we can associate each tree node with an interval, the interval of possible key values that can be reached through this node. The interval of root is $]-\infty, \infty[$, and if *n is an interior node associated with interval $[a, b[$, then n->key $\in [a, b[$, and n->left and n->right have as associated intervals $[a, $ n->key$[$ and $[$n->key$, b[$. With the exception of the intervals starting in $-\infty$, all these intervals are half-open, containing the left endpoint but not the right endpoint. This implicit structure on the tree nodes is very helpful in understanding the operations on the trees.

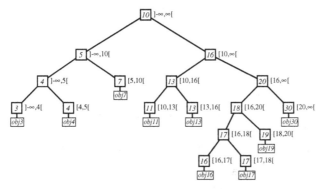

INTERVALS ASSOCIATED WITH NODES IN A SEARCH TREE

The same set of (key, object) pairs can be organized in many distinct correct search trees: the leaves are always the same, containing the (key, object) pairs in increasing order of the keys, but the tree connecting the leaves can be very different, and we will see that some trees are better than others. There are two operations – the left and right rotations – that transform a correct search tree in a different correct search tree for the same set. They are used as building blocks of more complex tree transformations because they are easy to implement and universal.

Suppose *n is an interior node of the tree and n->right is also an interior node. Then the three nodes n->left, n->right->left, and n->right->right have consecutive associated intervals whose union is the associated interval of *n. Now instead of grouping the second and third intervals (of n->right->left and n->right->right) together in node n->right, and then this union together with the interval of n->left in *n, we could group the first two intervals together in a new node, and that then together with the last interval in *n. This is what the left rotation does: it rearranges three nodes below a given node *n, the rotation center. This is a local change done in constant time; it does not affect either the content of those three nodes or anything below them or above the rotation center *n. The following code does a left rotation around *n:

```
void left_rotation(tree_node_t *n)
{   tree_node_t *tmp_node;
    key_t        tmp_key;
    tmp_node = n->left;
    tmp_key  = n->key;
    n->left  = n->right;
```

```
    n->key    = n->right->key;
    n->right  = n->left->right;
    n->left->right = n->left->left;
    n->left->left  = tmp_node;
    n->left->key   = tmp_key;
}
```

Note that we move the content of the nodes around, but the node *n still needs to be the root of the subtree because there are pointers from higher levels in the tree that point to *n. If the nodes contain additional information, then this must, of course, also be updated or copied.

The right rotation is exactly the inverse operation of the left rotation.

```
void right_rotation(tree_node_t *n)
{   tree_node_t *tmp_node;
    key_t          tmp_key;
    tmp_node = n->right;
    tmp_key  = n->key;
    n->right = n->left;
    n->key   = n->left->key;
    n->left  = n->right->left;
    n->right->left = n->right->right;
    n->right->right  = tmp_node;
    n->right->key    = tmp_key;
}
```

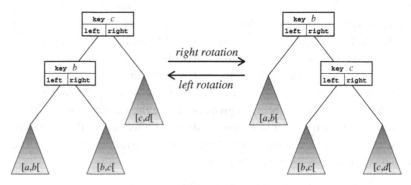

LEFT AND RIGHT ROTATIONS

Theorem. The left and right rotations around the same node are inverse operations. Left and right rotations are operations that transform a correct search tree in a different correct search tree for the same set of (key, object) pairs.

The great usefulness of the rotations as building blocks for tree operations lies in the fact that they are universal: any correct search tree for some set of (key, object) pairs can be transformed into any other correct search tree by a sequence of rotations. But one needs to be careful with the exact statement of this property because it is obviously false: in our model of search trees, we can change the key values in the interior nodes without destroying the search tree property as long as the order relation of the comparison keys with the object keys stays the same. But the rotations, of course, do not change the key values. The important structure is the combinatorial type of the tree; any system of comparison keys is transformed correctly together with the tree.

Theorem. Any two combinatorial types of search trees on the same system of (key, object) pairs can be transformed into each other by a sequence of rotations.

But this is easy to see: if we apply right rotations to the search tree as long as any right rotation can be applied, we get a degenerate tree, a path going to the right, to which the leaves are attached in increasing order. So any search tree can be brought into this canonical shape using only right rotations. Because right and left rotations are inverse, this canonical shape can be transformed into any shape by a sequence of left rotations.

The space of combinatorial types of search trees, that is, of binary trees with n leaves, is isomorphic to a number of other structures (a Catalan family). The rotations define a distance on this structure, which has been studied in a number of papers (Culik and Wood 1982; Mäkinen 1988; Sleator, Tarjan, and Thurston 1988; Luccio and Pagli 1989); the diameter of this space is known to be $2n - 6$ for $n \geq 11$ (Sleator et al. 1988). The difficult part here is the exact value of the lower bound; it is simple to prove just $\Theta(n)$ bounds (see, e.g., Felsner 2004, Section 7.5).

2.3 Height of a Search Tree

The central property which distinguishes the different combinatorial types of search trees for the same underlying set and which makes some search trees good and others bad is the height. The height of a search tree is the maximum length of a path from the root to a leaf – the maximum taken over all leaves. Usually not all leaves are at the same distance from the root; the distance of a specific tree node from the root is called the depth of that node. As already observed in Section 2.1, the maximum number of leaves of a search tree of height h is 2^h. And at the other end, the minimum number of leaves is $h + 1$

because a tree of height h must have at least one interior node at each depth $0, \ldots, h - 1$, and a tree with h interior nodes has $h + 1$ leaves. Together, this gives the bounds.

Theorem. A search tree for n objects has height at least $\lceil \log n \rceil$ and at most $n - 1$.

It is easy to see that both bounds can be reached.

The height is the worst-case distance we have to traverse to reach a specific object in the search tree. Another related measure of quality of a search tree is the average depth of the leaves, that is, the average over all objects of the distance we have to go to reach that object. Here the bounds are:

Theorem. A search tree for n objects has average depth at least $\log n$ and at most $\frac{(n-1)(n+2)}{2n} \approx \frac{1}{2}n$.

To prove these bounds, it is easier to take the sum of the depths instead of the average depth. Because the sum of depths can be divided in the depth of the a leaves to the left of the root and the depth of the b leaves to the right of the root, these sums satisfy the following recursions:

$$depthsum^{\min}(n) = n + \min_{\substack{a,b \geq 1 \\ a+b=n}} depthsum^{\min}(a) + depthsum^{\min}(b)$$

and

$$depthsum^{\max}(n) = n + \max_{\substack{a,b \geq 1 \\ a+b=n}} depthsum^{\max}(a) + depthsum^{\max}(b);$$

with these recursions, one obtains

$$depthsum^{\min}(n) \geq n \log n$$

and

$$depthsum^{\max}(n) = \frac{1}{2}(n - 1)(n + 2)$$

by induction. In the first case, one uses that the function $x \log x$ is convex, so $a \log a + b \log b \geq (a + b) \log (a + b)/2$.

2.4 Basic Find, Insert, and Delete

The search tree represents a set of (key, object) pairs, so it must allow some operations with this set. The most important operations that any search tree needs to support are as follows:

- find (tree, query_key): Returns the object associated with query_key, if there is one;
- insert (tree, key, object): Inserts the (key, object) pair in the tree; and
- delete (tree, key): Deletes the object associated with key from the tree.

We will now describe here the basic find, insert, and delete operations on the search trees, which will be extended in Chapter 3 by some rebalancing steps. The simplest operation is the find: one just follows the associated interval structure to the leaf, which is the only place that could hold the right object. Then one tests whether the key of this only possible candidate agrees with the query key, in which case we found the object, or not, in which case there is no object for that key in the tree.

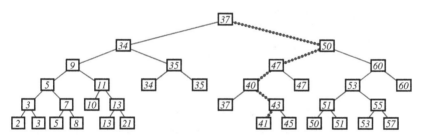

SEARCH TREE AND SEARCH PATH FOR UNSUCCESSFUL find(tree, 42)

```
object_t *find(tree_node_t *tree,
               key_t query_key)
{  tree_node_t *tmp_node;
   if( tree->left == NULL )
     return(NULL);
   else
   {  tmp_node = tree;
      while( tmp_node->right != NULL )
      {   if( query_key < tmp_node->key )
              tmp_node = tmp_node->left;
```

```
              else
                   tmp_node = tmp_node->right;
         }
         if( tmp_node->key == query_key )
            return( (object_t *) tmp_node->left );
         else
            return( NULL );
      }
   }
```

The descent through the tree to the correct level is frequently written as recursive function, but we avoid recursion in our code. Even with good compilers, a function call is much slower than a few assignments. Just as illustration we also give here the recursive version.

```
object_t *find(tree_node_t *tree,
                key_t query_key)
{   if( tree->left == NULL ||
       (tree->right == NULL &&
        tree->key != query_key ) )
       return(NULL);
    else if (tree->right == NULL &&
             tree->key == query_key )
       return( (object_t *) tree->left );
    else
    {   if( query_key < tree->key )
           return( find(tree->left, query_key) );
        else
           return( find(tree->right, query_key) );
    }
}
```

The insert operation starts out the same as the find, but after it finds the correct place to insert the new object, it has to create a new interior node and a new leaf node and put them in the tree. We assume, as always, that there are functions get_node and return_node available, as described in Section 1.4. For the moment we assume all the keys are unique and treat it as an error if there is already an object with that key in the tree; but in many practical applications we need to deal with multiple objects of the same key (see Section 2.6).

```
int insert(tree_node_t *tree, key_t new_key,
           object_t *new_object)
{  tree_node_t *tmp_node;
   if( tree->left == NULL )
   {  tree->left = (tree_node_t *) new_object;
      tree->key  = new_key;
      tree->right  = NULL;
   }
   else
   {  tmp_node = tree;
      while( tmp_node->right != NULL )
      {   if( new_key < tmp_node->key )
              tmp_node = tmp_node->left;
          else
              tmp_node = tmp_node->right;
      }
      /* found the candidate leaf. Test whether
         key distinct */
      if( tmp_node->key == new_key )
         return( -1 );
      /* key is distinct, now perform the insert */
      {  tree_node_t *old_leaf, *new_leaf;
         old_leaf = get_node();
         old_leaf->left = tmp_node->left;
         old_leaf->key = tmp_node->key;
         old_leaf->right  = NULL;
         new_leaf = get_node();
         new_leaf->left = (tree_node_t *)
         new_object;
         new_leaf->key = new_key;
         new_leaf->right  = NULL;
         if( tmp_node->key < new_key )
         {   tmp_node->left  = old_leaf;
             tmp_node->right = new_leaf;
             tmp_node->key = new_key;
         }
         else
         {   tmp_node->left  = new_leaf;
             tmp_node->right = old_leaf;
         }
      }
   }
   return( 0 );
}
```

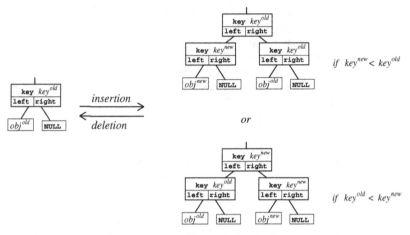

INSERTION AND DELETION OF A LEAF

The delete operation is even more complicated because when we are deleting a leaf, we must also delete an interior node above the leaf. For this, we need to keep track of the current node and its upper neighbor while going down in the tree. Also, this operation can lead to an error if there is no object with the given key.

```
object_t *delete(tree_node_t *tree,
                 key_t delete_key)
{  tree_node_t *tmp_node, *upper_node,
   *other_node;
   object_t *deleted_object;
   if( tree->left == NULL )
      return( NULL );
   else if( tree->right == NULL )
   {  if( tree->key == delete_key )
      {  deleted_object =
                     (object_t *) tree->left;
         tree->left = NULL;
         return( deleted_object );
      }
      else
         return( NULL );
   }
   else
   {  tmp_node = tree;
```

```
    while( tmp_node->right != NULL )
    {   upper_node = tmp_node;
        if( delete_key < tmp_node->key )
        {   tmp_node    = upper_node->left;
            other_node = upper_node->right;
        }
        else
        {   tmp_node    = upper_node->right;
            other_node = upper_node->left;
        }
    }
    if( tmp_node->key != delete_key )
        return( NULL );
    else
    {   upper_node->key    = other_node->key;
        upper_node->left   = other_node->left;
        upper_node->right = other_node->right;
        deleted_object = (object_t *)
        tmp_node->left;
        return_node( tmp_node );
        return_node( other_node );
        return( deleted_object );
    }
  }
}
```

If there is additional information in the nodes, it must also be copied or updated when we copy the content of the other_node into the upper_node. Note that we delete the nodes, but not the object itself. There might be other references to this object. But if this is the only reference to the object, this will cause a memory leak, so we should delete the object. This is the responsibility of the user, so we return a pointer to the object.

2.5 Returning from Leaf to Root

Any tree operation starts at the root and then follows the path down to the leaf where the relevant object is or where some change is performed. In all the balanced search-tree versions we will discuss in Chapter 3, we need to return along this path, from the leaf to the root, to perform some update or rebalancing operations on the nodes of this path. And these operations need to be done in that order, with the leaf first and the root last. But without additional measures, the basic search-tree structure we described does not contain any way to reconstruct this sequence. There are several possibilities to save this information.

1. A stack: If we push pointers to all traversed nodes on a stack during descent to the leaf, then we can take the nodes from the stack in the correct (reversed) sequence afterward. This is the cleanest solution under the criterion of information economy; it does not put any additional information into the tree structure. Also, the maximum size of the stack needed is the height of the tree, and so for the balanced search trees, it is logarithmic in the size of the search tree. An array-based stack for 200 items is really enough for all realistic applications because we will never have 2^{100} items. This is also the solution implicitly used in any recursive implementation of the search trees.

2. Back pointers: If each node contains not only the pointers to the left and right subtrees, but also a pointer to the node above it, then we have a path up from any node back to the root. This requires an additional field in each node. As additional memory requirement, this is usually no problem because memory is now large. But this pointer also has to be corrected in each operation, which makes it again a source of possible programming errors.

3. Back pointer with lazy update: If we have in each node an entry for the pointer to the node above it, but we actually enter the correct value only during descent in the tree, then we have a correct path from the leaf we just reached to the root. We do not need to correct the back pointers during all operations on the tree, but then the back pointer field can only be assumed to be correct for the nodes on the path along which we just reached the leaf.

Any of these methods will do and can be combined with any of the balancing techniques. Another method that requires more care in its combination with various balancing techniques is the following:

4. Reversing the path: We can keep back pointers for the path even without an extra entry for a back pointer in each node by reversing the forward pointers as we go down the tree. While going down in each node, if we go left, the left pointer is used as back pointer and if we go right, the right pointer is used as back pointer. When we go up again, the correct forward pointers must be restored.

This method does not use any extra space, so it found interest when space limitations were an important concern. In the early years of data structures, methods to work with trees without space for either back pointers or a stack have been studied in a number of papers (Lindstrom 1973; Robson 1973; Dwyer 1974; Burkhard 1975; Clark 1975; Soule 1977; Morris 1979; Chen 1986; Chen and Schott 1996). But this method causes many additional problems because the search-tree structure is temporarily destroyed. Space is now almost never a problem, so we list this method only for completeness, but advise against its use.

2.6 Dealing with Nonunique Keys

In practical applications, it is not uncommon that there are several objects with the same key. In database applications, we might have to store many objects with the same key value; there it is a quite unrealistic assumption that each object is uniquely identified by each of its attribute values, but there are queries to list all objects with a given attribute value. So any realistic search tree has to deal with this situation. The correct reaction is as follows:

- find returns all objects whose key is the given query key in output-sensitive time $O(h + k)$, where h is the height of the tree and k is the number of elements that find returns.
- insert always inserts correctly in time $O(h)$, where h is the height of the tree.
- delete deletes all items of that key in time $O(h)$, where h is the height of the tree.

The obvious way to realize this behavior is to keep all elements of the same key in a linked list below the corresponding leaf of the search tree. Then find just produces all elements of that list; insert always inserts at the beginning of the list; only delete in time independent of the number of deleted items requires additional information. For this, we need an additional node between the leaf and the linked list, which contains pointers to the beginning and to the end of the list; then we can transfer the entire list with $O(1)$ operations to the free list of our dynamic memory allocation structure. Again, this way we only delete the references to the objects contained in this tree. If we need to delete the objects themselves, we can do it by walking along this list, but not in $O(1)$ time independent of the number of objects.

2.7 Queries for the Keys in an Interval

Up to now we have discussed only the query operation find, which, for a given key, retrieves the associated object. Frequently, a more general type of query is useful, in which we give a key interval $[a, b[$ and want to find all keys that are contained in this interval. If the keys are subject to small errors, we might not know the key exactly, so we want the nearest key value or the next larger or next smaller key. Without such an extension, our find operation just answers that there is no object with the given key in the current set, which is correct but not helpful.

There are other types of dictionary structures, which we will discuss in Chapter 9 on hash tables that cannot support this type of query. But for search trees, it is a very minor modification, which can be done in several ways.

1. We can organize the leaves into a doubly linked list and then we can move in $O(1)$ time from a leaf to the next larger and the next smaller leaf. This requires a change in the insertion and deletion functions to maintain the list, but it is an easy change that takes only $O(1)$ additional time. The query method is also almost the same; it takes $O(k)$ additional time if it lists a total of k keys in the interval.

2. An alternative method does not change the tree structure at all but changes the query function: we go down the tree with the query interval instead of the query key. Then we go left if $[a, b[<$ node->key; right if node->key $\leq [a, b[$; and sometimes we have to go both left and right if $a <$ node->key $\leq b$. We store all those branches that we still need to explore on a stack. The nodes we visit this way are the nodes on the search path for the beginning of the query interval a, the search path for its end b, and all nodes that are in the tree between these paths. If there are i interior nodes between these paths, there must be at least $i + 1$ leaves between these paths. So if this method lists k leaves, the total number of nodes visited is at most twice the number of nodes visited in a normal find operation plus $O(k)$. Thus, this method is slightly slower than the first method but requires no change in the insert and delete operations.

Next we give code for the stack-based implementation of interval_find. To illustrate the principle, we write here just the generic stack operations; these need, of course, to be filled in. The output of the operation is potentially long, so we need to return many objects instead of a single result. For this, we create a linked list of the (key, object) pairs found in the query interval, which is linked here by the right pointers. After use of the results, the nodes of this list need to be returned to avoid a memory leak.

```
tree_node_t *interval_find(tree_node_t *tree,
                            key_t a, key_t b)
{  tree_node_t *tr_node;
   tree_node_t *result_list, *tmp;
   result_list = NULL;
   create_stack();
   push(tree);
   while( !stack_empty() )
   {  tr_node = pop();
      if( tr_node->right == NULL )
      {  /* reached leaf, now test */
         if( a <= tr_node->key &&
             tr_node->key < b )
         {  tmp = get_node();
            /* leaf key in interval */
            tmp->key  = tr_node->key; /*
            copy to output list */
            tmp->left = tr_node->left;
            tmp->right = result_list;
            result_list = tmp;
         }
      } /* not leaf, might have to follow down */
      else if ( b <= tr_node->key )
      /* entire interval left */
         push( tr_node->left );
      else if ( tr_node->key <= a )
      /* entire interval right */
         push( tr_node->right );
      else    /* node key in interval,
                 follow left and right */
      {  push( tr_node->left );
         push( tr_node->right );
      }
   }
   remove_stack();
   return( result_list );
}
```

Listing the keys in an interval is a one-dimensional range query. Higher-dimensional range queries will be discussed in Chapter 4. In general, a range query gives some set, the range, of a specific type, here intervals, and asks for all (key, object) pairs whose key lies in that range. For more complex ranges, such as rectangles, circles, halfplanes, and boxes, this is an important type of query.

2.8 Building Optimal Search Trees

Occasionally it is useful to construct an optimal search tree from a given set of (key, object) pairs. This can be viewed as taking search trees as static data structure: there are no inserts and deletes, so there is no problem of rebalancing the tree, but if we build it, knowing the data in advance, then we should build it as good as possible. The primary criterion is the height; because a search tree of height h has at most 2^h leaves, an optimal search tree for a set of n items has height $\lceil \log n \rceil$, where the log, as always, is taken to base 2.

We assume that the (key, object) pairs are given in a sorted list, ordered with increasing keys. There are two natural ways to construct a search tree of optimal height from a sorted list: bottom-up and top-down.

The bottom-up construction is easier: one views the initial list as list of one-element trees. Then one goes repeatedly through the list, joining two consecutive trees, until there is only one tree left. This requires only a bit of bookkeeping to insert the correct comparison key in each interior node. The disadvantage of this method is that the resulting tree, although of optimal height, might be quite unbalanced: if we start with a set of $n = 2^m + 1$ items, then the root of the tree has on one side a subtree of 2^m items and on the other side a subtree of 1 item.

Next is the code for the bottom-up construction. We assume here that the list items are themselves of type tree_node_t, with the left entry pointing to the object, the key containing the object key, and the right entry pointing to the next item, or NULL at the end of the list. We first create a list, where all the nodes of the previous list are attached as leaves, and then maintain a list of trees, where the key value in the list is the smallest key value in the tree below it.

```
tree_node_t *make_tree(tree_node_t *list)
{  tree_node_t *end, *root;
   if( list == NULL )
   {  root = get_node(); /* create empty tree */
      root->left = root->right = NULL;
      return( root );
   }
```

```
else if( list->right == NULL )
   return( list ); /* one-leaf tree */
else /* nontrivial work required: at least
        two nodes */
{  root = end = get_node();
   /* convert input list into leaves below
      new list */
   end->left = list;
   end->key = list->key;
   list = list->right;
   end->left->right = NULL;
   while( list != NULL )
   {  end->right = get_node();
      end = end->right;
      end->left = list;
      end->key = list->key;
      list = list->right;
      end->left->right = NULL;
   }
   end->right = NULL;
   /* end creating list of leaves */
   {  tree_node_t *old_list, *new_list, *tmp1,
                  *tmp2;
      old_list = root;
      while( old_list->right != NULL )
      {  /* join first two trees from
             old_list */
         tmp1 = old_list;
         tmp2 = old_list->right;
         old_list = old_list->right->right;
         tmp2->right = tmp2->left;
         tmp2->left  = tmp1->left;
         tmp1->left  = tmp2;
         tmp1->right = NULL;
         new_list = end = tmp1;
         /* new_list started */
         while( old_list != NULL )
         /* not at end */
         {  if( old_list->right == NULL )
```

```
                 /* last tree */
                 {  end->right = old_list;
                    old_list = NULL;
                 }
                 else /* join next two trees of
                         old_list */
                 {  tmp1 = old_list;
                    tmp2 = old_list->right;
                    old_list =
                          old_list-> right->right;
                    tmp2->right = tmp2->left;
                    tmp2->left  = tmp1->left;
                    tmp1->left  = tmp2;
                    tmp1->right = NULL;
                    end->right  = tmp1;
                    end =   end->right;
                 }
              } /* finished one pass through
                   old_list */
              old_list = new_list;
           } /* end joining pairs of trees
                together */
           root = old_list->left;
           return_node( old_list );
        }
     return( root );
  }
}
```

Theorem. The bottom-up method constructs a search tree of optimal height from an ordered list in time $O(n)$.

The first half of the algorithm, duplicating the list and converting all the original list nodes to leaves, takes obviously $O(n)$; it is just one loop over the length of the list. The second half has a more complicated structure, but in each execution of the body of the innermost loop, one of the n interior nodes created in the first half is removed from the current list and put into a finished subtree, so the innermost part of the two nested loops is executed only n times.

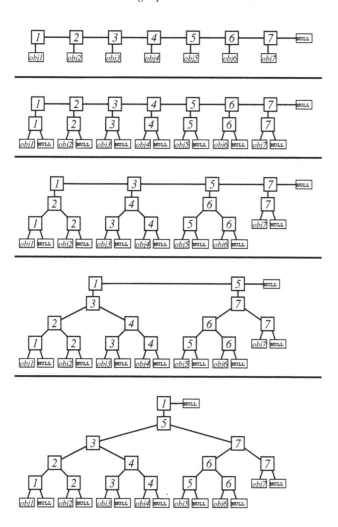

BOTTOM-UP CONSTRUCTION OF AN OPTIMAL TREE FROM A SORTED LIST

The top-down construction is easiest to describe recursively: divide the data set in the middle, create optimal trees for the lower and the upper halves, and join them together. This division is very balanced; in each subtree the number of items left and right differs by at most one, and it also results in a tree of optimal height. But if we implement it this way, and the data is given as list, it takes $\Theta(n \log n)$ time, because we get an overhead of $\Theta(n)$ in each recursion step to find the middle of the list. But there is a nice implementation with $O(n)$ complexity using a stack. We write here the generic stack operations push, pop, stack_empty, create_stack, remove_stack to illustrate how this method works. In a concrete implementation they should be replaced by one of the methods discussed in Chapter 1. In this case an array-based stack is the best method, and one should declare the stack as local array in the function, avoiding all function calls.

BOTTOM-UP AND TOP-DOWN OPTIMAL TREE WITH 18 LEAVES

The idea of our top-down construction is that we first construct the tree "in the abstract," without filling in any key values or pointers to objects. Then we do not need the time to find the middle of the list; we just need to keep track of the number of elements that should go into the left and right subtrees. We can build this abstract tree of the required shape easily using a stack. We initially put the root on the stack, labeled with the required tree size; then we continue, until the stack is empty, to take nodes from the stack, attach them to two newly created nodes labeled with half the size, and put the new nodes again on the stack. If the size reaches one, we have a leaf, so node should not be put back on the stack but should be filled with the next key and object from the list. The problem is to fill in the keys of the interior nodes, which become available only when the leaf is reached. For this, each item on the stack needs two pointers, one to the node that still needs to be expanded and one to the node higher up in the tree, where the smallest key of leaves below that node should be inserted as comparison key. Also, each stack item contains a number, the number of leaves that should be created below that node.

When we perform that step of taking a node from the stack and creating its two lower neighbors, the right-lower neighbor should and always go first on the stack, and then the left, so that when we reach a leaf, it is the leftmost unfinished leaf of the tree. This pointer for the missing key value propagates into the left subtree of the current node (where that smallest node comes from), whereas the smallest key from the right subtree should become the comparison key of the current node.

For this stack, an array-based stack of size 100 will be entirely sufficient because the size of the stack is the height of the tree, which is $\log n$, and we can assume $n < 2^{100}$.

```
tree_node_t *make_tree(tree_node_t *list)
{  typedef struct { tree_node_t  *node1;
                    tree_node_t  *node2;
                    int          number; }
                 st_item;
   st_item current, left, right;
   tree_node_t *tmp, *root;
   int length = 0;
   for( tmp = list; tmp != NULL;
   tmp = tmp->right )
      length += 1; /* find length of list */
   create_stack(); /* stack of st_item:
                    replace by array */
   root = get_node();
   /* put root node on stack */
   current.node1 = root;
   current.node2 = NULL;
   /* root expands to length leaves */
   current.number = length;
   push( current );
   while( !stack_empty() )
   /* there is still unexpanded node */
   {  current = pop();
      if( current.number > 1 )
      /* create (empty) tree nodes */
      { left.node1 = get_node();
        left.node2 = current.node2;
        left.number = current.number / 2;
        right.node1 = get_node();
        right.node2 = current.node1;
        right.number = current.number -
                       left.number;
        (current.node1)->left  = left.node1;
        (current.node1)->right = right.node1;
        push( right );
        push( left );
```

```
          }
          else /* reached a leaf, must be filled
                  with list item */
          { (current.node1)->left  = list->left;
            {/* fill leaf from list */}
            (current.node1)->key   = list->key;
            (current.node1)->right = NULL;
            if( current.node2 != NULL )
               /* insert comparison key in
                  interior node */
               (current.node2)->key   = list->key;
            tmp = list;
            /* unlink first item from list */
            list = list->right;
            /* content has been copied to */
            return_node(tmp);
            /* leaf, so node is returned */
          }
        }
        return( root );
      }
```

To analyze this algorithm, we just observe that in each step on the stack, we create either two new nodes, and there are only $n - 1$ new nodes created in total, or we attach a list item as leaf, and there are only n list items. So the total complexity is $O(n)$.

Theorem. The top-down method constructs a search tree of optimal height from an ordered list in time $O(n)$.

Several other methods to construct the top-down optimal tree from a list or to convert a given tree in a top-down optimal tree have been discussed in Martin and Ness (1972), Day (1976), Chang and Iyengar (1984), Stout and Warren (1986), Gerasch (1988), Korah and Kaimal (1992), and Maelbráncke and Olivié (1994). They differ mostly in the amount of additional space needed, which in our algorithm is the stack of size $\lceil \log_2 n \rceil$. Because this is a very minor amount, it is not an important consideration. One cannot avoid a worst-case complexity of $\Omega(n)$ if one wants to maintain an optimal search tree under insertions and deletions.

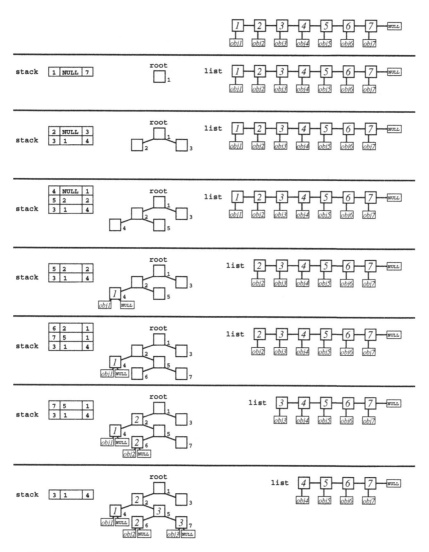

TOP-DOWN CONSTRUCTION OF AN OPTIMAL TREE FROM A SORTED LIST
FIRST STEPS, UNTIL THE LEFT HALF IS FINISHED

2.9 Converting Trees into Lists

Occasionally one also needs the other direction, converting a tree into an ordered list. This is very simple, using a stack for a trivial depth-first search enumeration of the leaves in decreasing order, which we insert in front of the list. This converts in $O(n)$ time a search tree with n leaves into a list of n

elements in increasing order. Again we write the generic stack functions, which in the specific implementation should be replaced by the correct method. If one knows in advance that the height of the tree is not too large, an array is the preferred method; the size of the array needs to be at least as large as the height of the tree.

```
tree_node_t *make_list(tree_node_t *tree)
{  tree_node_t *list, *node;
   if( tree->left == NULL )
   { return_node( tree );
     return( NULL );
   }
   else
   {  create_stack();
      push( tree );
      list = NULL;
      while( !stack_empty() )
      {  node = pop();
         if( node->right == NULL )
         { node->right = list;
           list = node;
         }
         else
         { push( node->left );
           push( node->right );
           return_node( node );
         }
      }
      return( list );
   }
}
```

2.10 Removing a Tree

We also need to provide a method to remove the tree when we no longer need it. As we already remarked for the stacks, it is important to free all nodes in such a dynamically allocated structure correctly, so that we avoid a memory leak. We cannot expect to remove a structure of potentially large size in constant time, but time linear in the size of the structure, that is, constant time per returned node, is easily reached. An obvious way to do this is using a stack, analogous

to the previous method to covert a tree into a sorted list. A more elegant method
is the following:

```
void remove_tree(tree_node_t *tree)
{   tree_node_t *current_node, *tmp;
    if( tree->left == NULL )
       return_node( tree );
    else
    {   current_node = tree;
        while(current_node->right != NULL )
        {   if( current_node->left->right == NULL )
            {   return_node( current_node->left );
                tmp = current_node->right;
                return_node( current_node );
                current_node = tmp;
            }
            else
            {   tmp = current_node->left;
                current_node->left = tmp->right;
                tmp->right = current_node;
                current_node = tmp;
            }
        }
        return_node( current_node );
    }
}
```

This essentially performs rotations in the root till the left-lower neighbor is
a leaf; then it returns that leaf, moves the root down to the right, and returns the
previous root.

3

Balanced Search Trees

In the previous chapter, we discussed search trees, giving `find`, `insert`, and `delete` methods, whose complexity is bounded by $O(h)$, where h is the height of the tree, that is, the maximum length of any path from the root to a leaf. But the height can be as large as n; in fact, a linear list can be a correct search tree, but it is very inefficient. The key to the usefulness of search trees is to keep them balanced, that is, to keep the height bounded by $O(\log n)$ instead of $O(n)$. This fundamental insight, together with the first method that achieved it, is due to Adel'son-Vel'skiĭ and Landis (1962), who in their seminal paper invented the height-balanced tree, now frequently called AVL tree. The height-balanced tree achieves a height bound $h \leq 1.44 \log n + O(1)$. Because any tree with n leaves has height at least $\log n$, this is already quite good. There are many other methods that achieve similar bounds, which we will discuss in this chapter.

3.1 Height-Balanced Trees

A tree is height-balanced if, in each interior node, the height of the right subtree and the height of the left subtree differ by at most 1. This is the oldest balance criterion for trees, introduced and analyzed by G.M. Adel'son-Vel'skiĭ and E.M. Landis (1962), and still the most popular variant of balanced search trees (AVL trees). A height-balanced tree has necessarily small height.

Theorem. A height-balanced tree of height h has at least
$\left(\frac{3+\sqrt{5}}{2\sqrt{5}}\right)\left(\frac{1+\sqrt{5}}{2}\right)^h - \left(\frac{3-\sqrt{5}}{2\sqrt{5}}\right)\left(\frac{1-\sqrt{5}}{2}\right)^h$ leaves.
    A height-balanced tree with n leaves has height at most
$\left\lceil \log_{\frac{1+\sqrt{5}}{2}} n \right\rceil = \left\lceil c_{Fib} \log_2 n \right\rceil \approx 1.44 \log_2 n$,
where $c_{Fib} = (\log_2(\frac{1+\sqrt{5}}{2}))^{-1}$.

Proof. Let $\mathcal{F}_h$ denote a height-balanced tree of height h with minimal number of leaves. Either the left or the right subtree of root($\mathcal{F}_h$) must have height $h - 1$, and because the tree is height balanced, the other subtree has height at least $h - 2$. So the tree $\mathcal{F}_h$ has at least as many leaves as the trees $\mathcal{F}_{h-1}$ and $\mathcal{F}_{h-2}$ together. And one can construct recursively a sequence of height-balanced trees $\mathcal{F}ib_h$, the Fibonacci trees, for which equality holds: just choose as left subtree of $\mathcal{F}ib_h$ a tree $\mathcal{F}ib_{h-1}$ and as right subtree a tree $\mathcal{F}ib_{h-2}$. Thus, the number of leaves *leaves*(h) of the height-balanced trees with minimum number of leaves satisfies the recursion *leaves*(h) = *leaves*($h - 1$) + *leaves*($h - 2$), with the initial values *leaves*(0) = 1 and *leaves*(1) = 2. Such recursions can be solved by a standard technique described in the Appendix; this recursion has the solution *leaves*(h) = $\left(\frac{3+\sqrt{5}}{2\sqrt{5}}\right)\left(\frac{1+\sqrt{5}}{2}\right)^h - \left(\frac{3-\sqrt{5}}{2\sqrt{5}}\right)\left(\frac{1-\sqrt{5}}{2}\right)^h$.

FIBONACCI TREES OF HEIGHT 0 TO 5

Thus, a height-balanced search tree is, at least for find operations, only a small factor (less than $\frac{3}{2}$) slower than an optimal search tree. But we need to explain how to maintain this property of height balancedness under insert and delete operations.

For this, we need to keep an additional information in each interior node of the search tree – the height of the subtree below that node. So the structure of a node is as follows:

```
typedef struct tr_n_t { key_t        key;
                        struct tr_n_t *left;
                        struct tr_n_t *right;
                        int           height;
                        /* possibly other information */
                      } tree_node_t;
```

The height of a node *n is defined recursively by the following rules:

– if *n is a leaf (n->left = NULL), then n->height = 0,
– else n->height is one larger than the maximum of the height of the left and right subtrees:
  n->height = 1 + max(n->left->height, n->right->height).

The height information must be corrected whenever the tree changes and must be used to keep the tree height balanced.

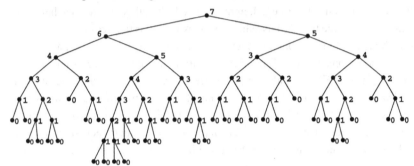

HEIGHT-BALANCED TREE WITH NODE HEIGHTS

The tree changes only by insert and delete operations, and by any such operation, the height can change only for the nodes that contain the changed leaf in their subtree, that is, only for the nodes on the path from the root to the changed leaf. As discussed in Section 2.5, we need to follow this path from the leaf back upward to the root and recompute the height information and possibly restore the balance condition.

At the leaf that was changed, or in the case of an insert, the two neighboring leaves, the height is 0. Now following the path up to the root, we have in each node the following situation: the height information in the left and right subtrees is already correct, and both subtrees are already height balanced: one because we restored balance in the previous step of going up and the other because nothing changed in that subtree. Also, the heights of both subtrees differ by at most 2 because previous to the update operation, the height differed by at most 1 and the update changed the height by at most 1. We now have to balance this node and update its height before we can go further up.

If *n is the current node, there are the following possibilities:

1. |n->left->height − n->right->height| ≤ 1.
   In this case, no rebalancing is necessary in this node. If the height also did not change, then from this node upward nothing changed and we can finish rebalancing; otherwise, we need to correct the height of *n and go up to the next node.
2. |n->left->height − n->right->height| = 2.
   In this case, we need to rebalance *n. This is done using the rotations introduced in Section 2.2. The complete rules are as follows:
   2.1 If n->left->height = n->right->height + 2 and
      n->left->left->height = n->right->height + 1.

Perform right rotation around n, followed by recomputing the height in n->right and n.

2.2 If n->left->height = n->right->height + 2 and n->left->left->height = n->right->height.
Perform left rotation around n->left, followed by a right rotation around n, followed by recomputing the height in n->right, n->left, and n.

2.3 If n->right->height = n->left->height + 2 and n->right->right->height = n->left->height + 1.
Perform left rotation around n, followed by recomputing the height in n->left and n.

2.4 If n->right->height = n->left->height + 2 and n->right->right->height = n->left->height.
Perform right rotation around n->right, followed by a left rotation around n, followed by recomputing the height in n->right, n->left, and n.

After performing these rotations, we check whether the height of n changed by this: if not, we can finish rebalancing; otherwise we continue with the next node up, till we reach the root.

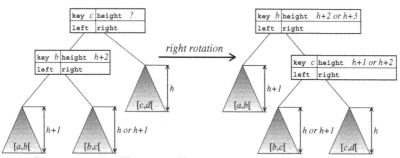

REBALANCING A NODE IN A HEIGHT-BALANCED TREE: CASE 2.1

Since we do only $O(1)$ work on each node of the path, at most two rotations and at most three recomputations of the height, and the path has length $O(\log n)$, these rebalancing operations take only $O(\log n)$ time. But we still have to show that they do restore the height balancedness.

We have to show this only for one step and then the claim follows for the entire tree by induction. Let $*n^{old}$ denote a node before the rebalancing step, whose left and right subtrees are already height balanced but their height differs by 2, and let $*n^{new}$ be the same node after the rebalancing step. By symmetry we can assume that

$$n^{old}\text{->left->height} = n^{old}\text{->right->height} + 2.$$

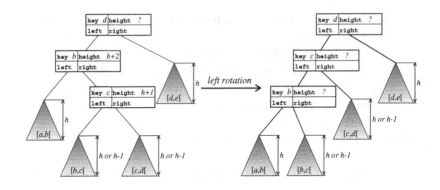

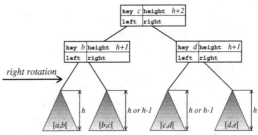

REBALANCING A NODE IN A HEIGHT-BALANCED TREE: CASE 2.2

Let $h = $ n^{old}->right->height. Because n^{old}->left->height = $h + 2$, we have max(n^{old}->left->left->height, n^{old}->left->right ->height) $= h + 1$, and because n^{old}->left is height balanced, there are the following cases:

(a) n^{old}->left->left->height $= h + 1$ and
    n^{old}->left->right->height $\in \{h, h + 1\}$.
    By rule 2.1 we perform a right rotation around n^{old}.
    By this n^{old}->left->left becomes n^{new}->left,
    n^{old}->left->right becomes n^{new}->right->left, and
    n^{old}->right becomes n^{new}->right->right.
    So n^{new}->left->height $= h + 1$,
    n^{new}->right->left->height $\in \{h, h + 1\}$,
    n^{new}->right->right->height $= h$.
    Thus, the node n^{new}->right is height-balanced, with
    n^{new}->right->height $\in \{h + 1, h + 2\}$.
    Therefore, the node n^{new} is height-balanced.
(b) n^{old}->left->left->height $= h$ and
    n^{old}->left->left->height $= h + 1$.

By rule 2.2 we perform left rotation around n^{old}->left, followed by a right rotation around n^{old}. By this
n^{old}->left->left becomes n^{new}->left->left,
n^{old}->left->right->left becomes n^{new}->left->right,
n^{old}->left->right->right becomes n^{new}->right->left, and
n^{old}->right becomes n^{new}->right->right.
So n^{new}->left->left->height $= h$,
n^{new}->left->right->height $\in \{h-1, h\}$,
n^{new}->right->left->height $\in \{h-1, h\}$,
n^{new}->right->right->height $= h$.
Thus, the nodes n^{new}->left and n^{new}->right are height-balanced, with n^{new}->left->height $= h+1$ and
n^{new}->right->height $= h+1$.
Therefore, the node n^{new} is height balanced.

This completes the proof that rebalancing can be done for height-balanced trees after insertions and deletions in $O(\log n)$ time.

Theorem. The height-balanced tree structure supports find, insert, and delete in $O(\log n)$ time.

A possible implementation of the insert in height-balanced trees is now as follows:

```
int insert(tree_node_t *tree, key_t new_key,
object_t *new_object)
{   tree_node_t *tmp_node;
    int finished;
    if( tree->left == NULL )
    {   tree->left = (tree_node_t *) new_object;
        tree->key  = new_key;
        tree->height = 0;
        tree->right  = NULL;
    }
    else
    {   create_stack();
        tmp_node = tree;
        while( tmp_node->right != NULL )
        {   push( tmp_node );
```

```
      if( new_key < tmp_node->key )
          tmp_node = tmp_node->left;
      else
          tmp_node = tmp_node->right;
}
/* found the candidate leaf. Test whether
   key distinct */
if( tmp_node->key == new_key )
   return( -1 );
/* key is distinct, now perform
   the insert */
{  tree_node_t *old_leaf, *new_leaf;
   old_leaf = get_node();
   old_leaf->left = tmp_node->left;
   old_leaf->key = tmp_node->key;
   old_leaf->right  = NULL;
   old_leaf->height = 0;
   new_leaf = get_node();
   new_leaf->left = (tree_node_t *)
   new_object;
   new_leaf->key = new_key;
   new_leaf->right  = NULL;
   new_leaf->height = 0;
   if( tmp_node->key < new_key )
   {   tmp_node->left  = old_leaf;
       tmp_node->right = new_leaf;
       tmp_node->key = new_key;
   }
   else
   {   tmp_node->left  = new_leaf;
       tmp_node->right = old_leaf;
   }
   tmp_node->height = 1;
}
/* rebalance */
finished = 0;
while( !stack_empty() && !finished )
{   int tmp_height, old_height;
    tmp_node = pop();
```

```
old_height= tmp_node->height;
if( tmp_node->left->height -
    tmp_node->right->height == 2 )
{  if( tmp_node->left->left->height -
       tmp_node->right->height == 1 )
   {  right_rotation( tmp_node );
      tmp_node->right->height =
      tmp_node->right->left->height + 1;
      tmp_node->height =
         tmp_node->right->height + 1;
   }
   else
   {  left_rotation( tmp_node->left );
      right_rotation( tmp_node );
      tmp_height =
         tmp_node->left->left->height;
      tmp_node->left->height  =
         tmp_height + 1;
      tmp_node->right->height =
         tmp_height + 1;
      tmp_node->height = tmp_height + 2;
   }
}
else if( tmp_node->left->height -
         tmp_node->right->height == -2 )
{  if( tmp_node->right->right->height -
       tmp_node->left->height == 1 )
   {  left_rotation( tmp_node );
      tmp_node->left->height =
      tmp_node->left->right->height + 1;
      tmp_node->height =
         tmp_node->left->height + 1;
   }
   else
   {  right_rotation( tmp_node->right );
      left_rotation( tmp_node );
      tmp_height =
         tmp_node->right->right->height;
```

```
                    tmp_node->left->height  =
                        tmp_height + 1;
                    tmp_node->right->height =
                        tmp_height + 1;
                    tmp_node->height = tmp_height + 2;
                }
            }
            else /* update height even if there
                    was no rotation */
            {   if( tmp_node->left->height >
                    tmp_node->right->height )
                    tmp_node->height =
                    tmp_node->left->height + 1;
                else
                    tmp_node->height =
                    tmp_node->right->height + 1;
            }
            if( tmp_node->height == old_height )
                finished = 1;
        }
        remove_stack();
    }
    return( 0 );
}
```

The basic delete function needs the same modifications, with the same rebalancing code while going up the tree. There is, of course, no change at all to the find function. Because we know that the height of the stack is bounded by $1.44 \log n$ and $n < 2^{100}$, this is a situation where an array-based stack of fixed maximum size is a reasonable choice.

In our implementation we chose to have in each node a field with the height of the node as balance information. It is possible to maintain height-balanced trees with less information in each node; each node really needs as balance information only the difference of left and right height, so one of three states. In older literature, various methods to minimize this space per node were discussed, but because space stopped being an important issue, it is now always preferable to have some explicit (and easily checkable) information.

Further analysis of the rebalancing transformation shows that the rotations can occur during an insert only on at most one level, whereas during a `delete` they might occur on every level if, for example, a leaf of minimum depth in a Fibonacci tree is deleted. The number of rotations or changed nodes has been studied by a number of papers, but it is of little significance for the actual performance of the structure. Also, even if there is only one level that requires rebalancing during an insert, there are many levels in which the nodes change because the height information must be updated.

The average depth of the leaves in a Fibonacci tree with n leaves is even better than $1.44 \log n$. By the recursive definition of the tree $\mathcal{F}ib_h$, it is easy to see that the sum $depthsum(h)$ of the depths of the leaves of $\mathcal{F}ib_h$ satisfies the recursion $depthsum(h) = depthsum(h - 1) + depthsum(h - 2) + leaves(h)$, where $leaves(h)$ is the number of leaves of $\mathcal{F}ib_h$, which we determined from the recursion $leaves(h) = leaves(h - 1) + leaves(h - 2)$ in the beginning of this section. One can eliminate the function $leaves$ from these two linear recursions to obtain

$$depthsum(h) - 2\, depthsum(h - 1) - depthsum(h - 2)$$
$$+ 2\, depthsum(h - 3) + depthsum(h - 4) = 0.$$

The initial values are $depthsum(0) = 0$, $depthsum(1) = 2$, $depthsum(2) = 5$, and $depthsum(3) = 12$. This recursion can be solved with standard methods (see Appendix) to give

$$depthsum(h) = \left(\frac{3}{5\sqrt{5}} + \frac{2+\sqrt{5}}{5}h\right)\left(\frac{1+\sqrt{5}}{2}\right)^h + \left(\frac{-3}{5\sqrt{5}} + \frac{2-\sqrt{5}}{5}h\right)\left(\frac{1-\sqrt{5}}{2}\right)^h$$
$$= \left(\frac{3}{5\sqrt{5}} + \frac{2+\sqrt{5}}{5}h\right)\left(\frac{1+\sqrt{5}}{2}\right)^h + o(1).$$

Thus the average depth of $\mathcal{F}ib_h$ is very near to the optimal depth of any binary tree with that number of leaves: $\frac{depthsum(h)}{leaves(h)} \approx 1.04 \log_2 (leaves(h)) + O(1)$.

This, however, is not true for height-balanced trees in general. In 1990, R. Klein and D. Wood constructed height-balanced trees whose average depth is almost the same as the worst-case depth of height-balanced trees (Klein and Wood 1990). So we cannot hope for any average-case improvement. They gave strong bounds for the maximum average depth of a height-balanced tree with n leaves. We will demonstrate here only the construction of 'bad' height-balanced trees.

Theorem. There are height-balanced trees with n leaves and average depth $c_{Fib} \log_2 n - o(\log n)$, where $c_{Fib} = (\log(\frac{1+\sqrt{5}}{2}))^{-1}$.

Proof. Let $\mathcal{B}in_h$ denote the complete binary tree of height h. In $\mathcal{B}in_h$, the left and right subtrees of the root are both $\mathcal{B}in_{h-1}$; in $\mathcal{F}ib_h$, the left subtree is $\mathcal{F}ib_{h-1}$ and the right subtree is $\mathcal{F}ib_{h-2}$. We now define a new family of height-balanced trees $\mathcal{G}_{k,h}$ by replacing a subtree of height $h-k$ containing the vertices of maximum depth by a complete binary tree of the same height. A recursive construction of these trees is the following:

- for $k=0$, we define $\mathcal{G}_{0,h} = \mathcal{B}in_h$, and
- for $k \geq 1$, we define $\mathcal{G}_{k,h}$ as the tree with left subtree $\mathcal{G}_{k-1,h-1}$ and right subtree $\mathcal{F}ib_{h-2}$.

The tree $\mathcal{G}_{k,h}$ is a height-balanced tree of height h with

$$
\begin{aligned}
leaves(\mathcal{G}_{h,k}) &= leaves(\mathcal{F}ib_h) - leaves(\mathcal{F}ib_{h-k}) + leaves(\mathcal{B}in_{h-k}) \\
&= leaves(h) - leaves(h-k) + 2^{h-k} \\
&= \left(\tfrac{3+\sqrt{5}}{2\sqrt{5}}\right)\left(\tfrac{1+\sqrt{5}}{2}\right)^h - \left(\tfrac{3+\sqrt{5}}{2\sqrt{5}}\right)\left(\tfrac{1+\sqrt{5}}{2}\right)^{h-k} + 2^{h-k} + o(1),
\end{aligned}
$$

and the sum of the depths of the leaves is

$$
\begin{aligned}
depthsum(\mathcal{G}_{h,k}) &= depthsum(\mathcal{F}ib_h) \\
&\quad - depthsum(\mathcal{F}ib_{h-k}) - k \cdot leaves(\mathcal{F}ib_{h-k}) \\
&\quad + depthsum(\mathcal{B}in_{h-k}) + k \cdot leaves(\mathcal{B}in_{h-k}) \\
&= depthsum(h) - depthsum(h-k) - k\, leaves(h-k) \\
&\quad + (h-k)2^{h-k} + k2^{h-k}.
\end{aligned}
$$

Denote $\phi = \tfrac{1+\sqrt{5}}{2}$ and $\gamma = \tfrac{2+\sqrt{5}}{5}$, $\delta = \tfrac{3}{5\sqrt{5}}$ and then we have

$$
\begin{aligned}
leaves(\mathcal{G}_{h,k}) &= \phi^h - \phi^{h-k} + 2^{h-k} + o(1) \\
&= \phi^h + 2^{h-k} + o(\phi^{h-k}), \\
depthsum(\mathcal{G}_{h,k}) &= \gamma h\phi^h + \delta\phi^h - \gamma(h-k)\phi^{h-k} - \delta\phi^{h-k} - k\phi^{h-k} \\
&\quad + h2^{h-k} + o(1) \\
&= \gamma h\phi^h + h2^{h-k} + O(\phi^h).
\end{aligned}
$$

We choose $k = k(h) = (1 - \log_2 \phi)h - \log_2 h$; then, $h - k = (\log_2 \phi)h + \log_2(h)$ and $2^{h-k} = h\phi^h$. Then,

$$
\begin{aligned}
leaves(\mathcal{G}_{h,k(h)}) &= h\phi^h + O(\phi^h), \\
depthsum(\mathcal{G}_{h,k(h)}) &= h^2\phi^h + O(h\phi^h).
\end{aligned}
$$

Therefore,

$$\log_2 \big(leaves(\mathcal{G}_{h,k(h)})\big) = \log_2(h\phi^h) + o(1) = (\log_2 \phi)h + \log_2 h + o(1),$$

so with $n = leaves(\mathcal{G}_{h,k(h)})$,

$$depthsum(\mathcal{G}_{h,k(h)}) = \frac{1}{\log_2 \phi} n \log_2 n \approx 1.44 n \log_2 n.$$

Several variants of the height-balanced trees were proposed relaxing the balance condition to some larger (but still constant) upper bound for the height difference in each node (Foster 1973; Karlton et al. 1976) or strengthening it to require that the nodes two levels below still have only height difference at most one (Guibas and Sedgewick 1978), but neither gives any interesting advantage. One-sided height-balanced trees, in which additionally the height of the right subtree is never smaller than the height of the left subtree, were subject of considerable study (Hirschberg 1976; Kosaraju 1978; Ottmann and Wood 1978; Zweben and McDonald 1978; Räihä and Zweben 1979), because it was not obvious how to update this structure in $O(\log n)$ time. But once that problem was solved, they lost interest, because they do not give any algorithmic advantages over the usual height-balanced trees.

3.2 Weight-Balanced Trees

When Adel'son-Vel'skiǐ and Landis invented the height-balanced search trees in 1962, computers were extremely memory limited, so the applicability of the structure at that time was small and only very few other papers on balanced search trees[1] appeared in the 1960s. But by 1970, technological development made it a feasible and useful structure, generating much interest in the topic, and several alternative ways to maintain search trees at $O(\log n)$ height were proposed. One natural alternative balance criterion is to balance the weight, that is, the number of leaves, instead of the height of the subtrees. Weight-balanced trees were introduced as "trees of bounded balance" or BB[α]-trees by Nievergelt and Reingold (1973) and Nievergelt (1974), and further studied in Baer (1975) and Blum and Mehlhorn (1980). Another variant of weight balance was proposed in Cho and Sahni (2000).

The weight of a tree is the number of its leaves, so in a weight-balanced tree, the weight of the left and right subtrees in each node should be "balanced".

---

[1] But there was a fashion of analyzing the height distribution of search trees without rebalancing under random insertions and deletions.

The top-down optimal search trees constructed in Section 2.7 are in this way as balanced as possible, with the left and right weights differing by at most 1; but we cannot maintain such a strong balance condition only with $O(\log n)$ rebalancing work during insertions and deletions. Instead of bounding the difference, the correct choice is to bound the ratio of the weights. This gives an entire family of balance conditions, the α-weight-balanced trees, where for each subtree the left and right sub-subtrees have each at least a fraction of α of the total weight of the subtree (and at most a fraction of $(1 - \alpha)$). An α-weight-balanced tree has necessarily small height.

Theorem. An α-weight-balanced tree of height $h \geq 2$ has at least $\left(\frac{1}{1-\alpha}\right)^h$ leaves.

An α-weight-balanced tree with n leaves has height at most $\log_{\frac{1}{1-\alpha}} n = \left(\log_2\left(\frac{1}{1-\alpha}\right)\right)^{-1} \log_2 n$.

Proof. Let T_h be an α-weight-balanced tree of height h with minimum number of leaves. Either left or right subtree of T_h must be of height $h - 1$, so the weight of that subtree is at least $leaves(T_{h-1})$ and at most $(1 - \alpha) leaves(T_h)$.

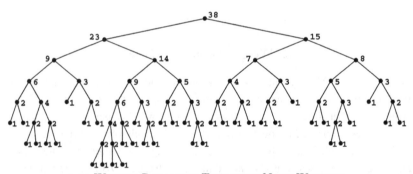

0.29-Weight-Balanced Tree with Node Weights

So the proof of the $O(\log n)$ height bound is even simpler than for the height-balanced trees. But the analysis of the rebalancing algorithm is more complicated and we cannot maintain the α-weight-balanced condition for all α. Already Nievergelt and Reingold (1973) observed $\alpha < 1 - \frac{1}{\sqrt{2}}$ as necessary condition for the rebalancing algorithm to work. But α should also not be chosen very small, otherwise rebalancing fails for small cases. Blum and Mehlhorn gave $\frac{2}{11} < \alpha$ as lower bound (Blum and Mehlhorn 1980), but indeed if we are willing to use a different rebalancing method for small trees, we could choose α smaller. In our model, we restrict ourselves to the small interval

$\alpha \in [\frac{2}{7}, 1 - \frac{1}{\sqrt{2}}] \supset [0.286, 0.292]$, but with additional work for the rebalancing of the trees of small weight, one could choose α arbitrary small.

To describe the rebalancing algorithm in this class, we first need to choose an α and a second parameter ε subject to $\varepsilon \leq \alpha^2 - 2\alpha + \frac{1}{2}$. As in height-balanced trees, we need to keep some additional information in each interior node of the search tree – the weight of the subtree below that node. So the structure of a node is as follows:

```
typedef struct tr_n_t { key_t        key;
                        struct tr_n_t  *left;
                        struct tr_n_t *right;
                        int           weight;
                        /* possibly other information */
                      } tree_node_t;
```

The weight of a node *n is defined recursively by the following rules:

– If *n is a leaf (n->left = NULL), then n->weight = 1.
– Else n->weight is the sum of the weight of the left and right subtrees:
  n->weight = n->left->weight + n->right->weight.

The node *n is α-weight-balanced if
n->left->weight $\geq \alpha$ n->weight   and   n->right->weight $\geq$ α n->weight,
or equivalently α n->left->weight $\leq (1 - \alpha)$ n->right->weight
and $(1 - \alpha)$ n->left->weight $\geq \alpha$ n->right->weight.

Again the weight information must be corrected whenever the tree is changed and is used to keep the tree weight balanced. And the information changes only by insert and delete operations, and only in those nodes on the path from the changed leaf to the root, and there only by at most 1. So, as in the height-balanced trees (Section 3.1) we use one of the methods of Section 2.5 to follow the path up to the root and restore in each node the balance condition, using inductively that below the current node the subtrees are already balanced.

If *n is the current node and we already corrected the weight of *n, there are the following cases for the rebalancing algorithm:

1. n->left->weight $\geq \alpha$ n->weight and
   n->right->weight $\geq \alpha$ n->weight.
   In this case, no rebalancing is necessary in this node; we go up to the next node.

2. `n->right->weight` $< \alpha$ `n->weight`

   2.1 If `n->left->left->weight` $> (\alpha + \varepsilon)$`n->weight`.
     Perform a right rotation around `n`, followed by recomputing the weight
     in `n->right`.

   2.2 Else perform a left rotation around `n->left`, followed by a right
     rotation around `n`, followed by recomputing the weight in `n->left`
     and `n->right`.

3. `n->left->weight` $< \alpha$ `n->weight`

   3.1 If `n->right->right->weight` $> (\alpha + \varepsilon)$`n->weight`.
     Perform a left rotation around `n`, followed by recomputing the weight
     in `n->left`.

   3.2 Else perform a right rotation around `n->right`, followed by a left
     rotation around `n`, followed by recomputing the weight in `n->left`
     and `n->right`.

Notice that, different from the height-balanced trees, we must always follow the
path up to the root and cannot stop early because the weight information, unlike
the height information, changes necessarily along the whole path. Because we
do only $O(1)$ work on each node of the path, at most two rotations and at most
three recomputations of the weight and the path has length $O(\log n)$, these
rebalancing operations take only $O(\log n)$ time. But again we still have to show
that they do restore the α-weight-balancedness.

Let $*n^{\mathrm{old}}$ be the node before the rebalancing step and $*n^{\mathrm{new}}$ the same
node after the rebalancing step. Denote the weight n^{old}`->weight` $= n^{\mathrm{new}}$`->`
`weight` by w. We need to analyze only case 2; in case 1, the node is already
balanced, and case 3 follows from case 2 by symmetry. In case 2, we have
n^{old}`->right->weight` $< \alpha w$, but the weight changed only by 1 and before
that the node was balanced; so n^{old}`->right->weight` $= \alpha w - \delta$ for some
$\delta \in {]}0, 1]$. We now have to check for cases 2.1 and 2.2 that all nodes changed
in that step are balanced afterwards.

2.1 We have n^{old}`->left->left->weight` $> (\alpha + \varepsilon)w$ and perform a
    right rotation around n^{old}. By this
       n^{old}`->left->left` becomes n^{new}`->left`,
       n^{old}`->left->right` becomes n^{new}`->right->left`, and
       n^{old}`->right` becomes n^{new}`->right->right`.
    Because n^{old}`->left` was balanced, with
    n^{old}`->left->weight` $= (1 - \alpha)w + \delta$, we have
       n^{new}`->right->left->weight` $\in$
    $[\alpha(1 - \alpha)w + \alpha\delta, (1 - 2\alpha - \varepsilon)w + \delta]$,
       n^{new}`->right->right->weight` $= \alpha w - \delta$,

n^{new}->right->weight $\in [\alpha(2 - \alpha)w - (1 - \alpha)\delta, (1 - \alpha - \varepsilon)w]$,
n^{new}->left->weight $\in [(\alpha + \varepsilon)w, (1 - \alpha)^2 w + (1 - \alpha)\delta]$.

Now for n^{new}->right the balance conditions are

a. $\alpha\, n^{\text{new}}$->right->left->weight

$$\leq (1 - \alpha)\, n^{\text{new}}\text{->right->right->weight, so}$$

$\alpha((1 - 2\alpha - \varepsilon)w + \delta) \leq (1 - \alpha)(\alpha w - \delta)$,
which is satisfied for $(\alpha^2 + \alpha\varepsilon)w \geq \delta$; and

b. $(1 - \alpha)\, n^{\text{new}}$->right->left->weight

$$\geq \alpha\, n^{\text{new}}\text{->right->right->weight, so}$$

$(1 - \alpha)\, (\alpha(1 - \alpha)w + \alpha\delta) \geq \alpha\, (\alpha w - \delta)$,
which is satisfied for $0 \leq \alpha \leq \frac{3 - \sqrt{5}}{2}$.

And for n^{new} the balance conditions are

c. $\alpha\, n^{\text{new}}$->left->weight $\leq (1 - \alpha)\, n^{\text{new}}$->right->weight, so

$$\alpha((1 - \alpha)^2 w + (1 - \alpha)\delta) \leq (1 - \alpha)(\alpha(2 - \alpha)w - (1 - \alpha)\delta),$$

which is satisfied for $\alpha w \geq \delta$; and

d. $(1 - \alpha)\, n^{\text{new}}$->left->weight $\geq \alpha\, n^{\text{new}}$->right->weight, so

$$(1 - \alpha)\, ((\alpha + \varepsilon)w) \geq \alpha\, ((1 - \alpha - \varepsilon)w),$$

which is satisfied for all α, with strict inequality for $\varepsilon > 0$. Together this shows that in the interesting interval $\alpha \in [0, 1 - \frac{1}{\sqrt{2}}]$, at least if the subtree is not too small (for $\alpha^2 w \geq 1$) in case 2.1, the α-weight-balance is restored.

2.2 We have n^{old}->left->left->weight $\leq (\alpha + \varepsilon)w$ and perform a left rotation around n^{old}->left, followed by a right rotation around n^{old}. By this

n^{old}->left->left becomes n^{new}->left->left,

n^{old}->left->right->left becomes n^{new}->left->right,

n^{old}->left->right->right becomes n^{new}->right->left,

and

n^{old}->right becomes n^{new}->right->right.

Because n^{old}->left was balanced, with
n^{old}->left->weight $= (1 - \alpha)w + \delta$, we have by the assumption of case 2.2

n^{new}->left->left->weight $\in [\alpha(1 - \alpha)w + \alpha\delta, (\alpha + \varepsilon)w]$,
n^{old}->left->right->weight $\in$
$[(1 - 2\alpha - \varepsilon)w + \delta, (1 - \alpha)^2 w + (1 - \alpha)\delta]$,
n^{new}->left->right->weight, n^{new}->right->left->weight

$$\in [\alpha(1 - 2\alpha - \varepsilon)w + \alpha\delta, (1 - \alpha)^3 w + (1 - \alpha)^2\delta],$$

n^{new}->right->right->weight $= \alpha w - \delta$,
n^{new}->left->weight $\in$
$[(2\alpha - 3\alpha^2 + \alpha^3)w + \alpha(2 - \alpha)\delta, (1 - 2\alpha + 2\alpha^2 + \alpha\varepsilon)w + (1 - \alpha)\delta]$,

n^{new}->right->weight $\in$

$[(2\alpha - 2\alpha^2 - \alpha\varepsilon)w - (1 - \alpha)\delta, (1 - 2\alpha + 3\alpha^2 - \alpha^3)w + \alpha(\alpha - 2)\delta].$

Then the balance conditions for n^{new}->left are

a. $\alpha\, n^{new}$->left->left->weight

$$\leq (1 - \alpha)\, n^{new}\text{->left->right->weight, so}$$

$\alpha\,((\alpha + \varepsilon)w) \leq (1 - \alpha)(\alpha(1 - 2\alpha - \varepsilon)w + \alpha\delta),$

which is satisfied for $\alpha \in [0, 1 - \frac{1}{\sqrt{2}}[$ and $\varepsilon \leq \alpha^2 - 2\alpha + \frac{1}{2}$; and

b. $(1 - \alpha)\, n^{new}$->left->left->weight

$$\geq \alpha\, n^{new}\text{->left->right->weight, so}$$

$(1 - \alpha)(\alpha(1 - \alpha)w + \alpha\delta) \geq \alpha\left((1 - \alpha)^3 w + (1 - \alpha)^2\delta\right),$

which is satisfied for $\alpha \in [0, 1]$.

The balance conditions for n^{new}->right are

c. $\alpha\, n^{new}$->right->left->weight

$$\leq (1 - \alpha)\, n^{new}\text{->right->right->weight, so}$$

$\alpha\left((1 - \alpha)^3 w + (1 - \alpha)^2\delta\right) \leq (1 - \alpha)(\alpha w - \delta),$

which is satisfied at least for $(2 - \alpha)\alpha^2 w \geq (1 + \alpha - \alpha^2)\delta$; and

d. $(1 - \alpha)\, n^{new}$->right->left->weight

$$\geq \alpha\, n^{new}\text{->right->right->weight, so}$$

$(1 - \alpha)(\alpha(1 - 2\alpha - \varepsilon)w + \alpha\delta) \geq \alpha\,(\alpha w - \delta),$

which is satisfied for $\alpha \in [0, 1 - \frac{1}{\sqrt{2}}[$ and $\varepsilon \leq 2\alpha^2 - 4\alpha + 1.$

And the balance conditions for n^{new} are

e. $\alpha\, n^{new}$->left->weight $\leq (1 - \alpha)\, n^{new}$->right->weight, so

$\alpha\left((1 - 2\alpha + 2\alpha^2 + \alpha\varepsilon)w + (1 - \alpha)\delta\right)$

$$\leq (1 - \alpha)\left((2\alpha - 2\alpha^2 - \alpha\varepsilon)w - (1 - \alpha)\delta\right),$$

which is satisfied for $\alpha(1 - 2\alpha - \varepsilon)w \geq 1$, and

f. $(1 - \alpha)\, n^{new}$->left->weight $\geq \alpha\, n^{new}$->right->weight, so

$(1 - \alpha)\left((2\alpha - 3\alpha^2 + \alpha^3)w + \alpha(2 - \alpha)\delta\right)$

$$\geq \alpha\left((1 - 2\alpha + 3\alpha^2 - \alpha^3)w + \alpha(\alpha - 2)\delta\right),$$

which is satisfied for $\alpha \in [0, \frac{3 - \sqrt{5}}{2}].$

Together this shows that in the interesting interval $\alpha \in\ ]0, 1 - \frac{1}{\sqrt{2}}[$ with $\varepsilon \leq \alpha^2 - 2\alpha + \frac{1}{2}$, at least if the subtree is not too small (for $\alpha^2 w \geq 1$, which implies $(2 - \alpha)\alpha^2 w \geq (1 + \alpha - \alpha^2)\delta$), and $\alpha(1 - 2\alpha - \varepsilon)w \geq 1$ in the interval of interest) in case 2.2, the α-weight-balance is restored.

But we still have to show that the rebalancing algorithm works for $w < \alpha^{-2}$. This, unfortunately, is in general not the case. It is, however, true for $\alpha \in\ ]\frac{2}{7}, 1 - \frac{1}{\sqrt{2}}[$; here we need to check it only for $w \leq 12$ and n->right->weight = $\lfloor \alpha w \rfloor$.

In case 2.1, we have additionally n^{old}->left->left->weight $\geq \lceil \alpha w \rceil$, and there is only one balance inequality (a) that could fail: we have to check that n^{new}->right->right->weight $>$ $\alpha\, n^{new}$->right->weight, so $\lfloor \alpha w \rfloor > \alpha\,(w - \lceil \alpha w \rceil)$, which is easily tested.

In case 2.2, we have additionally n^{old}->left->left->weight $\leq$ $\lfloor \alpha w \rfloor$. Because n^{old}->left->weight $= w - \lfloor \alpha w \rfloor$, the balance condition in n->left determines the weights of n^{old}->left->left and n^{old}->left->right, and it is easily tested for these trees that the balance is restored.

This completes the proof that rebalancing can be done for weight-balanced trees after insertions and deletions in $O(\log n)$ time.

Theorem. The weight-balanced tree structure supports find, insert, and delete in $O(\log n)$ time.

A possible implementation of the insert in weight-balanced trees is now as follows:

```
#define ALPHA     0.288
#define EPSILON   0.005

int insert(tree_node_t *tree, key_t new_key,
           object_t *new_object)
{  tree_node_t *tmp_node;
   if( tree->left == NULL )
   {  tree->left = (tree_node_t *) new_object;
      tree->key  = new_key;
      tree->weight = 1;
      tree->right  = NULL;
   }
   else
   {  create_stack();
      tmp_node = tree;
      while( tmp_node->right != NULL )
      {   push( tmp_node );
          if( new_key < tmp_node->key )
               tmp_node = tmp_node->left;
          else
               tmp_node = tmp_node->right;
      }
      /* found the candidate leaf. Test whether
```

```
         key distinct */
  if( tmp_node->key == new_key )
     return( -1 ); /* key alreay exists,
     insert failed */
  /* key is distinct, now perform
     the insert */
  {  tree_node_t *old_leaf, *new_leaf;
     old_leaf = get_node();
     old_leaf->left = tmp_node->left;
     old_leaf->key = tmp_node->key;
     old_leaf->right  = NULL;
     old_leaf->weight = 1;
     new_leaf = get_node();
     new_leaf->left = (tree_node_t *)
     new_object;
     new_leaf->key = new_key;
     new_leaf->right  = NULL;
     new_leaf->weight = 1;
     if( tmp_node->key < new_key )
     {   tmp_node->left  = old_leaf;
         tmp_node->right = new_leaf;
         tmp_node->key = new_key;
     }
     else
     {   tmp_node->left  = new_leaf;
         tmp_node->right = old_leaf;
     }
     tmp_node->weight = 2;
  }
  /* rebalance */
  while( !stack_empty())
  {  tmp_node = pop();
     tmp_node->weight =
        tmp_node->left->weight
        + tmp_node->right->weight;
     if( tmp_node->right->weight
        < ALPHA*tmp_node->weight )
     {  if(tmp_node->left->left->weight >
           (ALPHA+EPSILON) *tmp_node->weight)
```

```
{   right_rotation( tmp_node );
    tmp_node->right->weight =
    tmp_node->right->left->weight
    + tmp_node->right->right->weight;
}
else
{   left_rotation( tmp_node->left );
    right_rotation( tmp_node );
    tmp_node->right->weight =
    tmp_node->right->left->weight
    + tmp_node->right->right->weight;
    tmp_node->left->weight =
    tmp_node->left->left->weight
    + tmp_node->left->right->weight;
}
}
else if ( tmp_node->left->weight
        < ALPHA*tmp_node->weight )
{   if( tmp_node->right->right->weight
        > (ALPHA+EPSILON)
        *tmp_node->weight )
    {   left_rotation( tmp_node );
        tmp_node->left->weight =
        tmp_node->left->left->weight
        + tmp_node->left->right->weight;
    }
    else
    {   right_rotation( tmp_node->right );
        left_rotation( tmp_node );
        tmp_node->right->weight =
        tmp_node->right->left->weight
        + tmp_node->right->right->weight;
        tmp_node->left->weight =
        tmp_node->left->left->weight
        + tmp_node->left->right->weight;
    }
}

} /* end rebalance */
```

```
        remove_stack();
    }
    return( 0 );
}
```

Again the basic `delete` function needs the same modifications, with the same rebalancing code while going up the tree, and there is no change to the `find` function. Because we know that the height of the stack is bounded by $(\log \frac{1}{1-\alpha})^{-1} \log n$, which is less than $2.07 \log n$ for our interval of α, and $n < 2^{100}$, again an array-based stack of fixed maximum size is a reasonable choice.

The rebalancing algorithm described here was similar to the rebalancing of height-balanced trees in two phases: going down to the leaf and then rebalancing bottom-up. In principle, weight-balanced trees also allow a top-down rebalancing, which takes place while going down to the leaf and makes the second phase unnecessary. This is possible because we already know the correct weight of a subtree while going down, so we see whether it will need rebalancing, whereas the height of a subtree is available only when we reach the leaf. The algorithm was originally outlined for BB[α] trees that way (Nievergelt and Reingold 1973) and discussed in Lai and Wood (1993), but a correct analysis that balance is restored is even more work for top-down rebalancing because the assumption we have below the current node is weaker: the node below is not necessarily balanced, because we have not performed rebalancing below, but at most one off from balance.

With respect to the maximum height, the weight-balanced trees are not as good as the height-balanced trees; for our interval of α, the coefficient $(\log \frac{1}{1-\alpha})^{-1}$ is approximately 2 instead of 1.44, and for larger α, it would get even worse. It was already observed in Nievergelt and Reingold (1973) that the average depth of the leaves is slightly better than for the height-balanced trees.

Theorem. The average depth of an α-weight-balanced tree with n leaves is at most $\frac{-1}{\alpha \log \alpha + (1-\alpha) \log(1-\alpha)} \log n$.

For our interval of α, this coefficient is approximately 1.15, whereas for height-balanced trees we had also 1.44.

Proof. We again use the maximal depthsum instead of the average depth. It satisfies the recursive bound $depthsum(n) \leq n + depthsum(a) + depthsum(b)$

for some a, b with $a + b = n, a, b \geq \alpha n$. We show $depthsum(n) \leq cn \log n$ for the above c by induction, using that

$$depthsum(n) \leq n + ca \log a + cb \log b$$
$$= cn \left(\tfrac{1}{c} + \tfrac{a}{n} \log a + \tfrac{b}{n} \log b \right)$$
$$= cn \log n + cn \left(\tfrac{1}{c} + \tfrac{a}{n} \log \tfrac{a}{n} + \tfrac{b}{n} \log \tfrac{b}{n} \right).$$

Because the function $x \log x + (1 - x) \log(1 - x)$ is negative and decreasing on $x \in [0, 0.5]$, the second term is nonpositive for $c = \frac{-1}{\alpha \log \alpha + (1 - \alpha) \log(1 - \alpha)}$.

A more remarkable property of weight-balanced trees is the following:

Theorem. In the time from one rebalancing of a specific node to the next rebalancing of this node, a positive fraction of all leaves below that node are changed.

This is remarkable because it forces almost all rebalancing operations to occur near the leaves. This was observed in Blum and Mehlhorn (1980).

Proof. It is easy to check that the rebalancing operations leave each of the changed nodes not only α weight balanced, but even α^* weight balanced for some $\alpha^*(\alpha, \varepsilon) > \alpha$. But then the weight must change by a positive fraction to violate the balance condition, so a positive fraction of the leaves must be inserted or deleted before that node needs to be rebalanced again. This is the reason for the additional $\varepsilon > 0$ used in the rebalancing algorithm; without it, in case 2.1 one of the nodes would not have this stronger balance property.

For the height-balanced trees, we bounded the difference of the heights, whereas for weight-balanced trees, we bounded the ratio of the weights. Because in any sort of balanced tree the height will be logarithmic in the weight, it is not surprising that these conditions have the same effect. The much weaker condition of bounding the ratio of the heights was studied in Gonnet, Olivié, and Wood (1983). It turns out that this condition is not strong enough to give a logarithmic height; the maximum height of a height-ratio balanced tree with n leaves is $2^{\Theta(\sqrt{\log n})}$ instead of $\Theta(\log n) = 2^{\log \log n + \Theta(1)}$.

3.3 (a, b)- and B-Trees

A different method to keep the height of the trees small is to allow tree nodes of higher degree. This idea was introduced as B-trees by Bayer and McCreight (1972) and turned out to be very fruitful. It was originally intended as external memory data structure, but we will see in Section 3.4 that it has interesting uses also as normal main memory data structure. The characteristic of external memory is that access to it is very slow, compared to main memory, and is done in blocks, units much larger than single main memory locations, which are simultaneously transferred into main memory. In the 1970s, computers were still very memory limited but usually already had a large external memory, so that it was a necessary consideration how a structure operates when a large part of it is not in main memory, but on external memory. This situation is now less important, but it is still relevant for database applications, where B-tree variants are still much used as index structures.

The problem with normal binary search trees as external memory structure is that each tree node could be in a different external memory block, which becomes known only when the previous block has been retrieved from the external memory. So we might need as many external memory block accesses as the height of the tree, which is more than $\log_2(n)$, and would be interested in each of these blocks, which are large enough to hold many nodes, in just a single node. The idea of B-trees is to take each block as a single node of high degree. In the original version, each node has degree between a and $2a - 1$, where a is chosen as large as possible under the condition that a block must have room for $2a - 1$ pointers and keys. Then balance was maintained by the criterion that all leaves should be at the same depth.

The degree interval a to $2a - 1$ is the smallest interval for which the re-balancing algorithm from Bayer and McCreight (1972) works. Because each block has room for at most $2a - 1$ elements and is at least half full this way, it sounded like a good choice to optimize the space utilization. But then it was discovered by Huddleston and Mehlhorn (1982) and independently by Maier and Salveter (1981) that choosing the interval a bit larger makes an important difference for the rebalancing algorithm; if one allows node degrees from a to b for $b \geq 2a$, then rebalancing changes only amortized $O(1)$ blocks, whereas for $b = 2a - 1$, the original choice, $\Theta(\log n)$ block changes can be necessary. For a main memory data structure, the number of changes in rebalancing makes little difference, although it has been studied in many papers; but for an external memory structure it is essential because all changed blocks have to be written again to the external memory device. So these trees, known as (a, b)-trees, are the method of choice.

An (a, b)-tree is a nonbinary search tree in which all leaves have the same depth; each nonroot node has degree between a and b, with $b \geq 2a$, and the root has degree at most b and at least 2 (unless the tree is empty or has only one leaf). An (a, b)-tree has necessarily small height.

Theorem. An (a, b)-tree of height $h \geq 1$ has at least $2a^{h-1}$ and at most b^h leaves. An (a, b)-tree with $n \geq 2$ leaves has height at most
$\lceil \log_a(n) + (1 - \log_a 2) \rceil \approx \frac{1}{\log_2 a} \log n$.

This follows immediately from the definition.

Because these trees are not binary search trees, they do not fall in the framework described in Chapter 2, and we have to define their structure and our conventions for their representation in addition to the rebalancing algorithm. A node has the following structure:

```
typedef struct tr_n_t {  int           degree;
                         int           height;
                         key_t         key[B];
                         struct tr_n_t * next[B];
                  /* possibly other information */
                  } tree_node_t;
```

We describe the (a, b)-tree here as a main memory structure; for an external-memory version, we would need to establish a correspondence between the main memory nodes and the external memory blocks, and would need functions to recover a node from external memory and write it back.

The node structure contains the degree of the node, which is at most B, and space for up to B outgoing edges. It also contains space for B key values. Usually we need only one key value less than the degree to separate the outgoing edges, but in the node at the lowest level, we avoid having separate leaf nodes and instead place the object references together with their associated key values in that node. We need a convention to identify the nodes on the lowest level; for this reason we include the height of the node above the lowest level in the node.

As in the case of binary search trees, we associate with each node a half-open interval of the possible key values that can be reached through that node or pointer. If $*n$ is a node with associated interval $[a, b[$, then the associated intervals of the nodes referenced to by next pointers are as follows:

– for n->next[0], the interval $[a, $n->key[1][$;

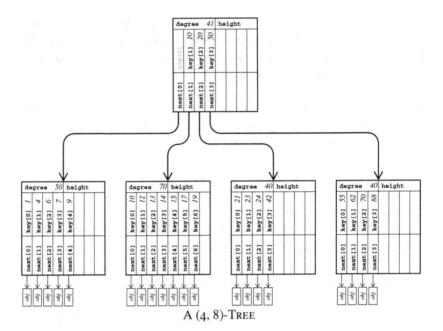

A (4, 8)-Tree

– for n->next [i], with $1 \le i \le$ n->degree $- 2$, the interval
  [n->key [i], n->key [$i + 1$] [; and
– for n->next [n->degree-1] the interval
  [n->key [n->degree-1], b[.

Then the find operation looks as follows:

```
object_t *find(tree_node_t *tree,
               key_t query_key)
{  tree_node_t *current_node;
   object_t *object;
   current_node = tree;
   while( current_node->height >= 0 )
   {  int lower, upper;
      /* binary search among keys */
      lower = 0;   upper = current_node->degree;
      while( upper > lower +1 )
      {  if ( query_key <
             current_node->key[ (upper+lower)/2 ] )
             upper = (upper+lower)/2;
```

```
      else
         lower = (upper+lower)/2;
   }
   if( current_node->height > 0)
      current_node =
      current_node->next[lower];
   else
   {  /* block of height 0, contains the
      object pointers */
      if( current_node->key[lower] ==
         query_key )
         object = (object_t *)
         current_node->next[lower];
      else
         object = NULL;
      return( object );
   }
}
   }
}
```

By performing binary search on the keys within the node, the find operation is as fast as a find in a binary tree.

Now we finally have to describe the insert and delete operations and the rebalancing that keeps the structure of the (a, b)-tree. Insert and delete begin straightforward as in the binary search-tree case: first one goes down in the tree to find the place where a new leaf should be inserted or an old one should be deleted. This is in a node of height 0. If there is still room in the node for the new leaf or after the deletion the leaf still contains at least a objects, there is no problem, but the node could overflow during an insertion or become underfull during a deletion. In these cases we have to change something in the structure of the tree and possibly propagate the structure upward. The restructuring rules for these situations are as follows:

− For an insertion: if the current node overflows

a. If the current node is the root, create two new nodes, copy into each half the root entries, and put into the root just pointers to these two new nodes together with the key that separates them. Increase the height of the root by 1.

   b. Else create a new node and move half the entries from the overflowing node to the new node. Then insert the pointer to the new node into the upper neighbor.

The case b is known as "splitting."

– For a deletion: if the current node becomes underfull

   a. If the current node is the root, it is underfull if it has only one remaining pointer. Copy the content of the node to which the pointer points into the root node and return the node to the system.

   b. Else find the block of the same height that immediately precedes or follows it in the key order and has the same upper neighbor. If that block is not already almost underfull, move a key and its associated pointer from that block and correct the key value separating these two blocks in the upper neighbor.

   c. Else copy entries of the current node into that almost underfull neighboring node of the same height, return the current node to the system, and delete the reference to it from the upper neighbor.

The cases b and c are known as "sharing" and "joining," respectively.

It is clear that this method does restore the (a, b)-tree property; if the node is overfull, then it contains enough entries to be split into two nodes, and if the node is underfull and its neighbor does not have an element to spare, then they can be joined together into a single node. These operations work even for $b = 2a - 1$ (the original B-trees) and because we change at most two blocks on each level, it is also clear that the number of changed blocks is $O(\log_a(n))$. For the original B-trees, this bound is also best possible: if $b = 2a - 1$, then both new blocks obtained from splitting an overflowing block (with $b + 1 = 2a$ entries) are at the lower degree limit, so deleting the element that was just inserted forces them to be joined again. It is easy to construct an example where along the entire path every block is split by an insertion; so by deleting the same element each of these block pairs is joined again.

   It was the remarkable observation of Huddleston and Mehlhorn (1982) and Maier and Salveter (1981) that if we allow at least one position more space ($b \geq 2a$), we get a much better bound with only amortized $O(1)$ blocks changed. To prove this amortized bound, we define a potential function on the search tree and analyze how this potential changes during the changes by the various operations of an insert or delete. We follow the development of the structure always immediately before the next operation (split, share, join, etc.), so the node degrees $a - 1$ (after a delete) and $b + 1$ (after an insert) are possible. We do not count the operation on the root: creating a new root or deleting the old root, but there is only at most one root operation per insertion or deletion.

We define the potential of the tree as the sum of the potentials of its nodes, where the potential of node *n is defined as

$$pot(*n) = \begin{cases} 4 & \text{if n->degree} = a - 1 \text{ and *n is not the root} \\ 1 & \text{if n->degree} = a \text{ and *n is not the root} \\ 0 & \text{if } a < \text{n->degree} < b \text{ or *n is the root} \\ 3 & \text{if n->degree} = b \text{ and *n is not the root} \\ 6 & \text{if n->degree} = b + 1 \text{ and *n is not the root.} \end{cases}$$

Now each operation starts with an insert or delete on the lowest level; before any restructuring operations are done, this is just a change of the degree of a single node by one, so the potential of the tree increases by at most three.

We claim now that each restructuring operation decreases the potential of the tree by at least two; because the potential of the tree is nonnegative and initially bounded by $6n$, this implies that each insert or delete can on the average cause at most $\frac{3}{2}$ restructuring operations, plus possibly one root operation. We have to check this claim for each of the following restructuring operations:

− For insertions the current node has degree $b + 1$.

  a. We do not count the root operation.
  b. A splitting operation takes the current node of degree $b + 1$ and splits it into two nodes of degree $\lceil \frac{b+1}{2} \rceil$ and $\lfloor \frac{b+1}{2} \rfloor$. Also, it increases the degree of the upper neighbor node. This removes a node of potential 6 and creates two new nodes, of which at most one has potential 1 (degree a) and the other has potential 0 (degree between $a + 1$ and $b - 1$), and it increases the degree of the upper neighbor node by 1 and so its potential by at most 3: in total the potential decreases by at least 2.

− For deletions the current node has degree $a - 1$ if it is not the root.

  a. Again we do not count the root operation.
  b. A sharing operation takes the current node of degree $a - 1$ and its neighbor of degree at least $a + 1$ and at most b, and creates two new nodes, each of degree at least a and less than b. This removes a node of potential 4 and a node of nonnegative potential, and creates two new nodes, each with potential at most 1: in total the potential decreases by at least 2.
  c. A joining operation takes the current node of degree $a - 1$ and its neighbor of degree a, and creates one new node of degree $2a - 1 < b$, and decreases the degree of the upper neighbor node by one. This

removes two nodes of potential 4 and 1, and creates one new node of potential 0 and increases the potential of the upper neighbor by at most 3: in total the potential decreases by at least 2.

Together this proves that the (a, b)-tree structure can be maintained efficiently.

Theorem. The (a, b)-tree structure supports find, insert, and delete with $O(\log_a n)$ block read or write operations and needs only an amortized $O(1)$ block writes per insert or delete.

We finally have to show one possible implementation of this structure.

```
tree_node_t *create_tree()
{   tree_node_t *tmp;
    tmp = get_node();
    tmp->height = 0;
    tmp->degree = 0;
    return( tmp );
}

int insert(tree_node_t *tree, key_t new_key,
            object_t *new_object)
{   tree_node_t *current_node, *insert_pt;
    key_t   insert_key;
    int finished;
    current_node = tree;
    if( tree->height == 0 && tree->degree == 0 )
    {   tree->key[0]  = new_key;
        tree->next[0] = (tree_node_t *) new_object;
        tree->degree  = 1;
        return(0); /* insert in empty tree */
    }
    create_stack();
    while( current_node->height > 0 )
    /* not at leaf level */
    {   int lower, upper;
        /* binary search among keys */
        push( current_node );
        lower = 0;   upper = current_node->degree;
        while( upper > lower +1 )
        {   if( new_key <
```

```
         current_node->key[(upper+lower)/2 ] )
            upper = (upper+lower)/2;
         else
            lower = (upper+lower)/2;
      }
      current_node = current_node->next[lower];
   } /* now current_node is leaf node in which
        we insert */
   insert_pt = (tree_node_t *) new_object;
   insert_key = new_key;
   finished = 0;
   while( !finished )
   {  int i, start;
      if( current_node->height > 0 )
         start = 1;
         /* insertion in non-leaf starts at 1 */
      else
         start = 0;
         /* insertion in non-leaf starts at 0 */
      if( current_node->degree < B )
           /* node still has room */
      {  /* move everything up to create
         the insertion gap */
         i = current_node->degree;
         while((i > start)&&
         (current_node->key[i-1] > insert_key))
         {  current_node->key[i]   =
            current_node->key[i-1];
            current_node->next[i] =
            current_node->next[i-1];
            i -= 1;
         }
         current_node->key[i]  = insert_key;
         current_node->next[i] = insert_pt;
         current_node->degree +=1;
         finished = 1;
      } /* end insert in non-full node */
      else /* node is full, have to split
      the node*/
```

```
{   tree_node_t *new_node;
    int j, insert_done=0;
    new_node = get_node();
    i= B-1; j = (B-1)/2;
    while( j >= 0 )
    /* copy upper half to new node */
    {   if( insert_done ||
        insert_key < current_node->key[i] )
        {   new_node->next[j]   =
            current_node->next[i];
            new_node->key[j--] =
            current_node->key[i--];
        }
        else
        {   new_node->next[j]   = insert_pt;
            new_node->key[j--] = insert_key;
            insert_done = 1;
        }
    } /* upper half done, insert in lower
    half, if necessary*/
    while( !insert_done)
    {   if( insert_key < current_node->key[i]
        && i >= start )
        {   current_node->next[i+1] =
            current_node->next[i];
            current_node->key[i+1]  =
            current_node->key[i];
            i -=1;
        }
        else
        {   current_node->next[i+1] =
            insert_pt;
            current_node->key[i+1]  =
            insert_key;
            insert_done = 1;
        }
    } /*finished insertion */
    current_node->degree = B+1 - ((B+1)/2);
    new_node->degree = (B+1)/2;
```

```
          new_node->height = current_node->height;
          /* split nodes complete, now insert the
          new node above */
          insert_pt  = new_node;
          insert_key = new_node->key[0];
          if( ! stack_empty() )
          /* not at root; move one level up*/
          {   current_node = pop();
          }
          else /* splitting root: needs copy to
          keep root address*/
          {   new_node = get_node();
              for( i=0; i < current_node->degree;
                   i++ )
              {   new_node->next[i] =
                  current_node->next[i];
                  new_node->key[i]  =
                  current_node->key[i];
              }
              new_node->height =
              current_node->height;
              new_node->degree =
              current_node->degree;
              current_node->height += 1;
              current_node->degree  = 2;
              current_node->next[0] = new_node;
              current_node->next[1] = insert_pt;
              current_node->key[1]  = insert_key;
              finished =1;
          } /* end splitting root */
       } /* end node splitting */
    } /* end of rebalancing */
    remove_stack();
    return( 0 );
}


object_t *delete(tree_node_t *tree,
key_t delete_key)
{   tree_node_t *current, *tmp_node;
```

```
int finished, i, j;
current = tree;
create_node_stack(); create_index_stack();
while( current->height > 0 ) /* not
at leaf level */
{   int lower, upper;
    /* binary search among keys */
    lower = 0;    upper = current->degree;
    while( upper > lower +1 )
    {   if( delete_key <
        current->key[ (upper+lower)/2 ] )
            upper = (upper+lower)/2;
        else
            lower = (upper+lower)/2;
    }
    push_index_stack( lower );
    push_node_stack( current );
    current = current->next[lower];
} /* now current is leaf node from
which we delete */
for( i=0; i < current->degree ; i++ )
    if( current->key[i] == delete_key )
        break;
if( i == current->degree )
{   return( NULL ); /* delete failed;
    key does not exist */
}
else /* key exists, now delete from
leaf node */
{   object_t *del_object;
    del_object = (object_t *) current->next[i];
    current->degree -=1;
    while( i < current->degree )
    {   current->next[i] = current->next[i+1];
        current->key[i]  = current->key[i+1];
        i+=1;
    } /* deleted from node, now rebalance */
    finished = 0;
    while( ! finished )
```

```
{   if(current->degree >= A )
    {  finished = 1; /* node still full
       enough, can stop */
    }
    else /* node became underfull */
    {  if( stack_empty() )
       /* current is root */
       {  if(current->degree >= 2 )
              finished = 1; /* root
              still necessary */
          else if ( current->height == 0 )
              finished = 1; /* deleting
              last keys from root */
          else /* delete root, copy to
          keep address */
          {   tmp_node = current->next[0];
              for( i=0; i< tmp_node->degree;
                   i++ )
              {   current->next[i] =
                  tmp_node->next[i];
                  current->key[i] =
                  tmp_node->key[i];
              }
              current->degree =
              tmp_node->degree;
              current->height =
              tmp_node->height;
              return_node( tmp_node );
              finished = 1;
          }
       } /* done with root */
       else /*  delete from non-root node */
       {  tree_node_t *upper, *neighbor;
          int curr;
          upper = pop_node_stack();
          curr  = pop_index_stack();
          if( curr < upper->degree -1 )
          /* not last*/
          {  neighbor = upper->next[curr+1];
```

```
if( neighbor->degree >A )
{  /* sharing possible */
   i = current->degree;
   if( current->height > 0 )
      current->key[i] =
      upper->key[curr+1];
   else /* on leaf level,
   take leaf key */
   {  current->key[i]  =
      neighbor->key[0];
      neighbor->key[0] =
      neighbor->key[1];
   }
   current->next[i] =
   neighbor->next[0];
   upper->key[curr+1] =
   neighbor->key[1];
   neighbor->next[0] =
   neighbor->next[1];
   for( j = 2; j <
   neighbor->degree; j++)
   {  neighbor->next[j-1] =
      neighbor->next[j];
      neighbor->key[j-1]  =
      neighbor->key[j];
   }
   neighbor->degree -=1;
   current->degree+=1;
   finished  =1;
} /* sharing complete */
else /* must join */
{  i = current->degree;
   if( current->height > 0 )
      current->key[i] =
      upper->key[curr+1];
   else /* on leaf level,
   take leaf key */
      current->key[i] =
      neighbor->key[0];
```

```
      current->next[i] =
      neighbor->next[0];
      for( j = 1;
      j < neighbor->degree; j++)
      {  current->next[++i] =
         neighbor->next[j];
         current->key[i]   =
         neighbor->key[j];
      }
      current->degree = i+1;
      return_node( neighbor );
      upper->degree -=1;
      i = curr+1;
      while( i < upper->degree )
      {  upper->next[i] =
         upper->next[i+1];
         upper->key[i]   =
         upper->key[i+1];
         i +=1;
      } /* deleted from upper,
      now propagate up */
      current = upper;
   } /* end of share/joining
   if-else*/
}
else /* current is last entry
in upper */
{  neighbor = upper->next[curr-1];
   if( neighbor->degree >A )
   {  /* sharing possible */
      for( j = current->degree;
      j > 1; j--)
      {  current->next[j] =
         current->next[j-1];
         current->key[j]   =
         current->key[j-1];
      }
      current->next[1] =
      current->next[0];
```

```
              i = neighbor->degree;
              current->next[0] =
              neighbor->next[i-1];
              if( current->height > 0 )
              {  current->key[1] =
                 upper->key[curr];
              }
              else /* on leaf level,
              take leaf key */
              {  current->key[1] =
                 current->key[0];
                 current->key[0] =
                 neighbor->key[i-1];
              }
              upper->key[curr] =
              neighbor->key[i-1];
              neighbor->degree -=1;
              current->degree+=1;
              finished  =1;
          } /* sharing complete */
          else /* must join */
          {  i = neighbor->degree;
             if( current->height > 0 )
                neighbor->key[i] =
                upper->key[curr];
             else /* on leaf level,
             take leaf key */
                neighbor->key[i] =
                current->key[0];
             neighbor->next[i] =
             current->next[0];
             for( j = 1;
             j < current->degree; j++)
             {  neighbor->next[++i] =
                current->next[j];
                neighbor->key[i]   =
                current->key[j];
             }
             neighbor->degree = i+1;
```

```
                    return_node( current );
                    upper->degree -=1;
                    /* deleted from upper,
                    now propagate up */
                    current = upper;
                  } /* end of share/joining
                    if-else */
                } /* end of current is (not)
                  last in upper if-else*/
              } /* end of delete root/non-root
                if-else */
            } /* end of full/underfull if-else */
          } /* end of while not finished */
          return( del_object );
      } /* end of delete object exists if-else */
  }
```

We used here in the delete operation two stacks, one for the node and one for the index within the node. Again all stacks in the insert and delete operations should be chosen as arrays; the necessary size is the maximum height, so it depends on a, the minimum degree of the nodes. But in a normal application, the disk blocks are currently chosen as 4–8 kB, so a value in the range $a \approx 500$ is reasonable, in which case our assumption $n < 2^{100}$ implies a maximum height of 12. In most real applications, a height of 3 is already large. Because accessing a single disk block is slow but accessing many consecutive disk blocks takes only slightly longer, the size of the nodes can also be chosen much larger than the blocks in which the disk is organized if the operating system allows to keep these groups of consecutive blocks together.

The (a, b)-tree structure allows for $b \geq 2a$, also a top-down rebalancing method, where all the rebalancing is done on the way from the root to the leaf and no pass back from the leaf to the root is necessary. This sounds convenient and it avoids the use of a stack, but it has the disadvantage that the number of changed nodes is larger. The idea is simple: for insertion, we split any node of degree b we encounter along the path down. This splitting does not propagate up because the node above was already split before, so it still has room for an additional entry. And at the bottom level, we arrive with a node that still has room for the new leaf that we insert. In the same way, for deletion, we perform joining or sharing for each node on the path down that has degree a; again this does not propagate up because the node above already has degree at least $a + 1$, and on the bottom level we arrive with a node that can spare the entry that we delete. Thus we perform a preemptive splitting or joining; we still change only $O(\log_a n)$ nodes, but the amortized $O(1)$ bound no longer holds. Also, we require $b \geq 2a$, so this method does not apply to classical B-trees (with $b = 2a - 1$). A potential useful aspect of the top-down method is that it requires only a lock on the current node and its neighbors, instead of the entire path to the root.

A number of alternative solutions have been proposed for the problem of blockwise memory access. Instead of creating a new tree structure like the (a, b)-trees that is explicitly adapted to the memory block setting, one could use any normal binary tree structure, like height-balanced trees, and try to group their nodes into blocks in such a way that the maximum number of distinct blocks along any path from root to leaf becomes small (Knuth 1973; Sprugnoli 1981; Diwan et al. 1996; Gil and Itai 1999). Because the implicit representation of a subtree in an (a, b)-tree node as an array of keys and an array of pointers is very dense, they have a slight advantage over any method that stores a subtree explicitly in a block. But a method that takes any tree and groups the tree nodes into blocks can reuse the results on the underlying tree structure and can also be applied to overlay structures on trees, as described in Chapter 4. Replicating tree nodes so that they occur in several blocks improves the query performance but makes updates difficult (Hambrusch and Liu 2003).

A different balance criterion for the same type of block nodes as (a, b)-trees was proposed in Culik, Ottmann, and Wood 1981; their r-dense m-ary multiway trees also have all leaves at the same depth, but balancing is achieved by the property that any nonroot node that is not of maximum degree (which is m) has at least r nodes with the same upper neighbor that are of maximum degree. This criterion is similar to the brother trees (Ottmann and Six 1976; Ottmann, Six, and Wood 1978; Ottmann et al. 1984) and inherits from there an inefficiency in the deletion algorithm ($O((\log n)^{m-1})$ for m-ary trees instead of $O(\log n)$).

A method proposed for small block size is to use search trees following the second model, with the objects in the nodes, but keep several consecutive keys and objects in each node (Jung and Sahni 2003). Then each node still has only two lower neighbors – one for all keys less than the smallest node key and one for all keys larger than the largest node key. Because it is essentially still a binary tree, it can be combined with any rebalancing scheme like height-balanced trees. The motivation given for this structure was that the processor cache is organized in the same way as the external memory, only with much smaller blocks. But a single block in the cache might still have room for more than a normal tree node, so packing more information in the node requires fewer cache load operations. But this improvement could as well have been reached by taking an (a, b)-tree with small b like a $(4, 8)$-tree. For large block size this method is clearly less efficient than the (a, b)-tree because the depth of the tree is between $\log_2(n/b)$ and $1.4 \log_2(n/a)$ (for the height-balanced version) instead of between $\log_b(n)$ and $\log_a(n)$.

3.4 Red-Black Trees and Trees of Almost Optimal Height

As already observed in the previous section, the idea of trees with variable-degree nodes is also a useful idea for normal main memory binary search trees. A node of an (a, b)-tree can be resolved into a small binary search tree with a to b leaves. This was already observed by Bayer (1971) simultaneously with the definition of B-trees as external memory structure (Bayer and McCreight 1972). He proposed the smallest special case, $(2, 3)$-trees, as a binary search tree, where any node of degree 3 is replaced by two binary nodes connected by an edge, which he called a "horizontal" edge, because it connected two nodes on the same level of the underlying $(2, 3)$-tree. In Bayer (1972a) he then extended the idea to $(2, 4)$-trees as underlying structure and called the derived binary search trees "symmetric binary B-trees" (SBB-trees). In these binary search trees, the edges are labeled as "downward" or "horizontal" with the restrictions:

– the paths from the root to any leaf have the same number of downward edges, and
– there are no two consecutive horizontal edges.

This structure directly corresponds to $(2, 4)$-trees; if we take such a tree and collapse all edges at the lower end of a horizontal edge into the previous node, we obtain a search tree with nodes of degree ranging from 2 to 4, in which all leaves are on the same level. We know from the previous chapter that such trees have height at most $\log_2 n$, so the derived binary search tree has height at most $2 \log_2 n$. And we inherit from the underlying $(2, 4)$-tree structure a rebalancing algorithm.

A further reformulation was done by Guibas and Sedgewick (1978), who labeled the nodes instead of the edges, making the top node of each small binary tree replacing a $(2, 4)$-node black and the other nodes red. This is the red-black tree now used in many textbooks: a binary search tree with nodes colored red and black such that

– the paths from the root to any leaf have the same number of black nodes,
– there are no two consecutive red nodes, and
– the root is black.

We also assign colors to the leaves; this breaks the complete analogy to (2, 4)-trees but is convenient for the rebalancing algorithm.

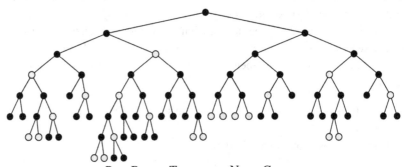

REPLACEMENT OF (2, 4)-NODES TO RED-BLACK-LABELED BINARY TREES

We can collapse any red node in the black node above it and obtain a (2, 4)-tree apart from the nodes on leaf level. So a red-black tree has height at most $2 \log n + 1$. And we have from the underlying (2, 4)-tree structure a rebalancing algorithm with $O(\log n)$ worst-case complexity and that changes amortized only $O(1)$ nodes. The only disadvantage with regard to our previous framework is that this rebalancing algorithm uses instead of rotations the more complex operations of split, share, and join. But there is also a rotation-based algorithm with the same properties that we will describe later.

RED-BLACK TREE WITH NODE COLORS

Other equivalent versions of the same structure are the half-balanced trees by Olivié (1982), characterized by the property that for each internal node, the longest path to a leaf is at most twice as long as the shortest path, whose equivalence to the red-black trees was noticed by Tarjan (1983a) and the standard son-trees by Ottmann and Six (1976) and Olivié (1980), which are trees with unary and binary nodes, whose all leaves are at the same depth, and there are no unary nodes on the even levels. Several alternative rebalancing algorithms for these structures have been proposed in Tarjan (1983a), Zivani, Olivié, and Gonnet (1985), Andersson (1993), Chen and Schott (1996).

Guibas and Sedgewick (1978) also observed that several other rebalancing schemes could be expressed as color labels on the vertices associated with certain rebalancing actions. For the height-balanced trees, it was already long known that one need not store the height in each node but just the information whether the two subtrees have equal height, or the left or the right height is smaller (by one). This was originally intended as memory-saving encoding, but it brings the height-balanced trees also into the node-coloring framework. In a height-balanced tree if one colors every node of odd height whose upper neighbor is of even height red and all other nodes black, then it satisfies the conditions of a red-black tree. But not all red-black trees are height-balanced; an additional restriction is that if a node is black and both of its lower neighbors are black, then at least one of their lower neighbors must be red. Under these conditions, it is possible to reconstruct the height balance of a node from the colors of the lower neighbors and their lower neighbors, and with this information one can restore the height balance of the tree. Guibas and Sedgewick (1978) gave several other rebalancing schemes based on red-black colorings of vertices, most interesting among them top-down rebalancing methods, which can be executed already while going down from the root to the leaf, making the second pass back to the root unnecessary.

A different development derived from the main memory reinterpretation of (a, b)-trees is trees of small height. We have seen in Chapter 2 that the height of a binary search tree with n leaves is at least $\log n$, and we can maintain an upper height bound of $1.44 \log n$ using the height-balanced trees. The bounds for the weight-balanced trees and for the red-black trees are both somewhat worse – $2 \log n$ for the red-black tree and at least $2 \log n$ (depending on the choice of α) for the weight-balanced trees. This suggests the question whether we can do better than $1.44 \log n$ while keeping the $O(\log n)$ update time. Without that, we could just rebuild an optimal tree after each update. The first scheme that reached $(1 + \frac{1}{k}) \log n$ for any $k \geq 1$ (the algorithms depending on k) were the k-trees by Maurer, Ottmann, and Six (1976), but a much simpler solution was discovered by Andersson et al. (1990). They just take a $(2^k, 2^{k+1})$-tree as underlying structure and replace each of the high-degree nodes by a small search tree of optimal height (which is $k + 1$). For the underlying tree, we have again the general rebalancing algorithm of (a, b)-trees, using split, join, and share operations, and on the embedded binary trees these transformations can be reproduced by rotations because we showed in Section 2.2 that any transformation of search trees on the same set of leaves can be realized by rotations. So this search tree structure has height at most $(k + 1) \log_{2^k}(n) = (1 + \frac{1}{k}) \log_2 n$, with fixed k rebalancing done in $O(\log n)$, with amortized only $O(1)$ rotations. Choosing $k = \log \log n$, they get further down to height $(1 + o(1)) \log_2 n$, and Andersson and Lai reduced in their dissertations and a series of papers with varying coauthors the $o(\log n)$ term further. The last word seems to be that height $\lceil \log_2 n \rceil$ cannot be maintained with $o(n)$ rebalancing work, because for $n = 2^k$, the unique search trees of height k for $\{1, \ldots, n\}$ and $\{2, \ldots, n + 1\}$ differ in $\Omega(n)$ positions; but height $\lceil \log_2 n \rceil + 1$ can be maintained with $O(\log n)$

rebalancing work (Andersson 1989a; Lai and Wood 1990; Fagerberg 1996a). All this is, of course, irrelevant for practical applications; the algorithms are too complicated to code, and the small gain in the query time for the find operations (which do not get more complex) would not be justified by the large loss in the update operations.

We already mentioned the height bound of $2 \log n + 1$.

Theorem. A red-black tree of height h has at least $2^{(h/2)+1} - 1$ leaves for h even and at least $\left(\frac{3}{2}\right) 2^{(h-1)/2} - 1$ leaves for h odd.

The maximum height of a red-black tree with n leaves is $2 \log n - O(1)$.

Proof. We already observed that the height bound follows from the height bound on the (a, b)-trees: a $(2, 4)$-tree with n leaves has height at most $\log n$ and each $(2, 4)$-node is replaced by a binary tree of height 2, so the underlying binary tree has at most height $2 \log n$. But we have to show that this does not overestimate the height: the $(2, 4)$-tree of height $\log n$ has only nodes of degree 2, so the binary tree underlying the extremal $(2, 4)$-tree also has height only $\log n$. But we can determine the extremal red-black tree. Let $T_h^{\text{red–black}}$ be the red-black tree of height h with minimal number of leaves. Then there is a path from the root to a leaf of depth h, and all red nodes have to occur along this path; otherwise we can reduce the number of leaves. So the structure of $T_h^{\text{red–black}}$ is that there is this path of length h, and off this path there are only complete binary trees, colored all black, of height i, so with 2^i leaves. Because the height of the binary tree, together with the number of black nodes along the path above the tree, is the same for all these binary trees, the total number of leaves is of the form

$$1 + 2^{i_1} + 2^{i_2} + 2^{i_3} + \cdots + 2^{i_h},$$

where $i_j \leq i_{j+1}$ and each exponent occurs at most twice, once below a red node and once below its black upper neighbor. So for h even the number of leaves of $T_h^{\text{red–black}}$ is

$$1 + 2(2^0 + 2^1 + 2^2 + \cdots + 2^{(h/2)-1}) = 2^{(h/2)+1} - 1,$$

and for h odd it is

$$1 + 2(2^0 + 2^1 + 2^2 + \cdots + 2^{((h-1)/2)-1}) + 2^{(h-1)/2} = \frac{3}{2} 2^{(h-1)/2} - 1.$$

So the worst-case height of a red-black tree is really $2 \log n - O(1)$.

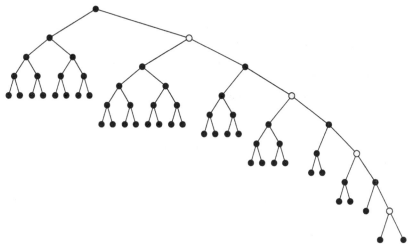

RED-BLACK TREE OF HEIGHT 8 WITH MINIMUM NUMBER OF LEAVES

As in the case of height-balanced trees, not only this worst-case height bound is tight, but it is possible that almost all leaves are at that depth; such a red-black tree was constructed in Cameron and Wood (1992).

We will describe now the red-black tree with its standard bottom-up rebalancing method because it is classical textbook material, and in Section 3.5 an alternative top-down rebalancing method. Both work on exactly the same structure. The node of a red-black tree contains as rebalancing information just that color entry.

```
typedef struct tr_n_t { key_t            key;
                 struct tr_n_t      *left;
                 struct tr_n_t      *right;
                 enum {red, black}  color;
               /* possibly other information */
               } tree_node_t;
```

We have to maintain the following balancedness properties:

(1) each path from the root to a leaf contains the same number of black nodes, and

(2) if a red node has lower neighbors, they are black.

It is also convenient to add the condition

– the root is black.

This is no restriction because we can always color the root black without affecting the other conditions; but this assumption guarantees that each red node has an upper neighbor that is black, so we can conceptually collapse all red nodes into their upper neighbors to get the isomorphism with (2, 4)-trees.

The rebalancing operations are different for insert and delete operations. For insert, we perform the basic insert and color both new leaves red. This possibly violates condition (2), but preserves condition (1); so the rebalancing after the insert starts with a red node with red lower neighbors and moves this color conflict up along the path to the root till it disappears.

For delete, we perform the basic delete but retain the colors of the nodes; if the deleted leaves were black, this violates condition (1) but preserves condition (2); again we will move this violation up along the path to the root till it disappears.

The insert-rebalance method works as follows: If the violation of (2) occurs in the root, we color the root black. Else let `*upper` be a node with lower neighbors `*current` and `*other`, where `*current` is the upper node of a pair of red nodes violating (2). Because there is only one pair of nodes violating (2), `*upper` is a black node. Now the rules are as follows:

1. If `other` is red, color `current` and `other` black and `upper` red.
2. If `current = upper->left`
   2.1 If `current->right->color` is black,
       perform a right rotation around `upper` and color `upper->right` red.
   2.2 If `current->right->color` is red,
       perform a left rotation around `current` followed by a right rotation around `upper`, and color `upper->right` and `upper->left` black and `upper` red.
3. If `current = upper->right`
   3.1 If `current->left->color` is black,
       perform a left rotation around `upper` and color `upper->left` red.
   3.2 If `current->left->color` is red,
       perform a right rotation around `current` followed by a left rotation around `upper`, and color `upper->right` and `upper->left` black and `upper` red.

It is easy to see that condition (1) is preserved by these operations, and the violation of condition (2) is moved two nodes up in the tree for cases 1, 2.2, and 3.2 and disappears for cases 2.1 and 3.1 or if it was in the root. Because we need only $O(1)$ work on each level along the path to the root of length $O(\log n)$, this rebalancing takes $O(\log n)$ time.

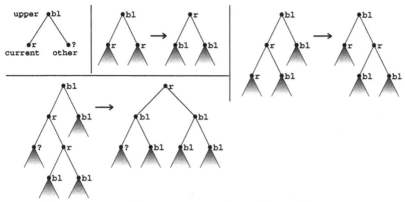

SITUATION AND CASES 1, 2.1, AND 2.2 OF INSERT-REBALANCE
current HAS A RED LOWER NEIGHBOR

Indeed, with the same argument as for (a, b)-trees in general, we can show that the amortized number of rotations is only $O(1)$. Associate with each black node the number of red nodes for which this node is the next black node above it, and give black nodes potential 1, 0, 3, 6 if they are associated with 0, 1, 2, 3 red nodes, respectively. Then each basic insert increases the sum of potentials by at least 3, whereas operations 1, 2.2, and 3.2 decrease the sum of potentials by at least 2, and operations 2.1 and 3.1 can occur only once during the rebalancing. This same analysis works although the rebalancing method by rotations is not equivalent to the rebalancing by split, join, and share.

By a slight complication of the rebalancing rules, we could even get a worst-case number of four rotations in an insert rebalancing. In the cases 2.2 and 3.2, which are the only rotation cases that propagate the color conflict, we need to color upper->right and upper->left black because it is possible that both lower neighbors of current are red; but that can happen only once on the leaf level. After that, there is always at most one red lower neighbor. Then we could color in the cases 2.2 and 3.2 upper->right and upper->left red and upper black; with that change, all rotation cases above the leaf level would remove the color conflict.

The delete rebalance is unfortunately much more complicated.[2] In this situation we have a violation of property (1): a node *current for which all paths through that node to a leaf contain one black node less than they should. There are two simple situations:

1. If current is red, we color it black.
2. If current is the root, then (1) holds anyway.

---

[2]It is very easy to make an error among these many cases; in a well-known algorithms textbook, one of the delete-rebalance cases is wrong.

Otherwise we can assume that *current is black and it has an upper neighbor
*upper, which itself has another lower neighbor *other. Because all paths
from *other to a leaf contain at least two further black vertices, all vertices
below *other referenced in the following cases do indeed exist. The cases
and transformation rules are the following:

3. If current = upper->left
   3.1 If upper is black, other is black, and other->left is black,
       perform a left rotation around upper and color upper->left red
       and upper black. Then the violation of (1) occurs in upper.
   3.2 If upper is black, other is black, and other->left is red,
       perform a right rotation around other, followed by a left rotation
       around upper, and color upper->left, upper->right and
       upper black. Then (1) is restored.
   3.3 If upper is black, other is red, and other->left->left is
       black, perform a left rotation around upper, followed by a left
       rotation around upper->left, and color upper->left->left
       red, upper->left and upper black. Then (1) is restored.
   3.4 If upper is black, other is red, and other->left->left is red,
       perform a left rotation around upper, followed by a right rotation
       around upper->left->right, and a left rotation around
       upper->left, and color upper->left->left and
       upper->left->right black, upper->left red, and upper
       black. Then (1) is restored.
   3.5 If upper is red, other is black, and other->left is black,
       perform a left rotation around upper and color upper->left red
       and upper black. Then (1) is restored.
   3.6 If upper is red, other is black, and other->left is red,
       perform a right rotation around other, followed by a left rotation
       around upper, and color upper->left and upper->right
       black and upper red. Then (1) is restored.
4. If current = upper->right
   4.1 If upper is black, other is black, and other->right is black,
       perform a right rotation around upper and color upper->right
       red and upper black. Then the violation of (1) occurs in upper.
   4.2 If upper is black, other is black, and other->right is red,
       perform a left rotation around other, followed by a right rotation
       around upper, and color upper->left, upper->right and
       upper black. Then (1) is restored.
   4.3 If upper is black, other is red, and other->right->right is
       black, perform a right rotation around upper, followed by a right

rotation around `upper->right`, and color `upper->right->`
`right` red, `upper->right` and `upper` black. Then (1) is restored.

4.4 If `upper` is black, `other` is red, and `other->right->right` is
red, perform a right rotation around `upper`, followed by a left rotation
around `upper->right->left`, and a right rotation around
`upper->right`, and color `upper->right->right` and
`upper->right->left` black, `upper->right` red, and `upper`
black. Then (1) is restored.

4.5 If `upper` is red, `other` is black, and `other->right` is black,
perform a right rotation around `upper` and color `upper->right`
red and `upper` black. Then (1) is restored.

4.6 If `upper` is red, `other` is black, and `other->right` is red,
perform a left rotation around `other`, followed by a right rotation
around `upper`, and color `upper->left` and `upper->right`
black and `upper` red. Then (1) is restored.

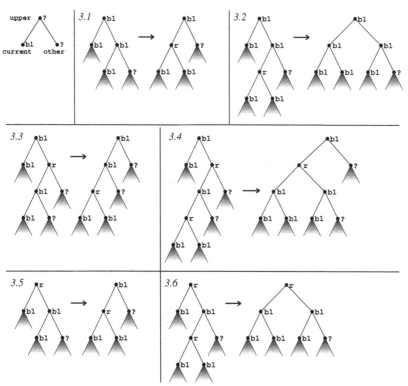

SITUATION AND CASES 3.1 TO 3.6 OF DELETE REBALANCE:
THE PATHS THROUGH `current` HAVE ONE BLACK NODE TOO FEW

Again we perform only $O(1)$ work per level along the path from the leaf to the root, so $O(\log n)$ in total. Only the operations 3.1 and 4.1 can occur more than once, but these can indeed occur $\Omega(\log n)$ times, as one can see when one starts with a complete binary tree, colored entirely black, and removes one vertex. This completes the proof that rebalancing can be done for red-black trees after insertions and deletions in $O(\log n)$ time.

Theorem. The red-black tree structure supports f ind, insert, and delete in $O(\log n)$ time.

Again we give an implementation of insert in red-black trees.

```
int insert(tree_node_t *tree, key_t new_key,
object_t *new_object)
{   tree_node_t *current_node;
    int finished = 0;
    if( tree->left == NULL )
    {   tree->left = (tree_node_t *) new_object;
        tree->key  = new_key;
        tree->color = black;
        /* root is always black */
        tree->right  = NULL;
    }
    else
    {   create_stack();
        current_node = tree;
        while( current_node->right != NULL )
        {   push( current_node );
            if( new_key < current_node->key )
                current_node = current_node->left;
            else
                current_node =
                current_node->right;
        }
        /* found the candidate leaf.
           Test whether key distinct */
        if( current_node->key == new_key )
            return( -1 );
        /* key is distinct,
           now perform the insert */
```

```
{   tree_node_t *old_leaf, *new_leaf;
    old_leaf = get_node();
    old_leaf->left = current_node->left;
    old_leaf->key = current_node->key;
    old_leaf->right  = NULL;
    old_leaf->color = red;
    new_leaf = get_node();
    new_leaf->left = (tree_node_t *)
    new_object;
    new_leaf->key = new_key;
    new_leaf->right  = NULL;
    new_leaf->color = red;
    if( current_node->key < new_key )
    {   current_node->left  = old_leaf;
        current_node->right = new_leaf;
        current_node->key = new_key;
    }
    else
    {   current_node->left  = new_leaf;
        current_node->right = old_leaf;
    }
}
/* rebalance */
if( current_node->color == black ||
    current_node == tree )
    finished = 1;
/* else: current_node is upper node of
red-red conflict*/
while( !stack_empty() && !finished )
{   tree_node_t *upper_node, *other_node;
    upper_node = pop();
    if(upper_node->left->color ==
        upper_node->right->color)
    {   /* both red, and upper_node black */
        upper_node->left->color = black;
        upper_node->right->color = black;
        upper_node->color = red;
    }
    else /* current_node red,
```

```
other_node black */
{   if ( current_node == upper_node->left)
    {   other_node = upper_node->right;
        /* other_node->color == black */
        if ( current_node->right->color ==
        black )
        {   right_rotation ( upper_node ) ;
            upper_node->right->color = red;
            upper_node->color = black;
            finished = 1;
        }
        else /* current_node->right->color
        == red */
        {   left_rotation ( current_node ) ;
            right_rotation ( upper_node ) ;
            upper_node->right->color =
            black;
            upper_node->left->color =
            black;
            upper_node->color = red;
        }
    }
    else /* current_node ==
    upper_node->right */
    {   other_node = upper_node->left;
        /* other_node->color == black */
        if ( current_node->left->color ==
        black )
        {   left_rotation ( upper_node ) ;
            upper_node->left->color = red;
            upper_node->color = black;
            finished = 1;
        }
        else /* current_node->left->color
        == red */
        {   right_rotation ( current_node ) ;
            left_rotation ( upper_node ) ;
            upper_node->right->color =
            black;
```

```
                    upper_node->left->color =
                    black;
                    upper_node->color = red;
                  }
                } /* end current_node left/right
                of upper */
                current_node = upper_node;
              } /*end other_node red/black */
              if( !finished && !stack_empty() )
              /* upper is red, conflict possibly
              propagates upward */
              {  current_node = pop();
                 if( current_node->color == black )
                    finished = 1;
                    /* no conflict above */
                    /* else: current is upper node of
                    red-red conflict*/
              }
            } /* end while loop moving back to root */
            tree->color = black; /* root is
            always black */
      }
      remove_stack();
      return( 0 );
}
```

We do not give code for the delete function, which works in the same way but with the numerous cases given in the delete rebalance description. Again, as in the previous chapter, the stack should be chosen as array.

3.5 Top-Down Rebalancing for Red-Black Trees

The method of the previous section was again very similar to the height-balanced and weight-balanced trees discussed in Sections 3.1 and 3.2; it separates the finding of the leaf from the rebalancing, which is done in a bottom-up way, returning from the leaf back to the root. But red-black trees also allow a top-down rebalancing, as did weight-balanced trees and (a, b)-trees, which performs the rebalancing on the way down to the leaf, without the need to return to the root. This method is a special case of the method we mentioned in Section 3.3, but we will describe it now in detail for the red-black trees.

For insertion, we go down from the root to the leaf and ensure by some transformations that the current black node has at most one red lower neighbor. So each time we meet a black node with two red lower neighbors, we have to apply some rebalancing transformation; this corresponds to the splitting of (2, 4)-nodes of degree 4. Thus, at the leaf level we always arrive at a black leaf, so we can insert a new leaf below that black node without any further rebalancing.

For deletion, we go down from the root to the leaf and ensure by some transformations that the current black node has at least one red lower neighbor. So each time we meet a black node with two black lower neighbors, we have to apply some rebalancing transformation; this corresponds to the joining or sharing of (2, 4)-nodes of degree 2. Thus we arrive at the leaf level in a black node that has at least one red lower neighbor, so we can delete a leaf below that black node without any further rebalancing.

The following are the rebalancing rules for the top-down insertion: Let *current be the current black node on the search path and *upper be the black node preceding it (with perhaps a red node between these two black nodes). By our rebalancing, *upper has already at most one red lower neighbor.

1. If at least one of current->left and current->right is black, no rebalancing is necessary.
2. If current->left and current->right are both red, and current->key < upper->key
   2.1 If current = upper->left
       color current->left and current->right black and current red.
       If upper->left->key < new_key
       − set current to upper->left->left, else
       − set current to upper->left->right.
   2.2 If current = upper->left->left
       perform a right rotation in upper, and color upper->left and upper->right red, and upper->left->left and upper->left->right black.
       If upper->left->key < new_key
       − set current to upper->left->left, else
       − set current to upper->left->right.
   2.3 If current = upper->left->right
       perform a left rotation in upper->left followed by a right rotation

in upper, and color upper->left and upper->right red, and
upper->left->right and upper->right->left black.
If upper->key < new_key
  – set current to upper->left->right, else
  – set current to upper->right->left.

3. Else current->left and current->right are both red, and
   current->key ≥ upper->key

   3.1 If current = upper->right
       color current->left and current->right black and
       current red.
       If upper->right->key < new_key
         – set current to upper->right->left, else
         – set current to upper->right->right.

   3.2 If current = upper->right->right
       perform a left rotation in upper, and color upper->left and
       upper->right red, and upper->right->left and
       upper->right->right black.
       If upper->right->key < new_key,
         – set current to upper->right->left, else
         – set current to upper->right->right.

   3.3 If current = upper->right->left
       perform a right rotation in upper->right, followed by a left
       rotation in upper, and color upper->left and upper->right
       red, and upper->left->right and upper->right->left
       black.
       If upper->key < new_key,
         – set current to upper->left->right, else
         – set current to upper->right->left.

The new current in cases 2 and 3 was previously a red node, so both
its lower neighbors are black. After this rebalancing transformation, we set
upper to current and move current further down along the search path
until it meets either a black node or a leaf. If it meets a black node, we
repeat the rebalancing transformation, and if it meets a leaf, we perform the
insertion. The insertion creates a new interior node below upper, which we
color red. If upper is the upper neighbor of that new red node, we are finished,
else the single red node below upper is the node above the new node; then
we perform a rotation around upper, and have restored the red-black tree
property.

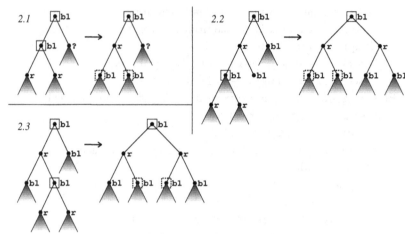

CASES 2.1 TO 2.3 OF TOP-DOWN INSERTION:
upper AND current ARE MARKED WITH current MOVING DOWN

Next we give an implementation of insert in red-black trees with top-down rebalancing.

```
int insert(tree_node_t *tree, key_t new_key,
           object_t *new_object)
{   if( tree->left == NULL )
    {   tree->left = (tree_node_t *) new_object;
        tree->key  = new_key;
        tree->color = black;
        /* root is always black */
        tree->right  = NULL;
    }
    else
    {   tree_node_t *current, *next_node, *upper;
        current = tree;
        upper = NULL;
        while( current->right != NULL )
        {   if( new_key < current->key )
                next_node = current->left;
            else
                next_node = current->right;
            if( current->color == black )
            {   if( current->left->color == black ||
                    current->right->color == black )
```

```
{   upper = current;
    current = next_node;
}
else /* current->left
and current->right red */
{   /* need rebalance */
    if( upper == NULL )
    /* current is root */
    {   current->left->color = black;
        current->right->color = black;
        upper = current;
    }
    else if (current->key <
    upper->key )
    {   /* current left of upper */
        if( current == upper->left )
        {   current->left->color =
            black;
            current->right->color =
            black;
            current->color = red;
        }
        else if( current ==
        upper->left->left )
        {   right_rotation( upper );
            upper->left->color = red;
            upper->right->color = red;
            upper->left->left->color =
            black;
            upper->left->right->color =
            black;
        }
        else /* current ==
        upper->left->right */
        {   left_rotation
            (upper->left );
            right_rotation( upper );
            upper->left->color = red;
            upper->right->color = red;
```

```
              upper->right->left->color =
              black;
              upper->left->right->color =
              black;
          }
      }
      else /* current->key >=
      upper->key */
      {   /* current right of upper */
          if( current == upper->right )
          {   current->left->color =
              black;
              current->right->color =
              black;
              current->color = red;
          }
          else if( current ==
          upper->right->right )
          {   left_rotation( upper );
              upper->left->color = red;
              upper->right->color = red;
              upper->right->left->color =
              black;
              upper->right->right->color =
              black;
          }
          else /* current ==
          upper->right->left */
          {   right_rotation(
              upper->right );
              left_rotation( upper );
              upper->left->color = red;
              upper->right->color = red;
              upper->right->left->color =
              black;
              upper->left->right->color =
              black;
          }
      } /* end rebalancing */
      current = next_node;
```

```
                upper = current;
                /*two black lower neighbors*/
            }
        }
        else /* current red */
        {  current = next_node; /*move down */
        }
    } /* end while; reached leaf. always
    arrive on black leaf*/
    /* found the candidate leaf. Test
    whether key distinct */
    if( current->key == new_key )
        return( -1 );
    /* key is distinct, now perform the
    insert */
    {  tree_node_t *old_leaf, *new_leaf;
        old_leaf = get_node();
        old_leaf->left = current->left;
        old_leaf->key = current->key;
        old_leaf->right  = NULL;
        old_leaf->color = red;
        new_leaf = get_node();
        new_leaf->left = (tree_node_t *)
        new_object;
        new_leaf->key = new_key;
        new_leaf->right  = NULL;
        new_leaf->color = red;
        if( current->key < new_key )
        {   current->left  = old_leaf;
            current->right = new_leaf;
            current->key = new_key;
        }
        else
        {   current->left  = new_leaf;
            current->right = old_leaf;
        }
    }
}
return( 0 );
}
```

The rebalancing rules for the top-down deletion are again more complicated. Let *current be the current black node on the search path and *upper be the black node preceding it (with perhaps a red node between these two black nodes). We need to maintain that below that at least one of upper->left and upper->right is red.

1. If at least one of current->left and current->right is red, no rebalancing is necessary. Set upper to current and move current down the search path to the next black node.
2. If current->left and current->right are both black, and current->key < upper->key
   2.1 If current = upper->left, and
       2.1.1 upper->right->left->left and upper->right->left->right are both black:
             Perform a left rotation in upper and color upper->left black, and upper->left->left and upper->left->right red, and set current and upper to upper->left.
       2.1.2 upper->right->left->left is red:
             Perform a right rotation in upper->right->left, followed by a right rotation in upper->right and a left rotation in upper, and color upper->left and upper->right->left black, and upper->right and upper->left->left red, and set current and upper to upper->left.
       2.1.3 upper->right->left->left is black and upper->right->left->right is red:
             Perform a right rotation in upper->right, followed by a left rotation in upper, and color upper->left and upper->right->left black, and upper->right and upper->left->left red, and set current and upper to upper->left.
   2.2 If current = upper->left->left, and
       2.2.1 upper->left->right->left and upper->left->right->right are both black: Color upper->left->left and upper->left->right red, and upper->left black, and set current and upper to upper->left.
       2.2.2 upper->left->right->right is red:
             Perform a left rotation in upper->left, and color

upper->left->left and upper->left->right black,
and upper->left and upper->left->left->left red,
and set current and upper to upper->left->left.

2.2.3 upper->left->right->left is red and
upper->left->right->right is black: Perform a right
rotation in upper->left->right, followed by a left
rotation in upper->left, and color upper->left->left
and upper->left->right black, and upper->left and
upper->left->left->left red, and set current and
upper to upper->left->left.

2.3 If current = upper->left->right, and

2.3.1 upper->left->left->left and
upper->left->left->right are both black: Color
upper->left->left and upper->left->right red,
and upper->left black, and set current and upper to
upper->left.

2.3.2 upper->left->left->left is red:
Perform a right rotation in upper->left, and color
upper->left->left and upper->left->right black
and upper->left and upper->left->right->right
red, and set current and upper to
upper->left->right.

2.3.3 upper->left->left->left is black and
upper->left->left->right is red: Perform a left
rotation in upper->left->left, followed by a right
rotation in upper->left, and color upper->left->left
and upper->left->right black, and upper->left and
upper->left->right->right red, and set current
and upper to upper->left->right.

3. Else current->left and current->right are both black, and
   current->key ≥ upper->key

3.1 If current = upper->right, and

3.1.1 upper->left->right->right and
upper->left->right->left are both black:
Perform a right rotation in upper, and color upper->right
black, and upper->right->right and
upper->right->left red, and set current and upper
to upper->right.

3.1.2 upper->left->right->right is red:
Perform a left rotation in upper->left->right, followed

by a left rotation in `upper->left` and a right rotation in
`upper`, and color `upper->right` and
`upper->left->right` black,
and `upper->left` and `upper->right->right` red,
and set `current` and `upper` to `upper->right`.

3.1.3 `upper->left->right->right` is black and
`upper->left->right->left` is red:
Perform a left rotation in `upper->left`, followed by a right
rotation in `upper`, and color `upper->right` and
`upper->left->right` black, and `upper->left` and
`upper->right->right` red, and set `current` and `upper`
to `upper->right`.

3.2 If `current = upper->right->right`, and

3.2.1 `upper->right->left->right` and
`upper->right->left->left` are both black:
Color `upper->right->right` and
`upper->right->left` red, and
`upper->right` black, and set `current` and `upper` to
`upper->right`.

3.2.2 `upper->right->left->left` is red:
Perform a right rotation in `upper->right` and color
`upper->right->right` and `upper->right->left`
black, and `upper->right` and
`upper->right->right->right` red, and set `current`
and `upper` to `upper->right->right`.

3.2.3 `upper->right->left->right` is red and
`upper->right->left->left` is black:
Perform a left rotation in `upper->right->left`, followed
by a right rotation in `upper->right`, and color
`upper->right->right` and `upper->right->left`
black, and `upper->right` and
`upper->right->right->right` red,
and set `current` and `upper` to `upper->right->right`.

3.3 If `current = upper->right->left`, and

3.3.1 `upper->right->right->right` and
`upper->right->right->left` are both black:
Color `upper->right->right` and
`upper->right->left` red, and
`upper->right` black, and set `current` and `upper` to
`upper->right`.

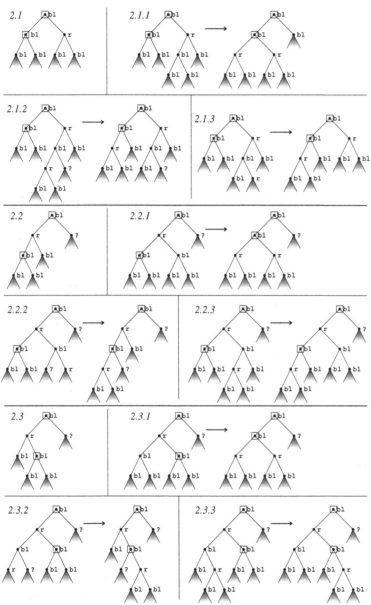

CASES 2.1 TO 2.3 AND THEIR SUBCASES OF TOP-DOWN DELETION:
upper AND current ARE MARKED

3.3.2 `upper->right->right->right` is red:
Perform a left rotation in `upper->right`, and color
`upper->right->right` and `upper->right->left`
black, and `upper->right` and
`upper->right->left->left` red, and set `current` and
`upper` to `upper->right->left`.

3.3.2 `upper->right->right->right` is black and
`upper->right->right->left` is red:
Perform a right rotation in `upper->right->right`,
followed by a left rotation in `upper->right`, and
color `upper->right->right` and
`upper->right->left` black,
and `upper->right` and
`upper->right->left->left` red, and set `current` and
`upper` to `upper->right->left`.

After this rebalancing transformation, we move `current` further down along
the search path until it either meets a black node or a leaf. If it meets a black
node, we repeat the rebalancing transformation, and if it meets a leaf, we
perform the deletion. The deletion removes a leaf and an interior node below
`upper`, but there is at least one red node below `upper`. If the leaf is below that
red node, we just delete it and the red node; otherwise, we perform a rotation
around `upper` to bring the red node above the leaf and then we delete the leaf
and the red node. By this, we have maintained the red-black tree property.

3.6 Trees with Constant Update Time at a Known Location

We have seen that (a, b)-trees need only an amortized constant number of
node changes during any update. This essentially also holds for the structures
derived from them like red-black trees, but here we have to distinguish between
structural changes, that is, rotations, and recolorings. In the bottom-up rebalancing algorithms described in the previous section, we need only an amortized
constant number of rotations but still have to recolor nodes all along the path.
With another rebalancing algorithm, Tarjan (1983a) managed to reduce the
number of rotations for the update of red-black trees from amortized $O(1)$ to
worst-case $O(1)$, but this disregards the time spent in finding the nodes that
should be rotated and the recoloring of nodes along the path, so even if we
know the leaf where we performed the update, it is not a constant update time,
not even in the amortized sense.

Overmars (1982) observed a very simple argument that converts any binary search tree with an $O(\log n)$ query and update time in a tree with an amortized $O(1)$ update time for updates at a known location, while keeping the $O(\log n)$ query time, with just some increase in the multiplicative constant. The technique he introduced is bucketing in the leaves; instead of storing individual elements in the leaves, he stores consecutive elements in a sorted linked list, so the lowest levels of the search tree are replaced by a sorted list. The length of these lists is limited by $\log n$. Then the search time is still $O(\log n)$ because the search consists of going to the correct leaf of the original tree and then following the linked list. The insertion of an element consists of inserting it in the correct ordered list, in time $O(\log n)$, followed by a splitting of the list if the length of the list is above the threshold $\log n$, and a rebalancing of the tree to insert the new list as new leaf, also in time $O(\log n)$. Because the lists overflow on the average only every $\frac{1}{2} \log n$ insertions, the rebalancing of the tree happens amortized only every $\Omega(\log n)$ steps and costs each time $O(\log n)$, so the amortized cost of the rebalancing of the tree after an insertion is $O(1)$. This assumes, of course, that we already know the exact place where the insertion happens.

The same method cannot be used for deletions because a list can become short but all its neighboring lists remain too long to join it to them. Instead, there is a much stronger transformation, also invented by Overmars (Overmars and van Leeuwen 1981b; Overmars 1983), a global rebuilding analog to the shadow copies of array-based structures that we introduced in Section 1.5. The important insight is that in any balanced search treelike structure the rebalancing after deletions, unlike insertions, can be deferred quite a lot. Without rebalancing, a sequence of l insertions in a balanced search tree with m leaves might increase the height of the tree from $c \log m$ to $l + c \log m$, where the rebalanced height should increase only to $c \log(m + l)$. But a sequence of l deletions without rebalancing does not increase the height at all, and the rebalanced height should decrease to $c \log(m - l)$. Thus, we can delete half the elements of the tree without any rebalancing and have still at most only an error $c = O(1)$ in the height of the tree. Thus, we can set a threshold for the number of deletions, for example, $\frac{1}{2} m$, and when the threshold is met, we start building a new tree, while still working with the old tree, copying $O(1)$ elements at a time, for example, four, so that the new tree is finished while the old tree still contains more than, for example, $\frac{1}{4} m$ elements. Then we switch the tree and start unbuilding and returning the nodes of the old tree, again only a constant number of nodes at a time. This way we have only a worst-case overhead of $O(1)$ for deletion of a known leaf. And again this technique can be combined with any balanced search tree, and indeed with a much more general class of objects like the tree with $\Theta(\log n)$-buckets for the leaves described earlier for which we have $m = \Theta(\frac{n}{\log n})$. The main implementation difficulty is that the current tree changes while we copy it.

So worst-case constant-time deletion in balanced search trees is in principle no problem, but worst-case constant insertion was an open problem for some time, finally solved by Levcopoulos and Overmars (1988) using a two-level bucketing scheme, and by Fleischer (1996) using $(a, 4a)$-trees with a single-level bucketing scheme and a deferred splitting of nodes, which become eligible for splitting as soon as they contain at least $2a + 1$ elements. Both methods are quite complicated especially because they have to be combined with the global rebuilding technique for deletions, so we do not give their details.

3.7 Finger Trees and Level Linking

The underlying idea of finger trees is that searching for an element should be faster if the position of a nearby element is known. This nearby element is known as the "finger." The search time should not depend on the total size of the underlying set S, but only on the neighborhood or distance from the finger f to the element q that is searched. The reasonable way to measure the distance is the number of elements between the finger and the query element. And the best we can hope for is a search time that is logarithmic in that distance, $O(\log |S \cap [f, q]|)$. Because finger search contains the usual find operation as special case (we could just add $-\infty$ to any set and take it as finger), it cannot be faster, but the logarithmic query time can be reached.

This needs, however, some additional structure on the search tree. As we have defined it, there is no connection from the leaf to any other node in the tree. We even had to keep the path back to the root on the stack because it was not recoverable from the leaf alone. But adding back pointers is no solution to the problem either because we still may have to go all the way back to the root to come from one leaf to its neighbor, as in the case of the rightmost leaf of the left subtree of root to its right neighbor. We need even more connections in the tree – a structure known as level linking.

Finger trees were invented by Guibas et al. (1977) for a structure based on B-trees and later discussed by Brown and Tarjan (1980) and Kosaraju (1981) for $(2, 3)$-trees, and the concept of level linking is really easiest to explain in the context of (a, b)-trees. In an (a, b)-tree, all leaves are at the same depth. Suppose now we create for each depth i a doubly linked list of nodes at depth i and also add back pointers to each node. Then a finger search method could have the following outline: go from the finger leaf several levels up, move in the list of nodes at level i in the right direction till the subtree with the query element is found, and then go down in the tree again to the query element. The importance of the level lists is that the higher up the list, the larger the distance between consecutive entries in the list: they give views of the set at various resolutions and allow moving large distances with few steps if one chooses the right list.

This idea does not directly transfer to binary search trees because the paths from the root to the leaves have different lengths. But we do not need to assign each node to some level – many nodes can be between levels. We need to maintain two conditions:

1. within each level, the intervals associated with the nodes form a partition of $]-\infty, \infty[$; and
2. along each path from the root to a leaf, the number of nodes between two nodes of consecutive levels is bounded by a constant C.

These conditions are obviously satisfied for (a, b)-trees: there condition (2) is empty. They are also satisfied for red-black trees because the black nodes are arranged in levels, and between two black nodes in consecutive levels there is at most one red node. Because we observed in the previous chapter that height-balanced trees allow a red-black coloring, we can also perform level linking on height-balanced trees (Tsakalidis 1985). So many of the balanced search trees we have discussed allow level linking. The structure of a node in a level linked tree is as follows:

```
typedef struct tr_n_t { key_t             key;
                struct tr_n_t          *left;
                struct tr_n_t          *right;
                struct tr_n_t          *up;
                struct tr_n_t   *level_left;
                struct tr_n_t  *level_right;
                /* some balancing information */
                /* possibly other information */
                } tree_node_t;
```

So in addition to the `left` and `right` pointers going downward, we have an up pointer and two pointers `level_left` and `level_right` that are the links for the doubly linked list within the level. We use the convention that `level_left` = NULL and `level_right` = NULL for nodes between levels, and one of them is NULL for nodes at the beginning or end of the level lists. For the root, the up pointer is NULL.

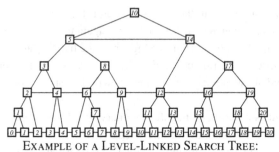

The strategy for the finger search is now that we go up from the finger as long as on each level the next node in the level list in the direction of the query key separates the finger key and the query key. Then below this separating node there is a subtree whose all leaves are between the finger leaf and the query leaf, and this subtree has a number of leaves that is exponential in its height, which is proportional to the length of the search path.

By property (1), each path from a leaf to the root intersects each level. Let n_i be the node on the ith level from the leaf on the path from the finger to the root. We have for each level that

```
nᵢ->level_left->key < finger->key < nᵢ->level_right->key
```

- If `finger->key < query_key`, let i be the last level for which
  `nᵢ->level_right->key ≤ query_key`, then all leaves of the subtree
  below `nᵢ->level_right->left` have key values between
  `finger->key` and `query_key`. So there are at least 2^{i-1} leaves between
  the finger and the query. Now one level higher, we have
  `query_key < nᵢ₊₁->level_right->key`, so the query key falls
  either in the subtree below n_{i+1} or in the subtree below
  `nᵢ₊₁->level_right->left`.
  Each of these trees has by property (2) height at most $C(i + 1)$. Together
  with the path from the finger up to n_{i+1} and all the neighbor comparisons
  on the levels, we have used $O(i)$ work to find a query key whose distance to
  the finger is at least 2^{i-1}, giving the
  $O(\log(\text{distance}(\text{finger}, \text{query})))$-bound we claimed.
- Similarly, if `finger->key > query_key`, let i be the last level for
  which `nᵢ->level_left->key > query_key`, then all leaves of
  subtree below `nᵢ->level_left->right` have key values between

`finger->key` and `query_key`. So there are at least 2^{i-1} leaves between the finger and the query. Now one level higher, we have n_{i+1}`->level_left->key` $\leq$ `query_key`, so the query key falls either in the subtree below n_{i+1}`->level_left->right` or in the subtree below n_{i+1}. Each of these trees has by property (2) height at most $C(i + 1)$. Together with the path from the finger up to n_{i+1} and all the neighbor comparisons on the levels, we again used $O(i)$ work to find a query key whose distance to the finger is at least 2^{i-1}, giving the O (log (distance(`finger`, `query`)))-bound we claimed.

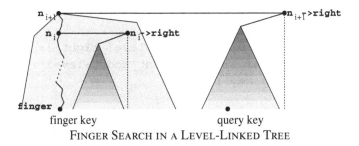

finger key   query key

FINGER SEARCH IN A LEVEL-LINKED TREE

Theorem. A level-linked tree supports finger search in time O (log (distance(`finger`, `query`))).

Next we give code for the finger search. In addition, the tree should of course also support the normal find, insert, and delete operations, and when implementing these, one needs to keep track of the level-linking information. In our finger search implementation, we use the normal find function, which, for this application, should be changed not to return the object pointer but the pointer to the leaf node, otherwise we have no method to obtain the finger pointers.

```
tree_node_t *finger_search(tree_node_t *finger,
                           key_t query_key)
{   tree_node_t *current_node, *tmp_result;
    current_node = finger;
    if (finger->key == query_key )
       return( finger );
    else if( finger->key < query_key )
    { while( current_node->up != NULL &&
             ( (current_node->level_right == NULL
```

```
                    &&
                    current_node->level_left == NULL )
                    ||
                    (current_node->level_right!= NULL
                      &&
                    current_node->level_right->
                    key < query_key) ) )
              current_node = current_node->up;
        /* end of while */
        if( (tmp_result = find( current_node,
        query_key ) ) != NULL )
              return( tmp_result );
        else if (current_node->level_right != NULL )
              return( find( current_node->level_right,
              query_key ) );
        else
              return( NULL );
   } /* end of: if query is right of finger */
   else /* query_key < finger->key */
   { while( current_node->up != NULL &&
                 ( (current_node->level_right == NULL
                   &&
                   current_node->level_left  == NULL )
                   ||
                   (current_node->level_left != NULL
                      &&
                      query_key < current_node->
                      level_left->key) ) )
              current_node = current_node->up;
        /* end of while */
        if( (tmp_result = find( current_node,
        query_key ) ) != NULL )
              return( tmp_result );
        else if (current_node->level_left != NULL )
              return( find( current_node->level_left,
              query_key ) );
        else
              return( NULL );
   } /* end of: if query is left of finger */
}
```

Finger search has been studied in a number of papers; for any search-tree structure or property, one can ask how to combine it with finger search and what the update cost of the finger structure is. This was finally optimally solved in Brodal (1998) and Brodal et al. (2002), where all update operations were done in $O(1)$ time in addition to the time to find the relevant leaf. But in truth, finger search has little practical relevance unless the access is extremely local, for instead of going once down from the root, we go up from the finger to some turning point and then down again (in a most optimistic estimate, the work is really about four times that distance). So this can be more effective than going down from the top only if the way we went up from the bottom is less than half the total height. So if there are in total $c^h = n$ leaves and we go up at most to $h/2$, then the distance between finger and query should be less than $n^{1/2}$ (really much smaller). Otherwise, the trivial find is more efficient than the finger search.

A final problem with the use of finger trees as described here is that the finger is a pointer into the structure, so it is only valid as long as the structure, at least in the memory location of the leaves, does not change. So if one wants the pointers to be valid after any insert, additional care has to be taken to keep the leaf node as leaf. This is different from what we did, which was just splitting the old leaf on insertion. To keep the leaf as leaf, one would have to change the pointer in the upper neighbor of the old leaf. Keeping the fingers valid after deletion introduces the additional problem that the finger element could have been deleted.

A variant proposed in Blelloch, Maggs, and Woo (2003) replaces the finger by a larger structure and instead does not need all those pointers added to the tree itself, making it more space efficient. In our level-linked trees, we really needed only the path back to the root for the evaluation of a finger query, and the level neighbors of that path on all levels; apart from that, we just used the normal pointers of the underlying tree. So the main problem is to make an efficient update of that access structure after a finger query.

3.8 Trees with Partial Rebuilding: Amortized Analysis

An entirely different method to keep the search trees balanced is to rebuild them. Of course, rebuilding the entire tree takes $\Omega(n)$ time, so it is no reasonable alternative to the update methods of $O(\log n)$ complexity if we do it in each update for the entire tree. But it turns out to be comparable in the amortized complexity if we only occasionally rebuild and rebuild only subtrees. This was first observed by Overmars, who studied partial rebuilding as a very general method to turn static data structures (not allowing updates) into dynamic data structures (supporting update operations) (Overmars 1983). We lose by this the worst-case guarantee on the update time but still have an amortized bound over a sequence of updates. Every single one of them could, however, take $\Theta(n)$ time.

The use of partial rebuilding for balanced search trees was rediscovered in a different context by Andersson (1989b, 1990, 1999) and Galperin and Rivest (1993). They were interested in the question how little information is sufficient to rebalance the tree. The red-black trees still needed one bit per node, but indeed no information in the nodes is necessary. One can keep the tree balanced with only the total number of leaves as balancing information because this is sufficient to detect when a leaf is too low.

Given the number n of elements, one can set a height threshold $c \log n$ for some c sufficiently large. Then we can decide, whenever we go down the tree to a leaf, whether the depth of this leaf is too large for the current number of elements. In that case some subtree containing the leaf requires rebalancing, but we do not know where this subtree starts. It could be possible that the next $\log n$ levels above the leaf are a complete binary tree; only this perfectly balanced tree is attached by a long path to the root. So we have to go up along the path from the leaf to the root and check for each node whether the subtree below that node is sufficiently unbalanced that rebalancing will give a significant improvement. This sounds very inefficient, but because the subtrees we are looking at are exponentially growing in size, the total work is really determined by the last subtree – the one which we decide to rebalance.

Our measure for the balancedness is α-weight-balance. Because we use a different rebalancing strategy, the restrictions on α of Section 3.2 do not apply here. We are here interested in $\alpha < \frac{1}{4}$. For α-weight-balance, our depth bound is $\left(\log \frac{1}{1-\alpha}\right)^{-1} \log n$, as in Section 3.2: if along the path all nodes are α-weight-balanced, then this is an upper bound for the length of the path. But we cannot directly use the violation of α-weight-balance as criterion for rebuilding because it is not sufficient to guarantee a height reduction by optimal rebuilding. The bottom-up optimal tree with $2^k + 1$ leaves is extremely unbalanced in the root, but it is still of optimal height. Instead, we accept a subtree as requiring rebuilding if its height is larger than the maximum height of an α-weight-balanced tree with the same number of leaves or equivalently if its number of leaves is less than the minimum number of leaves of an α-weight-balanced tree with the same height, which is $(\frac{1}{1-\alpha})^h$. This guarantees that rebuilding decreases the height.

So the method for insertion is the following: We perform the basic insertion, keeping track of the depth and the path up. If after the insertion the depth of the leaf is still below the threshold, no rebalancing is necessary. If the leaf has a depth above the threshold, we again go up the path and convert the subtree below the current node into a linked list. When we move up to the next node, we convert the other subtree of that node also into a linked list, using the method from Section 2.8, and concatenate the two lists of the left and right subtrees. If the node is the ith node along the path from the leaf and the number of leaves in this list is greater than $(\frac{1}{1-\alpha})^i$, we move up to the next node on the path to the root, else convert the list into an optimal tree using the top-down method from Section 2.7 and finish rebalancing. Because the length of the path is above the threshold of $\left(\log \frac{1}{1-\alpha}\right)^{-1} \log n$, there must be a node along the path where the number of leaves is too small for the height (at latest, the root).

We observe that the height bound $\left(\log \frac{1}{1-\alpha}\right)^{-1} \log n$ is maintained by this method over any sequence of insertions. If the height bound was satisfied before the insertion, then after the insertion it is violated by at most one; but if it is violated, then an unbalanced subtree will be found and optimally rebuilt, which will decrease the height of that subtree by at least one.

Now we prove that the amortized complexity of an insertion is $O(\log n)$. For this we introduce a potential function on the search trees. The potential of a tree is the sum over all interior nodes of the absolute value of the difference of the weights of the left and right subtrees. The potential of any tree is nonnegative, and a single insertion will change only the potential of the nodes along its search path, each by at most one, so it will increase the potential of the tree by at most $\left(\log \frac{1}{1-\alpha}\right)^{-1} \log n$. But the subtree that gets rebalanced is the first along the path that has height too large to be α-weight-balanced, so it is not α-weight-balanced in its root. So this subtree has potential at least $(1 - 2\alpha)w$ if it has w leaves. If we select this tree for rebalancing, we perform $O(w)$ work to obtain a top-down optimal tree on these w nodes.

Theorem. A top-down optimal tree with w leaves has potential at most $\frac{1}{2}w$.

Proof. In a top-down optimal tree, any interior node has potential 0 or 1, depending on whether the number of leaves in the subtree is even or odd. But one of the lower neighbors of an odd node must be even, so there are at least as many even nodes as odd nodes.

So the rebalancing reduces the potential from at least $(1 - 2\alpha)w$ to at most $\frac{1}{2}w$. So if $\alpha < \frac{1}{4}$, we have an $\Omega(w)$ decrease in potential using $O(w)$ work. But the average decrease over a sequence of insertions cannot be larger than the average increase, so the average work per rebalancing after an insertion is $O(\log n)$.

For deletions, the situation is even simpler; deletions do not increase the height of the tree, but decrease very slowly our reference measure for the maximum allowable height. So in order to keep the height restriction even after deleting many elements, we occasionally completely rebuilt the tree, whenever sufficiently many elements have been deleted that the required height would be decreased by one. For this we keep a second counter, which is set to αn after completely rebuilding the tree when it has n leaves. Each time we perform a basic delete, we decrease this counter, and when it reaches 0, we again completely rebuilt the tree as top-down optimal tree. When the counter reaches 0, there are still at least $(1 - \alpha)n$ leaves, possibly more if there were insert operations. So the height bound cannot have decreased by more than one since the last rebuilding. So this operation preserves the height bound. But its amortized complexity is very small, only $O(1)$ per delete operation, because we are performing one complete rebuild, taking $O(n)$ time, every $\Omega(n)$ operations. Of course, an amortized $O(1)$ deletion cost does not imply any advantage over $O(\log n)$ because the amortized insertion cost is $O(\log n)$ and there are at least as many insertions as there are deletions. But we get this amortized $O(\log n)$ update time with very simple tools, just top-down optimal complete rebuilding and counting the leaves of subtrees, together with two global counters for the number of leaves and the number of recent deletions.

Theorem. We can maintain by partial rebuilding search trees of height at most $\left(\log \frac{1}{1-\alpha}\right)^{-1} \log n$, for $\alpha \in]0, \frac{1}{4}[$, with amortized $O(\log n)$ `insert` and `delete` operations, without any balance information in the nodes.

Saving the bits of balancing information in the nodes is not a serious practical consideration, so this structure should not be seen as an alternative to height-balanced trees. But it is a demonstration of the power of occasional rebuilding, which gives only amortized bounds, but which is also available on much more complex static data structures, and in many cases the best tool we have to make static structures dynamic.

3.9 Splay Trees: Adaptive Data Structures

The idea of an adaptive data structure is that it adapts to the queries so that queries that occur frequently are answered faster. So an adaptive structure changes not only by the update operations, but also while answering a query. The first adaptive search tree was developed by Allen and Munro (1978), who showed that a search tree of model 2 that moves after each query the queried element to the root will behave on a sequence of independent queries that are generated according to a fixed distribution, only a constant factor worse than the optimal search tree for that distribution. Similar structures were also found by Bitner (1979) and Mehlhorn (1979), whose D-trees combine the adaptivity with regard to queries with a reasonable behavior under updates. The D-trees, as well as biased search trees (Bent, Sleator, and Tarjan 1985), and Vaishnavi's weighted AVL trees (Vaishnavi 1987) achieve this performance also for individual operations with explicitly given access probabilities, as well as supporting updates on those probabilities.

The most famous adaptive structures are the splay trees invented by Sleator and Tarjan (1985); they also move the queried element to the top in a slightly more complicated way and have several additional adaptiveness properties. A number of other structures with similar properties were found (Mäkinen 1987; Hui and Martel 1993; Schoenmakers 1993; Iacono 2001), as well as some general classes of transformation rules that generate the same properties (Subramanian 1996; Georgakopoulos and McClurkin 2004); also there are versions with block nodes similar to B-trees (Martel 1991; Sherk 1995).

Splay trees have a number of adaptiveness properties; perhaps the most natural is that if the queries come according to some fixed distribution on the set of keys, then the expected query time for a splay tree is only a constant factor worse than the expected query time of a tree that is optimal for that distribution. Of course, as with the finger trees, to make up for the loss of a constant factor, the distribution must be far from uniform, otherwise any balanced search tree has that property.

The other remarkable property of splay trees is that they are simple and do not have any balance information, neither in the nodes nor any global counters. They just follow some simple transformation rules that miraculously balance the tree, at least in the amortized sense.

Splay trees are unlike all other trees in this book in that they necessarily follow the model 2 for search trees, with the objects together with the keys in the nodes. For the various other balancing criteria, we could combine them with either model, but this is not possible for the standard model of splay trees. The adaptiveness of splay trees hinges on the use of the fact that in a model 2 tree, some objects are encountered much earlier than the average depth suggests. There is an object in the root which, if queried, is already found after two comparisons. And the splay tree query moves the queried object to the root, performing some rearrangements on the way, so that if this object is queried again not too much later, it will still be in some node near the root.

A node of a splay tree contains just the key, the pointer to the associated object, and the usual left and right pointers; no balancing information is necessary. So its structure is as follows:

```
typedef struct tr_n_t { key_t          key;
                        struct tr_n_t  *left;
                        struct tr_n_t  *right;
                        object_t       *object;
                      /* possibly other information */
                      } tree_node_t;
```

The left and right rotations must be adapted that they move not only the key, but also the object pointer. We keep the convention to mark the leaves by using NULL as right pointer. The intervals associated with the nodes are now open intervals. The insert and delete operations are just the basic insert and delete with the appropriate changes for this tree model. There is no rebalancing after insert or delete; the only place where the tree structure changes is the find operation.

The rules for find are as follows: We first go down to the node containing the object, keeping track of the way up. Let current initially denote this node. We repeat the following steps, which always keep current as the node that contains the queried object, until current becomes the root and we return the queried object.

1. If current is the root, we return current->object.
2. Else current has an upper neighbor upper.
   If upper is the root, and
   2.1 if current = upper->left,
       perform a right rotation in upper, set current to upper, and
       return current->object,
   2.2 else current = upper->right,
       perform a left rotation in upper, set current to upper, and return
       current->object.
3. Else upper itself has an upper neighbor upper2.
   3.1 If current = upper->left and upper = upper2->left,
       perform two consecutive right rotations in upper2 and set current
       to upper2.
   3.2 If current = upper->left and upper = upper2->right,
       perform a right rotation in upper, followed by a left rotation in
       upper2, and set current to upper2.

3.3 If `current = upper->right` and `upper = upper2->left`, perform a left rotation in `upper`, followed by a right rotation in `upper2`, and set `current` to `upper2`.

3.4 If `current = upper->right` and `upper = upper2->right`, perform two consecutive left rotations in `upper2` and set `current` to `upper2`.

The cases 2.1 and 2.2 are known as "zig," 3.1 and 3.4 as "zig-zig," and 3.2 and 3.3 as "zig-zag" operations.

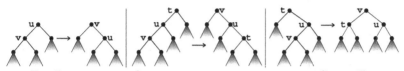

THE REBALANCING OPERATIONS 2.1, 3.1, AND 3.2 ON A SPLAY TREE

We have to show now that these operations restructure the tree in a way that is efficient in the amortized sense. We will obtain several such results by a single proof choosing different weight functions. The weight function w is defined on the objects with the sum of all weights normalized to n and all weights nonnegative.

For any given weight function and search tree, we define several derived functions:

- the weight sum $s(n)$ of node n is the sum of all weights of objects in the subtree below n;
- the rank $r(n)$ of node n is the logarithm of the weight sum: $r(n) = \log(s(n))$; and
- the potential *pot* of the tree is the sum of all ranks of the nodes of the tree.

Now the central tool is the following lemma that describes the potential change by the rebalancing of a query operation. In the following we use pot_{before}, r_{before}, s_{before} and pot_{after}, r_{after}, s_{after} to denote, respectively, the potential, rank function, and weight sum before and after rebalancing.

Lemma 3.1 If the query operation accessing node v used k rotations, then we have

$$k + (pot_{\text{after}} - pot_{\text{before}}) \le 1 + 3\left(r_{\text{after}}(v) - r_{\text{before}}(v)\right).$$

Proof. The rebalancing consists of a sequence of operations, and by the telescoping structure of the claimed inequality, it is sufficient to prove

$$2 + (pot_{\text{after}} - pot_{\text{before}}) \leq 3 \, (r_{\text{after}}(v) - r_{\text{before}}(v))$$

for any operation of type 3.1, 3.2, 3.3, and 3.4, which take two rotations each, and

$$1 + (pot_{\text{after}} - pot_{\text{before}}) \leq 1 + 3 \, (r_{\text{after}}(v) - r_{\text{before}}(v))$$

for the operation of type 2.1 or 2.2, which occurs at most once and which takes one rotation.

– For operations of type 2.1 and 2.2, let u be the upper neighbor of v.
  Because $r_{\text{before}}(u) = r_{\text{after}}(v)$, $r_{\text{after}}(v) \geq r_{\text{after}}(u)$, and $r_{\text{after}}(v) \geq r_{\text{before}}(v)$, the claimed inequality follows:

$$
\begin{aligned}
pot_{\text{after}} - pot_{\text{before}} &= r_{\text{after}}(v) - r_{\text{before}}(v) + r_{\text{after}}(u) - r_{\text{before}}(u) \\
&= r_{\text{after}}(u) - r_{\text{before}}(v) \\
&\leq r_{\text{after}}(v) - r_{\text{before}}(v) \\
&\leq 3 \, (r_{\text{after}}(v) - r_{\text{before}}(v)) \,.
\end{aligned}
$$

– For operations of type 3.1 and 3.4, let u be the upper neighbor of v and t be the upper neighbor of u. Then we note that

$$s_{\text{before}}(t) = s_{\text{after}}(v) \geq s_{\text{before}}(v) + s_{\text{after}}(t),$$

so

$$
\begin{aligned}
(r_{\text{before}}(v) &- r_{\text{after}}(v)) + (r_{\text{after}}(t) - r_{\text{after}}(v)) \\
&= \log \left(\frac{s_{\text{before}}(v)}{s_{\text{after}}(v)} \right) + \log \left(\frac{s_{\text{after}}(t)}{s_{\text{after}}(v)} \right) \\
&\leq \max_{\substack{\alpha, \beta > 0 \\ \alpha + \beta \leq 1}} (\log \alpha + \log \beta) \quad \leq -2.
\end{aligned}
$$

Using this, and $r_{\text{before}}(v) \leq r_{\text{before}}(u)$ and $r_{\text{after}}(u) \leq r_{\text{after}}(v)$, we again obtain the claimed inequality:

$$
\begin{aligned}
pot_{\text{after}} - pot_{\text{before}} &= r_{\text{after}}(v) + r_{\text{after}}(u) + r_{\text{after}}(t) \\
&\quad -r_{\text{before}}(v) - r_{\text{before}}(u) - r_{\text{before}}(t) \\
&= r_{\text{after}}(u) + r_{\text{after}}(t) - r_{\text{before}}(v) - r_{\text{before}}(u) \\
&= 3 \, (r_{\text{after}}(v) - r_{\text{before}}(v)) \\
&\quad + (r_{\text{before}}(v) - r_{\text{after}}(v)) + (r_{\text{after}}(t) - r_{\text{after}}(v))
\end{aligned}
$$

$$+ (r_{\text{before}}(v) - r_{\text{before}}(u)) + (r_{\text{after}}(u) - r_{\text{after}}(v))$$

$$\leq 3 \, (r_{\text{after}}(v) - r_{\text{before}}(v)) - 2.$$

– For operations of type 3.2 and 3.3, let u be the upper neighbor of v and t be the upper neighbor of u. Then we note that

$$s_{\text{before}}(t) = s_{\text{after}}(v) \geq s_{\text{after}}(u) + s_{\text{after}}(t),$$

so

$$(r_{\text{after}}(u) - r_{\text{after}}(v)) + (r_{\text{after}}(t) - r_{\text{after}}(v))$$

$$= \log \left(\frac{s_{\text{after}}(u)}{s_{\text{after}}(v)} \right) + \log \left(\frac{s_{\text{after}}(t)}{s_{\text{after}}(v)} \right)$$

$$\leq \max_{\substack{\alpha, \beta > 0 \\ \alpha + \beta \leq 1}} (\log \alpha + \log \beta) \quad \leq -2.$$

Using this, and $r_{\text{before}}(v) \leq r_{\text{after}}(v)$ and $r_{\text{before}}(v) \leq r_{\text{before}}(u)$, we again obtain the claimed inequality:

$$pot_{\text{after}} - pot_{\text{before}} = r_{\text{after}}(v) + r_{\text{after}}(u) + r_{\text{after}}(t)$$

$$- r_{\text{before}}(v) - r_{\text{before}}(u) - r_{\text{before}}(t)$$

$$= r_{\text{after}}(u) + r_{\text{after}}(t) - r_{\text{before}}(v) - r_{\text{before}}(u)$$

$$= 3 \, (r_{\text{after}}(v) - r_{\text{before}}(v))$$

$$+ (r_{\text{after}}(u) - r_{\text{after}}(v)) + (r_{\text{after}}(t) - r_{\text{after}}(v))$$

$$+ (r_{\text{before}}(v) - r_{\text{after}}(v)) + (r_{\text{before}}(v) - r_{\text{before}}(u))$$

$$\leq 3 \, (r_{\text{after}}(v) - r_{\text{before}}(v)) - 2.$$

This completes the proof of the lemma.

Now we can use the lemma to prove amortized bounds on the complexity of any sequence of find operations. The complexity of the operations is proportional to the number of rotations made in these operations. According to the lemma, the number of rotations in a single find operation is bounded by the potential change of the tree, plus three times the difference of the rank of the root minus the rank of the queried node before it became the new root, plus 1. Over a sequence of operations this becomes

$$\text{number of rotations} \leq \sum_{\text{operations}} (pot_{\text{before}} - pot_{\text{after}})$$

$$+ \sum_{\text{operations}} (r(\text{root}) - r_{\text{before}}(\text{queried node}))$$

$$+ \text{number of operations.}$$

The first sum is a telescoping sum, which reduces to the potential in the beginning minus the potential in the end, and can be bounded independent of the sequence of operations by the maximum potential of a tree with the given weights minus the minimum potential of such a tree. For an amortized bound on the complexity of a find operation, that is, the number of rotations it uses, we have to bound the other sum.

If we give each of the n objects in the tree the weight 1, then the weight of the root is n and the weight of any node is at least 1. So the ranks are numbers between 0 and $\log n$, and the rank difference of the root and the queried node is at most $\log n$. Also, the tree has n nodes, so its potential, that is, the sum of its ranks, is between 0 and $n \log n$ and any potential difference is $O(n \log n)$. This gives an amortized $O(\log n)$ bound.

Theorem. Any sequence of m find operations in a splay tree with n objects needs time $O(m \log n + n \log n)$.

A different model is that the queries come according to some probability distribution $(p_i)_{i=1}^n$ on the objects. Then we give object i as weight $p_i n$. Again the sum of weights is n, so the rank of the root is $\log n$, and with probability p_i the queried object has rank $\log(p_i n) = \log(p_i) + \log n$, so the expected rank difference is

$$\sum_{i=1}^n p_i \left(\log n - \log(p_i n)\right) = -\sum_{i=1}^n p_i \log p_i =: H(p_1, \ldots, p_n),$$

which is the entropy of the distribution. The maximum and minimum potential of a tree with these weights depends on the distribution $(p_i)_{i=1}^n$, and we have no simple bound on them but that maximal potential difference is some number $\Delta pot_{\max}(p_1, \ldots, p_n)$ that is independent of the sequence of the find operations. This gives the following bound:

Theorem. The expected complexity of a sequence of m find operations in a splay tree if the queries are chosen independently at random according to a distribution $(p_i)_{i=1}^n$ is $O\left(\Delta pot_{\max}(p_1, \ldots, p_n) + m(1 + H(p_1, \ldots, p_n))\right)$.

But the entropy $H(p_1, \ldots, p_n) = -\sum_{i=1}^n p_i \log p_i$ is essentially the expected depth of the optimal tree with the given distribution. It is a lower bound even in a weaker model, when we are using a tree of model 1, and are allowed to change the order of the keys and only have to keep the probability distribution; that is, the situation in variable-length codes and the lower bound is a consequence of Kraft's inequality. In that model, that depth, plus at most one, can be reached by Huffman or Shannon-Fano trees. By changing from model 1 to model 2 trees, we lose at most a factor 2 because each model 2 tree can be transformed in a model 1 tree by replacing each model 2 node by two model 1 nodes. Constructing optimal or near-optimal search trees, especially of model 2, was a much-studied subject (see Knuth (1973) or Mehlhorn (1979) for numerous references). So the splay tree needs an average expected access time within a constant factor of the optimum expected access time for that distribution for which $H(p_1, \ldots, p_n)$ is a lower bound. The splay tree achieves this by adapting to the query sequence without knowing the distribution. We used the distribution only in the analysis to define the weight function, not in the algorithm.

Yet another model of the adaptiveness is the finger search. Splay trees support finger search without knowing the finger. Consider a fixed element finger and assign each element x the weight $\frac{n}{\text{distance}(\text{finger, x})^2 + 1}$, where distance(finger, x) denotes the number of elements between finger and x. Then the weight sum is $\Theta(n)$ because $\sum_{v=1}^{\infty} \frac{1}{v^2} = \frac{\pi^2}{6} < \infty$, so the rank of the root is $\log n - O(1)$ and the rank of the query element q is

$$\log\left(\frac{n}{\text{distance}(\text{finger, q})^2 + 1}\right) = \log n - O(\log(\text{distance}(\text{finger, q}))).$$

So the rank difference is $O(\log(\text{distance}(\text{finger, q})))$. Because each node has a rank between $\log n$ and $\log \frac{n}{(n-1)^2+1} > -\log n$, the potential of the tree is between $n \log n$ and $-n \log n$, so any potential difference is $O(n \log n)$. This implies the following:

Theorem. A sequence of m find operations for elements $q_1, \ldots, q_m$ in a splay tree with n elements requires time

$O(n \log n + \sum_{i=1}^{m} \log(\text{distance}(\text{finger, } q_i)))$.

So the splay tree adapts to nonuniformness or locality of the queries in a number of ways at least in amortized sense.

Up to now we have only analyzed sequences of queries for a fixed set, implicitly excluding the update operations. We can perform updates by the basic insert and delete, possibly followed by the same moving to the top done for the queries. And if we use a constant weight one, the same amortized analysis applies, because there is really no difference between the query and the insert or delete. For the adaptive analysis, however, even the model becomes less clear, because we cannot change the weight function whenever the current set changes.

We finally give the code for the find in splay trees together with the basic insert and delete for these trees of model 2. Our conventions need to be changed for this node-tree model; because every node contains the object together with the key, the rotations need to move the object and the key, and we use a NULL pointer in the object field to encode the empty tree. The deletion is more complicated than in our preferred leaf tree model because keys from interior nodes can be deleted; in that case, it is necessary to move another key up to replace it.

```
object_t *find(tree_node_t *tree,
               key_t query_key)
{   int finished = 0;
    if( tree->object == NULL )
      return(NULL); /* tree empty */
    else
    {   tree_node_t *current_node;
        create_stack();
        current_node = tree;
        while( ! finished )
        {   push( current_node );
            if( query_key < current_node->key
                  && current_node->left != NULL )
              current_node = current_node->left;
            else if( query_key > current_node->key
                  && current_node->right != NULL )
              current_node = current_node->right;
            else
              finished = 1;
        }
        if( current_node->key != query_key )
          return( NULL );
        else
        {   tree_node_t *upper, *upper2;
            pop(); /* pop the node containing
            the query_key */
            while( current_node != tree )
            {   upper = pop(); /* node
                above current_node */
                if( upper == tree )
                {   if( upper->left == current_node )
```

```
                right_rotation( upper );
            else
                left_rotation( upper );
            current_node = upper;
        }
        else
        {   upper2 = pop(); /* node
            above upper */
            if( upper == upper2->left )
            {   if( current_node ==
                upper->left )
                    right_rotation( upper2 );
                else
                    left_rotation( upper );
                right_rotation( upper2 );
            }
            else
            {   if( current_node ==
                upper->right )
                    left_rotation( upper2 );
                else
                    right_rotation( upper );
                left_rotation( upper2 );
            }
            current_node = upper2;
        }
    }
    return( current_node->object );
    }
  }
}


int insert(tree_node_t *tree, key_t new_key,
object_t *new_object)
{   tree_node_t *tmp_node, *next_node;
    if( tree->object == NULL )
    {   tree->object =  new_object;
        tree->key  = new_key;
```

```
      tree->left   = NULL;
      tree->right  = NULL;
   }
   else /* tree not empty: root contains a key */
   {  next_node = tree;
      while( next_node != NULL )
      {    tmp_node = next_node;
           if( new_key < tmp_node->key )
              next_node = tmp_node->left;
           else if( new_key > tmp_node->key )
              next_node = tmp_node->right;
           else /* new_key == tmp_node->key:
           key already exists */
              return(-1);
      }
      /* next_node == NULL. This should
      point to new leaf */
      {  tree_node_t *new_leaf;
         new_leaf = get_node();
         new_leaf->object =  new_object;
         new_leaf->key = new_key;
         new_leaf->left   = NULL;
         new_leaf->right = NULL;
         if( new_key < tmp_node->key )
            tmp_node->left  = new_leaf;
         else
            tmp_node->right = new_leaf;
      }
   }
   return( 0 );
}

object_t *delete(tree_node_t *tree,
key_t delete_key)
{  tree_node_t *tmp_node, *upper_node,
   *next_node, *del_node;
   object_t *deleted_object;
   if( tree->object == NULL )
      return( NULL ); /* delete from empty tree */
```

```
else
{  next_node = tree; tmp_node = NULL;
   while( next_node != NULL )
   {  upper_node = tmp_node;
      tmp_node = next_node;
      if( delete_key < tmp_node->key )
         next_node = tmp_node->left;
      else if( delete_key > tmp_node->key )
         next_node = tmp_node->right;
      else /* delete_key == tmp_node->key */
         break; /* found delete_key */
   }
   if( next_node == NULL )
      return( NULL );
      /* delete key not found */
   else /* delete tmp_node */
   {  deleted_object = tmp_node->object;
      if( tmp_node->left == NULL
      && tmp_node->right == NULL )
      {  /* degree 0 node: delete */
         if( upper_node != NULL )
         {  if( tmp_node == upper_node->left )
               upper_node->left = NULL;
            else
               upper_node->right = NULL;
            return_node( tmp_node );
         }
         else /* delete last object,
         make tree empty */
            tmp_node->object = NULL;
      }
      else if ( tmp_node->left == NULL )
      {  tmp_node->left =
         tmp_node->right->left;
         tmp_node->key   =
         tmp_node->right->key;
         tmp_node->object =
         tmp_node->right->object;
         del_node = tmp_node->right;
```

```
            tmp_node->right =
            tmp_node->right->right;
            return_node( del_node );
        }
        else if ( tmp_node->right == NULL )
        {   tmp_node->right =
            tmp_node->left->right;
            tmp_node->key  = tmp_node->left->key;
            tmp_node->object =
            tmp_node->left->object;
            del_node = tmp_node->left;
            tmp_node->left =
            tmp_node->left->left;
            return_node( del_node );
        }
        else /* interior node needs to
        be deleted */
        {   upper_node = tmp_node;
            del_node = tmp_node->right;
            while( del_node->left != NULL )
            {   upper_node = del_node;
                del_node = del_node->left;
            }
            tmp_node->key = del_node->key;
            tmp_node->object = del_node->object;
            if( del_node = tmp_node->right )
                tmp_node->right = del_node->right;
            else
                upper_node->left =
                del_node->right;
            return_node( del_node );
        }
        return( deleted_object );
    }
  }
}
```

Here we cannot use an array-based stack because the depth of the element can be $n - 1$ in the worst case. We have to use one of the linked-list implementations for the stack. In fact, using back pointers instead of a stack to keep track of the path up would be preferable, but then we cannot claim that we do not use additional space in the nodes for rebalancing.

3.10 Skip Lists: Randomized Data Structures

The skip list is based on the idea that adding forward pointers to a sorted linked list that skip many in-between elements may allow a fast access to any element of the list. If we have just a sorted linked list of length n, then finding a query element will take up to n comparisons. If we add a second list on the same items that contains only every second item of the first list, we need at most $\lceil \frac{1}{2}n \rceil$ comparisons on the second list, plus one additional comparison on the first list. If we iterate the construction, adding lists that contain only every 2^i th element for $i = 1, \ldots, k$ to the original sorted list, then we need at most $\lceil \frac{1}{2^k}n \rceil$ comparisons on the kth list, plus one additional comparison on each of the lower lists. For $k = \log n$, this gives a $\log n$ find operation. Indeed, this system of lists is very similar to the bottom-up optimal search tree turned sideways, with a step down to a lower-order list corresponding to a left pointer, and a step to the next item on the current list corresponding to a right pointer. But, of course, we cannot maintain this structure in $O(\log n)$ time under insertions and deletions. Because updates change the distance between elements, we would have to rebuild all those lists from the changed item on.

The idea by which Pugh made this a useful structure, the skip list (Pugh 1990), is that we do not need to maintain the distances that the higher-level lists jump as exactly 2^i on the ith level, but just maintain the average. Here the average is an expectation over a sequence of random choices that the data structure makes; the skip list is a randomized data structure that achieves $O(\log n)$ complexity for the find, insert, and delete operations in the expected value. This expected value is for a fixed sequence of operations, so the same sequence of operations will take varying time depending on the random choices made by the structure.

The skip list assigns each item a level $i \geq 1$ during the insertion of that item. This level will not change while it exists and the item will be included in all lists up to that level. The distribution of the levels is a geometric distribution with Prob(level $= i$) $= (1 - p)p^{i-1}$. A simple interpretation for this distribution is that each item starts with level 1 and then repeats throwing a coin with success probability p to increase its level until it fails, so Prob(level $\geq i$) $= p^{i-1}$.

Now any access to an item, given a query key, starts on the list of maximum level that currently exists. On this list we move until the key of the next item on the list will be past the query key; then we go down a level and repeat the procedure until we are at the bottom level. There we either find the queried item, or, when the next item is already past the query key, no such item exists.

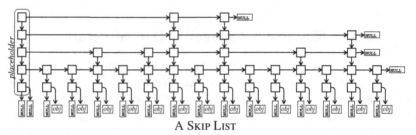

A Skip List

To analyze the structure, we first observe that if there are n elements, then the expected number of items on level i and above is $p^{i-1}n$, so the maximum level where we still expect to meet an item is $1 + \log_{\frac{1}{p}} n = 1 + \frac{-1}{\log p} \log n$, suggesting an expected height of the structure of $O(\log n)$. To make this argument precise, we need the expectation of the maximum level of n elements of the skip list, that is, the maximum of n independent random variables X_j with $\text{Prob}(X_j \geq i) = p^i$. Then we obtain, using Bernoulli's inequality $(1 - x)^n \geq 1 - nx$ for $x \in [0, 1]$, the following bound:

Exp(maximum level of skip list with n items)

$$= \text{Exp}\left(\max_{j=1,\dots,n} X_j\right) = \sum_{i=1}^{\infty} i\,\text{Prob}\left(\max_{j=1,\dots,n} X_j = i\right)$$

$$= \sum_{i=1}^{\infty} \text{Prob}\left(\max_{j=1,\dots,n} X_j \geq i\right) = \sum_{i=1}^{\infty}\left(1 - \text{Prob}\left(\max_{j=1,\dots,n} X_j < i\right)\right)$$

$$= \sum_{i=1}^{\infty} (1 - (1 - p^i)^n) < \sum_{i=1}^{\log_{\frac{1}{p}} n} 1 + \sum_{i=\log_{\frac{1}{p}} n+1}^{\infty} (1 - (1 - p^i)^n)$$

$$< \log_{\frac{1}{p}} n + \sum_{i=\log_{\frac{1}{p}} n+1}^{\infty} (1 - (1 - np^i)) = \log_{\frac{1}{p}} n + \sum_{i=\log_{\frac{1}{p}} n+1}^{\infty} p^i n$$

$$= \log_{\frac{1}{p}} n + p^{\log_{\frac{1}{p}} n} n \sum_{i=1}^{\infty} p^i \quad = \quad \log_{\frac{1}{p}} n + \frac{p}{1 - p}.$$

Within each of these $\log_{\frac{1}{p}} n + O(1)$ levels, the expected number of steps is bounded from above by the distance in that level to the next element of higher level, for within a level we will never go past an element of higher level.

Because we are on a lower-level list, all items on the higher-level lists must be beyond the query key. But each item on a list has probability p to reach the next higher level, so the number of steps on the list before we meet an item of higher level is negative exponentially distributed, with j steps with probability $p(1 - p)^{j-1}$. This argument also bounds the length of the top-level list because there is no element of higher level. Thus, on each level, the expected number of steps is $\frac{1}{p} = O(1)$ and the expected number of levels is $\frac{-1}{\log p} \log n = O(\log n)$, so the expected total number of steps is $O(\log n)$ for any choice of $p \in]0, 1[$. The coefficient $\frac{-1}{p \log p}$ has a minimum for $p = \frac{1}{e} \approx 0.3678$ for which we get an expected number of $1.88 \log n$ comparisons, but the choice does not matter much, $\frac{1}{2}, \frac{1}{3}$, or $\frac{1}{4}$ are good choices for p.

By this we find an element, given its key, or find the place where the element should be. To insert an element, we just need to make the random choice of its level and then insert it in all lists up to that level. To delete the element, we just have to unlink it from all the lists up to its level. Both operations use $O(1)$ work on each level, so $O(\log n)$ in total.

Theorem. The skip list structure supports `find`, `insert`, and `delete` operations on an n-element set in expected time $O(\log n)$.

We still need to describe how the element is represented in the various lists. In the original paper, Pugh (1990) proposed fat nodes that have links for all the lists we might require up to some predetermined maximum level. This, of course, suffers from all the drawbacks of array-based fixed-size structures: if we limit the number of levels of the skip list, then for sufficiently large n it really degenerates in a linked list with a few shortcuts, which give only a constant-factor speedup to the $\Theta(n)$ search time in a sorted list. So instead we represent the element itself by a linked list, which starts on the list whose level is the level of the element, and then connects by `down` pointers to the lower-level lists, until at the bottom we reach the element itself. This does not significantly increase the space requirements of the structure because the expected length of a list is the expected level of the element, that is $\frac{1}{1-p}$. We duplicate the key of the object in each node on this downgoing list. We attach leaf nodes for the objects below the level 1 list. Each of these downgoing lists belonging to the same object ends in a leaf node with NULL as `down` pointer and the object pointer in the `next` field; and each of the level lists ends in a node with NULL as the `next` pointer. At the beginning of each level list, there is a placeholder node that just serves as entry point with connection to the lower-order lists. The structure of the node is as follows:

```
typedef struct tr_n_t { key_t         key;
                        struct tr_n_t  *next;
                        struct tr_n_t  *down;
                   /* possibly other information */
                      } tree_node_t;
```

Now the code for find, insert, and delete in skip lists could look like this.

```
object_t *find(tree_node_t *tree,
               key_t query_key)
{  tree_node_t *current_node;
   int beyond_placeholder = 0;
   if( tree->next == NULL ) /* empty skip list */
     return(NULL);
   else
   {  current_node = tree;
      while( current_node->down != NULL )
      {  while( current_node->next != NULL
              && current_node->next->key
                 <= query_key )
         {  current_node = current_node->next;
            beyond_placeholder = 1;
         }
         current_node = current_node->down;
      }
      if( beyond_placeholder
         && current_node->key == query_key )
          return( (object_t *)
          current_node->next );
      else
          return( NULL );
   }
}

tree_node_t *create_tree(void)
{  tree_node_t *tree;
   tree = get_node();
```

```
    tree->next = NULL;
    tree->down = NULL;
    return( tree );
}

int insert(tree_node_t *tree, key_t new_key,
           object_t *new_object)
{  tree_node_t *current_node,
   *new_node, *tmp_node;
   int max_level, current_level, new_node_level;
   /* create downward list for new node */
   {  new_node = get_node();
      new_node->key  = new_key;
      new_node->down = NULL;
      new_node->next = (tree_node_t *)
      new_object;
      new_node_level = 0;
      do
      {  tmp_node = get_node();
         tmp_node->down = new_node;
         tmp_node->key = new_key;
         new_node = tmp_node;
         new_node_level += 1;
      }
      while( random(P) );
      /* random choice, probability P */
   }
   tmp_node = tree;
   /* find the current maximum level */
   max_level = 0;
   while( tmp_node->down != NULL )
   {  tmp_node = tmp_node->down;
      max_level +=1;
   }
   while( max_level < new_node_level )
   /* no entry point */
   {  tmp_node = get_node();
      tmp_node->down = tree->down;
      tmp_node->next = tree->next;
```

```
        tree->down = tmp_node;
        tree->next = NULL;
        max_level += 1;
    }
    {   /* find place and insert at all
        relevant levels */
        current_node = tree;
        current_level = max_level;
        while( current_level >= 1 )
        {   while( current_node->next != NULL
                    && current_node->next->key
                    < new_key )
                current_node = current_node->next;
            if( current_level <= new_node_level )
            {   new_node->next = current_node->next;
                current_node->next = new_node;
                new_node = new_node->down;
            }
            if( current_level >= 2 )
                current_node = current_node->down;
            current_level -= 1;
        }
    }
    return( 0 );
}

object_t *delete(tree_node_t *tree,
                 key_t delete_key)
{   tree_node_t *current_node, *tmp_node;
    object_t *deleted_object = NULL;
    current_node = tree;
    while( current_node->down != NULL )
    {   while( current_node->next != NULL
                && current_node->next->key
                < delete_key )
            current_node = current_node->next;
        if( current_node->next != NULL
            && current_node->next->key ==
            delete_key )
```

```
{  tmp_node = current_node->next;
   /*unlink node */
   current_node->next = tmp_node->next;
   if( tmp_node->down->down == NULL )
   /* delete leaf */
   {  deleted_object = (object_t *)
      tmp_node->down->next;
      return_node( tmp_node->down );
   }
   return_node( tmp_node );
}
current_node = current_node->down;
}
/* remove empty levels in placeholder */
while( tree->down != NULL  &&
       tree->next == NULL )
{  tmp_node = tree->down;
   tree->down = tmp_node->down;
   tree->next = tmp_node->next;
   return_node( tmp_node );
}
return( deleted_object );
}
```

We could have included a level field in each node; then, we could have put the object pointers in the level 1 list instead of creating leaf nodes for them, and the insert would have been slightly simplified. Instead, we chose the greater regularity of NULL-terminated lists in both directions.

Notice that the insert does not test whether the inserted key already exists; it is always successful. Dealing with multiple identical keys correctly in the skip list is inconvenient for several reasons: if we insert top-down as here, we find out only in the last level whether the key already exists. We could, of course, put the relevant nodes on a stack, and then we could remove them again if the key was already there. Or we could make the insert bottom-up, keeping all relevant nodes on the stack on all levels and inserting nodes in the level lists and making random choices only on the way up again. Unlike the other search trees, the delete operation is simpler than the insert.

This version of the skip list is related to our model 1 trees; a skip-list variant similar to model 2 trees was proposed in Cho and Sahni (1998). Another similar structure, which avoids the multiple levels of lists, is the jump lists sketched in Brönnimann, Cazals, and Durand (2003).

The running time distribution of the skip list has been subject of a number of papers (Sen 1991; Devroye 1992; Papadakis, Munro, and Poblete 1992; Kirschenhofer and Prodinger 1994), but it is quite well-behaved. The skip list also allows simple adaptation to known access probability distributions: if we skew the assignment of levels accordingly, we can make objects queried with high probability have shorter access paths (Ergun et al. 2001; Bagchi, Buchsbaum, and Goodrich 2002). Also, if we add backward pointers in both directions, the skip list is easily adapted for finger search. So if we are satisfied with good behavior in the expected case, the skip list is a very convenient structure.

The skip list can also be derandomized (Munro, Papadakis, and Sedgewick 1992); we only need to maintain the property that on each ith level list, the number of items of level i between two items of higher level is between lower and upper bounds a and b. If we insert an element, we insert it on level 1, and if the number of level 1 items between two items of level at least 2 becomes too large, we insert it in level 2, and so on. And the same in the other direction for deletion. This is very similar to an (a, b)-tree, but worse because we cannot do binary search within the (a, b)-nodes, but must use linear search. For the general similarity of the skip list to (a, b)-trees, note that during find operations we never follow the link in the ith level list that leads to an element of a higher level, so when breaking those links, we really get an (a, b)-tree, but the links are necessary during update operations. By derandomizing the skip list, we lose the simplicity of the random choice, so there is no advantage to the deterministic skip list.

Another randomized search-tree structure is the treap invented by Seidel and Aragon (1996) that is a search tree where the elements are assigned random priorities upon insertion. Then in each subtree the root contains the key of the element of the highest priority in the subtree. This essentially corresponds to taking a uniformly random cut in the elements in that subtree, which on the average distributes the elements sufficiently well to give an $O(\log n)$ expected depth. In the original version, this is described as a tree following model 2, but again the idea can be combined with either model. This structure is represented by a tree in which each node has two values: the key and the randomly chosen priority. With respect to the key values, the nodes are in search-tree order, and with respect to the priorities they are in heap order, which will be defined in Section 5.3; this combination of tree and heap gave the name. As a structure on pairs, so with given priorities instead of randomly chosen, this type of tree was named Cartesian tree by Vuillemin (1980); if n pairs are given in sorted order according to the key component, the structure can be build in $O(n)$ time

(Weiss 1994). Yet another randomized search tree was proposed in Martinez and Roura (1998).

Randomized variants of the splay tree with the same adaptivity properties were analyzed in Fürer (1999) and Albers and Karpinski (2002).

3.11 Joining and Splitting Balanced Search Trees

Up to now we have discussed only the find, insert, and delete operations on the sets stored by balanced search trees. There are some additional useful operations that can be supported by most of the search trees described in this chapter. We already mentioned in Section 2.7 the interval_find query to list all keys in a query interval and the related queries for the next smaller or next larger key. The methods described there also work for any of the balanced search trees.

Theorem. Any balanced search tree can be extended with $O(1)$ overhead in the find, insert, and delete operations to support additionally the operations find_next_larger and find_next_smaller in time $O(\log n)$ and interval_find in output-sensitive time $O(\log(n) + k)$ if there are k objects in the query interval.

Level-linked trees have the links for the doubly linked list of leaves anyway; they are the lowest level. Skip lists have these links in one direction, which is sufficient. So these structures do not need any modification to support interval queries.

More complex operations are the splitting of a set at a given threshold into the set of smaller elements and the set of larger elements, and in the other direction the joining of two sets whose keys are separated by a threshold. Both operations, split and join, can be implemented for most balanced search trees described in this chapter in time $O(\log n)$.

This is easiest for the skip list because the elements of the skip list are assigned their levels independently. To split, we just find the point to split and insert a new placeholder element for the lists that extend past the splitting threshold, and insert NULL pointers to terminate all those level lists we have cut. And the other direction, joining two skip lists where all keys in the first are smaller than all keys in the second, is just as easy; we remove the placeholder elements in the beginning of the second skip list and connect all level lists, possibly inserting additional placeholder elements in the first skip list if its maximum level was smaller than the maximum level of the second skip list.

The total work in either operation is just $O(\log n)$: we have to find the point where to split and then perform $O(1)$ work on each level.

Theorem. The skip list structure supports splitting at a threshold and joining two separated skip lists in expected time $O(\log n)$.

For the worst-case balanced trees, splitting and joining require a bit more thought, but the splitting follows once we have the joining. In the case of height-balanced trees, it works as follows. Suppose we have two height-balanced search trees T_1 and T_2 of height h_1 and h_2, which are separated, with all keys in T_1 smaller than all keys in T_2.

1. If h_1 and h_2 differ by at most one, we can add a new common root, whose key is the key of the leftmost leaf in T_2.
2. If $h_1 \leq h_2 - 2$, we follow the leftmost path in T_2, keeping track of the way back up to the root until we find a node whose height is at most h_1. Because any two consecutive nodes on this path differ in height by one or two, the following cases are possible:
   2.1 The node on the leftmost path of T_2 has height h_1 and its upper neighbor has height $h_1 + 2$: Then we just create a new node with height $h_1 + 1$ below the upper neighbor on the path, which has as right lower neighbor the node of height h_1 on the path, as left lower neighbor the root of T_1, and as key the key of the leftmost leaf in T_2. The new tree is again height-balanced.
   2.2 The node on the leftmost path of T_2 has height h_1 and its upper neighbor has height $h_1 + 1$: Then we just create a new node with height $h_1 + 1$ below the upper neighbor on the path, which has as right lower neighbor the node of height h_1 on the path, as left lower neighbor the root of T_1, and as key the key of the leftmost leaf in T_2. Then we correct the height of the upper neighbor to $h_1 + 2$ and perform the rebalancing, going up to the root.
   2.3 The node on the leftmost path of T_2 has height $h_1 - 1$ and its upper neighbor has height $h_1 + 1$: Then we just create a new node with height $h_1 + 1$ below the upper neighbor on the path, which has as right lower neighbor the node of height $h_1 - 1$ on the path, as left lower neighbor the root of T_1, and as key the key of the leftmost leaf in T_2. Then we correct the height of the upper neighbor to $h_1 + 2$ and perform the rebalancing, going up to the root.
3. If $h_2 \leq h_1 - 2$, we follow the rightmost path in T_1, keeping track on the way back up to the root until we find a node whose height is at most h_2.

Because any two consecutive nodes on this path differ in height by one or two, the following cases are possible:

3.1 The node on the rightmost path of T_1 has height h_2 and its upper neighbor has height $h_2 + 2$: Then we just create a new node with height $h_2 + 1$ below the upper neighbor on the path, which has as left lower neighbor the node of height h_2 on the path, as right lower neighbor the root of T_2, and as key the key of the leftmost leaf in T_2. The new tree is again height-balanced.

3.2 The node on the rightmost path of T_1 has height h_2 and its upper neighbor has height $h_2 + 1$: Then we just create a new node with height $h_2 + 1$ below the upper neighbor on the path, which has as left lower neighbor the node of height h_2 on the path, as right lower neighbor the root of T_2, and as key the key of the leftmost leaf in T_2. Then we correct the height of the upper neighbor to $h_2 + 2$ and perform the rebalancing, going up to the root.

3.3 The node on the leftmost path of T_1 has height $h_2 - 1$ and its upper neighbor has height $h_2 + 1$: Then we just create a new node with height $h_2 + 1$ below the upper neighbor on the path, which has as left lower neighbor the node of height $h_2 - 1$ on the path, as right lower neighbor the root of T_2, and as key the key of the leftmost leaf in T_2. Then we correct the height of the upper neighbor to $h_2 + 2$ and perform the rebalancing, going up to the root.

So the idea is just to insert a new node branching off to the smaller tree on the correct outermost path of the higher tree and use the rebalancing methods to restore the balance condition. We need to go to the bottom of the right tree only to recover the key value we use to separate the trees; if that key value is already known, the complexity is just $O(|h_1 - h_2| + 1)$.

Theorem. Two separated height-balanced search trees can be joined in time $O(\log n)$. If the separating key is already known, this time reduces to $O(|\text{height}(T_1) - \text{height}(T_1)| + 1)$.

We can reduce the splitting of a single search tree at a given threshold into a split along the search path into two sets of search trees, followed by sequence of join operations to collect these trees together into the left and right trees of the split. This works as follows: Given key_{split}, we follow the search path for this key from the root to the leaf. Each time we follow the `left` pointer, we insert the `right` pointer in front of the right tree list, together with the key that separated the right subtree from everything to the left in the original tree. And

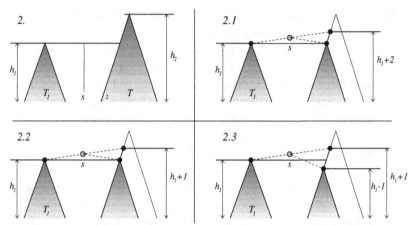

JOINING TWO HEIGHT-BALANCED TREES WHOSE KEYS ARE SEPARATED BY s.
CASES 2.1, 2.2, 2.3: INSERTING THE TREE ALONG THE LEFT BOUNDARY PATH

each time we follow the `right` pointer, we insert the `left` pointer in front of the left tree list, together with the key that separated the left subtree from everything to the right in the original tree.

When we reach the leaf with this splitting along key_{split}, we have created two lists of balanced search trees of increasing search trees. We now join these search trees in order of increasing size (as they are on the list), using as separating key the key associated with the next tree we take from the list. The key of the first tree on the list is discarded. Then the complexity of constructing the two lists is $O(\log n)$ because we just follow the path down to the leaf, and the total complexity of the join operations is $O(\log n)$ as it is a telescoping sum of the heights of the trees on the list. Here we use that the height of the join of two trees is at least the height of the larger tree. Together this implies the following:

Theorem. A height-balanced search tree can be split at a given key value into two balanced search trees in time $O(\log n)$.

For red-black trees and (a, b)-trees, a similar method works.

A final variant that has been studied in a number of papers is the separation of the update and the rebalancing, known as relaxed balance. This is motivated by the external memory model: In order to minimize the number of block transfers and to move them to a time when the system load is otherwise small, one would like to perform just the necessary insertions and deletions but perform the rebalancing later in a decoupled "clean-up" run (Nurmi, Soisalon-Soininen,

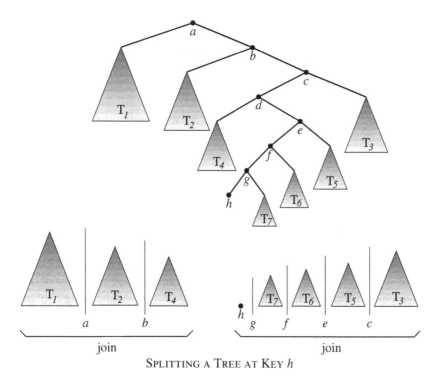

SPLITTING A TREE AT KEY *h*

and Wood 1987). The algorithmic problem here is that in the description and analysis of the rebalancing methods, we always assumed that previous to the insertion, the tree was balanced, so in order to apply those methods, we need to rebalance before making the next insertion (Larsen and Fagerberg 1996). Relaxed balance versions exist for most of the trees discussed here (Nurmi et al. 1987; Nurmi and Soisalon-Soininen 1996; Soisalon-Soininen and Widmayer 1997; Larsen 1998, 2000, 2002, 2003), although for main memory structures this question is only of theoretical interest because problems with rebalancing would occur only in parallel system where several processors act on a search tree stored in shared memory. Related is also the lazy rebalancing, performed only during following queries, proposed in Kessels (1983).

4

Tree Structures for Sets of Intervals

The importance of balanced search trees does not come primarily from the importance as dictionary structures – they are just the most basic application. Balanced search trees provide a scaffolding on which many other useful structures can be built. These other structures can then take advantage of the logarithmic depth and the mechanisms that preserve it, without going into the details of studying the underlying search-tree balancing methods. In this chapter we describe several structures that are built on top of a balanced search tree and that implement different queries or even an entirely different abstract structure.

4.1 Interval Trees

The interval tree structure stores a set of intervals and returns for any query key all the intervals that contain this query value. The structure is in a way dual to the one-dimensional range queries we mentioned in Section 2.7: they keep track of a set of values and return for a given query interval all key values in that interval, whereas we now have a set of intervals as data and a key value as query. In both cases the answer can be potentially large, so we have to aim for an output-sensitive complexity bound. Interval trees were invented by Edelsbrunner[1] and McCreight.[2]

The idea of the interval tree structure is simple. Suppose the underlying set of intervals is the set $\{[a_1, b_1], [a_2, b_2], \ldots, [a_n, b_n]\}$. Let $\mathcal{T}$ be any balanced

---

[1] In the frequently cited but almost inaccessible technical report, H. Edelsbrunner: Dynamic Data Structures for Orthogonal Intersection Queries, Report F59, Institut für Informationsverarbeitung, Technische Universität Graz, Austria, 1980. The first published reference is their use in Edelsbrunner and Maurer (1981).
[2] Again only in an inaccessible technical report, E.M. McCreight: Efficient Algorithms for Enumerating Intersecting Intervals and Rectangles, Report CSL-80-9, Xerox Palo Alto Research Center, USA, 1980.

search tree for the set of interval endpoints $\{a_1, a_2, \ldots, a_n, b_1, \ldots, b_n\}$. With each interior node of this search tree we associate, as described in Section 2.2, the interval of possible key values that can reach this node. Each interval $[a_i, b_i]$ of our set is now stored in a node that satisfies

1. the key of the node is contained in $[a_i, b_i]$, and
2. the interval $[a_i, b_i]$ is contained in the interval associated with the node.

Such a node is easy to find: given $[a_i, b_i]$ and $\mathcal{T}$, we start with the root as current node. The interval associated with the root is $] - \infty, \infty[$, so property 2 is initially satisfied by the current node. If the key in the current node is contained in $[a_i, b_i]$, then this node satisfies both properties and we choose it; otherwise, $[a_i, b_i]$ is either entirely to the left or entirely to the right of the key of the current node, so it is contained in the interval associated with the left or right lower neighbor, which we choose as new current node. Thus, each interval moves down in the search tree till we find a node for which properties 1 and 2 are satisfied. This node might not be unique; if during this descent the key of the current node occurs as endpoint of the interval, then some node below the current node will also satisfy both properties. For the interval tree structure, it makes no difference which node we choose.

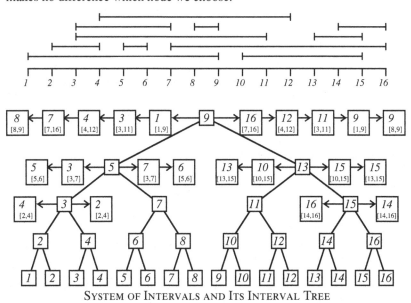

SYSTEM OF INTERVALS AND ITS INTERVAL TREE

Within the node there might be multiple intervals that should be stored in that node. We keep the intervals in two lists – one list of the left endpoints in increasing order and one list of the right endpoints in decreasing order. Each interval stored in that node appears on both lists. All left endpoints are smaller than or equal to the key in the node, and all right endpoints are larger than or equal to the key in the node.

By this we have specified the abstract structure of an interval tree. To implement it, we need two different types of nodes: the search-tree nodes augmented by the left and right list pointers, and the list nodes. The list nodes contain, in addition to the interval endpoint, a pointer to the object associated with the interval. The nodes have the following structure:

```
typedef struct ls_n_t { key_t        key;
                struct ls_n_t  *next;
                object_t       *object;
                } list_node_t;

typedef struct tr_n_t { key_t        key;
                struct tr_n_t   *left;
                struct tr_n_t   *right;
                list_node_t    *left_list;
                list_node_t    *right_list;
                /* balancing  information */
                } tree_node_t;
```

Given the interval tree, we can now describe the query algorithm. For a given value query_key, we follow the underlying search-tree structure with its usual find algorithm. In each tree node *n we visit, we output intervals as follows:

1. If query_key < n->key
   we set list to n->left_list,
   while list $\neq$ NULL and list->key $\leq$ query_key.
   1.1 We output list->object and set list to list->next.
2. Else query_key $\geq$ n->key
   we set list to n->right_list,
   while list $\neq$ NULL and list->key $\geq$ query_key.
   2.1 We output list->object and set list to list->next.

In each tree node, we perform $O(1)$ work for each object we list, so the total time is $O(h + k)$, where h is the height of the tree and k is the number of objects listed, so using any balanced search tree as underlying structure, we get an output-sensitive complexity of $O(\log n + k)$.

We still have to show that the output given by this method is correct. For this we observe that if an interval $[a_i, b_i]$ contains the query key, then it will be stored in one of the tree nodes along the path followed by the query key. On each level there is at most one node whose associated interval contains $[a_i, b_i]$, and if the query key is in that interval, this path will pass through that node. But for each node, we need to consider only those intervals for which the query key is between the interval endpoint and the node key. Because the node key is contained in all intervals stored in that node, we do not need to check the other interval endpoint. Thus

1. If the query key is less than the node key,
   1.1 and the list item key is less than the query key, we have

       left endpoint $\leq$ query key $<$ node key $\leq$ right endpoint,

   1.2 if the list item key is larger than the node key, this holds by the increasing order of the left list also for all following keys, so none of the remaining intervals contains the query key.
2. If the query key is larger than the node key,
   2.1 and the list item key is larger than the query key, we have

       left endpoint $\leq$ node key $\leq$ query key $\leq$ right endpoint,

   2.2 if the list item key is smaller than the node key, this holds by the decreasing order of the right list also for all following keys, so none of the remaining intervals contains the query key.

So this algorithm lists exactly the intervals (or associated objects) that contain the query key.

So far we gave only the structure and the query algorithm. The interval tree is a static data structure, we can build it once, but there is no update operation; insertion and deletion of intervals are not possible. To build it from a given list of n intervals, we first build the search tree for the interval endpoints in $O(n \log n)$ time. Next we construct a list of the intervals sorted in decreasing order of their left interval endpoints, in $O(n \log n)$, and find for each interval the node where it should be stored, and insert it there in front of the left list, in $O(\log n)$ per interval. Finally, we construct a list of the intervals sorted in increasing order of their right interval endpoints, in $O(n \log n)$, and find for each interval the node where it should be stored, and insert it there in front of the right list, in $O(\log n)$ per interval. By this initial sorting and inserting in that order, all node lists are in the correct order. The total work needed to construct the interval tree structure is $O(n \log n)$. The total space needed by the interval tree is $O(n)$ because the search tree needs $O(n)$ space and each interval occurs only on two lists. This completes the analysis of the interval tree structure.

Theorem. The interval tree structure is a static data structure that can be built in time $O(n \log n)$ and needs space $O(n)$. It lists all intervals containing a given query key in output-sensitive time $O(\log n + k)$ if there are k such intervals.

Before we now give the code for the query function find_intervals, we need to decide how to return multiple results – a question that occurs whenever our query operation has potentially many results. Our preferred solution is to construct a list of all results and return that list as answer. This has the advantage of conceptual clarity, but it depends on the list nodes being correctly returned by the program that gets this list to avoid a memory leak. The alternative would be to divide the query function in two: one to start the query and one to get the next result.

```
list_node_t *find_intervals(tree_node_t *tree,
 key_t query_key)
{   tree_node_t *current_tree_node;
    list_node_t *current_list, *result_list,
                *new_result;
    if( tree->left == NULL )
       return(NULL);
    else
    {   current_tree_node = tree;
        result_list = NULL;
        while( current_tree_node->right != NULL )
        {   if( query_key < current_tree_node->key )
            {   current_list =
                    current_tree_node->left_list;
                while( current_list != NULL
                      && current_list->key
                      <= query_key )
                {   new_result = get_list_node();
                    new_result->next = result_list;
                    new_result->object =
                             current_list->object;
                    result_list = new_result;
                    current_list = current_list->next;
                }
                current_tree_node =
                current_tree_node->left;
            }
            else
```

```
{   current_list =
            current_tree_node->right_list;
        while( current_list != NULL
            && current_list->key
            >= query_key )
        {   new_result = get_list_node();
            new_result->next = result_list;
            new_result->object =
                        current_list->object;
            result_list = new_result;
            current_list = current_list->next;
        }
        current_tree_node =
        current_tree_node->right;
    }
  }
  return( result_list );
  }
}
```

There are several problems in making this static data structure dynamic. The simpler problem is that to insert a new interval at the correct node, we need to insert it in the two ordered lists of left and right endpoints. The length of this ordered list can be anything up to n and inserting in an ordered list of length l takes up to $\Omega(l)$ time. This could be reduced to $O(\log l)$ if we represent the left and right endpoints in a balanced search tree with a doubly connected list of leaves and a pointer to the first and last leaf: then we still have $O(k)$ time to list the first k elements of the list and insertion or deletion time of $O(\log l) = O(\log n)$.

The other, essentially unsolved, problem consists of the restructuring of the underlying tree. The interval tree structure depends on each interval containing some key of a tree node. So although not every interval endpoint needs to be a key of the underlying search tree because many tree nodes will not store any intervals, we can be forced to add keys to the underlying search tree. And the tree can become unbalanced by this. But if we wish to rebalance the tree, for example, by rotations, we have to correct the associated lists and this requires that we join two ordered lists which are not separated and that we take apart an ordered list in two, depending on whether the intervals associated with the list items contain some key value. There is no known way to do this in sublinear time.

If we know in advance some superset of all the interval endpoints that might occur during our use of the structure, we can, of course, build the underlying tree for that superset and that tree will never need to be restructured. This can be a quite efficient solution if that superset is not too large. For the left and right lists in each node, we still need search trees to efficiently insert and delete new intervals.

Several external-memory versions of the interval tree structure were proposed in Ang and Tan (1995) and Arge and Vitter (2003).

4.2 Segment Trees

The primary task performed by a segment tree is the same as that done by an interval tree: keeping track of a set of n intervals, here assumed to be half-open, and listing for a given query key all the intervals that contain that key in output-sensitive time $O(\log n + k)$ if the output consisted of k intervals. It is slightly worse at this task than the interval tree having a space requirement of $O(n \log n)$ instead of $O(n)$. But the segment tree, or the idea of the canonical interval decomposition on which it is based, is really a framework on which a number of more general tasks can be performed. Again it is a static data structure. Segment trees were invented by Bentley.[3]

Assume a set $X = \{x_1, \ldots, x_n\}$ of key values and a search tree T for $\{-\infty\} \cup X$. As usual, with each node of T we associate the interval of all key values for which the query path would go through that node. Any interval $[x_i, x_j[$ can be expressed in many ways as union of node intervals,[4] so it can be represented by subsets of the tree nodes. In any such representation, a node that is in the tree below some other node is redundant because its node interval is contained in that higher-up node. Among all such representations there is one that is highest: just take all nodes whose intervals are contained in the interval $[x_i, x_j[$ we want to represent and eliminate the redundant nodes. This representation consists of all those nodes whose node interval is contained in $[x_i, x_j[$, but the node interval of their upper neighbor is not contained in $[x_i, x_j[$. This is the canonical interval decomposition of the interval $[x_i, x_j[$ relative to that search tree T.

Theorem. The canonical interval decomposition is a representation of the interval as union of disjoint node intervals. Any search path for a value in the

---

[3] In another frequently cited inaccessible technical report, J.L. Bentley: Solution to Klee's Rectangle Problems, Technical Report, Carnegie-Mellon University, Pittsburgh, USA, 1977.

[4] Here we need the key $-\infty$ as leaf of the search tree; otherwise there would be no node interval starting at x_1.

interval will go through exactly one node that belongs to the canonical interval decomposition.

The canonical interval decomposition is easy to construct. We start with the interval $[x_i, x_j[$ at the root:

1. Each time the node interval of the current node is entirely contained in $[x_i, x_j[$, we take that node into our representation and stop following that path down because all nodes below are redundant;
2. Each time the node interval of the current node partially overlaps $[x_i, x_j[$, we follow both paths down;
3. Each time the node interval of the current node is disjoint from $[x_i, x_j[$, we stop following that path down.

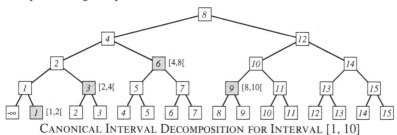

CANONICAL INTERVAL DECOMPOSITION FOR INTERVAL $[1, 10]$

It is easy to see that this operation selects exactly the nodes of the canonical interval decomposition. It remains to bound the size of the decomposition and the time necessary to construct it. For this we look at case 2, because it is the only case that does not immediately terminate. Case 2 happens only for those nodes whose node interval contains an endpoint of the interval $[x_i, x_j[$ that we wish to represent, so the nodes for which case 2 is followed are the nodes along the search paths of x_i and x_j. Each of these nodes causes both its lower neighbors to be visited. Because the only way a node that belongs to case 1 or case 3 can be visited is by being lower neighbor of a node of case 2, the total number of visited nodes is less than $4\,\text{height}(\mathcal{T})$ and the total number of selected nodes is less than $2\,\text{height}(\mathcal{T})$.

Theorem. Let $X = \{x_1, \ldots, x_n\}$ be a set of key values and $\mathcal{T}$ a search tree for $\{-\infty\} \cup X$. Then for any interval bounded by values from X, the canonical decomposition has size at most $2\,\text{height}(\mathcal{T})$ and can be constructed in time $O\,(\text{height}(\mathcal{T}))$. If $\mathcal{T}$ is of height $O(\log n)$, the canonical interval decomposition has size $O(\log n)$ and can be found in time $O(\log n)$.

Now we have the canonical interval decomposition; the segment tree structure that represents a set of intervals $\{[a_1, b_1[, [a_2, b_2[, \ldots, [a_n, b_n[\}$ is easy to describe. It consists of some balanced search tree $\mathcal{T}$ for the extended set of interval endpoints $\{-\infty, a_1, a_2, \ldots, a_n, b_1, \ldots, b_n\}$ in which each node carries a list of all those intervals $[a_i, b_i[$ for which this node is part of the canonical interval decomposition.

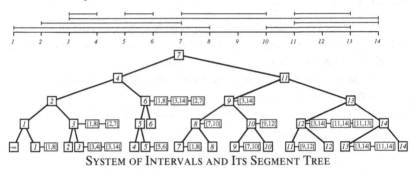

SYSTEM OF INTERVALS AND ITS SEGMENT TREE

With this structure, the interval containment queries are very easy: given a query key, we follow the search-tree structure down and for each node on the search path, we output all intervals on its list. All these intervals contain the query key, and each interval that contains the query key is met in exactly one node. Thus, the output does not contain any duplicates and the query time is $O(\log n + k)$ to follow the search path down and list k intervals. This would work just the same for any other interval decomposition that does not contain redundant elements, but we need the canonical interval decomposition because it is small and easy to build. Unlike the interval tree, each interval is stored in the segment tree many times, so the required space is not only $O(n)$. Each interval generates at most $O(\log n)$ parts in its canonical interval decomposition, so the total required space is $O(n \log n)$. And the segment tree structure can be built in $O(n \log n)$ time, first building the balanced search tree and then inserting the n intervals, constructing the canonical interval decomposition of each in $O(\log n)$.

Theorem. The segment tree structure is a static data structure that can be built in time $O(n \log n)$ and needs space $O(n \log n)$. It lists all intervals containing a given query key in output-sensitive time $O(\log n + k)$ if there are k such intervals.

To implement the segment tree structure, we again need two types of nodes – the tree nodes and the interval lists attached to each tree node.

```
typedef struct ls_n_t { key_t   key_a, key_b;
                        /* interval [a,b[ */
                        struct ls_n_t  *next;
                        object_t       *object;
                      } list_node_t;
```

```
typedef struct tr_n_t { key_t        key;
                struct tr_n_t   *left;
                struct tr_n_t   *right;
                list_node_t    *interval_list;
                /* balancing information */
                    } tree_node_t;
```

Then the query algorithm is as follows:

```
list_item_t *find_intervals(tree_node_t *tree,
                            key_t query_key)
{  tree_node_t *current_tree_node;
   list_node_t *current_list, *result_list,
              *new_result;
   if( tree->left == NULL ) /* tree empty */
      return(NULL);
   else /* tree nonempty, follow search path */
   {  current_tree_node = tree;
      result_list = NULL;
      while( current_tree_node->right != NULL )
      {  if( query_key < current_tree_node->key )
            current_tree_node =
            current_tree_node->left;
         else
            current_tree_node =
            current_tree_node->right;
         current_list =
               current_tree_node->interval_list;
         while( current_list != NULL )
         {  /* copy entry from node list to
            result list */
            new_result = get_list_node();
            new_result->next = result_list;
            new_result->key_a =
                        current_list->key_a;
            new_result->key_b =
                        current_list->key_b;
            new_result->object =
                        current_list->object;
```

```
                    result_list = new_result;
                    current_list = current_list->next;
                }
            }
            return( result_list );
        }
    }
```

Notice that neither the root nor any node on the left or right boundary path of the tree can have any intervals of the canonical interval decomposition attached to it because their node intervals are unbounded and we are representing only finite intervals. Typically, nodes near the leaf level will have nonempty lists, whereas in the interval tree, the intervals tended to be stored in higher-up nodes.

The construction of the segment tree structure has two phases. First the underlying balanced search tree is built for which we can choose any method from the previous chapter or a method to build optimal trees from Section 2.8. We assume that initially all the interval_list fields of the tree nodes are NULL. Then the intervals are inserted one after another. Next is code for the insertion of an interval [a, b[in the tree; the insertion of an interval into the interval list of a node is written as separate function.

```
    void attach_intv_node(tree_node_t *tree_node,
                          key_t a, key_t b,
                          object_t *object)
    {   list_node_t *new_node;
        new_node = get_list_node();
        new_node->next = tree_node->interval_list;
        new_node->key_a = a; new_node->key_b = b;
        new_node->object = object;
        tree_node->interval_list = new_node;
    }


    void insert_interval(tree_node_t *tree,
                         key_t a, key_t b,
                         object_t *object)
    {   tree_node_t *current_node, *right_path,
                    *left_path;
```

```
list_node_t *current_list, *new_node;
if( tree->left == NULL )
   exit(-1); /* tree incorrect */
else
{  current_node = tree;
   right_path = left_path = NULL;
   while( current_node->right != NULL )
   /* not at leaf */
   {   if( b < current_node->key )
       /* go left: a < b < key */
           current_node = current_node->left;
       else if( current_node->key < a)
       /* go right: key < b < a */
           current_node = current_node->right;
       else if( a < current_node->key &&
            current_node->key < b )
            /* split: a < key < b */
       {   right_path = current_node->right;
           /* both right */
           left_path  = current_node->left;
           /* and left */
           break;
       }
       else if( a == current_node->key )
       /* a = key < b */
       {   right_path = current_node->right;
           /* no left */
           break;
       }
       else /*   current_node->key == b, so a
       < key = b */
       {   left_path  = current_node->left;
           /* no right */
           break;
       }
   }
   if( left_path != NULL )
   {  /* now follow the path of the left
         endpoint a*/
```

```
while( left_path->right != NULL )
{   if( a < left_path->key )
    {   /* right node must be
            selected */
        attach_intv_node(left_path->
        right, a,b,object);
        left_path = left_path->left;
    }
    else if ( a == left_path->key )
    {   attach_intv_node(left_path
        ->right, a,b,object);
        break; /* no further descent
        necessary */
    }
    else
        /* go right, no node selected */
        left_path = left_path->right;
}
/* left leaf of a needs to be selected
   if reached */
if( left_path->right == NULL &&
    left_path->key == a )
    attach_intv_node(left_path,
    a,b,object);
}   /* end left path */
if( right_path != NULL )
{   /* and now follow the path of the right
        endpoint b */
    while( right_path->right != NULL )
    {   if( right_path->key < b )
        {   /* left node must be selected */
            attach_intv_node(right_path->
            left, a,b, object);
            right_path = right_path->right;
        }
        else if ( right_path->key == b)
        {   attach_intv_node(right_path->
            left, a,b, object);
            break; /* no further descent
```

```
        necessary */
      }
      else /* go left, no node selected */
        right_path = right_path->left;
    }
    /* on the right side, the leaf of b is
      never attached */
  } /* end right path */
  }
}
```

Again, like the interval tree, the segment tree is a static structure, and we face the same problems in making it dynamic: we have to allow insertion and deletion in each node, and we have to support the restructuring of the underlying tree. For the insertion and deletion in the nodes, we can again use a search tree. But we have to insert or delete the $O(\log n)$ fragments of the canonical interval decomposition for a single insert or delete; so it would be efficient to use a search tree only for the first fragment and then have the remaining fragments on a linked list from the first fragment. Then each tree node would need two structures: a search tree for all those intervals whose canonical interval decomposition has its first fragment in that node and a doubly linked list, allowing $O(1)$ insertion and deletion, for those intervals that started somewhere else. This shows that we can perform $O(\log n)$ insertion and deletion of intervals as long as the underlying tree does not change. A rebalancing of the underlying tree by rotations again causes changes in the lists attached to the tree nodes that can be resolved only by looking at the entire list and so this is no efficient solution. The situation here is better than that for interval trees because the sequence of the intervals attached to a tree node does not matter. This allows a representation of the sets of intervals attached to nodes, which will be described in Section 6.2, which makes segment trees truly dynamic (van Kreveld and Overmars 1989, 1993).

In the aforementioned discussion we have always used half-open intervals because they mirror the structure of the node intervals. It is easy to adapt the segment tree structure to open or closed intervals, but for interval trees, the same is even easier.

An external memory version of the segment tree structure was discussed in Blankenagel and Güting (1994).

4.3 Trees for the Union of Intervals

Several of the early papers on intervals were motivated by a problem posed by Klee in a note in the *American Mathematical Monthly* (Klee 1977), which became known as "Klee's Measure Problem." He asked whether it is possible to determine the measure (length) of a union of n intervals in time better than $\Theta(n \log n)$.

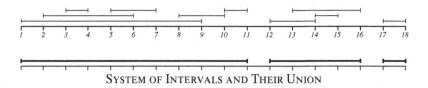

SYSTEM OF INTERVALS AND THEIR UNION

A simple solution in $O(n \log n)$ would be to sort the interval endpoints and then sweep from the smallest endpoint up, keeping track of the number of intervals that the current point belongs to. This number increases by 1 each time we pass a left interval endpoint and decreases by 1 each time we pass a right endpoint, and we compute the sum of the lengths from one endpoint to the next larger one for those points that belong to at least one interval.

The original question was answered in Fredman and Weide (1978), where an $\Omega(n \log n)$ lower bound in the decision tree model with linear comparisons was proved.[5] The higher-dimensional analog of this question, computing the area of a union of axis-aligned rectangles, or the measure of a union of d-dimensional orthogonal boxes was also stated by Klee (1977). The two-dimensional problem was solved by Bentley, who gave an $O(n \log n)$ algorithm for it,[6] and for $d \geq 3$, the best current result is an $O(n^{d/2} \log n)$ algorithm by Overmars and Yap (1991), improving an earlier result in van Leeuwen and Wood (1980b).

All methods for the higher-dimensional measure problem are based on the idea of sweeping the arrangement by a coordinate hyperplane, which intersects the arrangement of d-dimensional boxes in an arrangement of $(d-1)$-dimensional boxes. That induced arrangement changes whenever the hyperplane passes the beginning or end of a d-dimensional box, in which case a $(d-1)$-dimensional box is inserted into or deleted from the induced arrangement. If we have a structure that maintains the $(d-1)$-dimensional measure of the union of a system of $(d-1)$-dimensional boxes under insertion and deletion of these boxes, then we can use it to answer the d-dimensional measure problem.

---

[5] But this bound generalizes to the stronger algebraic decision tree model (Ben-Or 1983).
[6] In the same unpublished notes in which he invented the segment tree.

For the two-dimensional measure problem, we need a structure that maintains the measure of a union of intervals under insertion and deletion of intervals. Bentley's solution to this was based on his segment trees. As additional information, each node n contains the measure n->measure of the union of all node intervals of nodes in the subtree below n that have a nonempty list of intervals attached to them, that is, that are part of the canonical interval decomposition of some interval in the current set. For any node n, this information can easily be reconstructed from its lower neighbors:

- if n->interval_list $\neq$ NULL,
  then n->measure is the length of the node interval of n;
- if n is a leaf and n->interval_list = NULL, then n->measure
  is 0;
- if n is an interior node and n->interval_list = NULL, then
  n->measure = n->left->measure + n->right->measure.

So after any insertion or deletion of an interval, we just have to update the measure information in all nodes that were changed or that are above a changed node. These nodes are the nodes along the search path for the left interval endpoint, with their right lower neighbors, and the nodes on the search path for the right interval endpoint, with their left lower neighbors. This gives a structure with an insertion and deletion time of $O(\log n)$, which has the measure of the union of the current intervals in the root, so it can answer measure queries in $O(1)$ time. It has, however, a restriction that is inherited from the segment tree structure: we cannot change the underlying search tree, so all the interval endpoints must be known in advance. For the application in the measure problem, this is the case because all the rectangles are given.

A fully dynamic structure to maintain the measure of a union of intervals is the measure tree defined by Gonnet, Munro, and Wood (1983). That structure maintains a set of n intervals under insertion and deletion of intervals in $O(\log n)$ and measure queries in $O(1)$.

The construction of the measure tree begins with any balanced search tree on the endpoints of all intervals in the current set and $-\infty$. The associated intervals of a node are all those intervals in the current set that have at least one endpoint in the node interval; like the node interval, we do not store the associated intervals in the node, but just need them as concept. Notice that an interval that properly contains a node interval is not associated with the node; the interval $[a, b[$ is associated with exactly those nodes that are on the search paths of a or b.

Each node n of the search tree contains three additional fields:

- `n->measure` is the measure of the intersection of the node interval of n with the union of all its associated intervals.
- `n->rightmax` is the maximum right endpoint of all intervals associated with n.
- `n->leftmin` is the minimum left endpoint of all intervals associated with n.

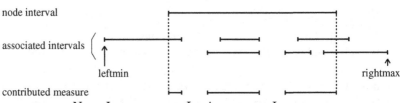

NODE INTERVAL AND ITS ASSOCIATED INTERVALS

For any interior node n, this information can be reconstructed from its lower neighbors. Two of the fields are easy:

- `n->rightmax =`
  max(`n->left->rightmax`, `n->right->rightmax`), and
- `n->leftmin = min(n->left->leftmin, n->right->leftmin)`.

The measure, however, needs several cases. Let x be any number in the node interval of n, which is contained in the union of the intervals associated with n, so it contributes to `n->measure`. Suppose x < `n->key`, so x is in the node interval of `n->left`. If x is contained in an interval associated with `n->left`, then it already contributed to `n->left->measure`. But it is also possible that x is contained in an interval associated with n, but not in an interval associated with `n->left`; in that case that interval must be associated with `n->right`, and contain the entire node interval of `n->left`. So the contribution of `n->left` to `n->measure` is either the length of the entire node interval of `n->left`, if `n->right->leftmin` is smaller than the left endpoint of the node interval of `n->left`, or it is `n->left->measure`. The corresponding situation holds for the contribution of `n->right`. Thus, if l and r are the left and right endpoints of the node interval of n, we have

1. if `n->right->leftmin` < l and `n->left->rightmax` $\geq r$,
   `n->measure` = $r - l$;
2. if `n->right->leftmin` $\geq l$ and `n->left->rightmax` $\geq r$,
   `n->measure` = $(r - $ `n->key`$) + $ `n->left->measure`;

3. if n->right->leftmin < *l* and n->left->rightmax < *r*,
n->measure = n->right->measure + (n->key − *l*); and
4. if n->right->leftmin ≥ *l* and n->left->rightmax < *r*,
n->measure = n->right->measure + n->left->measure.

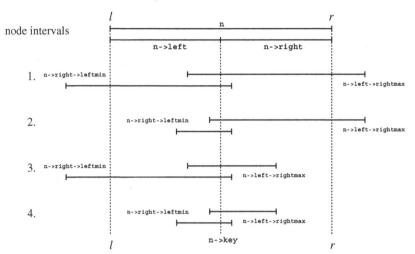

FOUR SITUATIONS FOR COMPUTATION OF n->measure

With these rules, we can now perform updates, inserting or deleting an interval [*a*, *b*[; we first update the leaves containing *a* and *b*, possibly inserting or deleting as necessary; then we go up to the root, rebalancing along the way and recomputing the three additional fields for each node we changed. Thus we get an $O(\log n)$ update time for any choice of the underlying balanced search tree; and the total measure of the union is in the root, so we have an $O(1)$ query time. If there are several intervals in the current set that have the same endpoint, the update of the leaf might become nontrivial because there might be many intervals associated with the same leaf; but we can arrange them again into a search tree, which gives an $O(\log n)$ update of the leaf, which does not change the total complexity. So we can summarize the performance of this structure as follows:

Theorem. The measure tree structure is a dynamic data structure that keeps track of a set of *n* intervals, supporting insertion and deletion of intervals in time $O(\log n)$, and that answers queries for the measure of the union of the intervals in $O(1)$ time. The structure has size $O(n)$.

Another related problem is to list the union of intervals instead of computing its measure. Here we want an output-sensitive query complexity: if the union is just one long interval, we want that answer fast, whereas if the union consists of many intervals, we cannot avoid the time required to list them all. But adding or deleting a single interval can change the structure of the union much. An optimal structure for this union-listing problem was given by Cheng and Janardan (1991); it supports insertions and deletions of intervals in $O(\log n)$ time and lists the union in output-sensitive time $O(k)$ if the union consists of k components.

The union tree structure we describe here is based on this structure in Cheng and Janardan (1991). We again start with any balanced search tree for the set $\{-\infty, x_1, \ldots, x_n\}$ of all interval endpoints and $-\infty$. As in the measure tree, we associate with each node all intervals in the current interval set that have at least one end point in the node interval. For a fixed node n, we consider the union of all intervals associated with that node; this union consists of connected components, which themselves are intervals with endpoints from the underlying set of intervals. Let $[x_i, x_j[$ be the leftmost component of the union and $[x_k, x_l[$ be the rightmost component. These intervals might coincide. Then the node n has the following additional fields:

– n->leftmin is the pointer to the leaf with key x_i.
– n->leftmax is the pointer to the leaf with key x_j.
– n->rightmin is the pointer to the leaf with key x_k.
– n->rightmax is the pointer to the leaf with key x_l.

There are also two further fields that are defined only if n is a leaf.

– n->next is the pointer to the leaf with the next larger key.
– n->transfer is the pointer to the highest node v with
  v->left->rightmin = n and
  v->left->rightmax->key $\geq$ v->key if such a node exists. A
  transfer pointer can exist only for those leaf nodes n that occur as
  v->left->rightmin for some node v.

With these definitions, the query algorithm is now easy, based on the observation that if $[x_i, x_j[$ is a connected component of the union of all intervals in the current set and n is the leaf node with key x_i, then n->transfer is defined and n->transfer->rightmax is the leaf node with key x_j. So if we know the beginning of a component of the union, then we find its end using the transfer pointers; and if we know the end of a component, then the next component must start at the next larger key, found by following the next pointer, because each key is beginning or end of some interval in the current interval set. The smallest key in the current set must be the beginning of the first component, so we can start at that node and work our way upward, with $O(1)$

time for each component we found. This gives the claimed output-sensitive $O(k)$ query time if the union of the current set consists of k components.

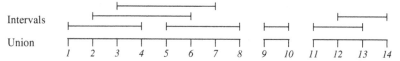

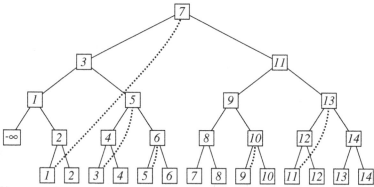

UNION OF INTERVALS WITH SEARCH TREE AND transfer POINTERS

The main difficulty is the update. To insert or delete an interval $[a, b[$, we first have to perform the insertion or deletion in the underlying tree, deleting a node only if there is no other interval in the current set with the same endpoint. We can also update the next pointer at this stage, that is, just maintaining a linked list of the leaves, as we mentioned in Section 3.11. Then we go back to the root, perform the rebalancing, and finally make a second upward pass over the nodes we passed on the search path and those neighboring nodes that were changed during the rebalancing to reconstruct all the other fields in a bottom-up way.

For this, we observe that the fields leftmin to rightmax can change only for those nodes for which the set of associated intervals changed, which are the nodes on the search path for a and b. For these nodes, bottom-up reconstruction is easy: if n->left and n->right already contain the correct information, then the information for n is given by the following rules:

1. n->leftmin
    1.1 if n->left->leftmin->key < n->right->leftmin->key, then set n->leftmin to n->left->leftmin;
    1.2 else set n->leftmin to n->right->leftmin.
2. n->leftmax
    2.1 if n->left->leftmax->key < n->right->leftmin->key, then set n->leftmax to n->left->leftmax;

2.2 else if
n->left->rightmax->key < n->right->leftmax->key,
then set n->leftmax to n->right->leftmax;

2.3 else if n->left->rightmax->key <
n->right->rightmax->key, then set n->leftmax to
n->left->rightmax;

2.4 else set n->leftmax to n->right->rightmax.

3. n->rightmin

   3.1 if n->left->rightmax->key <
n->right->rightmin->key, then set n->rightmin to
n->right->rightmin;

   3.2 else if
n->left->rightmin->key < n->right->leftmin->key,
then set n->rightmin to n->left->rightmin;

   3.3 else if
n->left->leftmax->key < n->right->leftmin->key,
then set n->rightmin to n->right->leftmin;

   3.4 else set n->rightmin to n->left->leftmin.

4. n->rightmax

   4.1 if n->left->rightmax->key <
n->right->rightmax->key, then set n->rightmax to
n->right->rightmax;

   4.2 else set n->rightmax to n->left->rightmax.

The update of the transfer pointer is more difficult because this happens not in the nodes along the search path, but in leaves. If n is a leaf, then n->transfer is a pointer to a node v with v->left->rightmin = n, so the only leaves that possibly need update of their transfer pointer are those that are reached as v->left->rightmin from a node v that is on the search path or changed during rebalancing. We take these $O(\log n)$ nodes v in sequence of decreasing depth, that is from the leaf to the root, and for each we perform the following step:

– if v->left->rightmax->key > v->key, then
set v->left->rightmin->transfer to v.

If for a leaf n there are several interior nodes v with v->left->rightmin = n and v->left->rightmax->key > v->key, then the highest of these overwrites all earlier entries in n->transfer, so we get the required property that n->transfer points to the highest node with these properties.

The complexity of any update is again only $O(\log n)$ because we spent a constant time on each level of the underlying balanced search tree. And the space requirement is $O(n)$ because we only augmented each of the $O(n)$ nodes of the search tree by six pointers. In total, this gives the following performance:

Theorem. The union tree is a dynamic data structure that keeps track of a set of n intervals, supporting insert and delete in time $O(\log n)$, and that lists the union of these intervals in output-sensitive time $O(k)$ if that union consists of k components. The structure has size $O(n)$.

4.4 Trees for Sums of Weighted Intervals

A simple but useful application of the canonical interval decomposition idea is a structure that keeps track of a piecewise constant function represented as sum of weighted intervals. We can identify an interval $[a, b[$ with its indicator function, which is 1 for $x \in [a, b[$ and 0 for $x \notin [a, b[$; with this convention, it is natural to define weighted intervals

$$\text{interval } [a, b[\text{ with weight } c \quad \equiv \quad f(x) = \begin{cases} c & x \in [a, b[\\ 0 & x \notin [a, b[\end{cases}$$

and we can use the sum of weighted intervals, whose value at x is the sum of the weights of the intervals that contain x. A typical use of this structure would be to keep track of the use of some resource like electricity; the resource is used by various systems, each for some time interval at a constant level, and the total amount used is at each moment the sum of the demands of all those systems active at that moment.

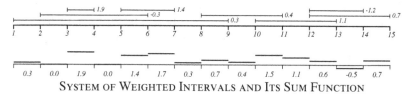

SYSTEM OF WEIGHTED INTERVALS AND ITS SUM FUNCTION

To construct the structure, we begin with the segment trees described in the previous section, but instead of requiring to report all covering intervals we ask only for the number of covering intervals. This way we do not need to keep in each tree node a list of the intervals, but just a single number. For a query we just go down the search path and sum up all the numbers in nodes we have visited. This gives us a structure of size $O(n)$, built in $O(n \log n)$, with query time $O(\log n)$, which gives for any query key the number of intervals that contain that key. Now we are not restricted to just counting the intervals;

we could give them arbitrary positive or negative weights and determine in the same way the sum of all the weights of intervals that contain the query key. This way we keep track of a piecewise constant function, with at most n jumps, and can evaluate this function at a given point in time $O(\log n)$. And we can easily make this data structure dynamic, for unlike the segment tree, where we needed to update the potentially large structures associated with each node in any rotation, here we just need to adjust the partial sums.

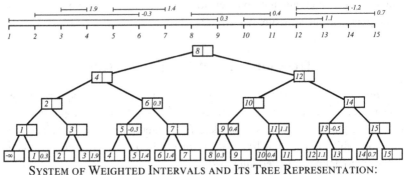

SYSTEM OF WEIGHTED INTERVALS AND ITS TREE REPRESENTATION:
SUMMAND FIELD OF NODES WITH WEIGHT 0 LEFT EMPTY

We arrive at the following structure: a search tree on the interval endpoints, or the places where the piecewise constant function jumps, with a number associated with each node. The value of the function at a query key is the sum of the numbers associated with nodes on the search path for that key. To increase the function on the interval $[a, b[$ by the value w, we find all nodes belonging to the canonical interval decomposition of $[a, b[$ and increase their associated numbers by w. If a, b were already keys of the underlying search tree, no further work is necessary during an insert; otherwise, we need to update the underlying search tree and adjust the numbers in the nodes in such a way that the sum along each path stays the same. To delete an interval, we just insert it with negative weight and delete unnecessary leaves. In total, this gives the following properties:

Theorem. There is a dynamic data structure that keeps track of a set of n weighted intervals, supporting insert and delete in time $O(\log n)$, and that evaluates the sum of the weights of all intervals containing a query point x in time $O(\log n)$. The structure has size $O(n)$.

The implementation of this structure is quite easy because we need to store and update only a single number in the tree nodes. So the structure of each tree node is the following:

```
typedef struct tr_n_t { key_t          key;
                         struct tr_n_t  *left;
                         struct tr_n_t *right;
                         number_t        summand;
                   /* some balancing information */
                         } tree_node_t;
```

As in the previous structures, we always need a node of key $-\infty$ in the underlying search tree, so we insert it when the tree is created. In this search tree, we do not use any objects associated with the keys, but we need a non-NULL object pointer to satisfy our search-tree convention. Here we just use the pointer to the tree root as object pointer.

```
tree_node_t *create_tree(void)
{  tree_node_t *tree;
   tree = get_node();
   tree->left = NULL;
   tree->summand = 0;
   /* need key -infty. use root as non-NULL
      object ptr */
   insert( tree, NEGINFTY, (object_t *) tree );
   return( tree );
}
```

Then the query algorithm is as follows:

```
number_t evaluate_sum(tree_node_t *tree,
key_t query_key)
{  tree_node_t *current_tree_node;
   number_t sum;
   if( tree->left == NULL )
      return(0);
   else
   {  current_tree_node = tree;
      sum = tree->summand;
      while( current_tree_node->right != NULL )
      {   if( query_key < current_tree_node->key)
             current_tree_node =
             current_tree_node->left;
         else
             current_tree_node =
```

```
                        current_tree_node->right;
                  sum += current_tree_node->summand;
        }
        return( sum );
  }
}
```

To insert a weighted interval, we first insert the interval endpoints into the underlying search tree if they are not there already. For this, we might have to split a previous leaf node, then the summand previously in the leaf nodes stays with that now-inner node, and the two new leaf nodes contain the summand 0, so that the sum along all the paths is not changed. Then we perform the necessary rebalancing, where we have to change the rotation code in such a way that the sums along the paths stay constant. But that is easy because we can push down summands in the search tree: given an interior node n, if we increase n->left->summand and n->right->summand each by n->summand and then set n->right->summand to 0, then along any path through n the sum has not changed.

PUSHING DOWN THE SUMMAND OF A NODE

So before the rotation, we push down the summands from the two nodes changed in the rotation, so their summands become 0. Then we can rotate without changing the sums along the paths because the nodes changed by the rotation do not contribute to the sums anyway. The following is the adapted code for the left rotation:

```
void left_rotation(tree_node_t *n)
{   tree_node_t *tmp_node;
    key_t        tmp_key;
    /* push down summand from n */
    n->left->summand += n->summand;
    n->right->summand += n->summand;
    n->summand = 0;
    tmp_node = n->right;
    /* push down summand from n->right */
    tmp_node->left->summand += tmp_node->summand;
    tmp_node->right->summand += tmp_node->summand;
```

```
    tmp_node->summand = 0;
    tmp_node = n->left;
    /* perform normal left rotation */
    tmp_key  = n->key;
    n->left  = n->right;
    n->key   = n->right->key;
    n->right = n->left->right;
    n->left->right = n->left->left;
    n->left->left  = tmp_node;
    n->left->key   = tmp_key;
}
```

Now we give the code for the insertion of an interval [a, b[with weight w.

```
void insert_interval(tree_node_t *tree,
                     key_t a, key_t b, number_t w)
{   tree_node_t *tmp_node;
    if ( find(tree, a) == NULL )
    {   insert( tree, a, (object_t *) tree );
    }   /* used treenode itself as non-NULL object
           pointer*/
    if ( find(tree, b) == NULL )
    {   insert( tree, b, (object_t *) tree );
    }
    tmp_node = tree;
    /* follow search path for a,*/
    while( tmp_node->right != NULL )
    {   /* add w to everything right of path */
        if( a < tmp_node->key )
        {   tmp_node->right->summand += w;
            tmp_node = tmp_node->left;
        }
        else
            tmp_node = tmp_node->right;
    }
    tmp_node->summand += w; /* leaf with key a */
    tmp_node = tree;
    /* follow search path for b, */
    while( tmp_node->right != NULL )
    {   /* subtract w from everything right of
           path */
```

```
        if ( b < tmp_node->key )
        {  tmp_node->right->summand -= w;
           tmp_node = tmp_node->left;
        }
        else
           tmp_node = tmp_node->right;
    }
    tmp_node->summand -= w; /* leaf with key b */
}
```

Here we reuse the find and insert functions of any of our balanced search trees, with the minor modification that the summand field of any newly created leaf is initialized to 0.

The deletion is just an insertion with weight $-w$. But this does not remove any leaves that became unnecessary. In a minimal tree representation, there should be leaves only for the places where the sum function changes. So, after the insertion of the interval [a, b[, we could evaluate the sum function for the leaf preceding a and the leaf following b. It is not sufficient to compare the summand fields of these leaves because they might be reached over different paths. If two consecutive leaves with the same sum are found, we push down the summands along the path to the leaf with the larger key and then delete that key from the tree, with the normal rebalancing.

A problem that looks similar but is more complicated is to maintain the maximum instead of the sum: given a set of weighted intervals, we want to find for a query key the maximum weight of an interval that contains the key. The problem here is to make the structure dynamic; as a static structure, we could reuse the canonical interval decomposition idea and store in each node the maximum weight of all intervals for which this node is part of the canonical interval decomposition. Then for a query, we would answer the maximum of all node values along the search path. This can be adapted to support insertions, but not for deletions. A structure that supports insertions and deletions with $O(\log n)$ amortized update time and $O(\log n)$ worst-case query time was described in Agarwal, Arge, and Yi (2005), improving an earlier structure in Kaplan, Molad, and Tarjan (2003).

4.5 Trees for Interval-Restricted Maximum Sum Queries

A structure on the same objects, piecewise constant functions or sets of weighted intervals, but supporting even stronger queries, was described in Bose et al.

(2003). Let σ be the current piecewise constant function, then this structure answers queries for the maximum value of σ in a query interval $[a, b[$, as well as for the argument x for which this maximum of $\sigma(x)$ is reached. This contains the evaluation queries supported by the previous structure as a special case when the interval degenerates to a single point. The update operation for structure is to increase or decrease σ for all $x \in [t, \infty[$ by c.

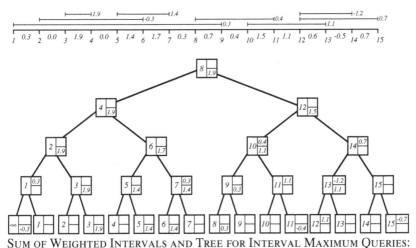

SUM OF WEIGHTED INTERVALS AND TREE FOR INTERVAL MAXIMUM QUERIES:
IN EACH NODE, LEFT IS key; TOP RIGHT IS summand;
BOTTOM RIGHT IS partial_sum; EMPTY FIELDS HAVE VALUE 0

This is again a dynamic data structure that consists of a balanced search tree, with the jumps of σ as keys, in which the nodes carry some additional information – the numbers partial_sum and summand. The central property of this structure is that for each node *n, the maximum of σ over the interval associated with this node equals n->partial_sum plus the sum of m->summand over all nodes *m on the path from the root to *n, including n->summand.

Thus, if the query interval $[a, b[$ is the interval associated with a node, we can answer the maximum value query simply by going down in the search tree to that node and adding up the correct terms. If the query interval is not a node interval, we use the canonical interval decomposition of the query interval: the maximum over the entire interval must occur in one of the subintervals of the canonical interval decomposition. We find the intervals of the decomposition, and the maximum values in them, again by going down in the tree and summing up the correct node values.

The structure of a node in this tree is the following:

```
typedef struct tr_n_t { key_t          key;
                        struct tr_n_t   *left;
                        struct tr_n_t   *right;
                        number_t        summand;
                        number_t  partial_sum;
                        /* balancing information */
                        } tree_node_t;
```

With this structure, the query algorithm is now similar to the insertion in segment trees: we just check for each node of the canonical interval decomposition whether it contributes a larger sum than the current maximum. The query function can be written as follows:

```
int max_value_interval(tree_node_t *tree,
key_t a, key_t b)
{   tree_node_t *current_node, *right_path,
                *left_path;
    number_t sum, left_sum, right_sum, tmp_sum,
             current_max;
    int first = 1;
    if( tree->left == NULL )
        exit(-1); /* tree incorrect */
    else
    {   current_node = tree;
        sum = 0;
        right_path = left_path = NULL;
        while( current_node->right != NULL )
        /* not at leaf */
        {   sum += current_node->summand;
            if( b < current_node->key )
            /* go left: a < b < key */
                current_node = current_node->left;
            else if( current_node->key < a )
            /* go right: key < b < a */
                current_node = current_node->right;
            else if( a < current_node->key &&
                    current_node->key < b )
                /* split: a < key < b */
```

```
    {   right_path = current_node->right;
        /* both right */
        left_path  = current_node->left;
        /* and left */
        break;
    }
    else if( a == current_node->key )
    /* a = key < b */
    {   right_path = current_node->right;
        /* no left */
        break;
    }
    else   /*   current_node->key == b, so a
    < key = b */
    {   left_path  = current_node->left;
        /* no right */
        break;
    }
}
if( left_path == NULL &&
    right_path == NULL)
    current_max = sum
                + current_node->summand
                + current_node->partial_sum;
left_sum = right_sum = sum;
if( left_path != NULL )
{   /* now follow the path of the left
        endpoint a*/
    while( left_path->right != NULL )
    {   left_sum += left_path->summand;
        if( a < left_path->key )
        {   /* right node possibly
                contributes */
            tmp_sum = left_sum
              + left_path->right->summand
              + left_path->right->partial_sum;
            if( first ||
                tmp_sum > current_max )
            {   current_max = tmp_sum;
```

```
              first = 0;
          }
          left_path = left_path->left;
      }
      else if ( a == left_path->key )
      {  tmp_sum = left_sum
            + left_path->right->summand
            + left_path->right->partial_sum;
          if( first ||
              tmp_sum > current_max)
          {  current_max = tmp_sum;
             first = 0;
          }
          break; /* no further descent
          necessary */
      }
      else /* go right, no node selected */
            left_path = left_path->right;
  }
  /* left leaf of a needs to be checked
     if reached */
  if( left_path->right == NULL )
  {  tmp_sum = left_sum
              + left_path->summand
              + left_path->partial_sum;
      if( first || tmp_sum > current_max )
      {  current_max = tmp_sum;  first = 0;
      }
  }
}  /* end left path */
if( right_path != NULL )
{  /* and now follow the path of the right
      endpoint b */
    while( right_path->right != NULL )
    {  right_sum += right_path->summand;
       if( right_path->key < b )
       {  /* left node possibly
          contributes */
          tmp_sum = right_sum
```

```
            + right_path->left->summand
            + right_path->left->partial_sum;
         if( first ||
             tmp_sum > current_max)
         {   current_max = tmp_sum;
             first = 0;
         }
         right_path = right_path->right;
      }
      else if ( right_path->key == b)
      {   tmp_sum = right_sum
             + right_path->left->summand
             + right_path->left->partial_sum;
         if( first ||
             tmp_sum > current_max )
         {   current_max = tmp_sum;
             first = 0;
         }
         break; /* no further descent
         necessary */
      }
      else /* go left, no node selected */
         right_path = right_path->left;
   }
   if( right_path->right == NULL &&
   right_path->key < b)
   {   tmp_sum = right_sum
             + right_path->summand
             + right_path->partial_sum;
      if( first || tmp_sum > current_max )
      {   current_max = tmp_sum;  first = 0;
      }
   }
}  /* end right path */
return( current_max );
}
}
```

This determines the maximum value of the current function σ over the query interval [a, b[, but does not tell us where this maximum is reached. The simplest way to implement the query for the argument x, which maximizes $\sigma(x)$, is to first perform a maximum value query and then make a second pass down. When we know the maximum value, we can find the interval of the canonical interval decomposition for which this value is reached and then go down in that interval to the leaf, always choosing that lower neighbor in whose associated interval we still find that maximum value.

We now need to describe the update, which is similar to the update in the previous section. To insert [a, b[with weight w, we add w to the current function σ for all $x \in [a, \infty[$ and then add $-w$ for all $x \in [b, \infty[$. We first insert a and b in the underlying search tree, with any of our balanced search-tree insert functions. This, as in the previous section, needs a modification for new leaves. If we split a leaf, both summand and partial_sum of the previous leaf stay with this now-interior node; the partial_sum is also copied to both new leaves, and the summand of the new leaves is 0. This preserves the sum property along the paths to the root. For the rebalancing of the underlying search tree, the standard rotations again need to be modified, pushing summands down and recomputing the partial_sum fields from the lower neighbors. An example code for the modified left rotation is as follows:

```
void left_rotation(tree_node_t *n)
{   tree_node_t *tmp_node;
    key_t        tmp_key;
    number_t tmp1, tmp2;
    tmp1 = n->summand;
    n->summand = 0;
    n->partial_sum += tmp1;
    tmp2 = n->right->summand;
    n->right->summand = 0;
    n->left->summand += tmp1;
    n->right->left->summand += tmp1 + tmp2;
    n->right->right->summand += tmp1 + tmp2;
    tmp_node = n->left;
    tmp_key  = n->key;
    n->left  = n->right;
    n->key   = n->right->key;
```

```
n->right = n->left->right;
n->left->right = n->left->left;
n->left->left  = tmp_node;
n->left->key   = tmp_key;
tmp1 = n->left->left->summand
       + n->left->left->partial_sum;
tmp2 = n->left->right->summand
       + n->left->right->partial_sum;
n->left->partial_sum = (tmp1 > tmp2) ?
tmp1 : tmp2 ;
}
```

These operations have up to now not changed the function σ represented by the tree and have preserved the sum property. To perform the actual update of the function, we proceed in a similar way as in the previous section. We add w to the summand for any node that belongs to the canonical interval decomposition of $[a, \infty[$. Then the path to any node whose associated interval lies entirely within $[a, \infty[$ will contain exactly one of these nodes. Because σ changed by w over the entire interval of the node, the maximum of $\sigma(x)$ over that interval will have changed by w, so the sum property is preserved for all these nodes.

For the nodes whose associated interval lies entirely outside the interval $[a, \infty[$ on which we changed the function σ, nothing changes; so only the nodes whose interval contains a remain. These are the nodes on the search path to a. For these we restore the sum property bottom-up by recomputing the partial_sum field from the lower neighbors.

Finally, we repeat the same steps to add $-w$ on the interval $[b, \infty[$.

This update does not remove leaves that have become unnecessary, at whose key the sum function σ does not change. The technique described in the previous section can also be used for this structure.

All the operations of the structure we have described take $O(h)$ time if h is the height of the underlying search tree. Choosing any balanced search tree from Chapter 3, we obtain an $O(\log n)$ time bound. The global maximum of the underlying function can even be determined in constant time; it is just the sum of the summand and partial_sum fields of the root. We could even add some further operations if they are supported by the underlying search tree, like splitting the function at a threshold or joining together two functions whose jumps are separated.

Theorem. There is a structure that keeps track of a piecewise constant function σ with n jumps, which supports interval-restricted maximum queries and maximum argument queries in $O(\log n)$ time and supports updates of the function by adding w to $\sigma(x)$ for all $x \geq [a, b[$ in time $O(\log n)$. It can answer queries for the global maximum in time $O(1)$.

4.6 Orthogonal Range Trees

We have already met the one-dimensional problem of range searching in Section 2.7: given a query interval, list all key values of the current set that lie in that interval. The higher-dimensional analog is the orthogonal range-searching problem: given an axis-aligned rectangle, or in general a box in d-dimensional space, list all the points in the current set that lie in that rectangle or box.

Orthogonal range searching has been much studied, not only for geometric applications, but indeed rather more for database index structures. In a database, there are frequently tuples with many number components, and there higher-dimensional range queries are quite normal, like "list all employees with salary between \$50,000 and \$75,000, age above 50, who made more than \$500,000 sales in each of the last three years": this is a five-dimensional orthogonal range query. Orthogonal range searching is also useful as preprocessing for queries, which really depend only on the neighborhood of the query point, to isolate the small subset of relevant points and then answer the query based on these points.

So the general situation is that we have a set of data points $p_1, \ldots, p_n$ given by their coordinates in d-dimensional space, $p_i = (p_{i1}, \ldots, p_{id})$, which is in some way stored by the data structure. We receive a d-dimensional query interval $[a_1, b_1[\times \cdots \times [a_d, b_d[$ and want to list all points p_i contained in that interval, so $a_1 \leq p_{i1} < b_1, \ldots, a_d \leq p_{id} < b_d$ in output-sensitive time $O(f_d(n) + k)$ if there are k such points, with $f_d(n)$ as slow-growing as possible. Many solutions have been proposed for data structures supporting this type of query. The canonical interval decomposition allows a particularly nice recursive construction, the orthogonal range trees, which were independently discovered by Bentley (1979), Lee and Wong (1980), Lueker (1978), and Willard.[7]

The idea of the orthogonal range tree is that in order to solve the d-dimensional orthogonal range-searching problem, we build a balanced search tree for the key values that occur in the first coordinate of the data points. Each node of the search tree has its associated interval for the first coordinate, and we store in that node all points whose first coordinate falls into that interval

---

[7] In an inaccessible technical report, D.E. Willard: The Super-B-Tree Algorithm, Report TR-03-79, Aiken Computer Laboratory, Harvard University, USA, 1979.

in a structure that allows $d - 1$-dimensional range searching on the remaining $d - 1$ coordinates.

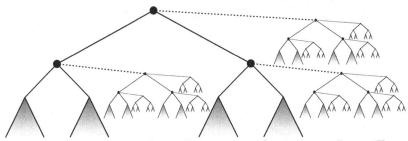

RECURSIVE STRUCTURE OF THREE-DIMENSIONAL ORTHOGONAL RANGE TREE:
EACH TREE NODE HAS ASSOCIATED TWO-DIMENSIONAL TREE, IN WHICH
EACH NODE HAS ASSOCIATED ONE-DIMENSIONAL TREE

If we have this structure, then the query for the d-dimensional interval $[a_1, b_1[\times \cdots \times [a_d, b_d[$ is simple: we find the $O(\log n)$ nodes that correspond to the canonical interval decomposition of $[a_1, b_1[$. In each of these nodes, we perform $d - 1$-dimensional range searching for $[a_2, b_2[\times \cdots \times [a_d, b_d[$. Each data point that occurs in the d-dimensional query interval occurs in exactly one of these nodes, where it will be found by the $d - 1$-dimensional query. And all the points that occur in the nodes have a first coordinate that lies in the interval $[a_1, b_1[$, so within the nodes we can disregard the first coordinate. Suppose now there are r nodes that belong to the canonical interval decomposition of $[a_1, b_1[$, with $r = O(\log n)$, and the ρth node returns k_ρ matching points in time $O(f_{d-1}(n) + k_\rho)$; then the total time is $O(\log n)$ for finding the canonical interval decomposition, plus $O(\sum_{\rho=1}^{r}(f_{d-1}(n) + k_\rho))$ for the $d - 1$-dimensional queries in the nodes. Because the total output size is just the sum of the output sizes of the subproblems, $k = \sum_{\rho=1}^{r} k_\rho$, we have in total an output-sensitive complexity of $O(f_d(n) + k)$, with $f_d(n) = O(f_{d-1}(n) \log n)$. If we use for the one-dimensional problem any balanced search tree, with any of the interval-query methods from Section 2.7, we get $f_1(n) = O(\log n)$, so $f_d(n) = O\left((\log n)^d\right)$. Thus, orthogonal range trees are a static structure that supports d-dimensional orthogonal range queries in a set of d-dimensional points in output-sensitive time $O\left((\log n)^d + k\right)$ if the output consists of k points. To build the structure for $d \geq 2$, we first build the tree on the first coordinates and insert each of the n points in all the $O(\log n)$ nodes along the search path for its first coordinate. Within each node, we build a $d - 1$-dimensional range tree structure. This gives a building time of $O\left(n(\log n)^d\right)$. The space requirement of this structure is $O\left(n(\log n)^{d-1}\right)$ because the one-dimensional structure needs an $O(n)$ space.

Theorem. Orthogonal range trees are a static structure that supports d-dimensional orthogonal range queries in a set of d-dimensional points in output-sensitive time $O\left((\log n)^d + k\right)$ if the output consists of k points. They can be built in $O\left(n(\log n)^d\right)$ time using $O\left(n(\log n)^{d-1}\right)$ space.

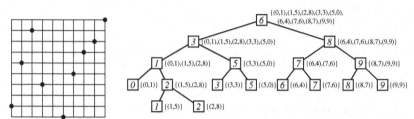

SET OF NINE POINTS, WITH SEARCH TREE FOR FIRST COORDINATE.
EACH NODE HAS SET OF POINTS WITH FIRST COORDINATE IN NODE INTERVAL;
FOR THESE, A SEARCH STRUCTURE FOR SECOND COORDINATE IS BUILT

Because the structure is defined inductively using a lower-dimensional structure in the nodes, we can improve the performance in all dimensions if we have a better low-dimensional range-searching structure to start the induction. The one-dimensional structure, the normal binary search tree, does not leave any room for improvement; at least in the comparison-based model assumed here, the $\Omega(n \log n)$ lower bound for comparison-based sorting implies a $\Omega(\log n)$ lower bound for one-dimensional range searching. But the two-dimensional structure can be improved, reducing the $O((\log n)^2 + k)$ query time to $O(\log n + k)$ using the technique of fractional cascading. This method was discovered by Willard[8] and Hart.[9]

The general idea of fractional cascading is that when we have to make a sequence of searches in different, but related, sets, we should avoid having to start each search from anew, but create links between these sets so that we can use the information from the previous search in the next set. A similar situation occurs in the two-dimensional orthogonal range tree because in each node of the canonical interval decomposition of the query interval in the first coordinate, we have to search among the second-coordinate values of points stored in that node for the second-coordinate query interval. The fractional cascading idea occurs in a number of other algorithms. The method was

[8] Another inaccessible technical report from 1978 is usually cited, but that dates the improved method before the basic method. The first published reference is Willard (1985).

[9] Another technical report, J.H. Hart: Optimal Two-Dimensional Range Queries Using Binary Range Lists, Technical Report 76–81, Department of Computer Science, University of Kentucky, USA, 1981.

discussed in a more general setting by Chazelle and Guibas (1986a, b), and later in Sen (1995).

In the two-dimensional orthogonal range tree, the searches we need to do are not themselves related in the required way: the sets in the nodes of the canonical interval decomposition are disjoint, so searching in one set does not give any information about the position in another set. But if we also search for the same second-coordinate query interval in all nodes along the search paths for the first-coordinate query interval, we find the structure we need.

For each node, we organize the points stored in that node into a list, sorted by increasing second coordinate. If the node is not a leaf, then each point on the list of the node occurs either on the list of the left lower neighbor or on the list of the right lower neighbor. We link each point on this sorted list

- to the same point on the list of the left or the right lower neighbor, where it occurs;
- to the point with the next smaller second coordinate if the point is missing on that list; or
- to the first point on the list if there is no point with a smaller coordinate.

With this information, we can follow down an interval, given in the list of the root, through all nodes we visit while determining the canonical interval decomposition of the first-coordinate interval. In each node, we have the first and last points of the interval, restricted to the list in the node, and we find in $O(1)$ time the first and last points in the list of the left or right lower neighbor, just following the pointers between the lists and possibly going one node up on the list. Thus, if we perform the search in the top node in $O(\log n)$ time, then each level of going down the tree takes only $O(1)$ time. There are two types of going down a level we need, following the path of the query interval endpoint, where we just keep track of the current position, which takes $O(1)$, and listing the contents of a node belonging to the canonical interval decomposition, which takes $O(1 + k)$ if there are k elements in that interval. So in total, the query takes $O(\log n + k)$ time if the output consists of k points.

Using this structure for the two-dimensional orthogonal range queries, we improve the bound by one $\log n$ factor.

Theorem. Orthogonal range trees with fractional cascading are a static data structure that supports d-dimensional orthogonal range queries in a set of d-dimensional points, $d \geq 2$, in output-sensitive time $O\left((\log n)^{d-1} + k\right)$ if the output consists of k points. They can be built in $O\left(n(\log n)^{d-1}\right)$ time using $O\left(n(\log n)^{d-1}\right)$ space.

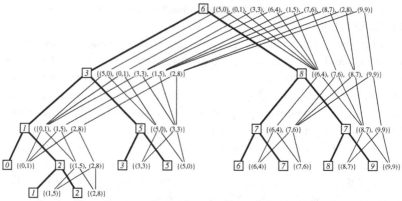

SET OF NINE POINTS: ORTHOGONAL RANGE SEARCH TREE WITH
FRACTIONAL CASCADING

To decribe the orthogonal range tree in more detail, we first give code
for the general recursive structure and then discuss the improvement of the
two-dimensional case by fractional cascading. In general, the d-dimensional
orthogonal range tree consists of any balanced search tree, with an additional pointer to a $d - 1$-dimensional orthogonal range tree in each node.
The one-dimensional orthogonal range tree is just a balanced search tree that
supports interval queries as in Section 2.7, so that one-dimensional range
queries can be answered. So a node of the d-dimensional tree looks as
follows:

```
typedef struct tr_n_t { key_t          key;
                struct tr_n_t    *left;
                struct tr_n_t    *right;
                struct tr_n_t    *1_dim_tree;
                /* balancing information */
                } tree_node_t;
```

The points stored in the tree are given by an array of coordinates and possibly
a pointer to some object associated with that point. We assume the dimension
to be a globally defined constant.

```
typedef struct { key_t     coordinate[DIMENSION];
                object_t object; } point_t;
```

We need again a list type to collect the output.

```
typedef struct p_ls_n_t { struct p_ls_n_t  *next;
                          point_t  *point;
                        } p_list_node_t;
```

For our recursive algorithms, it is always convenient to use the coordinates in backward order, evaluating the last coordinate first. So each point has an array of coordinates of unknown length, of which we look only at the first dimension entries.

Next is the code that constructs the orthogonal range tree from a list of points. It first creates a list of the key values in the last coordinate, then sorts these, build a search tree on the key values, augmented by $-\infty$, attaches to each search-tree node the list of all points that should go into that lower-dimensional tree, and finally calls itself to build all these lower-dimensional trees. The sorting function produces a sorted list of key values occurring in the last coordinate, with the list of points of that key value attached to each node of the sorted list. The function to build the search tree can be one of the functions of Section 2.8.

```
tree_node_t *build_or_r_tree(p_list_node_t
*pt_list, int dim )
{ if( pt_list == NULL )
      return( NULL );
      /* should not be called for empty tree*/
   else
   {  tree_node_t *o_tree, *t_tmp;
      tree_node_t *key_list, *k_tmp;
      p_list_node_t *p_tmp, *p_tmp2;
      /* create list of key values in dimension
         dim */
      key_list = NULL;  p_tmp = pt_list;
      while( p_tmp != NULL )
      {  k_tmp = get_node();
         k_tmp->key =
                 (p_tmp->point->coordinate)[dim];
         p_tmp2 = get_p_list_node();
         p_tmp2->point = p_tmp->point;
         p_tmp2->next  = NULL;
         k_tmp->left = (tree_node_t *) p_tmp2;
         k_tmp->right = key_list;
         key_list = k_tmp;
         p_tmp = p_tmp->next;
```

```
}  /* made copy of point list */
/* sort and remove duplicates*/
key_list = sort( key_list );
if( dim >=1 ) /* for interval decomposition,
need -infty key*/
{  k_tmp        = get_node();
   k_tmp->key   = NEGINFTY;
   k_tmp->right = key_list;
   k_tmp->left = NULL;
   key_list = k_tmp;
}
/* create search tree */
o_tree = make_tree( key_list );
/* initialize all lower-dimensional trees
   to NULL */
create_stack();
push( o_tree );
while( !stack_empty() )
{  t_tmp = pop();
   t_tmp->l_dim_tree = NULL;
   if( t_tmp->right != NULL )
   {  push( t_tmp->left );
      push( t_tmp->right );
   }
}
remove_stack();
if( dim == 0 )
   return( o_tree );
   /* for dimension one:finished */
else /* need to construct lower-dimensional
trees */
{  /* insert each point, initially attach as
      list to nodes */
   while(  pt_list != NULL )
   {  t_tmp = o_tree; /* tree not empty */
      while( t_tmp!= NULL )
      {  p_tmp = get_p_list_node();
         p_tmp->next = (p_list_node_t *)
```

```
            t_tmp->1_dim_tree;
            p_tmp->point = pt_list->point;
            t_tmp->1_dim_tree = (tree_node_t *)
            p_tmp;
            if( t_tmp->right != NULL &&
            pt_list->point->coordinate[dim] <
            t_tmp->key)
                t_tmp = t_tmp->left;
            else
                t_tmp = t_tmp->right;
         } /* attached point to each node
            on its search path */
         pt_list = pt_list->next; /* go to next
         point */
      }
      /* now create lower-dimensional trees for
         all nodes */
      create_stack();
      push( o_tree );
      while( !stack_empty() )
      { t_tmp = pop();
         if( t_tmp->1_dim_tree != NULL )
            t_tmp->1_dim_tree =
            build_or_r_tree((p_list_node_t *)
            t_tmp->1_dim_tree, dim-1);
         if( t_tmp->right != NULL )
         { push( t_tmp->left );
            push( t_tmp->right );
         }
      }
      remove_stack();
      /* finished */
      return( o_tree );
   }
 }
}
```

The keys of the query interval $[a_1, b_1[\times \cdots \times [a_d, b_d[$ are given as two pointers to arrays a[] and b[] of keys. For dimension greater than one, the query function is based on the canonical interval decomposition that we already used several times. One difference is that the query interval is not necessarily spanned by key values occurring in the tree, so at the left and right leaves, we need to test whether the key values really belong to our query interval. For dimension one, we call a different function, which is the one-dimensional range-searching function described in Section 2.7 adapted to the current situation.

```
p_list_node_t *find_points_1d(tree_node_t *tree,
                                key_t *a, key_t *b)
{   tree_node_t *tr_node;
    p_list_node_t *result_list, *tmp, *tmp2;
    result_list = NULL;
    create_stack();
    push( tree );
    while( !stack_empty() )
    {   tr_node = pop();
        if( tr_node->right == NULL )
        {   /* reached leaf, now test */
            if( a[0] <= tr_node->key &&
                tr_node->key < b[0] )
            {   /* must attach all points below this
                   leaf */
                tmp = (p_list_node_t *)
                tr_node->left;
                while( tmp != NULL )
                {   tmp2 = get_p_list_node();
                    tmp2->point = tmp->point;
                    tmp2->next  = result_list;
                    result_list = tmp2;
                    tmp = tmp->next;
                }
            }
        }
        else if ( b[0] <= tr_node->key )
            push( tr_node->left );
        else if ( tr_node->key <= a[0])
            push( tr_node->right );
```

```
      else
      {  push( tr_node->left );
         push( tr_node->right );
      }
   }
   remove_stack();
   return( result_list );
}


p_list_node_t *join_list(p_list_node_t *a,
                         p_list_node_t *b)
{  if( b == NULL )
      return(a);
   else
   {  p_list_node_t *tmp;
      tmp = b;
      while( tmp->next != NULL )
         tmp = tmp->next;
      tmp->next = a;
      return(b);
   }
}


p_list_node_t *find_points(tree_node_t *tree,
                   key_t *a, key_t *b, int dim)
{  tree_node_t *current_node, *right_path,
               *left_path;
   p_list_node_t *current_list, *new_list;
   current_list = NULL;
   if( tree->left == NULL )
      exit(-1); /* tree incorrect */
   else if( dim == 0 )
      return( find_points_1d( tree, a, b ) );
   else
   {  current_node = tree;
      right_path = left_path = NULL;
      while( current_node->right != NULL )
      /* not at leaf */
      {   if( b[dim] < current_node->key )
```

```
           /* go left: a < b < key */
           {    current_node = current_node->left;
           }
           else if( current_node->key < a[dim])
           /* go right: key < b < a */
           {    current_node =
                current_node->right;
           }
           else if( a[dim] < current_node->key &&
                current_node->key < b[dim]  )
                /* split: a < key < b */
           {    right_path = current_node->right;
                /* both right */
                left_path  = current_node->left;
                /* and left */
                break;
           }
           else if( a[dim] == current_node->key )
           /* a = key < b */
           {    right_path = current_node->right;
                /* no left */
                break;
           }
           else
/* current_node->key == b, so a < key = b */
           {    left_path  = current_node->left;
                /* no right */
                break;
           }
       }
    if( left_path != NULL )
    {   /* now follow the path of the left
        endpoint a */
        while( left_path->right != NULL )
        {   if( a[dim] < left_path->key )
            {   /* right node must be selected */
                new_list = find_points(
                    left_path->right->l_dim_tree,
                    a, b, dim-1);
```

```
              current_list = join_list(
                    new_list, current_list);
              left_path = left_path->left;
         }
         else if ( a[dim] == left_path->key )
         {   new_list = find_points(
                left_path->right->1_dim_tree,
                a, b, dim-1);
              current_list = join_list(
                    new_list, current_list);
              break; /* no further descent
                    necessary */
         }
         else /* go right, no node
              selected */
              left_path = left_path->right;
    }
    /* left leaf needs to be selected if
      reached in descent*/
    if( left_path->right == NULL &&
       left_path->key == a[dim] )
    {   new_list = find_points(
                      left_path->1_dim_tree,
                      a, b, dim-1);
         current_list = join_list( new_list,
                          current_list);
    }
}  /* end left path */
if( right_path != NULL )
{   /* and now follow the path of the right
      endpoint b */
    while( right_path->right != NULL )
    {   if( right_path->key < b[dim] )
         {   /* left node must be selected */
              new_list = find_points(
                  right_path->left->1_dim_tree,
                  a, b, dim-1);
              current_list = join_list(
                    new_list, current_list);
```

```
                    right_path = right_path->right;
                }
                else if ( right_path->key == b[dim])
                {   new_list = find_points(
                        right_path->left->l_dim_tree,
                        a, b, dim-1);
                    current_list = join_list(
                            new_list, current_list);
                    break; /* no further descent
                        necessary */
                }
                else /* go left, no node selected */
                    right_path = right_path->left;
            }
            if( right_path->right == NULL &&
                right_path->key < b[dim])
            {   new_list = find_points(
                            right_path->l_dim_tree,
                            a, b, dim-1);
                current_list = join_list( new_list,
                current_list);
            }
        } /* end right path */
    }
    return( current_list );
}
```

Notice that we must insert the results from the subproblems in front of the current result list. To concatenate the two lists, we have to follow one list to its end, so if we always follow the list of new results to the end, we touch each result on each level of the recursion only once and spend only $O(k)$ time on the k results. An alternative way would be to give back from the lower-dimensional subproblems pointers to front and rear of the list.

The two-dimensional range searching with fractional cascading is more difficult. We have a search tree for the first coordinate, where we have to select the nodes corresponding to the canonical interval decomposition of the query interval in the first coordinate. Attached to each node of the first tree is a structure for the search in the second coordinate, but these structures are linked together as needed for the fractional cascading, so that we need to search only in the set associated with the first node and then can reuse that information in all later searches.

It is sufficient to attach to each node of the first tree just a linked list of all points in the set of that node, ordered with increasing second coordinate, and each list item containing two pointers to the next list item in the two lists associated with the lower neighbors of the node. We also need a second tree, a search tree for the second coordinates of all points, to get the fractional cascading started by locating the query interval endpoints in the list of all points.

We have up to now only described the query algorithms for this data structure. To build the structure, we list all coordinate values in the last coordinate and build a search tree for these key values. Each node should contain a lower-dimensional search structure for all those points whose last coordinate lies in the interval associated with that node. Thus, each point occurs in all the sets of nodes along the search path of its last coordinate, and we can assign the n points to the nodes in $O(n \log n)$ time. Then we visit each node and build there the lower-dimensional search structure in the same way until we arrive at dimension one, in the simple structure, or dimension two, in the fractional cascading structure.

In the simple one-dimensional structure, we just build a normal balanced search tree whose leaves are connected in a linked list in time $O(n \log n)$.

In the two-dimensional fractional cascading structure, we first build the search tree for the second coordinates, whose leaves are arranged in a linked list, and the search tree for the first coordinates. The list of leaves of the second-coordinate tree is linked to the root of the first-coordinate tree. Then we go down the first-coordinate tree, and for each node, the list associated with that node is entirely copied and the items distributed over the list of the lower neighbors of the tree node, with pointers added from the list nodes to the copies or their next successors in the lists of the lower neighbors. Because the depth of the tree is $O(\log n)$ and we meet each of the n points on each level only in one list, the total time to build this structure is $O(n \log n)$.

Together with the recursion, the total time to build this structure is $O(n(\log n)^d)$ for the simple version and $O(n(\log n)^{d-1})$ for the fractional cascading version.

The structure, as described, is a static structure. One can make it dynamic, with amortized bounds, using the technique of partial rebuilding (Edelsbrunner 1981; Lueker and Willard 1982; Overmars 1983). If we do not ask for a list of points in our range, but only for their number (range counting), one can make the structure fully dynamic, with worst-case update bounds (Willard and Lueker 1985). If we are interested only in range-counting queries, we need to store in the nodes of the range tree only the numbers of points in the associated intervals, which are easier to update, because they can be added and subtracted. The maximum number of distinct range queries possible for a set of n points in d-dimensional space was studied by Saxe (1979). It is between $\frac{1}{2^d d^{2d}} n^{2d}$ and $\frac{1}{2(2d)!} n^{2d} + O(n^{2d-1})$.

4.7 Higher-Dimensional Segment Trees

In the previous section we studied the orthogonal range-searching problem: given a set of n points and a query range (a d-dimensional interval), list all points that lie in that range. The inverse problem is also quite natural: given a set of n ranges (d-dimensional intervals) and a query point, list all ranges that contain that point. This problem can be solved by d-dimensional segment trees, which are a straightforward generalization of the segment tree structure.

Like the orthogonal range tree, the d-dimensional segment tree is defined recursively; we have a balanced search tree whose keys are the first coordinates of the d-dimensional intervals, and each node of that tree contains a $d - 1$-dimensional segment tree. In this $(d - 1)$-dimensional segment tree associated with the node *n, all those d-dimensional intervals $[a_{i1}, b_{i1}[\times \cdots \times [a_{id}, b_{id}[$ are stored for which *n is part of the canonical interval decomposition of $[a_{i1}, b_{i1}[$. Because there are at most $2n$ keys in the first coordinate, the canonical interval decomposition has size $O(\log n)$, so each d-dimensional interval is stored in $O(\log n)$ $(d - 1)$-dimensional segment trees. Thus the space requirement, and the time to construct the d-dimensional segment tree of n intervals, is $O(n(\log n)^d)$.

Now for the query, we follow the search path of the first coordinate of the query point, and in each node we perform a $(d - 1)$-dimensional query with the remaining coordinates in the structure associated with the node. By the properties of the canonical interval decomposition, we will meet any d-dimensional interval that contains this point in exactly one of the associated structures. Because the search path contains $O(\log n)$ nodes, we perform that number of $(d - 1)$-dimensional queries, each of which takes an output-sensitive time $O((\log n)^{d-1} + k_j)$ if it lists k_j intervals. By induction it follows that the query time of the d-dimensional segment tree of n intervals is output-sensitive

$O((\log n)^d + k)$. This is again a static structure that can be made dynamic in the amortized sense by the technique of partial rebuilding.

Theorem. The d-dimensional segment tree structure is a static data structure that can be built in time $O(n(\log n)^d)$ and needs space $O(n(\log n)^d)$. It lists all d-dimensional intervals containing a given query key in output-sensitive time $O((\log n)^d + k)$ if there are k such intervals.

Again this allows an improvement for the two-dimensional case, which reduces the query time from $O((\log n)^2 + k)$ to $O(\log n + k)$. This can then be used in the recursive construction for the d-dimensional structure to get $O((\log n)^{d-1} + k)$ output-sensitive query time for $d \geq 2$. This structure, the S-tree, was developed by Vaishnavi (1982) and uses again a fractional cascading-like technique.

To describe this method for the two-dimensional problem, we start with the two-dimensional segment tree as described before. In a query, we follow the segment tree for the first coordinate, with the first coordinate q_x of the query point, and in each of the $O(\log n)$ nodes along this search path we make a query in the segment tree for the second coordinate q_y and list all the rectangles we found along that path. So this second-coordinate query goes again in a search tree down from the root to a leaf and gathers the rectangles listed in the nodes. If we knew which leaf we would end up in, we could also take the same path backward, going up from the leaf. And this is indeed easier because we always end in the same leaf: that one which contains the second-coordinate q_y of the query point.

So the first idea is to orient each second-coordinate tree backward, from leaves to root, and join the leaves of different trees together according to the first-coordinate tree; then we visit $O(\log n)$ second-coordinate trees, but in each we just follow a path upward and list all rectangles found on the way. With the upward pointers along these $O(\log n)$ paths, we can skip the empty nodes, so the time we spend on the ith path is $O(1 + k_i)$ if we list k_i rectangles on that path, which gives an $O(\log n + k)$ output-sensitive query time, $k = \sum_i k_i$, if we can visit the $O(\log n)$ leaves of the second-coordinate trees in $O(\log n)$ time, instead of the $O((\log n)^2)$ time we need if we locate each leaf in its tree individually.

The problem here is that, although in each tree we need the leaf that contains the second coordinate q_y of the query point, the individual trees might look quite different, because they do not use the same keys, but only those that are second coordinates of rectangles that are inserted in that specific second-coordinate tree. Thus it could happen that going down the first-coordinate tree, some of the second-coordinate trees have only one leaf, and then there are again big ones. If we want to go in $O(1)$ time from one leaf containing q_y to the corresponding leaf of the next tree, the interval associated with the previous leaf should intersect only $O(1)$ intervals of leaves in the next tree.

Because the leaf intervals are the intervals between the consecutive key values in the tree, we can achieve this if the set of key values that occur in the next second-coordinate tree is a subset of the key values used in the current tree. Then each leaf interval in the current tree is contained in a unique leaf interval in the next tree, and we can just create a pointer from the leaf in the current to the leaf in the next tree, for each of the two possible next trees we get from the first-coordinate tree.

To achieve this subset property for the key values, we need to enter the second coordinates of each rectangle not only in the second-coordinate trees, where it occurs by the canonical interval decomposition of its first coordinate, but also in the trees above it in the first-coordinate tree. But there are only another two nodes on each level where the rectangle is entered, so each rectangle occurs still in only $O(\log n)$ second-coordinate trees, where it contributes $O(\log n)$ occurences each, so the total size of the structure is still only $O(\log n)$. And the query time, as described earlier, is $O(\log n + k)$.

The construction we now ultimately arrived at is the following: given the rectangles $[a_i, b_i[\times [c_i, d_i[$, for $i = 1, \ldots, n$,

1. Create a balanced search tree T_1 for $\{a_1, b_1, a_2, b_2, \ldots, a_n, b_n\}$.
2. Attach to each node v of this tree an initially empty secondary search tree $T_2(v)$.
3. For each $i = 1, \ldots, n$,
   3.1 Start at the root of T_1 and put it on a stack. Then, as long as the stack is not empty, repeat.
   3.2 Take the current node v from the stack.
   Insert $\{c_i, d_i\}$ as keys into the tree $T_2(v)$.
   If the interval of the current node v is not contained in $[a_i, b_i[$, check for v->left and v->right whether their intervals have nonempty intersection with $[a_i, b_i[$; if yes, put them on the stack.
4. For each $i = 1, \ldots, n$,
   4.1 Insert rectangle $[a_i, b_i[\times [c_i, d_i[$ into the segment tree $T_2(v)$ for all those nodes v that belong to the canonical interval decomposition of $[a_i, b_i[$ in T_1.
5. For each node v of T_1,
   5.1 Create pointers from each leaf of $T_2(v)$ to the corresponding leaves of $T_2(v$->left) and $T_2(v$->right).

6. For each node v of T_1,

   6.1 For each node w of $T_2(v)$ create a pointer to the next node above w in $T_2(v)$ that has some rectangle associated with it.

This is already a quite complicated structure. The key insight for the analysis is that each pair $\{c_i, d_i\}$ is inserted in step 3 only $O(\log n)$ times, so the associated segment trees $T_2(v)$ together have only $O(n \log n)$ nodes. Each rectangle will again be inserted in at most $O((\log n)^2)$ node lists, so the total size and preprocessing time is $O(n(\log n)^2)$: the construction time is dominated by step 4; all others need only $O(n \log n)$. To summarize the performance of this structure see the following:

Theorem. The S-tree is a static data structure that keeps track of a set of n rectangles, using $O(n(\log n)^2)$ space and preprocessing time, and lists for a given query point all rectangles that contain this point in time $O(\log n + k)$ if there are k such intervals.

4.8 Other Systems of Building Blocks

In many of the preceding algorithms we used the canonical interval decomposition induced by a search tree on a set of numbers. The underlying abstract idea is to decompose an interval in a union of a small number of building blocks. If we want to answer a query for an arbitrary query interval, then we decompose that query interval into a union of building blocks and execute the query on those building blocks.

1	*2*	*3*	*4*	*5*	*6*	*7*	*8*	*9*	*10*	*11*	*12*	*13*	*14*

| *1* | *2* | *3* | *4* | *5* | *6* | *7* | *8* | *9* | *10* | *11* | *12* | *13* | *14* |

| *1* | *2* | *3* | *4* | *5* | *6* | *7* | *8* | *9* | *10* | *11* | *12* | *13* | *14* |

| *1* | *2* | *3* | *4* | *5* | *6* | *7* | *8* | *9* | *10* | *11* | *12* | *13* | *14* |

| *2* | *3* | *4* | *5* | *6* | *7* | | *9* | *10* | *11* | *12* | *13* | *14* |

INTERVALS IN A CANONICAL INTERVAL DECOMPOSITION OF $\{1, \ldots, 14\}$:
ANY INTERVAL CAN BE EXPRESSED AS UNION OF FIVE BLOCKS

This requires that we can decompose the queries and reconstruct the answer for the entire interval from the answers for the building blocks into which we decomposed the query.[10] Also, we need some structure that answers the query for a fixed block. And finally we need to be able to represent each interval as union of a small number of blocks.

The prototype of this situation is orthogonal range queries. With the canonical interval decomposition, we need only n distinct building blocks, of total size $O(n \log n)$, and a query for an arbitrary interval is reduced to $O(\log n)$ lower-dimensional queries to building blocks. There is a trade-off in the choice of building blocks: if we want to reduce our arbitrary interval query to a small number of block queries, then we need many building blocks, and for each block we have to build a structure to answer queries. In the extreme case, we can build a structure for each possible query interval. In the orthogonal range query example, there are $\binom{n}{2} = \Theta(n^2)$ possible query intervals for the first coordinate, and we could build for each of them a structure for the lower-dimensional query. Then we would need just one lower-dimensional query, instead of $\Theta(\log n)$, but would need much more preprocessing time to construct all these lower-dimensional structures.

This idea was first used by Bentley and Maurer in 1980 for d-dimensional orthogonal range searching, where they showed that one can reach an output-sensitive query time of $O(f(d, \varepsilon) \log n + k)$ with $O(n^{1+\varepsilon})$ preprocessing time. The same idea can be applied to many other problems, although the details depend, of course, on what we need to do with the building blocks.

To describe the method in more detail, we notice first that we need not deal with those arbitrary n coordinate values; we can always assume they are $1, \ldots, n$. We achieve this normalization by building a search tree for the coordinate values, which translate a query coordinate in its rank, that is, i for the ith smallest. This adds $O(\log n)$ to the query time, but as the query time is at least $\Omega(\log n)$, this is insignificant.

The system of blocks used in Bentley and Maurer (1980) is an r-level structure that can be interpreted as writing the numbers to the base $n^{\frac{1}{r}}$. On the top level, the blocks are the intervals

$$\left[an^{1-\frac{1}{r}}, bn^{1-\frac{1}{r}} \right] \qquad \text{with } 0 \le a < b \le n^{\frac{1}{r}}.$$

On the jth level, the blocks are intervals

$$\left[an^{1-\frac{j}{r}} + cn^{1-\frac{j-1}{r}}, bn^{1-\frac{j}{r}} + cn^{1-\frac{j-1}{r}} \right] \qquad \begin{array}{l} \text{with } 0 \le a < b \le n^{\frac{1}{r}} \text{ and} \\ 0 \le c < n^{\frac{j-1}{r}}, \text{ for } 2 \le j \le r. \end{array}$$

---

[10] This is different from the decomposable searching problems we discuss in Section 7.1. There, we decompose the underlying set; here, we decompose the query interval.

This gives $\binom{n^{\frac{1}{r}}}{2} = O(n^{\frac{2}{r}})$ blocks on the top level, each of size at most n, and $n^{\frac{i-1}{r}}\binom{n^{\frac{1}{r}}}{2} = O(n^{\frac{i+1}{r}})$ blocks on the jth level, each of size at most $n^{1-\frac{i-1}{r}}$. To answer a query, we need at most one block on the top level and two blocks each on the lower levels, which gives a total of $2r - 1$ queries on blocks. If the time to build the query-answering structure for a block of size m is preproc(m), we need in total

$$O\left(\sum_{j=1}^{r} n^{\frac{i+1}{r}} \text{ preproc}\left(n^{1-\frac{i-1}{r}}\right)\right) = O\left(rn^{1+\frac{2}{r}} \frac{\text{preproc}(n)}{n}\right)$$

time to build this structure.

INTERVALS IN A TWO-LEVEL BENTLEY–MAURER STRUCTURE OF $\{1, \ldots, 14\}$:
ANY INTERVAL CAN BE EXPRESSED AS UNION OF THREE BLOCKS

In the case of d-dimensional orthogonal range queries (Bentley and Maurer 1980), any normal balanced search tree gives us a structure that performs the one-dimensional queries in output-sensitive time $O(\log n + k)$, with preprocessing time $\text{preproc}_1(n) = O(n \log n)$. If we now use this r-level structure for the possible query intervals in the second coordinate, we obtain a structure that performs two-dimensional queries in output-sensitive time $O(r \log n + k)$ and requires preprocessing time $\text{preproc}_2(n) = O(rn^{1+\frac{2}{r}} \log n)$. We again use an r-level structure for the possible query intervals in the third coordinate, and the two-dimensional structure for the queries on each third-coordinate block in the first two coordinates, we obtain a structure that performs three-dimensional queries in output-sensitive time $O(r^2 \log n + k)$ and requires preprocessing time $\text{preproc}_3(n) = O(r^2 n^{1+\frac{4}{r}} \log n)$. Iterating this construction, we obtain a structure that performs d-dimensional orthogonal range searching in time $O(r^d \log n + k)$ and requires preprocessing time $O(r^d n^{1+\frac{2d-2}{r}} \log n)$. We now choose r large enough to obtain $O(f(d, \varepsilon) \log n + k)$ output-sensitive query time with $O(n^{1+\varepsilon})$ preprocessing time. Unfortunately, this method is advantageous only for very large n, because the multiplicative constants in those $O(\cdot)$ bounds are very large (Falconer and Nickerson 2005).

The same technique can be applied to other interval-based problems; indeed, the technique of decomposing a query domain into few building blocks and preprocessing the answers for all blocks is not restricted to intervals as query domains. But we must be able to find the block decomposition of the query domain fast and to answer the query from the answers on the blocks.

4.9 Range-Counting and the Semigroup Model

The range-counting problem asks just for the number of points in a range, instead of a list of these points. So in the complexity bound, we do not need any output-sensitive term; the output is always just one number. The orthogonal range tree idea can be directly adapted to that question instead of concatenating lists; we just add up the numbers contributed from the subproblems in the canonical interval decomposition. This can be immediately generalized, giving the points weights and asking for the total weight of the points in a query range or for the maximum weight. Indeed, if we have a commutative semigroup (like $+$, or max) and each point has an associated value, we can determine the semigroup sum of all points in the query range in exactly the same way, constructing the canonical interval decomposition of the first-coordinate query interval, executing lower-dimensional queries, and computing the semigroup sum of their results. In the one-dimensional version, this just asks for the number of keys in an interval, or the semigroup sum of their keys, which can be directly answered from the canonical interval decomposition, if those values are stored in the tree nodes. A special case is to maintain an array $a_1, \ldots, a_n$, together with the partial sums of its subarrays $a_i + \cdots + a_j$, under updates of the array elements a_k, a problem studied in various versions and models in Fredman (1979, 1982), Yao (1982, 1985c), Hampapuram and Fredman (1998), Burghardt (2001), and Pătraşcu and Demaine (2004).

There are two things that make range-counting problem interesting and different from range searching. First, it allows to make the structure dynamic, allowing insertions and deletions, as we can rebalance the trees. This was not possible in the range-searching problem because the structures associated to the tree nodes were large structures, which would have to be rebuilt; but for the range counting, it is just a single number, which can be recomputed from its lower neighbors. This was already observed by Lueker (1978) and Willard.[11] This structure performs `insert`, `delete`, and `range_count` all in amortized $O((\log n)^d)$ on a set of n points. More remarkable, however, is that in this model one can show lower bounds on the complexity of any algorithm solving this range-counting problem. In the range-searching model, the output-sensitive term hides some effects. This study of lower bounds was started by Fredman (1979, 1981a, b) and Yao (1982). For a lower bound, one needs to be specific about the model assumptions, which are rather strong and in each of these papers somewhat different. And the results show that details do matter. In the model of Fredman (1981a), any structure that solves the dynamic range-counting problem, supporting `insert`, `delete`, and `range_count` for any commutative semigroup, will need $\Omega(n(\log n)^d)$ for some sequence of n operations, starting from an empty set; and he gives one structure that gives $O((\log n)^d)$ worst-case complexity. But this complexity model is quite different from either pointer machines or algebraic decision trees because only arithmetic operations of a specific type are allowed and only these are counted. As an example, if we have a static array $a_1, \ldots, a_n$ and want to evaluate partial sums of subarrays $a_i + a_{i+1} + \cdots + a_j$, and are interested in the additional storage and the query time, then there is a trivial algorithm with n cells of additional storage, and $O(1)$ query time, if we are allowed to use subtractions: we just store all partial sums starting in a_1, then $a_i + \cdots + a_j = (a_1 + \cdots + a_j) - (a_1 + \cdots + a_{i-1})$. But if we are not allowed subtractions, and our query algorithm can only add some subset of the additional storage cells together, and these storage cells contain only nonnegative linear combinations of the a_i, then a bound on the complexity of the query related to the inverse Ackermann function of n and the number of additional storage cells was given in Yao (1982).[12] But this complexity then counts only the number of arithmetic operations, taking the sum of cells, not the time to select the cells, in dependence of the query, of which the sum is taken. Thus, the complexity results in these measures are not comparable to our other complexity bounds. The most important of these papers is Fredman (1981b), where a general technique for complexity bounds for dynamic range-counting problems in a class of arithmetic models is

---

[11] In a technical report mentioned earlier in Footnote 7.

[12] A related technical report, N. Alon, and B. Schieber: Optimal Preprocessing for Answering On-line Product Queries, Tel Aviv University, Israel, 1987, gives a similar result for partial products of static sequence of semigroup elements, using yet another relative of the inverse Ackermann function.

introduced. Many other models have been developed since; a survey of lower bounds in various models is given in Pătraşcu (2007). The space-query time trade-off in static d-dimensional range-query models was studied in Vaidya (1989), Chazelle (1990a, b) and in a quite different type of model in Hellerstein, Koutsoupias, and Papadimitriou (1997), Koutsoupias and Taylor (1998), and Samoladas and Miranker (1998).

4.10 kd-Trees and Related Structures

The kd-tree is another structure that supports orthogonal range searching. It is quite popular in practical applications and conceptually easy to understand and implement; but it is unsatisfactory because its worst-case performance is much worse than orthogonal range trees. In the two-dimensional version, the worst-case query time is $O(\sqrt{n} + k)$ instead of $O((\log n)^2 + k)$, and the d-dimensional analog is even worse, with $O(n^{(1-\frac{1}{d})} + k)$ instead of $O((\log n)^d + k)$. The empirical performance in database examples seems better than this worst-case complexity, so in database literature, this and related structures have been widely studied and used.

The kd-tree was invented by Bentley (1975)[13] as a direct analog of the normal balanced search tree, which is viewed as a one-dimensional tree: the name kd-tree was originally meant as k-dimensional tree. The lower bound for the query time was given by Lee and Wong (1977), and a first comparative analysis of several range-searching structures, among them the kd-tree, the orthogonal range tree (see Section 4.6), and the Bentley–Maurer structures (see Section 4.8), appears in Bentley and Friedman (1979). The bad worst-case query time places the kd-tree in any comparison far behind these structures, only under strong assumptions like uniformly distributed data points and small, "relatively square" query rectangles; its performance becomes comparable to them. Square query rectangles occur when we really aim at a nearest-neighbor query, or at least some filter for the neighborhood of the query point. Variants of the kd-tree structure are analyzed in numerous papers under input and query distribution assumptions (Silva-Filho 1979; Cunto, Lau, and Flajolet 1989; Gardy, Flajolet, and Puech 1989; Duch, Estivill-Castro, and Martinez 1998; Chanzy, Devroye, and Zamora-Cura 2001; Duch and Martinez 2002). Other aspects of the classical kd-tree structure have been studied in Silva-Filho (1981) and Hoshi and Yuba (1982). Much work went into making kd-trees a dynamic structure, allowing insertions and deletions of points starting with kd-trees

---

[13] Winning the second prize in an ACM best student paper competition.

(Robinson 1981), semidynamic kd-trees (Bentley 1990), divided kd-trees (van Kreveld and Overmars 1991), O-trees (Ravi Kanth and Singh 1999), and the structure in Grossi and Italiano 1997. External memory efficiency has also been a major consideration in these structures; further related structures supporting various types of range-restricted queries have been developed in the database community (Guttman 1984; Beckmann et al. 1990; Lomet and Salzberg 1990; Freeston 1995; Agarwal et al. 2002; Bozanis, Nanopoulas, and Manolopoulos 2003; Arge et al. 2004; Procopiuc et al. 2003); see also the books by Samet (1990, 2006) and the surveys by Gaede and Günther (1998) and Nievergelt and Widmayer (1999).

The idea of the kd-tree is that we have a search tree, where in each node we make a comparison and enter the left or right subtree, but unlike the normal search trees, we can compare in different nodes against different coordinates. The simplest choice is to cycle through the coordinates; in the root, we compare against the first coordinate, in the nodes below, we compare against the second coordinate, and so on. In each node, we choose as comparison key a value that divides the set of points below that node in a balanced way. As in the normal search trees, this defines a node interval for each node, which is now a d-dimensional half-open box – the set of all possible query points whose search path would go through that node. The comparison with the node key then divides the box by a hyperplane in the direction of that coordinate which we used in the comparison. So we get a hierarchy of possibly unbounded orthogonal boxes. In the two-dimensional version, these are rectangles alternatingly divided in the horizontal and vertical directions.

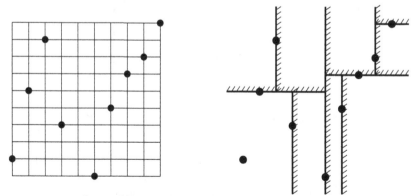

SET OF NINE POINTS WITH KD-TREE STRUCTURE:
ALL RECTANGLES ARE HALF-OPEN TO THE RIGHT AND THE TOP

If we have this structure, a range query can be answered just as in the one-dimensional case: starting in the root, we descend into each node whose node interval has a nonempty intersection with the query region and stop following any branch when that intersection becomes empty. This is a very natural and generic query algorithm that can be applied for any type of query ranges, not only for rectangles. This is a great strength of this type of structure, but it is not very efficient, for the number of leaves we visit without actually finding a point that should belong to the answer can be as large as $\Omega(\sqrt{n})$. And this is not only for specific bad point sets, or bad subdivision structures; it is a problem that always occurs: there is always a query rectangle that intersects $\Omega(\sqrt{n})$ of the cells without containing any point of the underlying set.

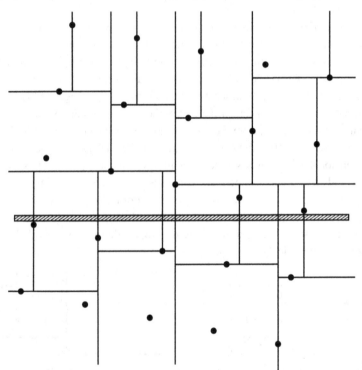

VERY REGULAR KD-TREE SUBDIVISION WITH BAD QUERY RECTANGLE:
EACH POINT BELONGS TO RECTANGLE ABOVE OR TO THE RIGHT OF IT

We now assume that all point coordinates are distinct, and that the kd-tree is constructed in such a way that in each node the key divides the number of points in both subtrees as evenly as possible, with horizontal and vertical cuts alternating. The tree has then height $\lceil \log n \rceil$.

To show that $O(\sqrt{n} + k)$ query time is indeed the worst case that can happen in this tree, we have to bound the number of nodes we visit in a query. We visit only such nodes whose node interval (rectangle) has nonempty intersection with the query interval (rectangle). Of these, the nodes whose node interval contains the query interval are few, only at most one per level of the tree, for the node intervals at each level form a partition of the plane. Because the tree has height $\lceil \log n \rceil$, there are only $O(\log n)$ such nodes. Nodes whose node interval is contained in the query interval are potentially more, but each of these contributes at least one point to the answer, so there are at most k such nodes. The only problem are those nodes whose node interval partially overlaps with the query interval. These nodes intersect one of the sides of the query interval, so we can bound the number of these nodes by four times the maximum number of times an axis-parallel line segment can be cut by node intervals. Let a_i be the number of such nodes at level i. Because the cutting direction alternates horizontal and vertical, in every second level this number does not increase at all, and in the other levels, it at most doubles. Thus $a_i \leq 2^{\lfloor (1/2)i \rfloor}$, and $a_0 + a_1 + \cdots + a_{\log n} \leq 2 * 2^{(1/2)\log n} = O(\sqrt{n})$.

Note that at this point we really needed the optimal height $\lceil \log n \rceil$; a weaker balance criterion in the nodes, with height $O(\log n)$, would not be enough to show the $O(\sqrt{n})$ bound on the sum. For this height bound, it was necessary that we could always divide the point sets in almost equal parts, which is enforced by assuming that all coordinates are distinct. This strong assumption can be removed by making each node a ternary comparison, with separate equality case; we can always choose the comparison key in such a way that both $<$ and $>$ cases contain at most half the remaining points and the $=$ case is a one-dimensional problem, which can be solved directly in $O(\log n)$ time.

To see that the $O(\sqrt{n})$ bound cannot be improved, we show that there is always a query rectangle that intersects $\Omega(\sqrt{n})$ leaf intervals without containing any point. We just follow the previous argument again. Take any horizontal or vertical line; let b_i be the number of nodes at level i of the tree that are intersected by the line. Then we have $b_2 = 2$ and $b_{i+2} = 2b_i$ for $i + 2 < \log n$. So at the leaf level, we have $b_{\log n} = \Omega(\sqrt{n})$. If we select a thin rectangle around this line, we have thus a very bad query rectangle, which forces us to visit $\Omega(\sqrt{n})$ leaves without containing any point.

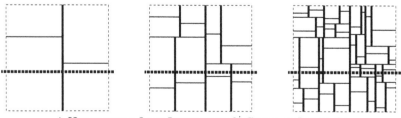

A Horizontal Line Intersects 2^i Cells at Level $2i$

We summarize the performance of the structure for the d-dimensional analog.

Theorem. kd-trees are a static structure that supports d-dimensional orthogonal range queries in a set of d-dimensional points in output-sensitive time $O\left(n^{1-\frac{1}{d}} + k\right)$ if the output consists of k points. They can be built in $O(n(\log n))$ time using $O(n)$ space.

5

Heaps

Heaps are, after the search trees, the second most studied type of data structure. As abstract structure they are also called priority queues, and they keep track of a set of objects, each object having a key value (the priority), and support the operations to insert an object, find the object of minimum key (find_min), and delete the object of minimum key (delete_min). So unlike the search trees, there are neither arbitrary find operations nor arbitrary delete operations possible. Of course, we can replace everywhere the minimum by maximum; where this distinction is important, one type is called the min-heap and the other the max-heap. If we need both types of operations, the structure is called a double-ended heap, which is a bit more complicated.

The heap structure was originally invented by Williams[1] (1964) for the very special application of sorting, although he did already present it as a separate data structure with possibly further applications. But it was recognized only much later that heaps have many other, and indeed more important, applications. Still, the connection to sorting is important because the lower bound of $\Omega(n \log n)$ on comparison-based sorting of n objects implies a lower bound on the complexity of the heap operations. We can sort by first inserting all objects in the heap and then performing find_min and delete_min operations to recover the objects, sorted in increasing order. So we can sort by performing n operations each of insert, find_min, and delete_min; thus, at least one of these operations must have (in a comparison-based model) a complexity $\Omega(\log n)$. This connection works in both directions; there is an equivalence between the speed of sorting and heap operations in many models – even those

---

[1] Usually Floyd (1964) is also cited, but his contribution is the adaptation of the heap to in-place sorting, continuing the line of development of his Treesort algorithm (Floyd 1962) previously improved by Kaupe (1962).

209

in which the comparison-based lower bound for sorting does not hold (Thorup 2002).

The various methods to realize the heap structure differ mainly by the additional operations they support. The most important of these are the merging of several heaps (taking the union of the underlying sets of objects), which is sometimes also called melding, and the change of the key of an object (usually decreasing the key), which requires a finger to the object in the structure.

The most important applications of heaps are all kinds of event queues, as they occur in many diverse applications: sweeps in computational geometry, discrete event systems (Evans 1986), schedulers, and many classical algorithms such as Dijkstra's shortest path algorithm.

5.1 Balanced Search Trees as Heaps

Because we have already studied balanced search trees in detail, it is easy to see that they also support the heap operations. They have the same underlying abstract structure, a set of objects associated with keys; but instead of find and delete of arbitrary objects, given by their keys, we need find and delete for the object with the smallest key. To find that object, we just need to always follow the left pointer in a search tree, and in the same way we find the largest key by always following the right pointer. Thus, we can use any balanced search tree to obtain a heap in which each of the operations insert, find_min, and delete_min takes $O(\log n)$ time. The find_min operation can even be made in $O(1)$ time: we just need to store the current minimum in a variable, and when we perform the next delete_min, we also look up the new current minimum in the same $O(\log n)$ time that the delete_min operation takes anyway. Indeed, it is a double-ended heap; we get find_max, delete_max in the same way, as well as all additional operations that are perhaps supported by the search tree (e.g., split).

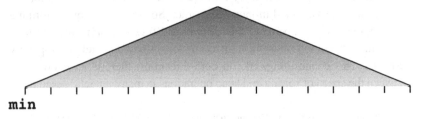

min

SEARCH TREE USED AS HEAP

Thus, it is trivial to reach $O(\log n)$ performance for all the heap operations by reusing balanced search trees, with the query operation find_min becoming even a constant-time operation. This is the standard of comparison: any interesting heap structure should perform better than this in some respect or support some type of operation not supported by balanced search trees.

Theorem. The heap structure can be realized using any balanced search tree with time $O(\log n)$ for insert and delete_min and $O(1)$ for find_min operations.

In addition to the normal balanced trees, splay trees and skip lists have been frequently used this way. Next is the code for this trivial heap implementation if we already have a balanced search tree available.

```
typedef struct {key_t        key;
                object_t    *object;
               }heap_el_t;
typedef struct {heap_el_t       current_min;
                tree_node_t    *tree;
               }heap_t;

heap_t *create_heap(void)
{  heap_t *hp;
   hp = (heap_t *) malloc( sizeof(heap_t) );
   hp->tree = create_tree();
   return( hp );
}

int heap_empty(heap_t *hp)
{  return( hp->tree->left == NULL );
}

heap_el_t find_min(heap_t *hp)
{  return( hp->current_min );
}

void insert_heap( key_t new_key,
                  object_t *new_obj, heap_t *hp)
{  if( hp->tree->left == NULL ||
       new_key < hp->current_min.key )
     {  hp->current_min.key = new_key;
        hp->current_min.object = new_obj;
```

```
        }
        insert(hp->tree, new_key, new_obj );
    }

    object_t *delete_min(heap_t *hp)
    {   object_t     *del_obj;
        tree_node_t *tmp_node;
        if( hp->tree->left == NULL )
            return( NULL ); /* heap empty */
        else
        {   del_obj = hp->current_min.object;
            delete(hp->tree, hp->current_min.key );
            tmp_node = hp->tree;
            if( tmp_node->left != NULL )
            /* update current_min */
            {   while( tmp_node->right != NULL )
                    tmp_node = tmp_node->left;
                hp->current_min.key    = tmp_node->key;
                hp->current_min.object = (object_t *)
                    tmp_node->left;
            }
            return( del_obj );
        }
    }

    void remove_heap(heap_t *hp)
    {   remove_tree( hp->tree );
        free( hp );
    }
```

As explained in the beginning, we cannot expect both delete_min and insert to be faster than $O(\log n)$. But it is possible to use balanced search trees to get the delete_min operation in $O(1)$ time. For this, we need to arrange the leaves in a linked list, and the underlying search tree has to support the split operation in $O(\log n)$, with splitting in the root in $O(1)$, as it is the case for height-balanced or red-black trees. Then we keep a pointer to the current minimal element in this list and just advance this pointer in the list when we perform the delete_min operation, without actually deleting the tree nodes. Such a strategy is called lazy deletion. Of course, at some point we must really delete all the invalid objects and return the nodes. But in principle any balanced binary search tree that supports a split operation and whose leaves are arranged in a linked list can be used to implement a heap with $O(1)$ find_min and delete_min operations, and $O(\log n)$ insert. This method was essentially already discovered in Guibas et al. (1977); it is best possible, and this is the reason why most later heap implementations proposed in literature discuss the other extremum – $O(1)$ insert and $O(\log n)$ delete_min.

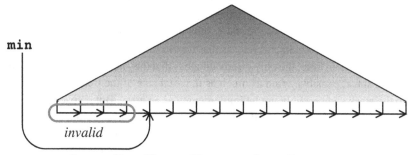

SEARCH TREE USED AS HEAP WITH LAZY DELETION:
INVALID ELEMENTS ARE ALREADY DELETED FROM HEAP

In more detail, we need a balanced search-tree structure that supports the splitting operation and whose leaves are arranged in a linked list from smallest to largest key, or, which is easier to update, a doubly linked list in both directions. We also need a pointer current_min to the current minimum in this list. Finally, we need an invalid nodes structure that allows us to add an entire subtree of nodes whose keys and objects have already been deleted, but which still need to be returned to the free list one by one. Then the heap operations are implemented as follows:

– find_min: return current_min->key and current_min->object.
– insert:

1. Split the search tree at current_min->key, and add the lower tree to the invalid nodes structure.
2. Insert the new key in search tree.
3. If the new key is below current_min->key, set current_min to the new key and object.

– delete_min:

1. Delete the object current_min->object.
2. Move current_min to the next list position.
3. If current_min->key is now larger than the key in the root of the balanced search tree, add the left subtree of the balanced search tree to

the invalid nodes structure; take the right subtree as new search tree; and
return the node of the old root to the free list.
4. Return several nodes from the invalid nodes structure to the free list.

This still leaves unspecified how to realize the invalid nodes structure. It has
to allow adding a subtree and removing a node both in constant time. The
simplest way to do this is to build a stack whose entries are pointers to roots of
the subtrees. To add a new subtree, one just puts it on the stack; to remove a node,
one takes the top root from the stack, puts both left and right subtrees on the
stack, if it was not a leaf, and returns that root to the free list. These operations
work in constant time; the only disadvantage is that they need additional storage
for the stack, possibly again as much as the total size of the trees on the stack.
So the stack can certainly not be implemented as an array. But if space is not an
essential restriction, this is only a constant-factor overhead, in the worst case
an increase of the space requirement by a factor of less than four.

It is obvious that the find_min operation takes only $O(1)$ time. The insert operation takes $O(\log n)$ for steps 1 and 2 each, and $O(1)$ for step 3, so
a total of $O(\log n)$. And each step of the delete_min operation takes only
$O(1)$. We observe that the current_min is always in the left subtree of the
search tree, so height of the search tree with all the invalid nodes is never more
than one larger than the height of a search tree without these nodes.

To summarize the performance of this structure, we obtained the following:

Theorem. The heap structure can be realized using a balanced search tree
with lazy deletion in time $O(\log n)$ for insert and $O(1)$ for find_min and
delete_min operations if the heap contains n elements.

An alternative way to reach the same performance is to use a search tree with
a constant time deletion of an element at a known location, as described in
Section 3.6.

5.2 Array-Based Heaps

The classical heap version that was originally invented for heapsort and that
is described in most algorithms textbooks is the array-based heap. By using
the array index instead of explicit pointers, it is a very compact representation
(an implicit data structure). In the heapsort application, it even fits exactly in
the space of the array to be sorted and does not require any additional space.
It supports insert and delete_min operations in time $O(\log n)$ and $O(1)$

find_min, and the number of key comparisons in the sorting application (n inserts followed by n deletes) is near the theoretical minimum, so it is a rather fast heap version, at the price of having a fixed maximum size and not supporting additional operations. Thus, the array-based heap is most important for the sorting application.

This heap works by embedding a complete binary tree structure in the array elements, establishing a key ordering called the heap order. Given a big array heap_key[MAX_SIZE], a correct heap satisfies the following conditions:

1. The entries used by the heap are a beginning interval of the array; if the heap currently contains n elements, it uses the array positions 0 to $n - 1$.
2. For all $i \geq 0$ have
   heap_key[i] < heap_key[$2i + 1$] if $2i + 1 < n$ and
   heap_key[i] < heap_key[$2i + 2$] if $2i + 2 < n$.

An immediate consequence of this is that the minimum key is always in index position 0, and the first unused entry of the array is the index position n. Each array element is subject to three heap-order conditions: the element at position i is smaller than the elements at positions $2i + 1$ and $2i + 2$, its upper[2] neighbors, if they exist, and larger than the element at position $\lfloor \frac{1}{2}(i - 1) \rfloor$, its lower neighbor, if it exists. This defines a binary tree of height $\log n$ on the array elements.

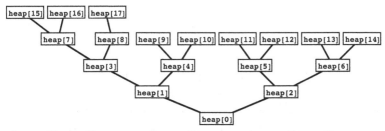

ARRAY-BASED HEAP WITH ORDER RELATION AMONG ARRAY ELEMENTS

The insert now works as follows: put the new element into position n and increase n; in this way, property 1 is maintained, but the new element might violate property 2, so we need to compare and possibly exchange it with the lower neighbor. If we do exchange the new element at position i with its lower neighbor at position $\lfloor \frac{1}{2}(i - 1) \rfloor$, this decreases the key value in that position, so the order conditions from there upward, in which this should be the smaller

---

[2]When visualizing an array, we always put the start of the array to the left, or to the bottom, and then number left to right, or from the bottom-up. This convention has as a consequence that the root of the implicit tree of the array heap is at the bottom, the only trees in this book, which grow in the right direction.

value, still hold; but again the order condition downward must be checked and possibly corrected by an exchange. This stops at the latest in position 0, if the new element is the new minimum, as there is no downward condition. This takes at most one comparison on each level, so at most $\log n$ key comparisons per insert operation.

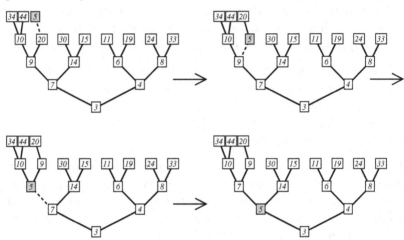

ARRAY-BASED HEAP: INSERTION OF NEW ELEMENT WITH KEY 5.
THE NEW ELEMENT IS PLACED IN THE LAST POSITION AND MOVES DOWN

For the delete_min, we have to delete the element at position 0 and fill this gap by moving elements into it. The problem with the trivial strategy, moving down the smaller of the two upper neighbors, is that this way we move up the gap and restore the order property 2, but the gap will not end up in position $n - 1$, so property 1 will be violated.

The classical method to avoid this problem is to move in the first step that last element from position $n - 1$ to position 0 and then have it move up to its correct place. Because we have to restore the two upward conditions in each step of moving up, we need two comparisons: we compare the upper neighbors and then the smaller of the upper neighbors with the current element. If the smaller upper neighbor has a smaller key than the current element, we exchange them, moving the current element up. This uses two comparisons per level, one to decide which of the upper neighbors should possibly move down and another to decide whether it should move down. This will almost always be the case because we moved the last element, which will be large, to the place of the smallest, so we probably have to move it back a long way. Thus, an alternative is to skip the second comparison and always exchange the current element with the smaller of its upper neighbors, moving the gap up to the top, fill in the last element, and then move that element in a second pass down to its proper place. In the worst case, this does not gain anything, but in the application of sorting, it was shown that this indeed decreases the total number of comparisons. This is known as bottom-up heapsort (Wegener 1993; Fleischer 1994). A similar method that gives a general improvement of the number of comparisons in the deletion was proposed in Xunrang and Yuzhang (1990); they move the gap up to $\frac{2}{3}$ of the possible height, insert the last element, and then move it up or down as necessary. This decreases the worst-case number of key comparisons in delete_min operation from $2 \log n$ to $\frac{4}{3} \log n$.

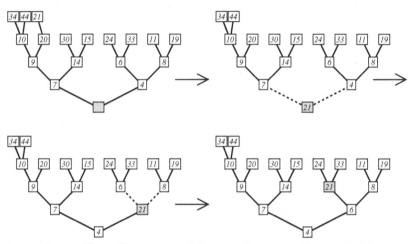

ARRAY-BASED HEAP: DELETION OF MINIMUM ELEMENT, CLASSICAL METHOD.
THE LAST ELEMENT IS PLACED INTO THE GAP AND MOVES UP

A very small improvement can be gained by avoiding elements with two lower neighbors on the highest level as long as possible, not filling the highest level sequentially, but first the odd and then the even positions. This requires a change of the order property 2 (Carlsson 1984) and saves one key comparison for half the values of n. Yet another possible modification is to use binary search in that process of moving down an element (Gonnet and Munro 1986; Carlsson 1987). By careful analysis it is even possible to find the exact minimum number of key comparisons for insert and delete (Gonnet and Munro 1986; Carlsson 1991), as well as bounds for some other operations, like constructing a heap from an unordered array (McDiarmid and Reed 1989; Carlsson and Chen 1992) or merging of two heaps (Sack and Strothotte 1985; Khoong and Leong 1994). But the number of key comparisons is not that important as a realistic measure of speed; this example of making a binary search on the path, but then having to move all elements in the path to perform the actual insertion at the correct place, shows that reducing the number of comparisons from $\log n$ to $\log \log n$ is not useful if the number of data movements does not also decrease. In a good implementation we should also avoid unnecessary data movements.

Yet another variant of the standard array-heap was proposed by Herman and Masuzawa (2001) and allows partial recovery of the heap structure even from corrupted states. An extension of array-heaps to other partially ordered sets was outlined by Noltemeier (1981).

Next is an implementation of this standard array-based heap structure, with a given maximum size. Each element of the heap consists of a key and a pointer to an object, and this is what we return with the query:

```
typedef struct {key_t key; object_t *object;
               }heap_el_t;
typedef struct {int     max_size;
                int     current_size;
                heap_el_t *heap;      } heap_t;

heap_t *create_heap(int size)
{   heap_t *hp;
    hp = (heap_t *) malloc( sizeof(heap_t) );
    hp->heap = (heap_el_t *)
    malloc( size * sizeof(heap_el_t) );
    hp->max_size = size;
    hp->current_size = 0;
    return( hp );
}


int heap_empty(heap_t *hp)
{   return( hp->current_size == 0 );
}


heap_el_t *find_min(heap_t *hp)
{     return( hp->heap );
}


int insert( key_t new_key, object_t *new_object,
            heap_t *hp)
{   if ( hp->current_size < hp->max_size )
    {  int gap;
```

```
      gap = hp->current_size++;
      while(gap > 0 &&
           new_key < (hp->heap[(gap-1)/2]).key )
      { (hp->heap[gap]).key    =
        (hp->heap[(gap-1)/2]).key;
        (hp->heap[gap]).object =
        (hp->heap[(gap-1)/2]).object;
        gap = (gap-1)/2;
      }
      (hp->heap[gap]).key    = new_key;
      (hp->heap[gap]).object = new_object;
      return( 0 ); /* insert successful */
   }
   else
      return( -1 ); /* Heap overflow */
}

object_t *delete_min(heap_t *hp)
{   object_t *del_obj;
    int reached_top = 0;
    int gap, newgap, last;
    if( hp->current_size == 0 )
      return( NULL );
      /*failed: delete from empty heap */
    del_obj = (hp->heap[0]).object;
    gap = 0;
    while( ! reached_top )
    {   if( 2*gap + 2 < hp->current_size )
        { if( (hp->heap[2*gap+1]).key <
              (hp->heap[2*gap+2]).key)
            newgap = 2*gap + 1;
          else
            newgap = 2*gap + 2;
          (hp->heap[gap]).key    =
          (hp->heap[newgap]).key;
          (hp->heap[gap]).object =
          (hp->heap[newgap]).object;
          gap = newgap;
        }
```

```
        else if ( 2*gap + 2 == hp->current_size )
        {   newgap = 2*gap + 1;
            (hp->heap[gap]).key    =
            (hp->heap[newgap]).key;
            (hp->heap[gap]).object =
            (hp->heap[newgap]).object;
            hp->current_size -= 1;
            return(del_obj);
            /* finished, came out exactly
               on last element */
        }
        else
            reached_top = 1;
    }
    /* propagated gap to the top, now move
       gap down again to insert last object in
       the right place */
    last = --hp->current_size;
    while(gap > 0 &&
            (hp->heap[last]).key <
            (hp->heap[(gap-1)/2]).key )
    {  (hp->heap[gap]).key    =
       (hp->heap[(gap-1)/2]).key;
       (hp->heap[gap]).object =
       (hp->heap[(gap-1)/2]).object;
       gap = (gap-1)/2;
    }
    (hp->heap[gap]).key    = (hp->heap[last]).key;
    (hp->heap[gap]).object =
    (hp->heap[last]).object;
    /* filled gap by moving last element in it*/
    return( del_obj );
}

void remove_heap(heap_t *hp)
{   free( hp->heap );
    free( hp );
}
```

This heap version again has all the disadvantages of any structure of fixed size, so it should only be used if the maximum size of the heap is known in advance, as it is for sorting or Dijkstra's algorithm. Neither of the update operations is $O(1)$, but it is still considered a fast implementation of the heap structure. To summarize the performance of this structure, we obtained the following:

Theorem. The heap structure of fixed maximum size can be realized using an array in time $O(1)$ for find_min and $O(\log n)$ for insert and delete_min operations.

We described here an array-based heap that is essentially a binary tree encoded in the array indices. One could construct in just the same way a k-ary tree (Luk 1999). Then the comparison condition 2 has to be replaced by

$2'$. For all $i \geq 0$ have
heap_key$[i] <$ heap_key$[ki + 1]$ if $ki + 1 < n$,
heap_key$[i] <$ heap_key$[ki + 2]$ if $ki + 2 < n, \ldots$ up to
heap_key$[i] <$ heap_key$[ki + k]$ if $ki + k < n$.

This decreases the height of the tree and makes, therefore, the insert faster, but the degree k of each node increases and therefore the delete_min gets slower. In Johnson (1975) it was proposed to keep the height of the heap constant and instead increase the degree of the vertices if the number of items n on the heap gets larger. That would give a constant time insert operation, but for a heap of height h and n elements, one would need a degree of $n^{\frac{1}{h}}$ and therefore a delete_min operation of time $\Omega(n^{\frac{1}{h}})$.

5.3 Heap-Ordered Trees and Half-Ordered Trees

Instead of an array-based implementation, we can again use a dynamically allocated structure. The heap is essentially just a tree, but there is an important difference, which actually makes the structure much simpler than a search tree. Each node contains a key and two pointers to other nodes, which itself are roots of some subheaps. But the key does not separate the keys in the subheaps; instead, it is smaller than either of them. There is no required relation between the nodes in the subheaps, and when we insert an element, we are free to choose either of them. This order condition is called a heap-ordered tree, and it is different from the search-tree order.

A consequence of heap order is that the key we are looking for is always in the root, and keys are not repeated further down in the tree. Thus, each key has to occur together with its object: there are no two possible models like they existed for search trees, but each node contains a key with its object. Thus, the structure of a node of a (binary) heap-ordered tree is as follows:

```
typedef struct hp_n_t {
                key_t           key;
                object_t        *object;
                struct hp_n_t   *left;
                struct hp_n_t   *right;
        /* possibly additional information */
                } heap_node_t;
```

We named the two pointers again left and right, but different from the search tree, there is no order relation between them. Again we define a heap-ordered tree recursively: the heap-ordered tree is either empty or contains in the root node a key, an object, and two pointers, each of which might be either NULL or point to another heap-ordered tree in which all keys are larger than the key in the root node.

Any structure with these properties is a heap-ordered tree for its objects and key values.

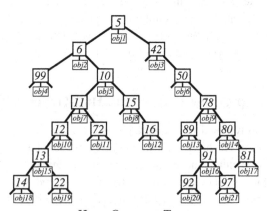

HEAP-ORDERED TREE

We have to establish some convention to mark the empty heap; this is different from the situation in the search trees, where we could use NULL fields in left and right pointers; but in a heap-ordered tree, both pointers might legitimately be NULL pointers. We could use the object field, but there might be legitimate uses with some NULL objects. Thus, we will decide on the empty heap convention only later in the specific structures, but it should always be something that can be tested just from the root node in time $O(1)$.

With these conventions we can now write down the functions create_heap, heap_empty and find_min – all of which are very simple constant-time operations. The find_min function is split in two operations find_min_key and find_min_object, which is more convenient than returning a structure.

```
heap_node_t *create_heap(void)
{  heap_node_t *tmp_node;
   tmp_node = get_node();
   tmp_node->object = NULL;
   /* or other mark for empty heap */
   return( tmp_node );
}

int heap_empty(heap_node_t *hp)
{  return( hp->object == NULL );
   /* or other test for empty heap*/
}

key_t find_min_key(heap_node_t *hp)
{  return( hp->key );
}

object_t *find_min_object(heap_node_t *hp)
{  return( hp->object );
}
```

For the insert and delete_min we need, however, more structure. In the array-based heap, we had the advantage that all paths from the root to a leaf were almost of the same length and we knew which of the paths would have to be lengthened or shortened by one when we insert or delete an element. For the heap-ordered tree, any operation has to start at the root because we do not have any direct access to a leaf.

The obvious method for insert would be to start at the root, select any path to a leaf by making arbitrary left-right choices, insert the new key and object in a new node at the right place on this path, and attach everything that was previously at this place as a subtree below this new node.

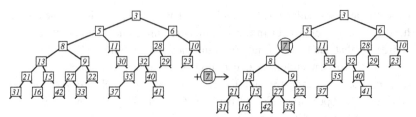

HEAP-ORDERED TREE: SIMPLE GENERIC INSERTION METHOD.
THE ENTIRE SUBTREE AT THE INSERTED NODE IS MOVED DOWN

This way, we do not even need to go down until we reach a leaf, but we increase the depth of everything below the newly inserted node by 1. Alternatively, we could insert the new key in the existing node and then push every following key one step downward to the leaf on this path, creating a new leaf in the end. Here the depth of the nodes stays the same; only the final leaf is a new node with possibly high depth. We do not violate the heap-order property by this pushing down along any path, because in each node we exchange the current key for a smaller key. The complexity of this operation is the length of the path taken, so we just need to be able to find one short path. Any tree with n nodes must contain some path of length $\lfloor \log(n + 1) \rfloor$; we just have to find it.

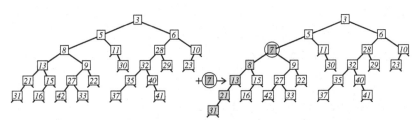

HEAP-ORDERED TREE: ALTERNATIVE GENERIC INSERTION METHOD.
THE ELEMENTS ALONG THE ARBITRARY CHOSEN PATH ARE PUSHED DOWN

For the delete_min operation, the situation is more difficult; the obvious method would be to remove the key and object from the root, compare the keys of its left and right lower neighbors, and move the smaller one down, deleting it recursively from its subtree. Thus we have no choice; we have to take the path from the root to a leaf that we get when we always take the smaller key, and along this path we move everything one step up to the root, deleting the last, now empty, node. Because we have no control over the path we take, this works only in $O(\log n)$ time if all paths from the root to any leaf have length $O(\log n)$.

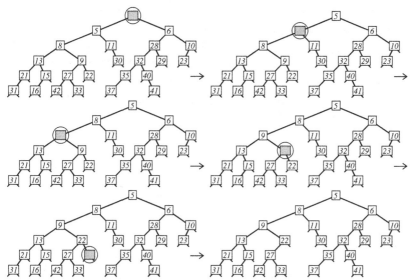

HEAP-ORDERED TREE: GENERIC DELETION METHOD.
THE ROOT IS DELETED, AND THE HOLE MOVES DOWN TO A LEAF

We thus need some sort of balancing information. We could attempt to reuse any of the balancing methods of the search trees, for example, creating a height-balanced heap-ordered tree. Because the height of the tree would be bounded by $O(\log n)$, we would support all the update operations in $O(\log n)$ time. The problem here is that the rotations cannot be applied to heap order. If we want to rotate a subtree, the key in the root of the subtree must stay the same by the heap-order condition, so the key in the other node of the rotation also stays the same. But this other node receives a new lower neighbor and that lower neighbor might violate the heap-order condition. Thus, we cannot just reuse the balancing methods we developed for search trees.

An alternative with a weaker order condition is the half-ordered trees. These are the same trees as before, but we demand only that for each node, every key in its right subtree should be larger. For the left subtree, there is no condition.

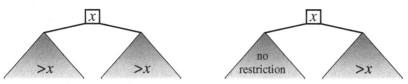

ORDER CONDITIONS BELOW A NODE: HEAP ORDER AND HALF ORDER

This way the minimum key need not be in the root, but it could be in any node along the leftmost path. This weaker structure is easier to maintain. It is possible to adapt the standard rotations to these structures, so we can reuse any form of balancing we used for search trees also for half-ordered trees. Because the tree then has depth $O(\log n)$, we can perform find_min by following the leftmost path, as well as insert and delete_min, in $O(\log n)$ time, for any method of balancing (Høyer 1995).

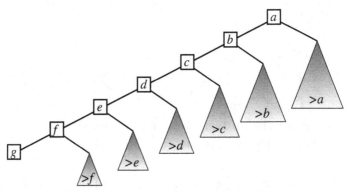

LEFTMOST PATH IN HALF-ORDERED TREE:
MAXIMUM MUST BE ON LEFTMOST PATH BY IMPLIED ORDER CONDITIONS

But the most important reason why this structure is used is that it is one representation for heap-ordered trees with nodes of arbitrary large degree. Many heaps, starting with the binomial heap, are presented in literature in that way, but to implement them, one has to represent them with binary (or fixed-size) nodes. The classical method to achieve this is to keep the lower neighbors of a node as a linked list, linked by their left pointer. The right pointer points to the first node on the list. By this representation, there is no order condition along left edges, because they are all just lower neighbors of the same node, but they are all in the right subtree of that node. A minor difference is that in any heap-ordered tree, the root will contain the smallest element, which is not the case in half-ordered trees. Indeed, the classical description of binomial and related heaps is that they are a list of heap-ordered trees with nodes of arbitrary large degree, so the common root is missing. And the half-ordered trees are isomorphic to these lists of heap-ordered trees with nodes of arbitrary degrees.

5.4 Leftist Heaps

One of the simplest and earliest methods is the leftist heaps. Leftist heaps were probably invented by C.A. Crane[3] and revised and named by D.E. Knuth (1973). They support `insert` and `delete_min` both in $O(\log n)$ time, which is not remarkable, but they support an additional operation, the merging of two heaps, also in $O(\log n)$. This we cannot do with either the search-tree-based heaps or the array heaps.

Leftist heaps are heap-ordered trees that use the distance to the *nearest* leaf, called rank, as balancing information. This is different from the height, which is the distance to the farthest leaf. Each node contains an additional field, the `rank`, which is defined by

- `n->rank = 1` if `n->left = NULL` or `n->right = NULL`.
- `n->rank = 1 + min(n->left->rank, n->right->rank)` if `n->left ≠ NULL` and `n->right ≠ NULL`.
  If we have this additional `rank` field, we can also use it to identify the root of an empty heap by `rank = 0`.

The leftist heap is characterized by the property that in each node the shortest path on the left side is at least as long as that on the right side:

- `n->left->rank ≥ n->right->rank` if both are defined; and
- if they are not both defined, then if one of them exists, it is the left one:
  `n->left = NULL` only if `n->right = NULL`.

Thus a leftist heap may be very unbalanced on the left side when always going to the left, but going always to the right, a heap with n elements contains a path of length at most $\lfloor \log(n + 1) \rfloor$.

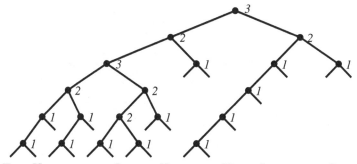

TREE UNDERLYING A LEFTIST HEAP WITH NODES LABELED BY RANK

---

[3] In the technical report, C.A. Crane: Linear Lists and Priority Queues as Balanced Binary Trees, CS-72-259, Stanford University, USA, 1972.

This structure is easy to restore after we have changed some node because we just have to follow the path back to the root, recompute the rank of each node, and exchange `left` and `right` fields wherever necessary. For an insertion, we follow the rightmost path down to the correct place for the new node and insert the node there, moving the rest of the rightmost path to the left below the new node. The new node has then rank 1. We then follow the path upward again, recomputing the ranks and restoring the leftist property along the path.

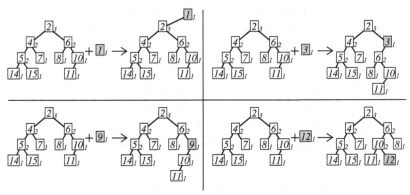

INSERTION IN A LEFTIST HEAP: FOUR EXAMPLES

The first phase is essentially the generic strategy for heap-ordered tree insertion, but for the second phase we need a method to return to the root of the tree, as we discussed in Section 2.5. Because we know that the length of the rightmost path is at most $\lfloor \log(n + 1) \rfloor$, we can safely use a stack to keep that return path and realize the stack as an array of size 100. We can now write down the code for the `insert` and other basic operations.

```
typedef struct hp_n_t {
                int             rank;
                key_t           key;
                object_t        *object;
                struct hp_n_t   *left;
                struct hp_n_t   *right;
                  } heap_node_t;

heap_node_t *create_heap(void)
{   heap_node_t *tmp_node;
    tmp_node = get_node();
    tmp_node->rank = 0;
```

```
      return( tmp_node );
}

int heap_empty(heap_node_t *hp)
{   return( hp->rank == 0 );
}

key_t find_min_key(heap_node_t *hp)
{   return( hp->key );
}

object_t *find_min_object(heap_node_t *hp)
{   return( hp->object );
}

void remove_heap(heap_node_t *hp)
{   heap_node_t *current_node, *tmp;
    if( hp->rank == 0 )
       return_node( hp );
    else
    {   current_node = hp;
        while(current_node != NULL )
        {   if( current_node->left == NULL )
            {   tmp = current_node->right;
                return_node( current_node );
                current_node = tmp;
            }
            else
            {   tmp = current_node;
                current_node = current_node->left;
                tmp->left = current_node->right;
                current_node->right = tmp;
            }
        }
    }
}

int insert( key_t new_key, object_t *new_obj,
            heap_node_t *hp)
```

```
   {
       if(hp->rank ==0) /* insert in empty heap */
       {  hp->object = new_obj;
          hp->key = new_key;
          hp->left = hp->right = NULL;
          hp->rank = 1;
       }
       else if( new_key < hp->key )
       /* new minimum, replace root */
       {  heap_node_t *tmp;
          tmp = get_node();
          tmp->left   = hp->left;
          tmp->right  = hp->right;
          tmp->key    = hp->key;
          tmp->rank   = hp->rank;
          tmp->object = hp->object;
          hp->left    = tmp;
          hp->right   = NULL;
          hp->key     = new_key;
          hp->object  = new_obj;
          hp->rank    = 1;
       }
       else /* normal insert */
       {  heap_node_t *tmp, *tmp2, *new_node;
          tmp = hp;
          create_stack();
          /* go down right path to the
             insertion point */
          while( tmp->right != NULL &&
          tmp->right->key < new_key)
          {  push( tmp ) ;
             tmp = tmp->right;
          }
          /* now create new node */
          new_node = get_node();
          new_node->key = new_key;
          new_node->object = new_obj;
          /* insert new node in path,
             everything below goes left */
```

```
new_node->left   = tmp->right;
new_node->right = NULL;
new_node->rank   = 1;
if( tmp->left == NULL )
    /* possible only at the end */
    tmp->left   = new_node;
    /* here tmp->right == NULL */
else /* insert right, restore
        leftist property */
{  tmp->right = new_node;
   tmp->rank   = 2;
   /* has rank at least one also left */
   /* completed insert, now move up,
      recompute rank and exchange left and
      right where necessary */
   while( !stack_empty() )
   {  tmp = pop();
      {  if(tmp->left->rank <
            tmp->right->rank )
         {  tmp2 = tmp->left;
            tmp->left = tmp->right;
            tmp->right = tmp2;
         }
         tmp->rank = tmp->right->rank +1;
      }
   }
}  /* end walking back to the root */
remove_stack();
}
return(0); /* insert always successful */
}
```

The key idea of leftist heaps is the merging; it is then easy to reduce the delete_min to merging: just delete the root and merge the left and right subtrees. For the merge, one just merges the right paths of both trees and then does the same cleanup as in the insert: recomputing the rank and restoring the leftist heap property by exchanging left and right pointers wherever necessary.

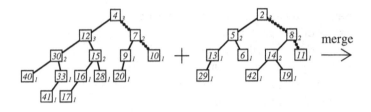

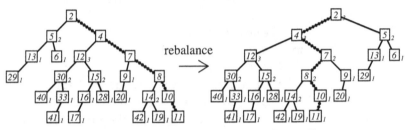

MERGING TWO LEFTIST HEAPS: MERGE THE RIGHT PATHS AND
RECOMPUTE RANKS AND RESTORE LEFTIST PROPERTY ALONG MERGED PATH

Again, both right paths have length at most $\lfloor \log(n+1) \rfloor$, so we can safely
use an array of size 200 as stack. Next is the code for merge and delete_min.

```
heap_node_t *merge( heap_node_t *hp1,
                    heap_node_t *hp2)
{   heap_node_t *root, *tmp1, *tmp2, *tmp3;
    if( hp1->rank == 0 ) /* heap 1 empty */
    {   return_node( hp1 );
        return( hp2 );
    }
    if( hp2->rank == 0 ) /* heap 2 empty */
    {   return_node( hp2 );
        return( hp1 );
    } /* select new root, setup merging */
    if( hp1->key < hp2->key )
    {   tmp1 = root = hp1;
        tmp2 = hp1->right;
        tmp3 = hp2;
    }
    else
    {   tmp1 = root = hp2;
        tmp2 = hp2->right;
        tmp3 = hp1;
```

```
}
create_stack();
while( tmp2 != NULL && tmp3 != NULL )
{  if( tmp2->key < tmp3->key )
   {  tmp1->right = tmp2;
      push( tmp1 );
      tmp1 = tmp2;
      tmp2 = tmp2->right;
   }
   else
   {  tmp1->right = tmp3;
      push( tmp1 );
      tmp1 = tmp3;
      tmp3 = tmp3->right;
   }
}
if( tmp2 == NULL)
   tmp1->right = tmp3;
else
   tmp1->right = tmp2;
/* merging of right paths complete,
   now recompute rank and restore leftist
   property */
push( tmp1 );
while( !stack_empty() )
{  tmp1 = pop();
   if( tmp1->left == NULL ||
     ( tmp1->left != NULL &&
       tmp1->right != NULL &&
       tmp1->left->rank <
       tmp1->right->rank ) )
   {  tmp2 = tmp1->left;
      tmp1->left = tmp1->right;
      tmp1->right = tmp2;
   }
   if( tmp1->right == NULL )
      tmp1->rank = 1;
   else
      tmp1->rank = tmp1->right->rank +1;
```

```
      }
      remove_stack();
      return( root );
}

object_t *delete_min(heap_node_t *hp)
{   object_t *del_obj;
    heap_node_t *heap1, *heap2, *tmp;
    del_obj = hp->object;
    heap1 = hp->left;
    heap2 = hp->right;
    if( heap1 == NULL && heap2 == NULL )
        hp->rank = 0;
    else
    {   if ( heap2 == NULL )
            tmp = heap1;
        else
            tmp = merge( heap1, heap2);
        /* now they are merged, need to copy
            root to correct place */
        hp->key    = tmp->key;
        hp->object = tmp->object;
        hp->rank   = tmp->rank;
        hp->left   = tmp->left;
        hp->right  = tmp->right;
        return_node( tmp );
    }
    return( del_obj );
}
```

To summarize the performance of this structure, we have the following:

Theorem. The leftist heap structure supports the operations find_min in $O(1)$ time and insert, merge, and delete_min in $O(\log n)$ time.

Leftist heaps use a balance criterion similar to the height; as with balanced search trees, one could instead use a weight balance. Weight-based leftist heaps, in which the number of nodes in the left subtree is always at least as large as in the right subtree, were studied in Cho and Sahni (1998). A related, but slower heap structure was developed by Jonassen and Dahl (1975).

5.5 Skew Heaps

The skew heaps were introduced by Sleator and Tarjan (1986) as an analog of the leftist heaps, but without balancing information. The interesting property here is that, as in the splay trees, one can do without this information if one accepts amortized bounds instead of worst-case bounds. And by omitting the balancing information, in principle the structure becomes simpler; we just always perform the same sequence of operations. The memory advantage of doing without balancing information is insignificant; memory is never a problem, and in the bottom-up variant of skew heaps, we actually need several additional pointers per node.

Without balancing information, one cannot decide whether the rank on the left or on the right is larger, so whether to exchange left and right subtree to restore the leftist heap property. In skew heaps, the strategy is just to exchange always. This leads to simpler code. We do not need a stack because there is no information propagated back to the root. Next is the code for `insert` and `merge`; the other operations are the same as before, and only the references to the `rank` field must be removed. For this reason, we must use the `object` field as mark for an empty heap.

```
typedef struct hp_n_t {
                 key_t           key;
                 object_t        *object;
                 struct hp_n_t   *left;
                 struct hp_n_t   *right;
                 } heap_node_t;

int insert( key_t new_key, object_t *new_obj,
            heap_node_t *hp)
{
    if(hp->object == NULL)
      /* insert in empty heap */
    {  hp->object = new_obj;
       hp->key  = new_key;
       hp->left = hp->right = NULL;
    }
    else if( new_key < hp->key )
            /* new minimum, replace root */
    {  heap_node_t *tmp;
       tmp = get_node();
```

```
        tmp->left   = hp->left;
        tmp->right  = hp->right;
        tmp->key    = hp->key;
        tmp->object = hp->object;
        hp->left    = tmp;
        hp->right   = NULL;
        hp->key     = new_key;
        hp->object  = new_obj;
    }
    else /* normal insert */
    {   heap_node_t *current, *tmp, *new_node;
        current = hp;
        /* go down right path to the insertion
           point */
        while( current->right != NULL &&
               current->right->key < new_key)
        {   tmp = current->right; /* exchange */
            current->right = current->left;
            current->left = tmp;
            current = tmp; /* and go down */
        }
        /* now create new node */
        new_node = get_node();
        new_node->key = new_key;
        new_node->object = new_obj;
        /* insert new node in path, everything
           below goes left */
        new_node->left  = current->right;
        new_node->right = NULL;
        current->right = new_node;
    }
    return(0);
}


heap_node_t *merge( heap_node_t *hp1,
                    heap_node_t *hp2)
{   heap_node_t *root, *tmp1, *tmp2, *tmp3;
    if( hp1->object == NULL ) /* heap 1 empty */
```

```
{   return_node( hp1 );
    return( hp2 );
}
if( hp2->object == NULL )  /* heap 2 empty */
{   return_node( hp2 );
    return( hp1 );
} /* select new root, setup merging */
if( hp1->key < hp2->key )
{   tmp1 = root = hp1;
    tmp3 = hp2;
}
else
{   tmp1 = root = hp2;
    tmp3 = hp1;
}
tmp2 = tmp1->right;
/* tmp1 is end of already merged right path
   tmp2 and tmp3 are next nodes in remaining
   right paths */
while( tmp2 != NULL && tmp3 != NULL )
{   tmp1->right = tmp1->left;
    /* exchange on the merged path*/
    if( tmp2->key < tmp3->key )
    {   /* attach tmp2 next, move down */
        tmp1->left  = tmp2;
        tmp1 = tmp2;
        tmp2 = tmp2->right;
    }
    else
    {   /* attach tmp3 next, move down */
        tmp1->left  = tmp3;
        tmp1 = tmp3;
        tmp3 = tmp3->right;
    }
} /* now one of the paths empty,
     attach the other */
if( tmp2 == NULL)
    tmp1->right = tmp3;
else
```

```
        tmp1->right = tmp2;
    return ( root );
}
```

Both `insert` and `merge` exchange `left` and `right` in each node along the path they visit; their complexity is $O(1 + k)$ if they exchanged `left` and `right` in k nodes.

The interesting part is now the analysis; as usual in an amortized analysis, we need a potential function on the trees, indeed on sets of trees, because we include the `merge` operation. The potential used by Sleator and Tarjan is the number of nodes that are "right-heavy": the right subtree contains more nodes than the left subtree. The key insight is now that on a right path there are at most $\log n$ "left-heavy" nodes because going right in a left-heavy node reduces the number of nodes in the subtree below the current node to less than half their previous number. So there are not too many left-heavy nodes on the right paths of the trees, but each time we touch them in any operation, left-heavy and right-heavy exchange, so there should be not too many right-heavy nodes either.

To make this idea precise, we keep track of the potential. For the analysis, we decompose both `insert` and `merge` in two phases: first the change of the right path, performing the insertion of the new element or the merging of the right paths, and then the exchange operation in all nodes of the right path that we visited.

In the first phase of either `insert` or `merge`, all nodes on the right path that were right-heavy stay right-heavy, because some nodes might be added in their right subtree whereas nothing changes in their left subtree. It is possible that left-heavy nodes on the right path become right-heavy, but there are only $O(\log n)$ such nodes, so this increases the potential by at most $O(\log n)$. The nodes that are not on the right path do not change their status.

In the second phase of either `insert` or `merge`, we exchange `left` and `right` in each node we visited. So these nodes exchange left-heavy and right-heavy status. Each left-heavy node that becomes right-heavy increases the potential by 1, but there are only $\log n$ left-heavy nodes among the nodes we visited. Each right-heavy node becoming left-heavy decreases the potential by 1. Thus, the second phase of either `insert` or `merge` also increases the potential by at most $O(\log n)$.

The `delete_min` finally just removes the root, generating two trees, which does not increase the potential, and then merges these two trees, so it increases the potential by at most as much as a `merge` operation.

If we have a sequence of m insert, merge, or delete_min operations, each of them exchanging left and right in k_i nodes, of which $k_i^{\mathcal{L}}$ are left-heavy and $k_i^{\mathcal{R}}$ are right-heavy, then the total time is $O(m + \sum_{i=1}^{m} k_i) = O(m + \sum_{i=1}^{m} k_i^{\mathcal{L}} + \sum_{i=1}^{m} k_i^{\mathcal{R}}) = O(m + m \log n) + O(\sum_{i=1}^{m} k_i^{\mathcal{R}})$. To bound the last sum, we notice that the potential is initially at most n, in the end it is at least 0, we subtract $\sum_{i=1}^{m} k_i^{\mathcal{R}}$ and add $\sum_{i=1}^{m} k_i^{\mathcal{L}} \leq m \log n$; thus, $\sum_{i=1}^{m} k_i^{\mathcal{R}} \leq n + m \log n$. The total time of m operations on n elements is therefore $O(n + m \log n)$. Together this shows the following:

Theorem. The skew heap structure supports the operations find_min in $O(1)$ time and insert, merge, and delete_min in amortized $O(\log n)$ time on a heap with n elements.

A more complicated variant, the bottom-up skew heaps, was also described in Sleator and Tarjan (1986); they achieve insert and merge in $O(1)$ amortized time. Because they contain additional pointers that need to be updated in a delete_min operation, for bottom-up skew heaps we cannot use the reduction of delete_min to merge; the delete_min operation still has $O(\log n)$ amortized complexity. None of these complexities are worst case; at worst they could be $\Omega(n)$. The structure was somewhat further studied in Jones (1987), Kaldewaij and Schoenmakers (1991), and Schoenmakers (1997).

5.6 Binomial Heaps

Binomial heaps are another classical, although somewhat complicated, method to achieve all heap operations including merge in $O(\log n)$ time. In contrast to the previous structure, the find_min operation also needs $\Theta(\log n)$ time. Binomial heaps were invented by Vuillemin (1978) and are mainly interesting for another type of additional operation, the change of key values, which will require a separate discussion in a later section.

Binomial heaps can again be written as binary trees with keys and objects in each node, but they are not heap-ordered trees, but only half-ordered trees:

1. If node w is in the right subtree of node v, then v->key < w->key.

This is a weaker condition than heap order: keys get larger to the right, but on a left path keys might appear in any order. The minimum key itself might occur anywhere along the path from the root to the left. This weaker order condition is coupled with a stronger balance condition.

2. If v is a node on the path from the root to the left, then v->right is root of a complete binary tree. The height of these trees is strictly decreasing along the path from the root to the left.

Thus the binomial heap consists of blocks of the following structure, which are put together on the left path: a node n_i on the path, whose right pointer points to a complete binary tree of height h_i, where this h_i is decreasing along the path. The complete binary tree of height h contains $2^{h+1} - 1$ nodes, so together with the node on the leftmost path the block has 2^{h_i+1} nodes. We also allow the empty tree as complete binary tree of height -1, so there might also be a block of $2^0 = 1$ node, just consisting of the node on the path. If the block sizes along the path are $2^{h_1} > 2^{h_2} > \cdots > 2^{h_k}$, then $2^{h_1} + 2^{h_2} + \cdots + 2^{h_k} = n$, so the block decomposition corresponds to the binary expansion of the total size n of the heap.

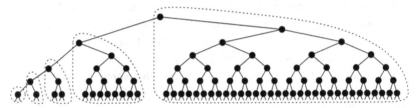

BINOMIAL HEAP STRUCTURE, WITH BLOCKS OF SIZE 2^0, 2^1, 2^2, 2^4, AND 2^6

The central property of these blocks is that one can combine in time $O(1)$ two blocks of the same size 2^h into one block of size 2^{h+1}: if n and m are the top nodes of two blocks, for which both n->right and m->right are complete binary trees of height h and n->key < m->key, then we can make n the new top node, whose right field points to m, and m becomes root of a complete binary tree of height $h + 1$, with the tree previously below n->right now below m->left. This is the point where the weaker order condition 1 is needed; if we required heap order, we could not just join these trees together because the heap-order relation between m and the new m->left could be violated, but condition 1 does not require any order along the left paths.

With this "adding" of two individual blocks in $O(1)$ time, we can merge two binomial heaps by performing an addition with carry of the two left paths.

The other operations, insert and delete_min, can be reduced to merge. An insert is just a merge with a single-node heap. For a delete_min, we have to find the minimum node from the leftmost path of the root, unlink that block, and delete its top node. Then the remaining block is a complete binary tree, which itself is a binomial heap, so it can be merged

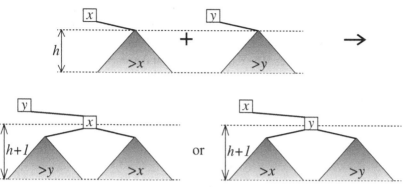

COMBINING TWO BLOCKS OF SIZE 2^h INTO ONE BLOCK OF SIZE 2^{h+1}

back with the original heap from which it was removed to get the heap resulting from the deletion.

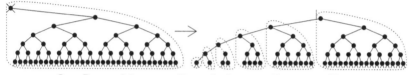

ONE BLOCK MINUS ITS ROOT IS AGAIN A BINOMIAL HEAP

We get an $O(\log n)$ bound for all operations, `insert`, `merge`, and `delete_min`, from observing that the binary addition with carry of two $\log n$-bit numbers requires $O(\log n)$ bit additions. This bound can be improved, in the amortized sense, for long sequences of `insert` operations, which correspond to repeated adding of 1 or counting in binary numbers. The total number of bits flipped while counting in binary from n to $n + i$ is $O(i + \log n)$, so the complexity of i consecutive insertions in a heap of initial size n is $O(i + \log n)$. Consider now a sequence of a `insert` and b `merge` or `delete_min` operations on a set of heaps with initial total size n, which at the end consists of k heaps. For each heap, each `delete_min` or `merge` operation, of complexity $O(\log n)$, is preceded by some sequence of a_j `insert` operations, of complexity $O(a_j + \log n)$. There are also some a_{final} `insert` operations that are not followed by any `delete_min` or `merge` involving that heap; these take at most $O(a_{\text{final}} + k \log n)$ time. Because $a = a_{\text{final}} + \sum_j a_j$, this gives a total complexity of $O(a + b \log n + k \log n)$. Because $k \leq n$, this shows that the amortized complexity of the `insert` operation is $O(1)$.

Next we give the code for the `merge` of two binomial heaps, as well as some elementary operations. Because the size of the blocks is decreasing along the paths, but we have to add starting from the blocks of smallest size, we put in a first phase just all blocks on a stack to invert the order. An alternative solution

would be to put the blocks in increasing size on the leftmost path; in that case
the blocks themselves would not be complete binary trees but very skewed
objects of twice the height. The total work is the same, and it is preferable to
use standard binary trees. The required height of the stack is only $2 \log n$.

```
typedef struct hp_n_t {
                  int             height;
                  key_t           key;
                  object_t        *object;
                  struct hp_n_t   *left;
                  struct hp_n_t   *right;
                      } heap_node_t;

heap_node_t *create_heap(void)
{   heap_node_t *tmp_node;
    tmp_node = get_node();
    tmp_node->height = -1;
    tmp_node->left = tmp_node->right = NULL;
    return( tmp_node );
}

int heap_empty(heap_node_t *hp)
{   return( hp->height == -1 );
}

key_t find_min_key(heap_node_t *hp)
{   heap_node_t *tmp;
    key_t          tmp_key;
    tmp     = hp;
    tmp_key = hp->key;
    while( tmp->left != NULL )
    {    tmp = tmp->left;
         if( tmp->key < tmp_key )
            tmp_key =  tmp->key;
    }
    return( tmp_key );
}

heap_node_t *merge( heap_node_t *hp1,
                    heap_node_t *hp2)
```

```
{  heap_node_t *tmp1, *tmp2, *current, *next;
   if( hp1->height == -1 ) /* heap 1 empty */
   {  return_node( hp1 );
      return( hp2 );
   }
   if( hp2->height == -1 ) /* heap 2 empty */
   {  return_node( hp2 );
      return( hp1 );
   }
   /* put all the blocks on the stack */
   create_stack();
   tmp1 = hp1; tmp2 = hp2;
   while( tmp1 != NULL && tmp2 != NULL )
   {  if( tmp1->height > tmp2->height )
      {  push( tmp1 );
         tmp1 = tmp1->left;
      }
      else
      {  push( tmp2 );
         tmp2 = tmp2->left;
      }
   }
   /* one list is empty, push the rest
      of the other */
   while( tmp1 != NULL )
   {  push( tmp1 );
      tmp1 = tmp1->left;
   }
   while( tmp2 != NULL )
   {  push( tmp2 );
      tmp2 = tmp2->left;
   }
   /* now all the blocks are on the stack */
   /* put them together, performing addition */
   current = pop();
   while( !stack_empty )
   {  next = pop();
      if( next->height > current->height )
      {  next->left = current;
```

```
      /* add in front of left list */
      current = next;
   }
   else if( next->height ==
           current->height )/* add blocks */
   {  if( next->key < current->key )
      {  next->left = current->left;
         current->left = next->right;
         next->right = current;
         next->height += 1;
         current = next;
      }
      else
      {  next->left = current->right;
         current->right = next;
         current->height +=1;
      }
   }
   else /* next->height < current->height */
   {  next->left = current->left;
      /* exchange current, next*/
      current->left = next;
      /* insert next just below current */
   }
 }
 return( current );
}
```

The delete_min code needs some care, because we have to preserve the
address of the root node, and the result of the merge could be a different
node. The same problem exists for the insert. Here we just copy the root
to a different node and then copy the result back. This could be avoided if
we used a placeholder node above the root. The placeholder could also point
to the current minimum node on the leftmost path, making find_min an
$O(1)$ operation by moving the minimum update time to the insert and
delete_min operations. For the greater regularity of the structure, we decided
to avoid a placeholder node. Next we give the code for the delete_min and
insert operations.

```
object_t *delete_min(heap_node_t *hp)
{  object_t *del_obj;
   heap_node_t *tmp1, *tmp2, *min1, *min2;
   key_t     tmp_key;
   if( hp->height == 0 )
       /* delete last object, heap now empty */
   {  hp->height = -1;
      return( hp->object );
   } /* can assume now that heap will
        not become empty */
   tmp1 = tmp2 = hp;
   tmp_key  = hp->key;
   min1 = min2 = hp;
   while( tmp1->left != NULL )
   {    tmp2 = tmp1;
        /* tmp2 node above tmp1 on left path */
        tmp1 = tmp1->left;
        if( tmp1->key < tmp_key)
        {  tmp_key =  tmp1->key;
           /* min1 is minimum node */
           min1 = tmp1; min2 = tmp2;
           /* min2 node above min1 */
        }
   }
   del_obj = min1->object;
   if( min1 != min2 ) /* min1 not root,
   so node above exists */
   {  min2->left = min1->left;
      /* unlinked min1 */
      if( min1->height > 0 )
          /* min1 has right subtree */
      {  tmp1 = min1->right;
         /* save its right tree */
         min1->key    = hp->key;
         /* copy root into min1 */
         min1->object = hp->object;
         min1->height = hp->height;
         min1->left   = hp->left;
         min1->right  = hp->right;
         tmp2 = merge( min1, tmp1 );
```

```
            /* and merge */
        }
        else /* min1 is leaf on left path */
        {   return_node( min1 );
            return( del_obj );
        }
    }   /* min1 is root node, has left
            and right subtrees */
    else if ( min1->left != NULL )
        tmp2 = merge( min1->left, min1->right );
    else /* min1 is root node, has only
                right subtree */
        tmp2 = min1->right;
     /* merge completed, now copy new root back */
    hp->key    = tmp2->key;
    hp->object = tmp2->object;
    hp->height = tmp2->height;
    hp->left   = tmp2->left;
    hp->right  = tmp2->right;
    return_node( tmp2 );
    return( del_obj );
}


int insert( key_t new_key, object_t *new_obj,
            heap_node_t *hp)
{   heap_node_t *new_node, *tmp, *tmp2;
    new_node = get_node();
    /* create one-element heap */
    new_node->height = 0;
    new_node->key    = new_key;
    new_node->object = new_obj;
    new_node->left = new_node->right = NULL;
    tmp = get_node();
    /* copy root into tmp_node */
    tmp->left   = hp->left;
    tmp->right  = hp->right;
    tmp->key    = hp->key;
    tmp->object = hp->object;
```

```
    tmp->height    = hp->height;
    tmp2 = merge( new_node, tmp );
    /* merge the heaps */
    hp->left = tmp2->left;
    /* merge completed, copy root back */
    hp->right = tmp2->right;
    hp->key = tmp2->key;
    hp->object = tmp2->object;
    hp->height = tmp2->height;
    return_node( tmp2 );
    return( 0 );
}
```

To summarize the performance of this structure, we have the following:

Theorem. The binomial heap structure supports the operations `insert`, `merge`, `find_min`, and `delete_min` in $O(\log n)$ time.
The amortized complexity of the `insert` operation is $O(1)$; any sequence of a `insert` and b `delete_min` or `merge` operations on a set of heaps of initial total size n, with k heaps remaining at the end, takes $O(a + b \log n + k \log n)$ time.

The key idea of the binomial heap structure is this decomposition of the heap into these blocks of canonical size (2^i for some i) that are guaranteed to have small height and that can be combined to the next larger size in constant time. With this block structure, we can then merge two heaps by performing binary addition on the lists of blocks. Several other implementations of this idea are possible, and some were discussed in Brown (1978). An array-based representation of the binomial heap structure was given in Strothotte and Sack (1985). One could also change the system of canonical sizes as long as we specify the block structure and the combination of a set of equal-sized blocks to a block of the next larger size; this gives a trade-off between the `insert` and the `delete_min` complexities that was studied in Fagerberg (1996b). Also the binomial heap structure formed the base of several other heaps, among them the Fibonacci heap (Fredman and Tarjan 1987) described in Section 5.8, the pairing heap (Fredman et al. 1986), and the relaxed heap (Driscoll et al. 1988). The pairing heap was especially popular for some time because it is easier to code; it is essentially related to the binomial heap in the same way as the skew heap is related to the leftist heap: a self-adjusting version in which no balance conditions are checked and updated. It has amortized $O(\log n)$ bounds instead of the worst-case bounds of the binomial heap. The pairing heap was the object of several experimental studies as well as theoretical bounds (Stasko and Vitter 1987; Liao 1992; Fredman 1998, 1999a; Iacono 2000; Pettie 2005). A parametrized variant of these structures was discussed in Elmasry (2004). A general transformation of binomial-heap-like structures that defers comparisons and sometimes makes the structure more efficient by this was studied in Fredman (1999b).

All these structures used half-ordered trees, or equivalently heap-ordered trees of variable degree, as the underlying model. A structure that combines this idea of a list of canonical building blocks with (binary) heap-ordered trees instead is the M-heaps (Bansil, Sreekanth, and Gupta 2003), which use a list of complete binary heap-ordered trees as block structure, with the block heights in increasing order and all distinct except possibly the first two. Then in an insert, one joins together the two blocks of the same height, if they exist, or creates a new block of height 0, if not. This structure again allows an $O(\log n)$ worst-case insert and delete_min.

Any of these heaps based on binary addition of blocks again allows the amortized analysis that gives an $O(1)$ amortized complexity for the insert operation.

5.7 Changing Keys in Heaps

There is an additional operation on heaps that received much interest and was the main motivation for the interest in binomial heaps and their various relatives, which is to change the keys of elements, especially to decrease keys, which is necessary for Dijkstra's single-source shortest path algorithm and many combinatorial optimization algorithms.

This operation is different from the other operations we discussed so far because we have to identify the element that we want to change. A heap does not support a find operation, so we need a pointer into the structure to the element, a finger as in the finger search trees. This finger is returned by the insert operations and must refer to the element until it is deleted. In any actual implementation this requires some care because the node that contains the element possibly changes during the operations on the heap:

- In the array-based heap, the item moves through the array.
- If we use rotations as rebalancing method on half-ordered trees, our standard rotations copy the item to a different node.

– Even the binomial heap implementation we just described moved at one point the item to a different node, although that could easily be changed.

Possible solutions to this problem of keeping the fingers correct are to

– Introduce one level of indirection: the finger points to a node that itself contains a pointer to the current node that contains the element; and the node that contains the element contains a pointer back to that indirection node, so the position can be updated.
– Rewrite the code in such a way that the content of a node is never copied to another node, but only the pointers are changed.

Especially the first solution can be combined with any heap, even with the array-based heap, for which the second solution would be impossible.

If we have solved the problem of identifying the element, the work necessary to change the key of an element depends on the heap we use. In the first solution we discussed, the use of balanced search trees as heaps, we can just delete the element with the old key and insert it with the new key, which gives an $O(\log n)$ change-key operation. This reduction of change-key to `delete` followed by `insert` works in any heap that allows the deletion of arbitrary elements. Indeed, the inverse reduction also exists: if the heap supports a `decrease_key` operation, we can also delete arbitrary elements: we decrease the key to the minimum possible key value and then perform a `delete_min`.

The classical array-based heap also supports key changes in $O(\log n)$, just moving the elements up or down as the heap-order condition demands until heap order is restored. This was already discussed in Johnson (1975), but no information is given on how to identify the element, a tradition followed by all later papers.

Any heap-ordered tree would support key changes if we introduced backward pointers in the nodes. Then we could move elements up or down, as required by the heap-order condition. The complexity of this, however, would be the length of the path along which we had to move the element, so at worst the height of the tree. Neither leftist heaps nor skew heaps allow a sublinear height bound, so they cannot be used to get efficient key change operations.

The binomial heap, however, does have a good height bound; as we described it, it even maintains the optimal height $\lfloor \log(n+1) \rfloor$. We again need back pointers to allow an element to move in the direction of the root. Because the order condition of binomial heaps is not quite the heap order, there is a difference between increase and decrease of keys. If the key of a node is decreased, we follow the path back to the root, but we need to check the order condition and possibly exchange the nodes only for those nodes for which the next edge is a right edge; no restrictions apply along the left edges. Thus, a decrease_key operation takes $O(\log n)$ time. But if we increase a key, we need to check the order condition for all nodes that can be reached by a single right edge followed by a left path, and possibly exchange with the node with smallest key among them and repeat until these left path conditions are all satisfied. This takes $O((\log n)^2)$ time, so decreasing the key to the minimum possible value, deleting the element, and reinserting it with the new key value would be faster than an increase key operation. But because the applications usually need only to decrease keys, that operation is more important. Thus, a binomial heap does all the usual heap operations, and in addition to that merge and decrease_key, in $O(\log n)$ time.

5.8 Fibonacci Heaps

The importance of the decrease_key operation in various combinatorial optimization algorithms motivated the development of a number of heap structures with a decrease_key operation that aim to be constant time instead of $O(\log n)$. These structures did not quite achieve their aim, insofar as the bounds were amortized, instead of worst case, but for the application of these structures in other algorithms, where we know how often the individual operations will be called, and especially that the decrease_key operation will be called more often than insert of delete_min, such amortized bounds for the structures are still sufficient to give worst-case bounds for the algorithm that uses them.

The oldest and best known of these structures is the Fibonacci heap (Fredman and Tarjan 1987). The Fibonacci heap is related to the binomial heap described in Section 5.6; it is again a half-ordered tree, and like a binomial heap, it consists of blocks arranged on the leftmost path, but the structure of the blocks is weaker and they are not necessarily of distinct size, and in decreasing order, as they were in binomial heaps. During the updates, almost all rebalancing of the structure will be deferred to the next delete_min operation; the leftmost path is a holding area where we can place blocks until that rebalancing phase and where they are subject to neither order conditions nor structural conditions.

The structure that we maintain in a Fibonacci heap is as follows: Each node n carries an integer field n->rank, as well as a state n->state, which can be either complete or deficient. Then the defining properties are:

F1. For any node n with n->rank > 1, or n->rank = 1 and
    n->state = complete, holds n->right $\neq$ NULL, and

F1.1 If n->state = complete, then on the left path below
n->right there are n->rank nodes, which have rank *at least*
n->rank − 1, n->rank − 2, ..., 0, in some sequence.

F1.2 If n->state = deficient, then on the left path below
n->right there are n->rank − 1 nodes, which have rank *at
least* n->rank − 2, n->rank − 3, ..., 0, in some sequence.

F2. For any node n with n->rank = 0, or n->rank = 1 and
n->state = deficient, holds n->right = NULL.

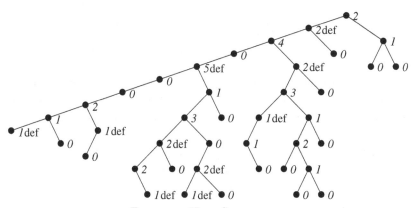

FIBONACCI HEAP STRUCTURE:
THE NODES ARE LABELED BY RANK AND DEFICIENCY STATUS

If we allow no deficient nodes, demand strictly decreasing rank along the
leftmost path, and strengthen F1 to the following property:

B1. For any node n of with n->rank > 0, holds n->right ≠ NULL, and
on the left path below n->right, there are n->rank nodes, which
have rank *exactly* n->rank − 1, n->rank − 2, ..., 0, in *decreasing*
sequence.

We get the binomial heap structure, so the Fibonacci heap is a structural relax-
ation of the binomial heap.

A block again consists of a node n and the subtree below n->right; then
we can add, exactly as in the case of binomial heaps, two blocks of rank k to
one block of rank $k + 1$ in $O(1)$ time.

A block of rank k consists of the top node n and at least $k − 2$ further blocks,
or $k − 1$, if n->state = complete that are arranged on the left path below
n->right and have rank at least 0, 1, ..., $k − 2$. So the minimum number
$f(k)$ of nodes in a block of rank k satisfies the recursion

$$f(k) = f(k − 2) + f(k − 3) + \cdots + f(1) + f(0) + 1.$$

Using

$$f(k-1) = f(k-3) + \cdots + f(1) + f(0) + 1,$$

we can rewrite this recursion as $f(k) = f(k-1) + f(k-2)$, which is the same recursion we already met in Section 3.1. Here the starting values are $f(0) = f(1) = 1$, so f is the classical sequence of Fibonacci numbers, which gives the name to this heap. By the methods of Section 10.4, we can solve this recursion and obtain

$$f(k) = \frac{1}{\sqrt{5}} \left(\frac{1 + \sqrt{5}}{2} \right)^{k+1} - \frac{1}{\sqrt{5}} \left(\frac{1 - \sqrt{5}}{2} \right)^{k+1}.$$

The key elements of the Fibonacci heap are the methods by which we maintain this structure. For that, each node needs two further fields: a normal back pointer up and another pointer upward in the tree structure, r_up, which for any node n not on the leftmost path points to that node m for which n is on the left path below m->right. If n is on the leftmost path, we set n->r_up to NULL. So the structure of a node in the Fibonacci heap is as follows:

```
typedef struct hp_n_t { key_t                  key;
                        object_t              *object;
                        struct hp_n_t         *left;
                        struct hp_n_t         *right;
                        struct hp_n_t         *up;
                        struct hp_n_t         *r_up;
                        int                    rank;
                  enum {complete, deficient}  state;
                      } heap_node_t;
```

Both the up and the r_up pointers can be adjusted in $O(1)$ time when adding two blocks of equal rank; although there are possibly many nodes whose r_up pointers point to the root nodes of the blocks we add, these nodes stay in the correct r_up relationship after adding and do not need to be changed.

In addition to the tree structure of the Fibonacci heap, we maintain a pointer to the node with the minimum element and a pointer to the last node on the leftmost path. Because the Fibonacci heap is a half-ordered tree, the node with the minimum element occurs somewhere on the leftmost path. With this minimum pointer, we can answer find_min queries in $O(1)$ time.

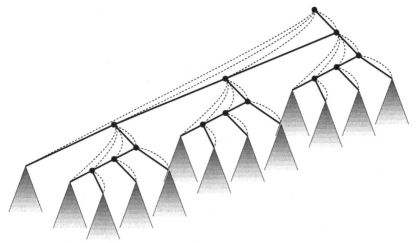

FIBONACCI HEAP: r_up POINTERS AND NORMAL TREE POINTERS

The insert operation is now very simple: we create a new node of rank 0, with the new key and object, and place it on top of the leftmost path. Then we check whether the new key is smaller than the previous minimum and adjust the minimum pointer, if necessary.

In the same way we realize the merge operation by just concatenating the leftmost paths; for this we need the left end pointer to the end of the leftmost path.

For the decrease_key operation, the situation is more complicated. The algorithm to decrease the key in node n works as follows:

1. Decrease the key in n as requested. If the new key is smaller than the previous minimum, we adjust the minimum pointer.
2. If n->r_up = NULL, then n is already on the leftmost path, so it is not subject to any condition and we are finished.
3. Else the half-ordered tree condition might be violated in n->r_up and possibly some nodes above. Set u to n->r_up. Unlink n from the left path to which it belongs, using the back pointer n->up, and place n on the leftmost path.
4. Now the property F1 is violated for u because it lost one node on the left path below u->right.
    4.1 If u->r_up = NULL, then u is on the leftmost path. Decrease u->rank by 1. Then property F1 is restored, and we are finished.
    4.2 Else if u->state = complete, then set u->state to deficient. Then property F1 is restored, and we are finished.

4.3 Else u->state = deficient. Decrease u->rank by 2, or only 1
   if it becomes negative, and then set u->state to complete. By
   this F1 is restored for node u.
   Unlink u from the left path to which it belongs, using the back pointer
   u->up, and place u on the leftmost path. Set u to u->r_up and
   repeat step 4.

This upward propagation of the unlinking is called a "cascading cut"; it happens
during the decrease_key of n if the nodes n->r_up, n->r_up->r_up, ...
are all deficient. We spend $O(1)$ time for each iteration of the unlinking
process. The upward propagation of the unlinking process ends when a node
n->r_up->·····->r_up is reached that is complete, which is then changed
to deficient, or when a node on the leftmost path is reached. This is the
only node changed to deficient, and all unlinked nodes are changed to
complete. So in each decrease_key operation, if we perform k unlinking
operations, we need time $O(k)$, change one node from complete to deficient, and change $k - 1$ nodes from deficient to complete. Because
each deficient node must have been created by an earlier decrease_key
operation, any sequence of operations that contains n decrease_key operations, and that starts on a heap with a deficient nodes and ends on a heap with
b deficient nodes, takes $O(n + a - b)$ time and places $O(n + a - b)$ nodes
on the leftmost path. This gives an amortized complexity of $O(1)$ for the
decrease_key operation.

   This speed is achieved by delaying all rebalancing, placing items without
any structure update on the leftmost list. So if we have sufficiently many
decrease_key operations, all items will finally be placed on that list in any
order. The difficult step is then to find a new minimum after the delete_min
operation. The new minimum can be in any node on the leftmost path, so
we have to go through all of them. We use this opportunity to shorten the
the leftmost path and perform the rebalancing, so that the next delete_min
operation does not again meet a very long leftmost path. In this operation, we
use that the maximum rank of any node occurring in this structure is $O(\log n)$,
because if there is a node of rank k, then its block contains at least $\frac{1}{\sqrt{5}}(\frac{1+\sqrt{5}}{2})^{k+1}$
nodes.

   The delete_min operation works as follows:

1. Unlink the current minimum node n, identified by the minimum pointer,
   from the leftmost path. Then place the nodes on the left path of
   n->right on top of the leftmost path and delete n.
2. Create an array of node pointers of size $\Theta(\log n)$, with an entry for each
   possible rank value.

3. Go down the leftmost path. Set n to the next node on the leftmost path.
    3.1 If the array does not contain an entry of rank n->rank, store n in the array and repeat step 3.
    3.2 Else remove the node m of that same rank and add the blocks below n and m. Set n to the node at the top of the new block and repeat step 3.1.
4. Now all nodes that were on the leftmost path are either stored in the array or have become part of blocks. Go through the array and link the nodes together to form the new leftmost path. Set the minimum pointer to the node of minimum key among them and the leftend pointer to the last node of the leftmost path.

Here, step 1 takes $O(\log n)$ time because that is the length of the left path below n->right. Step 2 takes $O(1)$ time. Step 4 takes $O(\log n)$ time because that is the size of the array. The key to the analysis of the complexity is the loop in step 3; in each iteration of this loop, we use up one node from the leftmost path, so if the length of the leftmost path was l before the delete_min operation, then step 3 takes $O(l)$ time. So the delete_min operation takes $O(l + \log n)$ time and leaves a heap structure with a leftmost path of length $O(\log n)$.

To analyze the total complexity of a sequence of operations on a heap with n elements, among these i insert operations, k decrease_key operations, and d delete_min operations, we observe

- Each insert takes $O(1)$ time and places one node on the leftmost path.
- Each decrease_key takes $O(1)$ time per item it places on the leftmost path, and the sequence of decrease_key operations places at most $O(k + n)$ times an item on the leftmost path.
- Each delete_min takes $O(\log n)$ time, plus $O(1)$ time per item it removes from the leftmost path.

So we can summarize the performance of this structure.

Theorem. The Fibonacci heap structure supports the operations find_min, insert, merge, delete_min, and decrease_key, with find_min, insert, and merge in $O(1)$ time, decrease_key in amortized $O(1)$ time, and delete_min in amortized $O(\log n)$ time.
Any sequence of m operations on a set of heap with a total of n elements, among which are d delete_min operations, takes $O(n + m + d \log n)$.

The Fibonacci heap does not fit in our pointer-machine model because we need the array to efficiently collect the nodes of equal rank; if we took a search tree on the ranks instead, the amortized complexity of decrease_key would increase to $O(\log \log n)$. But as we know the required array size in advance and it is not large, this is no signficant obstacle in the efficient use.

We finally give an implementation of a Fibonacci heap. We use a placeholder node that does not contain any key as entry point, with left pointing to the current minimum, up pointing to the end of the leftmost path, and right pointing to the root of the heap if the heap is not empty.

```
typedef struct hp_n_t { key_t               key;
                        object_t          *object;
                        struct hp_n_t     *left;
                        struct hp_n_t     *right;
                        struct hp_n_t     *up;
                        struct hp_n_t     *r_up;
                        int                rank;
              enum {complete, deficient}  state;
                        } heap_node_t;
heap_node_t *create_heap(void)
{   heap_node_t *tmp_node;
    tmp_node = get_node();
    tmp_node->right = NULL;
    return( tmp_node );
}


int heap_empty(heap_node_t *hp)
{   return( hp->right == NULL );
}


key_t find_min_key(heap_node_t *hp)
{   return( hp->left->key);
}


heap_node_t *insert(key_t new_key,
            object_t *new_obj, heap_node_t *hp)
{   heap_node_t *new_node;
    new_node = get_node(); /* create new node */
    new_node->right = NULL;
    new_node->key = new_key;
    new_node->object = new_obj;
    new_node->rank = 0;
```

```
    new_node->state = complete;
    if( hp->right == NULL )
        /* insert in empty heap */
    {  hp->right = hp->left = hp->up = new_node;
       new_node->left = NULL;
    }
    else /* heap nonempty, put on top
             of leftmost path */
    {  new_node->left = hp->right;
       hp->right = new_node;
       new_node->left->up = new_node;
       if( hp->left->key > new_key) /*
       update min-pointer */
          hp->left = new_node;
    }
    return( new_node );
}

heap_node_t *merge(heap_node_t *hp1,
                   heap_node_t *hp2)
{  if( hp1->right == NULL )        /* hp1 empty */
   {  return_node(hp1); return(hp2);
   }
   else if( hp2->right == NULL ) /* hp2 empty */
   {  return_node(hp2); return(hp1);
   }
   else /* both heaps nonempty */
   { hp1->up->left = hp2->right;
     /* concatenate leftmost paths */
     hp2->right->up = hp1->up;
     /* join their up-pointers */
     hp1->up = hp2->up;
     /* restore leftend pointer */
     if(hp1->left->key > hp2->left->key)
        hp1->left = hp2->left;
        /* update min-pointer */
     return_node(hp2); return(hp1);
   }
}
```

```
    void decrease_key( key_t new_key, heap_node_t *n,
                       heap_node_t *hp)
    {  heap_node_t *u, *tmp; int finished = 0;
       n->key = new_key; /* decrease key in n */
       if( new_key < hp->left->key )
       /* update min-pointer */
          hp->left = n;
       while( n->r_up != NULL && !finished )
       {  u = n->r_up;
          /* n on left path of u->right: unlink n */
          if( n == u->right )
              /* n on top of left path of u->right */
          {  u->right = n->left;
             if( n->left != NULL )
                n->left->up = u;
          }
          else /* n further down on left
                   path of u->right */
          {  n->up->left = n->left;
             if( n->left != NULL )
                n->left->up = n->up;
          } /* unlink n complete, now insert
                n on leftmost path */
          n->r_up = NULL;
          n->left = hp->right; n->left->up = n;
          hp->right = n;
          /* now repair u; if necessary, repeat cut */
          if( u->r_up == NULL )
              /* u already on leftmost path */
          {  u->rank -= 1;
             finished = 1;
          }
          else if( u->state == complete )
          /* u becomes deficient */
          {  u->state = deficient;
             finished =1;
          }
          else /* u deficient and not
                   on leftmost path */
```

```
{  if( u->rank >= 2 )
        u->rank -= 2;
    else
        u->rank = 0;
    u->state = complete;
    /* u rank information correct */
   } /* in this case, have to cut u from
        left list */
   n = u; /* so repeat unlink operation */
  }/* end of while loop, finished with
      'cascading cut' */
}

object_t *delete_min( heap_node_t *hp)
{  heap_node_t *min, *tmp, *tmp2;
   object_t *del_obj;
   heap_node_t *rank_class[100]; int i;
   key_t tmp_min;
   if( hp->right == NULL)
       /* heap empty, delete failed */
       return( NULL );
   min = hp->left;
   /* unlink min node from leftmost path */
   del_obj = min->object;
   if( min == hp->right )
       /* min on top of leftmost path */
   {  if( min->left != NULL )
       /* path continues after min */
       {  hp->right = min->left;
          min->left->up = hp;
       }
       else /* min only vertex on leftmost path */
       {  if( min->right != NULL )
              /* min not last node */
          {  hp->right = min->right;
             min->right->up = hp;
             min->right = NULL;
          }
          else /* min last node, heap now empty */
```

```
        {   hp->right = NULL;
            return_node( min );
            return( del_obj );
        }
    }
}
else /* min further down on leftmost path */
{   min->up->left = min->left;
    if( min->left != NULL )
        /* min not last vertex */
        min->left->up = min->up;
} /* unlink min complete */
/* now move left path of min->right
   to leftmost path */
if( min->right != NULL ) /* path nonempty */
{   tmp = min->right;
    while( tmp->left != NULL )
            /* find end of path */
        tmp = tmp->left;
    tmp->left = hp->right; tmp->left->up = tmp;
    hp->right = min->right;
    min->right->up = hp;
}
/* now path below min->right
   linked to leftmost path */
return_node( min ); /* minimum deleted */
/* now starts clean-up phase */
for( i = 0; i < 100; i++)
  rank_class[i] = NULL;
/* now unbuild leftmost path, collect
   nodes of equal rank*/
tmp = hp->right;
/* take first node from leftmost path */
hp->right = hp->right->left;
/* unlink that node */
while( tmp != NULL )
{   if( rank_class[tmp->rank] == NULL )
    {   /* no node of same rank found:
            store node */
```

```
      rank_class[tmp->rank] = tmp;
      tmp = hp->right; /* take new node */
      if( tmp != NULL)
         hp->right = hp->right->left;
         /* unlink that node */
   }
   else /* two nodes of same rank found,
           add blocks */
   {  tmp2 = rank_class[tmp->rank];
      rank_class[tmp->rank] = NULL;
      if( tmp->key < tmp2->key )
      {  tmp2->left = tmp->right;
         tmp->right = tmp2;
      }
      else /* tmp->key >= tmp2->key */
      {  tmp->left = tmp2->right;
         tmp2->right = tmp;
         tmp = tmp2;
      }
      tmp->rank += 1;
      /* increase rank of sum block */
   }
} /* all remaining blocks now
     in rank_class[] */
/* now rebuild the leftmost path */
hp->right = NULL;
for( i = 0; i < 100; i++)
{  if( rank_class[i] != NULL )
   {  tmp = rank_class[i];
      tmp->left = hp->right;
      hp->right = tmp;
   }
}
/* recompute pointers on new leftmost path */
hp->left = hp->right; tmp_min = hp->left->key;
for( tmp = hp->right; tmp->left !=NULL;
     tmp = tmp->left)
{  tmp->left->up = tmp;
   /* new up pointers */
```

```
        if ( tmp->left->key < tmp_min )
        {  hp->left = tmp->left;
           /* new min pointer */
           tmp_min = tmp->left->key;
        }
     }
     hp->up = tmp; /* end of leftmost path */
     /* finished with clean-up phase */
     return ( del_obj );
  }
```

5.9 Heaps of Optimal Complexity

We already noted in Section 5.1 that we cannot get all heap operations in sublogarithmic time. For the search trees with lazy deletion, we showed that delete_min is possible in constant time, together with insert in $O(\log n)$. Because there are necessarily more insert than delete_min operations, it became a much-studied question whether one could get insert and all other operations but deletion, in constant time, and delete_min in $O(\log n)$.

The answer to this question somewhat depends on the exact details of the question, but is "yes" (almost), with the best structures due to Brodal (1995, 1996a). The first step in this direction was the Fibonacci heap (Fredman and Tarjan 1987), which supported insert, find_min, and merge in $O(1)$ amortized time and delete_min, indeed arbitrary deletions, in $O(\log n)$ amortized time. The special importance of this structure comes from the fact that although the time bounds are only amortized, they are sufficient to obtain worst-case time bounds in algorithms where we know that the number of heap operations is large, for example, in Dijkstra's algorithm. Other developments are the pairing heap (Fredman et al. 1986) and the relaxed heap (Driscoll et al. 1988), and the 2-3-heap (Takaoka 2003). One reason for the pairing heap's popularity, besides the simpler implementation, was that although it has only $O(\log n)$ amortized bounds for the usual heap operations, it was conjectured to have an $O(1)$ time decrease_key; but finally an $\Omega(\log \log n)$ amortized lower bound was found (Fredman 1998). The relaxed heaps came in two variants, of which the run-relaxed heaps achieved $O(1)$ worst-case insert and decrease_key and $O(\log n)$ find_min and delete_min; but Fibonacci heaps and relaxed heaps are somewhat unsatisfactory because they do not work in the pointer-machine model but require dynamically allocated arrays of size $\Theta(\log n)$.

The almost final answer is the two structures of Brodal (1995, 1996a), of which the first works in the pointer-machine model and supports worst-case bounds of $O(1)$ for insert, find_min, and merge and $O(\log n)$ for delete_min and decrease_key. The second structure additionally reduces the complexity of decrease_key to constant time, but leaves the pointer-machine model and needs dynamically allocated arrays of size $\Theta(\log n)$. Other structures with the same performance are the ternary heap (Takaoka 2000) and the heaps based on the black-box transformation of Alstrup et al. (2005). We will describe here the first structure.

The underlying structure is again a heap-ordered tree with nodes of potentially large degree, but to allow an insert in constant time while keeping this structure and a delete_min in $O(\log n)$ time, we need a lot of additional structure, especially several additional pointers per node to reach all those other nodes that have to be corrected in constant time.

The structure is as follows:

- Each node has a smaller key than all its lower neighbors (a heap-ordered tree).
- Each node n has a nonnegative rank as balancing information.
- Each node has at most one special lower neighbor, which might be of arbitrary rank, and a number of normal lower neighbors, whose rank is smaller than the rank of the node.
- The normal lower neighbors are arranged in order of increasing rank in a doubly linked list. The ranks of the normal lower neighbors of n satisfy the following properties:

  1. Each rank less than the rank of n occurs at least once, and at most three times.
  2. Between two ranks that occur three times there is a rank that occurs only once.
  3. Before the first rank that occurs three times, there is a rank that occurs only once.

- For each node, the first-lower neighbors of each rank that occurs three times are arranged in a linked list, in increasing order.
- The root has rank 0.

To provide the necessary information, the structure of a node is the following:

```
typedef struct hp_n_t {
int             rank;
```

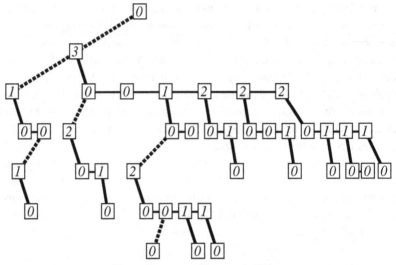

NODE RANKS IN BRODAL'S HEAP

```
key_t          key;
object_t       *object;
struct hp_n_t  *first; /* lower neighbors */
struct hp_n_t  *last;  /* lower neighbors */
struct hp_n_t  *next;  /* same level list */
struct hp_n_t  *previous; /* same level list */
struct hp_n_t
*thrice_repeated;
struct hp_n_t  *special;
               } heap_node_t;
```

By the heap order, the root contains the smallest key, so the find_min operation is trivial and in constant time. The insert operation is reduced in the
standard way to merge, creating a new one-element heap for the new element
and merging that heap with the old heap.

The merge is the main operation and it works as follows: let r_1 and r_2 be
the roots of the heaps we want to merge. Because the root has rank 0, it has
only one lower neighbor, the special lower neighbor that may be of arbitrary
rank, r_1->special and r_2->special. We want to insert the root of one
heap in the list of normal lower neighbors of the special lower neighbor of the

root of the other heap at the beginning of that list because it already has rank 0. But we have to preserve heap order and the rank sequence conditions on that list.

For the rank sequence, we observe that it is easy to combine the subtrees below two nonroot nodes of the same rank into one subtree below a rank one higher: just increase the rank of the node with the larger key and insert the node with the smaller key at the end of the sequence of lower neighbors, as new maximum-rank node.

The steps of the `merge` operation are as follows:

1. Compare r_1->key and r_2->key if necessary, exchange, so that r_1 is the root with smaller key. Then it must become the root of the merged tree.
2. Compare r_1->special->key and r_2->key, exchange, so that r_1->key < r_1->special->key < r_2->key.
3. If the list of three-time occurring ranks below r_1->special is not empty, go to the first rank on the list and convert two of its nodes into the next higher rank. Remove that rank from the list of three-time occurring ranks, and if the next higher rank now occurs three times, add that to the list.
   3.1 If that next higher rank is now the same as the rank of r_1->special, increase the rank of r_1->special by one.
4. Insert r_2 into the list of normal lower neighbors of r_1->special at r_1->special->first.
   4.1 If there were already two nodes of rank 0 on that list, combine them into one node of rank 1.
   4.2 If the rank of r_1->special was 1, increase it to 2.
   4.3 If there are now three nodes of rank 1 on the list, insert the first of them in front of the list of ranks occurring three times.

These operations restore the rank conditions; step 3 moves the first three-time repeated rank one step on, or destroys that repetition, while preserving that alternation of some rank occurring only once between any two ranks that occur three times and before the first such rank. This especially guarantees that rank 1 occurs at most two times, so we can combine two elements of rank 0, if necessary, because there is still room at rank 1.

The `delete_min` operation is more complicated. The general strategy is clear; one removes the root, moves the one lower neighbor of the root up, and finds among its lower neighbors the one of minimum key, and moves that up, and somehow merges the lists of all lower neighbors. There are, however, a number of difficulties along the way.

We observe first that the rank sequence conditions enforce that each node has only $O(\log n)$ lower neighbors. A node of rank k has at least one lower neighbor of each rank $0, \ldots, k - 1$, from this follows by induction that the subtree with a node of rank k as root contains at least 2^k nodes.

Let r be the original root, $n = r$->special its unique lower neighbor, and $m_1, \ldots, m_l$ the normal lower neighbors of n. The first step is to integrate n->special into the list of normal lower neighbors of n. The difficulty here is that n->special might violate the rank restriction for a normal lower neighbor of n. If n->special->rank $\geq$ n->rank, we cut the list of normal lower neighbors of n->special at the rank n->rank and attach the top half, those nodes with rank at least n->rank, to the top end of the list of lower neighbors of n. Then we can reduce the rank of n->special to n->rank by which the rank condition for the subtree below n->special is restored and correct n->special->thrice_repeated. Then we insert n->special at the correct place in the list of normal lower neighbors of n. Thus, n has no special lower neighbor any more, but the list of normal lower neighbors violates the rank condition. The ranks on that list are still in increasing order, and each rank up to the maximum occurs at least once, but they might occur more than three times and the alternation might be lost. Still, there are at most $O(\log n)$ nodes on the list because each node was previously a normal lower neighbor either of n or of n->special. We now go once through that list, from n->first to n->last, and whenever there are three consecutive nodes of the same rank, we combine two of them to the next larger rank, so that in the end each rank occurs either one or two times. Then we increase the rank n->rank to n->last->rank + 1, and the rank condition in n is restored. Finally we clear n->thrice_repeated. All this took $O(\log n)$ time and merely integrated n->special into the list of normal lower neighbors of n.

We now go once through that list, from n->first to n->last, and find and unlink the node with the smallest key. Let this node be m. We copy key and object from n to r, deleting the previous minimum, and from m to n. Then we merge the list of normal lower neighbors of m into that list for n, and copy m->special to n->special, and delete the node m. The list of normal lower neighbors of n is now again a list of $O(\log n)$ nodes, in order of increasing rank, which possibly violates the rank sequence condition, and also there might be a missing rank: if m was the only node of that rank on the list of n, this rank is now missing. In that case we take the next node on the list and split it, inverting the combining of two nodes into at most four nodes of one rank smaller. If this leaves again a missing rank, we repeat this until we reach the end of that list. Finally, we go again through the list from `n->first` to `n->last`, and whenever there are three consecutive nodes of the same rank, we combine them to the next larger rank, so that in the end each rank occurs either one or two times. Then we set the rank `n->rank` to `n->last->rank + 1`. After this, the heap again satisfies all the conditions. In total all these operations for the `delete_min` took $O(\log n)$ time.

To summarize the performance of this structure, we have the following:

Theorem. Brodal's heap structure supports the operations `insert`, `merge`, `find_min` in worst-case $O(1)$ and `delete_min` in worst-case $O(\log n)$ time.

If one adds upward pointers, one can also get the operations `decrease_key` and arbitrary deletions in $O(\log n)$ time. Some care is required; however, the structure does not give an $O(\log n)$ height bound, because a list of nodes of rank 0, which each have the special neighbor, would be a correct heap structure. The strategy is therefore to bubble up until one meets a special neighbor link, and then clear the special neighbor of `r->special` as described before, and insert the current node there instead.

An array-based heap of the same performance, $O(1)$ worst-case `insert` and `find_min`, and $O(\log n)$ `delete_min`, was developed in Carlsson, Munro, and Poblete (1988). As always in array-based heaps, we cannot merge two heaps in this structure, but the space requirement is significantly smaller by the implicit representation than in Brodal's heap, where we need at least six pointers per element.

5.10 Double-Ended Heap Structures and Multidimensional Heaps

The heap structures that we discussed so far allow fast access to one end of the set of keys to the minimum key element in the current set, the way we have presented it here, or the maximum key element if we reverse all the inequality conditions. This is sufficient for all natural applications, but an obvious generalization is to ask for fast access both to the minimum and to the maximum element. That structure is called a double-ended heap, and it must support at least the operations `insert`, `find_min`, `find_max`, `delete_min`, `delete_max`, and possibly additional operations like `merge` or `change_key`.

If we use balanced search trees as heap, as described in Section 5.1, we immediately get a double-ended heap with the heap operations all in $O(\log n)$, and with the lazy deletion improvement we can get insert and change_key in $O(\log n)$, and find_min, find_max, delete_min, delete_max in $O(1)$ worst-case time. And all this requires not much extra effort beyond the balanced search tree with leaves arranged in a doubly linked list.

Nonetheless, a large number of other double-ended heaps have been proposed.[4] The most obvious solution would be to have two heaps – a min-heap and a max-heap – and insert each element in both, linking the two copies together by pointers. This requires that the underlying heap structure supports not only delete_min, but deletion of arbitrary elements, given a pointer to that element. This element duplication reduces an insert to two insert operations in the underlying heaps, and a delete_min or delete_max to the corresponding deletion in one of the underlying heaps, and an arbitrary deletion in the other. A merge operation reduces to two merges of the underlying heaps, when these are supported, but decrease_key fails to generalize, unless the underlying heap allows key changes in both directions, because the min-heap and the max-heap have opposite preferred orientations. We discussed this in Section 5.7.

An alternative to element duplication is to group the elements into pairs, again linked by pointers, and the smaller element of each pair is inserted into the min-heap and the larger element into the max-heap. Then any delete_min in the min-heap or delete_max in the max-heap does indeed delete the global minimum or maximum, it breaks only one of these pairs, which has to be corrected. This might again require deletion of arbitrary elements from one heap, if that heap contained several unmatched elements, of which half have to be moved to the other heap. If the underlying structure is a heap-ordered tree, this can be avoided by matching only the leaves.

This idea, combined with array-based heaps, was already observed in Knuth (1973) and Carlsson (1987/88), also Carlsson, Chen, and Strothotte (1989), van Leeuwen and Wood (1993), Chang and Du (1993), Chen (1995), and Jung (2005). These structures differ essentially only in the way these heaps are mapped into an array and how the pairing between them is established; this influences the multiplicative constant in the $O(\log n)$ bound per operation. Because these structures are all based on the array-based heaps, they achieve $O(\log n)$ per insert, delete_min, delete_max, or even arbitrary deletions of elements with known positions, and $O(1)$ find_min and find_max. Arbitrary key changes of elements at known position can be done in $O(\log n)$ time by deleting and reinserting it.

---

[4]Frequently, the original note by Williams (1964), in which he first defined the heap, is also cited as the source of the first double-ended heap, but this is not true.

Array-based heaps are combined with a different order structure in Atkinson et al. (1986) and Arvind and Rangan (1999) to implement double-ended heaps. They again achieve the same $O(\log n)$ time for all operations supported by array-based heaps; the only differences are the multiplicative constants in the number of comparisons and possibly the difficulty of the implementation.

The idea of pairing elements in a min-heap and a max-heap structure is, of course, not restricted to array-based heaps. It is applied to binomial heaps in Khoong and Leong (1993) and to leftist heaps in Cho and Sahni (1999), where all three variants – element duplication, global element pairing, and leaves-only pairing – are discussed. The method is studied as general construction principle in Chong and Sahni (2000) and Makris, Tsakalidis, and Tsichlas (2003). If we have any underlying heap that supports `merge` and deletion of arbitrary elements, the derived double-ended heap consists of the following parts:

- at most one unmatched element,
- a min-heap,
- a max-heap, and
- a pairing of the elements of the min-heap and the max-heap, so that for each pair, the min-heap element is smaller than the max-heap element, and from any element we can access the other half of its pair in $O(1)$.

Now the operations work as follows:
- `insert`: If there is an unmatched element, the new element is paired with it, and the smaller part of the pair is inserted into the min-heap, the larger into the max-heap. If there is no unmatched element, the new element becomes the unmatched element.
- `find_min`: Performs a `find_min` in the min-heap and compares the result with the unmatched element if there is one and returns the smaller.
- `find_max`: Performs a `find_max` in the max-heap and compares the result with the unmatched element if there is one and returns the larger.
- `delete_min`: Performs a `find_min` in the min-heap and compares the result with the unmatched element if there is one. If the unmatched element is smaller, it deletes and returns the unmatched element. Otherwise it performs a `delete_min` in the min-heap, a general `delete` of the matched element in the max-heap, and again an `insert` of that element from the max-heap.
- `delete_max`: Performs a `find_max` in the max-heap and compares the result with the unmatched element if there is one. If the unmatched element is larger, it deletes and returns the unmatched element. Otherwise it performs a `delete_max` in the max-heap, a general `delete` of the

matched element in the min-heap, and again an insert of that element from the min-heap.

- merge: Performs a merge for the two min-heaps and another merge for the two max-heaps, and if there are two unmatched elements, one from each of the merged heaps, it matches them and inserts the smaller into the min-heap, the larger into the max-heap.

If we apply this construction to the heap invented by Brodal (1995) that we described in the previous section, which supported insert and merge in $O(1)$ and delete_min as well as arbitrary deletions in $O(\log n)$, we obtain a double-ended heap with insert, find_min, find_max, merge in $O(1)$ and delete_min, delete_max in $O(\log n)$ time (Chong and Sahni 2000; Makris et al. 2003). Brodal (1995) himself proposed element duplication instead, which gives exactly the same performance, but needs twice the space for the heap. But if the objects associated with the keys are larger, this does not matter because the objects themselves are not duplicated.

Theorem. There is a double-ended heap that supports insert, find_min, find_max, merge in $O(1)$ and delete_min, delete_max in $O(\log n)$ worst-case time.

Further pointer-based double-ended heaps were proposed in Olariu, Overstreet, and Wen (1991) and Ding and Weiss (1993), which reuses the alternative order structure of min-layers and max-layers developed in Atkinson et al. (1986) for array-based heaps. The heaps of Atkinson et al. (1986) were also studied in Hasham and Sack (1987) and Strothotte, Eriksson, and Vallner (1989).

A further generalization of the double-ended heap is the d-dimensional interval heaps proposed in van Leeuwen and Wood (1993) and discussed further by Ding and Weiss (1994). They model a set of objects, where to each object a d-tuple of key values is attached, and one can query for the objects with minimum or maximum ith coordinate for each $i = 1, \ldots, d$. This looks somewhat similar to range searching, and indeed van Leeuwen and Wood (1993) observed that their structure allows to solve complementary orthogonal range queries, that is, listing the points outside a given box in output-sensitive time $O(\log n + k)$. They are realized as array-based heaps, with insert, delete_min, and delete_max for each coordinate in $O(\log n)$ time.

A d-dimensional min-heap is the natural generalization of all these structures: a set of objects, each with d key values, in a structure that allows inserts, and query for and deletion of the object with minimum ith coordinate. A double-ended heap is a special case of a two-dimensional heap because we can replace each key by the pair $(key, -key)$. Then the maximum queries translate into minimum queries for the second coordinate. In the same way, the queries supported by a d-dimensional interval heap are a special case of the queries in a $2d$-dimensional min-heap.

Again, one can implement this using several heaps whose elements are linked, one heap for each coordinate (Brass 2007). The main difference is that we cannot group the elements into d-tuples and insert one in each heap, because it is possible that the same element is minimal for each coordinate and has thus to be entered in each heap. The simplest way to realize this structure is element duplication. We have d min-heaps, one for each coordinate, and we insert each element in each heap, joining the nodes that refer to the same element in a cyclic linked list. Then each insert reduces to d insertions in the underlying heaps, and each delete_min in one coordinate reduces to one delete_min in one heap, which gives us the beginning of the list of copies, and $d - 1$ general deletions at known places in the other heaps. And for a merge, we just merge the d coordinate-heaps. Using again Brodal's heap as the underlying heap structure, we obtain the following bounds:

Theorem. There is a d-dimensional min-heap that supports insert, merge, and find_min in each coordinate in $O(1)$ and delete_min in each coordinate in $O(\log n)$ worst-case time.

5.11 Heap-Related Structures with Constant-Time Updates

Several structures have been studied that keep track of the minimum key in a dynamically changing set if the changes are subject to some restrictions. In general, because we can use a search tree to allow arbitrary insertions and deletions in $O(\log n)$ and find the minimum in $O(1)$, we are interested in such situations where the updates are significantly faster than $O(\log n)$, at best in time $O(1)$.

The simplest example of such a structure is to keep track of the minimum value of elements on a stack. One can view the stack as a set that changes in a very restricted way: if y is inserted after x, then it must be deleted before x. For the minimum of the key values of the current set, this implies that either the insertion of y decreases the minimum, then the previous minimum becomes irrelevant until y is deleted, or the minimum stays the same. So we can keep track of the current minimum by using a second stack, which contains the current minimum. For each push on the stack, we compare the current

minimum, that is, the top of the second stack, with the new element and push
the smaller value on the second stack. For each pop, we also pop the element
of the second stack. And for a find_min, we return the value on top of the
second stack. All these operations take only constant time.

Theorem. The doubled stack structure supports push, pop, and find_min
in $O(1)$ worst-case time.

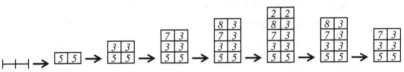

DOUBLED STACK TO MAINTAIN THE MINIMUM ELEMENT ON THE STACK:
LEFT STACK CONTAINS ELEMENT, RIGHT STACK THE CURRENT MINIMUM

The same problem for a queue instead of a stack is more difficult, but
also more important. A minqueue is a structure that supports the operations
enqueue, dequeue, and find_min. It models a sliding window over a
sequence of items, where we want to keep track of the smallest key value in
that window. One application of a minqueue is to partition a sequence of objects
into groups of consecutive objects such that each group has a certain size and
the breakpoints have small values. There, each potential breakpoint defines
an interval of potential next breakpoints, which is a queue, and we need the
minimum value of the next breakpoint as function of the previous breakpoint.
This type of problem was first discussed by McCreight (1977) in the context
of choosing page breaks in an external-memory index structure; there, normal
heaps were used (Diehr and Faaland 1984). The same problem occurs in many
other contexts, for example, in text formatting, breaking text into lines.

A simple version of a minqueue with amortized $O(1)$ time works as follows:
We have a queue for the objects and additionally a double-ended queue for the
minimum key values (it really needs only one-and-a-half ends). The operations
are as follows:

- enqueue: Enqueue the object in the rear of the object queue; remove from
  the rear of the minimum key queue all keys that are larger than the key of the
  new object, and then add the new key in the rear of the minimum key queue.
- dequeue: Dequeue and return the object from the front of the object
  queue; if its key is the same as the key in front of the minimum key queue,
  dequeue that key.
- find_min: Return the key value in front of the minimum key queue.

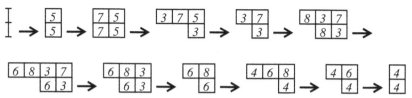

<small>DOUBLED QUEUE TO MAINTAIN THE MINIMUM ELEMENT IN A QUEUE:
TOP QUEUE CONTAINS ELEMENT, BOTTOM QUEUE THE CURRENT MINIMUM</small>

This doubled queue structure takes amortized $O(1)$ time because each object and each key is just inserted and deleted once; but in a single enqueue operation, there are possibly many key values removed from the minimum key queue. Here is an implementation of the doubled queue structure.

```
typedef struct qu_t { key_t       key;
                      object_t    *object;
                      struct qu_t *next;
                      struct qu_t *prev; } queue_t;

queue_t *create_minqueue()
{    queue_t *entrypoint;
     entrypoint = get_node();
     /* create empty object queue below
        entrypoint->next */
     entrypoint->next = get_node();
     entrypoint->next->next = entrypoint->next;
     entrypoint->next->prev = entrypoint->next;
     /* create empty minkey queue below
        entrypoint->prev */
     entrypoint->prev = get_node();
     entrypoint->prev->next = entrypoint->prev;
     entrypoint->prev->prev = entrypoint->prev;
     /* minimum over empty set is +infty */
     entrypoint->prev->key = POSINFTY;
     /* empty minqueue created */
     return( entrypoint );
}

int queue_empty(queue_t *qu)
{    return( qu->next->next == qu->next );
```

```
}

key_t find_min_key(queue_t *qu)
{   return( qu->prev->prev->key );
}

object_t *find_min_obj(queue_t *qu)
{   return( qu->prev->prev->object );
}

void enqueue( object_t *new_obj, key_t new_key,
              queue_t *qu)
{   queue_t *new, *tmp; tmp = NULL;
    /* create and fill new node with new
       object and key */
    new = get_node();
    new->object = new_obj; new->key = new_key;
    /* insert node in rear of object queue,
       as qu->next->next */
    new->prev = qu->next;
    qu->next->next->prev = new;
    new->next = qu->next->next;
    qu->next->next = new;
    /* remove all larger keys from rear
       of minkey queue */
    while( qu->prev->next != qu->prev &&
           qu->prev->next->key > new_key)
    {   if( tmp != NULL )
            /* return node only if we get another*/
            return_node( tmp );
        tmp = qu->prev->next;
        /* now unlink tmp */
        qu->prev->next = tmp->next;
        qu->prev->next->prev = qu->prev;
    }
    /* create node with new key */
    new = ( tmp != NULL ) ? tmp : get_node();
    new->object = new_obj; new->key = new_key;
    /* insert node in rear of minkey queue,
```

```
        as qu->prev->next */
    new->prev = qu->prev;
    qu->prev->next->prev = new;
    new->next = qu->prev->next;
    qu->prev->next = new;
}


object_t *dequeue(queue_t *qu)
{   queue_t *tmp; object_t *tmp_object;
    if( qu->next->next == qu->next)
      return( NULL );
      /* dequeue from empty queue */
    else
    {  /* unlink node from front of
           object queue */
       tmp = qu->next->prev;
       tmp_object = tmp->object;
       qu->next->prev = tmp->prev;
       qu->next->prev->next = qu->next;
       /* test front of minqueue,
          unlink node if equal */
       if( tmp->key == qu->prev->prev->key )
       {  return_node( tmp );
          tmp = qu->prev->prev;
          qu->prev->prev = tmp->prev;
          qu->prev->prev->next = qu->prev;
       }
       return_node( tmp );
       return( tmp_object );
    }
}


void remove_minqueue(queue_t *qu)
{   queue_t *tmp;
    /* link all queues together
        to a list connected by next */
    qu->next->prev->next = qu->prev;
    qu->prev->prev->next = NULL;
    /* follow the next pointers
```

```
        and return all nodes*/
    do
    { tmp = qu->next;
      return_node( qu );
      qu = tmp;
    }
    while ( qu != NULL );
}
```

Theorem. The doubled queue is a minqueue that supports enqueue, dequeue, and find_min in $O(1)$ amortized time.

A structure that supports all double-ended queue operations and find_min
in $O(1)$ worst-case time is described in Gajewska and Tarjan (1986), and a
further extension to allow concatenation, but only in amortized $O(1)$ time,
occurs in Buchsbaum, Sundar, and Tarjan (1992). A different $O(1)$ worst-case
generalization is a min-heap that discards on each insert all those elements that
have a larger key than the new element (Sundar 1989). That is exactly what
the minimum key queue did in the previously described version of a minqueue;
replacing it by the structure (Sundar 1989) gives another $O(1)$ worst-case
minqueue. A minqueue that additionally supports key change operations, also
in $O(1)$ amortized time, was given, together with some applications in Suzuki,
Ishiguro, and Nishizeki (1992).

Some heap structures have been proposed that support the general heap
operations, but take advantage of some special update pattern if it is present.
The queaps of Iacono and Langerman (2002) give $O(1)$ time insert and
amortized $O(\log k)$ time delete_min, where k is the number of items in
the heap that are in it longer than the current minimum item. Thus, the queap
is fast if the minimum item is always one of the oldest, so the items are
inserted approximately in increasing order. This is achieved by having separate
structures for "old" and "new" elements, converting all "new" to "old" whenever
the current minimum lies in the "new" part. This way, a delete_min operation
needs to look up the minimum in both parts, but in most cases it has to perform
the deletion only on the small "old" part.

The fishspear structure by Fischer and Paterson (1994) performs better in
the opposite case, when current minimum usually is in the heap only for a
short time. This will happen if the inserted elements are chosen from a fixed
distribution. The fishspear takes an amortized $O(\log m)$ time for an insert,

where m is the maximum number of elements smaller than the inserted element that exist at any moment before it is deleted again, and amortized $O(1)$ time for a delete_min.

A similar property was proved by Iacono (2000) for pairing heaps: the amortized complexity of delete_min in a pairing heap is $O(\log \min(n, m))$, where n is the size of the heap at the time of the deletion, and m is the number of operations between the insertion and the deletion of the element.

As with finger trees and splay trees, this advantage for special update patterns given by a queap or a fishspear is too small to perform better than a good ordinary heap unless the update pattern is extremely strong.

6

Union-Find and Related Structures

The problem known as "union-find" is to keep track of a partition of a set, in which partition classes may be merged, and we want to answer queries whether two elements are in the same class. This problem was first discussed in Arden, Galler, and Graham (1961)[1] and Galler and Fisher (1964) with the motivation of keeping track of the equivalence of identifiers, because in Fortran and several other early languages it was possible to give several names to the same variable. Later, much more important applications were found, and this step of keeping track of a partition of a set whose classes grow together can be found, for example, in the minimum-spanning-tree algorithms of Kruskal and Borůvka.

The large number of papers generated by this problem and its relatives are not so much motivated by the difficult structures they use, but by the difficulties of the analysis. Also, it turned out that the correct answer very much depends on the exact question and the computational model. This is one of the two places in algorithms[2] where the inverse Ackermann function occurs, an extremely slow-growing function, and it not only occurs as a technical device, but also gives the correct order of the amortized complexity of the classical solution to this problem.

The structures related to the union-find problem are again, like the binary search trees, useful building blocks in the construction of more complicated data structures. But here one has to be more careful about which operations exactly need to be supported.

---

[1] One of the earliest algorithms paper in our references.
[2] And almost the rest of mathematics. The other place is in Davenport–Schinzel sequences, which occur by their application to the complexity of arrangements in a number of computational geometry results.

6.1 Union-Find: Merging Classes of a Partition

The classical version of the union-find structure works in the following model: there is a set of items on which some partition is maintained. Items can be inserted into that set, each initially forming a one-element partition class. Items are identified by a pointer, a finger into the structure, which is obtained from the insertion operation. This makes access to an item a constant-time operation; there is no key involved in this structure. The underlying partition can be changed by joining two classes, the classes identified by giving items in these classes. And the partition can be queried by asking whether two items are in the same class. So we have the following operations:

- `insert`: Takes an item, returns pointer to the node representing the item, and creates a one-element class for it.
- `join`: Takes two pointers to nodes and joins the classes containing these items.
- `same_class`: Takes two pointers to nodes and decides whether their items are in the same class.

One could implement these operations in many different ways. One possibility would be to keep a table with the class for each item; then one could query fast, just looking up two table entries and checking whether they are the same, but to join two classes, one would have to change all entries in one class. Or one could just keep the graph of pairs of items that were joined, allowing very fast updates by inserting one edge, and then decide at query time whether two items are in the same connected component.

But a much better class of methods is based on the following idea, which occurred first in Galler and Fisher (1964). We represent each class by a directed tree, with all edges oriented to the root. Then each node representing an item

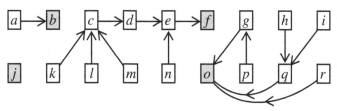

CLASSES $\{a, b\}$, $\{c, d, e, f, k, l, m\}$, $\{g, h, i, o, p, q, r\}$, $\{j\}$
WITH MARKED ROOT NODES

needs just one outgoing pointer to that neighbor in the tree that is nearer to the root; for the root itself we use the NULL pointer.

Given this representation, we can query whether two items are in the same class by following from both nodes the path to their respective roots; they are in the same class if they reach the same root. And we can join two classes by connecting the root of one tree to the root of the other tree.

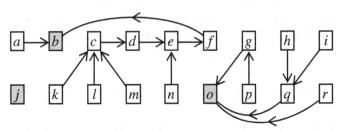

JOINING TWO CLASSES BY CONNECTING ONE ROOT TO THE OTHER

This outline still leaves a lot of freedom: we have to decide on joining two trees, which of the two roots should become the root of the union. And we can restructure the tree, ideally making all vertices point directly to the root, because the time taken by the query is the length of the path to the root. In the best-known solution, we use the following two techniques:

– *Union by rank*: Each node has another field, the rank, which starts on insertion as 0. Each time we join two classes, the root with the larger rank becomes the new root, and if both roots have the same rank, we increase the rank in one of them.
– *Path compression*: In each query and each update, when we followed a path to the root, we go along that path a second time and make all the nodes point directly to the root.

Both heuristics were introduced separately, but simultaneously, in several papers,[3] for example, Bayer (1972b), they were combined in Hopcroft and Ullman (1973).

With this, we can now write down an implementation of this very simple structure.

---

[3] And inaccessible technical reports and personal communications.

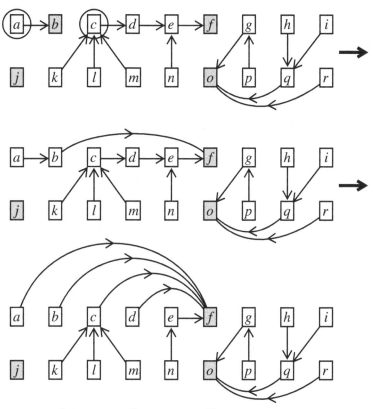

JOINING THE CLASSES WITH ELEMENTS *a* AND *c*:
UNION BY RANK FOLLOWED BY PATH COMPRESSION

```
typedef struct uf_n_t {
                int             rank;
                item_t          *item;
                struct uf_n_t   *up;     } uf_node_t;

uf_node_t *insert(item_t *new_item)
{   uf_node_t *new_node;
    new_node = get_node();
    new_node->item = new_item;
    new_node->rank = 0;
    new_node->up = NULL;
    return( new_node );
}
```

```
int same_class( uf_node_t *node1,
                uf_node_t *node2 )
{  uf_node_t *root1, *root2, *tmp;
   /* find both roots */
   for( root1 = node1; root1->up != NULL;
   root1 = root1->up)
      ; /* follow path to root for node1 */
   for( root2 = node2; root2->up != NULL;
   root2 = root2->up)
      ; /* follow path to root for node2 */
   /* make both paths point directly to
   their respective roots */
   tmp = node1->up;
   while( tmp != root1 && tmp != NULL )
   {  node1->up = root1;
      node1 = tmp; tmp = node1->up;
   }
   tmp = node2->up;
   while( tmp != root2 && tmp != NULL )
   {  node2->up = root2;
      node2 = tmp; tmp = node2->up;
   }
   /* return result */
   return( root1 == root2 );
}

void join( uf_node_t *node1, uf_node_t *node2 )
{  uf_node_t *root1, *root2, *new_root, *tmp;
   /* find both roots */
   for( root1 = node1; root1->up != NULL;
   root1 = root1->up)
      ; /* follow path to root for node1 */
   for( root2 = node2; root2->up != NULL;
   root2 = root2->up)
      ; /* follow path to root for node2 */
   /* perform union by rank */
   if( root1->rank > root2->rank )
   {  new_root = root1; root2->up = new_root;
   }
```

```
else if( root1->rank < root2->rank )
{    new_root = root2; root1->up = new_root;
}
else /* same rank */
{    new_root = root1; root2->up = new_root;
     new_root->rank += 1;
}
/* make both paths point directly to
the new root */
tmp = node1->up;
while( tmp != new_root && tmp != NULL )
{   node1->up = new_root;
    node1 = tmp; tmp = node1->up;
}
tmp = node2->up;
while( tmp != new_root && tmp != NULL )
{   node2->up = new_root;
    node2 = tmp; tmp = node2->up;
}
}
```

The complexity of each of these operations is of the order of the length of the path taken to reach the root, so its worst-case complexity is the height of the trees that result from these operations. It is easy to see that the height of these trees, even without path compression, is $O(\log n)$. When constructing bad trees by a sequence of these operations, we can avoid path compression if we always perform the join operations on the roots. By this we can construct trees of height $\Omega(\log n)$, so the worst-case performance of this structure is indeed $O(\log n)$. Union by rank is just one of several very similar rules, as union by height or union by weight, to select in a join operation which of the roots to become the new root; any of these rules has the same effect: a tree of height h has at least 2^h nodes.

This $O(\log n)$ upper bound on the complexity of an operation in this structure is tight, but only for a single operation: after we performed an operation in which we took a long time, we leave the tree representation in a much better state by the path compression. We cannot have a long sequence of operations, each of them taking $\Omega(\log n)$ time. This suggests that a better amortized bound should be possible, and indeed it is. After earlier bounds in Fischer (1972), Hopcroft and Ullman (1973), and Lao (1979), Tarjan (1975) obtained a famous result that expresses the amortized complexity in a version of the inverse Ackermann function.

The inverse Ackermann function is an extremely slow-growing function. The classical Ackermann function was defined by Ackermann as an example of an extremely fast-growing function for a problem in computability by

$$A(m, 0) = 0 \quad \text{for } m \geq 1,$$
$$A(m, 1) = A(m - 1, 2) \quad \text{for } m \geq 1,$$
$$A(0, n) = 2n \quad \text{for } n \geq 0,$$
$$A(m, n) = A(m - 1, A(m, n - 1)) \quad \text{for } m \geq 1, n \geq 2.$$

Because this Ackermann function has two variables, it is unfortunately not quite as clear what its inverse is. Several distinct functions exist under this name, some of them for technical reasons quite strange (e.g., Tarjan (1975) used $\alpha^{\text{Tarjan}}(m, n) = \min\{k \mid A(k, 4\lceil\frac{m}{n}\rceil) > \log n\}$). We define as inverse Ackermann function the function

$$\alpha(n) = \min\{i \mid A(i, 1) > n\}.$$

With this function, we can now state the performance of the given union-find structure.

Theorem. The union-find structure with union by rank and path compression supports the operations insert in $O(1)$ and same_set and join in $O(\log n)$ time on a set with n elements. A sequence of m same_set or join operations on a set with n elements takes $O((m + n)\alpha(n))$ time.

We have already observed the first part; the maximum length of any path on a set with n elements is $O(\log n)$, so the time of any single operation is $O(\log n)$.

To prove the second part, the amortized bound, we define a sequence of partitions $(\mathcal{B}_i)_{i=0}^{\infty}$ of $\mathbb{N}$. Each $\mathcal{B}_i$ is a partition of $\mathbb{N}$ into blocks that are intervals; the jth block in $\mathcal{B}_i$ is the interval $[A(i, j), A(i, j + 1) - 1]$. Each block in the ith partition is a union of blocks in the $(i - 1)$th partition, because

$$[A(i, 0), A(i, 1) - 1] = [A(i - 1, 0), A(i - 1, 2) - 1]$$
$$= [A(i - 1, 0), A(i - 1, 1) - 1]$$
$$\cup [A(i - 1, 1), A(i - 1, 2) - 1]$$

and

$$[A(i, j), A(i, j + 1) - 1] = [A(i - 1, A(i, j - 1)), A(i - 1, A(i, j)) - 1]$$
$$= [A(i - 1, A(i, j - 1)), A(i - 1, A(i, j - 1) + 1) - 1]$$
$$\cup \cdots \cup [A(i - 1, A(i, j) - 1), A(i - 1, A(i, j)) - 1].$$

Let b_{ij} denote the number of blocks in $\mathcal{B}_{i-1}$ that together form the jth block of $\mathcal{B}_i$, then $b_{i0} = 2$ and $b_{ij} = A(i, j) - A(i, j - 1)$. Now $\alpha(n)$ is the smallest i such that $\{1, \ldots, n\}$ is contained in the 0th block of $\mathcal{B}_i$.

Define the *level* of a node v at a moment in our sequence of operations by

$$level(\text{v}) = \begin{cases} 0 & \text{if } \text{v->next} = \text{NULL} \\ \min \left\{ i \mid \begin{array}{l} \text{v->rank and} \\ \text{v->next->rank are in} \\ \text{the same class of } \mathcal{B}_i \end{array} \right\} & \text{else.} \end{cases}$$

If we follow a node v over a sequence of operations, initially its rank is 0 and then it increases by some join operations, but only while v is still the root of its tree. Once v becomes a nonroot node, its rank cannot change further and it is not possible for a nonroot node to become root again. So the rank of v is monotone increasing while it is a root node, and then becomes fixed. Up to that moment, the *level*(v) is 0; once v becomes a nonroot node, *level*(v) increases. Now v->next->rank exists, and by further operations, it can only increase. Because v->rank is now fixed, *level*(v) can only increase.

To measure the total work done with a node v over a sequence of m operations, we first observe that the work done with v while v is a root node is $O(1)$ in each operation and each operation touches at most two root nodes, and so the part of the work done on root nodes by the m operations is $O(m)$. The main contribution is the work on nonroot nodes, that is, the path compression.

Consider a path being compressed; this requires $O(1)$ work for each node on the path. Classify the nodes on the path in two groups as follows:

– v belongs to group 1 if there is a node w on the same path, nearer to the root, with *level*(v) = *level*(w).
– Else v is the last node with its level on the path and belongs to group 2.

Each operation performs at most two path compressions, and on each path there are at most $\alpha(n)$ nodes of group 2 because there are only $\alpha(n)$ distinct levels. So the total work spent in m operations on group 2 nodes is $O(m\alpha(n))$.

It remains to bound the work done on nodes during path compression while they belong to group 1. Suppose x is such a node and at the moment of this path compression *level*(x) = i. Thus, x->rank and x->next->rank belong to the same class in $\mathcal{B}_i$, but not in $\mathcal{B}_{i-1}$. Because x is of group 1, there is another node y on the path, nearer to the root, which also has $level(\texttt{y}) = i$. Let z be the root. Because along the path the ranks are increasing, we have

```
x->rank < x->next->rank ≤ y->rank < y->next->rank ≤ z->rank,
```

and along this chain we move at least twice in $\mathcal{B}_{i-1}$ one class on. So z->rank and x->next->rank are not in the same class of $\mathcal{B}_{i-1}$. Because after the path compression z will be x->next, this implies that in each path compression in which x participates as vertex of group 1, and while being on level i, the rank of x->next moves to a higher class in $\mathcal{B}_{i-1}$, but stays in the same class of $\mathcal{B}_i$.

If x is a nonroot node for which x->rank is contained in the jth class of $\mathcal{B}_i$, then x can participate as vertex of group 1, while being on level i, in at most $b_{ij} - 1$ path compressions.

Let n_{ij} be the number of nodes whose rank is in the jth class of $\mathcal{B}_i$ when they become nonroot nodes and the rank becomes fixed. Then the total work done by our m operations on these nodes by path compressions in which they belong to group 1 is

$$\sum_{i=0}^{\alpha(n)} \sum_j n_{ij}(b_{ij} - 1).$$

To bound the n_{ij}, we observe that there are at most $\frac{n}{2^k}$ nodes of rank k; for any node that reaches rank k is root of a tree of at least 2^k nodes, and these node sets are disjoint. So

$$n_{ij} \leq \sum_{k=A(i,j)}^{A(i,j+1)-1} \frac{n}{2^k} < \sum_{k=A(i,j)}^{\infty} \frac{n}{2^k} = \frac{n}{2^{A(i,j)-1}}.$$

Putting these bounds, and the trivial $n_{i0} \leq n$, together, we obtain for the work on group 1 nodes

$$\sum_{i=0}^{\alpha(n)} \sum_{j\geq 0} n_{ij}(b_{ij} - 1) = \sum_{i=0}^{\alpha(n)} n_{i0}(b_{i0} - 1) + \sum_{i=0}^{\alpha(n)} \sum_{j\geq 1} n_{ij}(b_{ij} - 1)$$

$$\leq (\alpha(n) + 1)n + \sum_{i=0}^{\alpha(n)} \sum_{j\geq 1} \frac{n}{2^{A(i,j)-1}}(A(i,j) - A(i,j-1) - 1)$$

$$\leq (\alpha(n) + 1)n + \sum_{i=0}^{\alpha(n)} 2n \sum_{j\geq 1} \frac{1}{2^{A(i,j)}}(A(i,j))$$

$$\leq (\alpha(n) + 1)n + \sum_{i=0}^{\alpha(n)} 2n \sum_{k\geq A(i,1)} \frac{k}{2^k}$$

$$= (\alpha(n) + 1)n + \sum_{i=0}^{\alpha(n)} 2n \frac{A(i, 1) + 1}{2^{A(i,1)-1}}$$

$$= (\alpha(n) + 1)n + 8n \sum_{i=0}^{\alpha(n)} \frac{A(i, 1) + 1}{2^{A(i,1)+1}}$$

$$< (\alpha(n) + 1)n + 8n \sum_{i=0}^{\infty} \frac{A(i, 1) + 1}{2^{A(i,1)+1}}$$

$$< (\alpha(n) + 1)n + 8n \frac{A(0, 1) + 2}{2^{A(0,1)}} = n(\alpha(n) + 1 + 8).$$

Together with the $O(m)$ work done in the roots and the $O(m\alpha(n))$ work done in group 2 nodes, this gives a total complexity of $O((m + n)\alpha(n))$.

This proof followed Tarjan (1975, 1983b). Alternative methods of analysis of this structure were proposed in Harfst and Reingold (2000) and Seidel and Sharir (2005); they all lead to the same result. Path compression is, like union by rank, just one of several rules that have the same effect and lead to the same bounds, but require different proofs (Tarjan and van Leeuwen 1984). This amortized bound is, subject to some restrictions on m, n, known to be best possible in several computation models (Tarjan 1979a, b; Banachowski 1980; Tarjan and van Leeuwen 1984; Fredman and Saks 1989; La Poutré 1990a, b), so the occurrence of the inverse Ackermann function is not an artifact of the proof.

The amortized bound, as it is stated, is useful only if the number of operations m is at least as large as the number of elements n. But the number of nontrivial join operations is at most $n - 1$, so the interesting case is the diagonal case. Our model differs from the model underlying the published papers on this problem because they create a separate find operation to find the root and perform path compression and then allow the join operation only on roots. The amortized bound is certainly not best possible if the number of operations is small compared to the size of the set.

The amortized complexity of the classical union-find structure is best possible, but the single-operation complexity is not. Structures with a worst-case complexity of $O(\frac{\log n}{\log \log n})$ for a join or same_set operation were proposed in Blum (1986) and Smid (1990). Again these complexities are best possible in some sense. An attempt to simultaneously achieve optimal amortized and worst-case complexity was made in Alstrup, Ben-Amram, and Rauhe (1999).

To reduce the worst-case complexity of the union-find operations, while keeping the same representation as set of trees oriented to their roots, we need to reduce the height of the trees. The height is essentially determined by the number of nodes and the indegree of the nodes. So we need to increase the indegree of the nodes. The idea used in Smid (1990) to achieve this is that in those join operations in which both roots have the same height and a small indegree, we redirect all incoming edges of one root to the other root, so that the new root has the sum of the previous indegrees and the height is still the same. For this, we need a list of all nodes whose outgoing edge points to the root because we need to change all these edges. So the time of a join is proportional to the length of this list (indegree of the root) plus the height of the tree. Because the height of a tree with n interior nodes, all interior nodes of degree k, is $\Theta(\log_k(n)) = \Theta(\frac{\log n}{\log k})$, we cannot do better than $O(\frac{\log n}{\log\log n})$ with this representation, which corresponds to $k = \Theta(\frac{\log n}{\log\log n})$.

There are a number of problems to realize that structure. Our indegree requirement for the nodes changes with n, so we cannot keep this property in the lower nodes if n increases. Also, we specified only the way to join two trees of the same height. We do not want to insert a tree of smaller height in the list of lower neighbors of the root, because it would increase the length of the list without giving many new nodes in its subtree. We overcome the first problem by requiring that a node at height h that is not a root has at least $h!$ nodes in its subtree. If we maintain this condition, which is independent of n, for all nodes, the height bound is satisfied because the total number of nodes is at most n and $h! \leq n$ implies that $h = O(\frac{\log n}{\log\log n})$. The second problem we overcome by making the root of small trees point not to the root of the large tree, but to some node on the list, which points to the root of the large tree. This way, the list does not get any longer, and if the smaller tree has height at most $h - 2$, the height does not increase, either.

To give the structure in more detail now, each node has two pointers:

- up, which is NULL for a root, points to the next node on the path to the root for all other nodes.
- list, which points to its list of lower neighbors for a root, points to the next on that list for a node that is lower neighbor of the root and is unspecified otherwise.

The node also contains two numbers: the height and the indegree. Then the rules for joining two components with roots r and s are as follows: Let r->height $\geq$ s->height ≥ 2, then

- If r->height > s->height, all lower neighbors of s, as well as s itself, are made to point to a lower neighbor of r.

– Else r->height = s->height. All lower neighbors of s are added to the list of lower neighbors of r,
  – If r->height > r->indegree, s is made to point to one lower neighbor of r.
  – Else s becomes the new root, with r as its only lower neighbor.

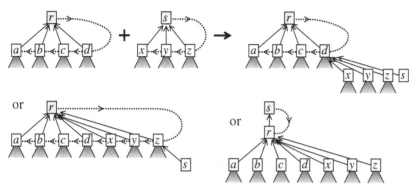

THREE CASES FOR JOINING THE CLASSES WITH ROOTS *r* AND *s*

With these definitions, we can now give the code for the operations of the structure.

```
typedef struct uf_n_t {
            int             height;
            int             indegree;
            item_t          *item;
            struct uf_n_t   *up;
            struct uf_n_t   *list; } uf_node_t;

uf_node_t *uf_insert(item_t *new_item)
{   uf_node_t *new_node;
    new_node = get_uf_node();
    new_node->item = new_item;
    new_node->height   = 0;
    new_node->indegree = 0;
    new_node->up = NULL;
    new_node->list = NULL;
    return( new_node );
}
```

```
int same_class( uf_node_t *node1,
                uf_node_t *node2 )
{  uf_node_t *tmp1, *tmp2;
   /* find both roots */
   for( tmp1 = node1; tmp1->up != NULL;
        tmp1 = tmp1->up)
      ; /* follow path to root for node1 */
   for( tmp2 = node2; tmp2->up != NULL;
        tmp2 = tmp2->up)
      ; /* follow path to root for node2 */
   /* return result */
   return( tmp1 == tmp2 );
}


void join( uf_node_t *node1, uf_node_t *node2 )
{  uf_node_t *root1, *root2, *tmp;
   int i;
   /* find both roots */
   for( root1 = node1; root1->up != NULL;
        root1 = root1->up)
      ; /* follow path to root for node1 */
   for( root2 = node2; root2->up != NULL;
        root2 = root2->up)
      ; /* follow path to root for node2 */
   if( root1->height < root2->height )
   {  tmp = root1; root1 = root2; root2 = tmp;
   }  /* now root1 is the larger subtree */
   if( root1->height >=2 )
   { /* inserting two levels below root 1,
   height stays the same */
      if( root2->height < root1->height )
      {  tmp = root2->list;
         /* go through list below root2 */
         while( tmp != NULL )
         {  tmp->up = root1->list;
            /* point to node on root1 list */
            tmp = tmp->list;
         }
         root2->up = root1->list;
```

```
      /* also point root2 to that node */
   }
   else /* root2->height == root1->height */
   {  /* join root2 list to root1 list,
      pointing to root1 */
      tmp = root2->list; tmp->up = root1;
      while( tmp->list != NULL )
      {  tmp = tmp->list;
         /* move to end of root2 list */
         tmp->up = root1;
      }
      tmp->list = root1->list;
      root1->list = root2->list;
      /* linked lists */
      root1->indegree += root2->indegree;
      /* now lists joined together
      below root 1 */
      if( root1->indegree <= root1->height )
         root2->up =root1->list;
         /* point to node on root1 list */
      else /* root2 becomes new root,
      root1 goes below */
      {  root1->up = root2;
         root1->list = NULL;
         root2->height += 1;
         root2->indegree = 1;
         root2->list = root1;
      }
   }
}
else /* root1->height <= 1*/
{  if( root1->height == 0 )
   {  root1->height = 1;
      root1->indegree = 1;
      root1->list = root2;
      root2->up = root1;
      /* root1 is new root */
   }
   else /* root1->height == 1 */
```

```
/* any root at height 1 has exactly
one lower neighbor */
{  if ( root2->height == 1 )
   /* both height 1 */
      root2->list->up = root1;
   /* now make root1 lower neighbor
   of root2 */
   root2->height = 2;
   root2->indegree = 1;
   root2->list = root1;
   root1->list = NULL;
   root1->up = root2;
   /* now root2 is the new root */
   }
  }
}
```

In this structure, each node at height h has indegree at least h once it becomes a nonroot node and has indegree at most h while it is the root. All the lower neighbors of a root, which has height h, themselves have height $h - 1$, although later further subtrees get attached that might have smaller height. So each nonroot node that is at height h has at any time at least h lower neighbors that are at height $h - 1$, in addition to some possible lower neighbors at smaller height. This implies that a tree of height h in this structure contains at least $(h - 1)!$ nodes; so with $(h - 1)! \leq n$ we have the claimed bound $h = O(\frac{\log n}{\log \log n})$. To summarize the performance of this structure, we state the following theorem:

Theorem. The union-find structure described before supports the operations insert in $O(1)$ and same_set and join in $O(\frac{\log n}{\log \log n})$ time on a set with n elements.

There have been many attempts to extend the structures for the union-find problem, but even deleting an item from a class is less trivial than expected if we expect the complexity to depend on the current size of the set after the deletions (Kaplan, Shafrir, and Tarjan 2002a). Both the worst-case and the amortized bounds can be adapted.[4] A survey of related results and variants is

---

[4] But Tarjan's cryptic two-variable inverse Ackermann function gains a third variable.

given in Galil and Italiano (1991). For special sequences of operations or if the sequence of unions is known in advance, algorithms with linear amortized bounds have been given in Gabow and Tarjan (1985) and Loebl and Nešetřil (1997). A version in which some unions might be undone, returning to an earlier state before those unions, was studied in Mannila and Ukkonen (1986), Gambosi, Italiano, and Talamo (1988, 1991), Westbrook and Tarjan (1989); there is an $\Omega(\frac{\log n}{\log \log n})$ lower bound on the amortized complexity in a restricted variant of the pointer machine, and this bound matches the worst-case bound of an algorithm (Apostolico et al. 1994). A variant of union-find in which the same-set queries are replaced by queries testing whether item x is in set Y was discussed in Kaplan et al. (2002b).

6.2 Union-Find with Copies and Dynamic Segment Trees

A structure that kept track of general set systems would be very useful. Up to now, our model is very restricted, the sets have to be disjoint, and we can take only unions of them. So we keep track of a sequence of coarser and coarser partitions until after $n - 1$ unions everything is in the same class. Another less obvious, but equally important, restriction is that our elements are presented by fingers, not by keys. There is no search-tree variant that supports the union of two sets. Of course, we can use a search tree to keep track of the fingers and then we get an $O(\log n)$ overhead on every operation, so the trivial $O(\log n)$ bound for the union-find structure would be sufficient.

It turns out that the details matter very much to decide what extension of union-find is possible and what not. If we want to keep track of a system of sets, allowing unions and copies (or nondestructive unions), and listing of the sets, as long as the unions occur only between disjoint sets, we can essentially keep the speed of the union-find structure (van Kreveld and Overmars 1993). On the other hand, if we allow arbitrary unions, there is a lower bound of $\Omega(n^2)$ for a sequence of n operations in a reasonable model (Lipton, Martino, and Neitzke 1997). So by allowing unions of overlapping sets, the complexity per operation increases from sublogarithmic to at least linear; a linear-time implementation using linked lists is trivial.

The assumption of disjointness of the sets of which unions are formed at first seems difficult to guarantee, but it has interesting applications.

The union-copy structure by van Kreveld and Overmars keeps track of a set of items, represented by fingers, and sets, also represented by fingers. It supports the following operations, which are symmetric with respect to the role of items and sets:

- `create_item`: Creates representation for a new item and returns a finger
  to it.
- `create_set`: Creates representation for a new set and returns a finger to it.
- `insert`: Inserts a given item in a given set. Requires that the item was not
  already contained in the set.
- `list_sets`: Lists all sets containing a given item.
- `list_items`: Lists all items contained in a given set.
- `join_sets`: Replaces the first set by the union of two given sets and
  destroys the other set. Requires the two sets to be disjoint.
- `join_items`: Replaces the first item by an item that is contained in all sets
  which contained one of the two given items, and destroys the other item.
  Requires that there is no set that contains both items.
- `copy_set`: Creates representation for a new set, which is a copy of the
  given set, and returns a finger to it.
- `copy_item`: Creates representation for a new item, which is a copy of the
  given item, and returns a finger to it.
- `destroy_set`: Destroys the given set.
- `destroy_item`: Destroys the given item.

Of these operations, the creation and insertion operations are $O(1)$, and the
complexity of the others depends on the complexity of the underlying union-
find structure, which is used as a building block of the union-copy structure. That
structure, however, cannot be directly plugged in – we need some modification.
The underlying union-find structure must also perform – in addition to the
normal operation of returning the current name (root) of the set containing a
given element – the reverse operation, listing all the elements of a set with a
given root. This is easy to add because we perform only disjoint unions: we
must attach to the root a list of pointers to the elements. These lists are just put
together in a union operation; to avoid pointers to beginning and end, we can
just use a cyclic linked list.

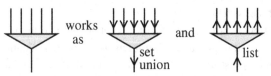

The underlying representation of the set system is as follows: The data structure consists of item nodes, set nodes, and sets in two extended union-find structures – labeled A and B – which allow both normal and listing queries. It is symmetric, like the operations supported by it, but because pointers are necessarily directed graph edges and the two union-find structures exchange their roles, we describe both directions.

If we wish to go from the items to the sets, the structure is as follows:

1. Each item node has exactly one outgoing edge.
2. Each set in the union-find structure A has at least two incoming edges (the elements of the set) and exactly one outgoing edge (the current name of the set).
3. Each set in the union-find structure B has exactly one incoming edge (the current name of the set) and at least two outgoing edges (the elements of the set).
4. Each set node has exactly one incoming edge.
5. An item belongs to a set if there is a directed path from the item node to the set node.
6. Between any item node and any set node there is at most one directed path.
7. There are no edges between sets in the same structure (from A to A or from B to B).

If we wish to go from the sets to the items, the properties 1–4 are replaced by their reflected versions:

1′. Each set node has exactly one outgoing edge.
2′. Each set in the union-find structure B has at least two incoming edges (the elements of the set) and exactly one outgoing edge (the current name of the set).
3′. Each set in the union-find structure A has exactly one incoming edge (the current name of the set) and at least two outgoing edges (the elements of the set).
4′. Each item node has exactly one incoming edge.

So the items are connected by unique alternating paths through structures A and B to their sets. The alternation property will be maintained in the updates by performing a set union whenever a set is directly connected to another set in the same structure; this preserves the existence and uniqueness of the paths between the item nodes and the set nodes.

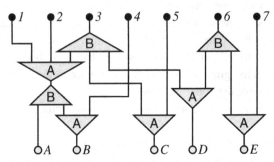

STRUCTURE REPRESENTING THE SET SYSTEM:
$A = \{1, 2, 3\}, B = \{1, 2, 3, 4\}, C = \{3, 5\}, D = \{3, 6\}, E = \{6, 7\}$

The alternation property is central because it allows us to bound the total number of edges between the structures and make our listing queries output sensitive. Consider all the items contained in a given set; they correspond to a set of directed paths, which by the uniqueness of these paths has to form a directed tree, from the set node through the nodes in A and B to the item nodes. In this tree, each node has only one incoming edge, and each node in B has also only one outgoing edge (by property 2′). There are no two consecutive B nodes (alternation property), so if we contract the incoming and outgoing edges of each B node to one edge, we get a graph on the A and item nodes, in which each A node has at least two outgoing edges (by property 3′). So if the total number of leaves in this tree, that is, item nodes corresponding to items contained in the set, is k, then total number of A nodes is at most $k - 1$. Because each B node subdivides an edge of this graph and each edge is subdivided at most once, there are at most $2k - 1$ B nodes in this tree. So if the set contains k elements, there are at most $3k - 2$ nodes in structures A and B that are traversed by the tree.

If we take the sum over all sets, this gives an immediate bound on the the total number of edges between the structures A and B and the set and item nodes: it is of the order of the total size of the set system. Let n be that total size, that is, the sum of the sizes of the sets in the system. Then both structures A and B are union-find structures on an underlying set of size n.

From this description follows immediately the algorithm for list_ items. To list all items for a given set, we perform the following steps:

0. Put the initial outgoing edge of the set node on the stack.
1. While the stack is not empty, take the next edge from the stack.
    1.1 If this edge goes to an item node, list that item.

1.2 If this edge goes to union-find structure A, perform a listing query and put all outgoing edges listed in the answer on the stack.

1.3 If this edge goes to union-find structure B, perform a naming query and put the one outgoing edge in the answer on the stack.

If we execute this algorithm and it lists k items that are contained in the set, we perform k times step 1.1, each taking $O(1)$, and by the aforementioned argument, at most $2k - 1$ times step 1.3, which is a normal naming (find) query in a set union structure. If the time for queries in the structure is $\mathrm{uf}(n)$, then we need at most $k\,\mathrm{uf}(n)$ for those queries. And we perform some $j \le k - 1$ listing queries in step 1.2, which produce $a_1, \ldots, a_j$ elements, with a listing query reporting a elements taking $O(1 + a)$ and $\sum_{i=1}^{j} a_i = 2k - 1$. Thus, step 1.2 takes in total $O(k)$. Thus, the total complexity of a list_items query that returns k items is output-sensitive $O(k\,\mathrm{uf}(n))$.

The same holds for the exactly symmetrical list_sets query.

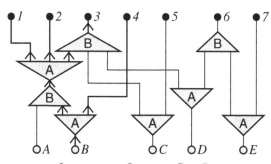

LISTING THE ITEMS IN SET B

The copy_set operation is also easy and takes only constant time. Given the set node, we follow the outgoing edge. There are only two cases:

1. The outgoing edge of the set node directly goes to an item node or to the structure A: We create a new set node and a set with two new elements in structure B. The two set nodes are joined to the elements in B, and the name of the set in B is the previous outgoing pointer of the node to be duplicated. Then we return the new set node.

2. The outgoing edge of the set node goes to the structure B: We create a new set node and a new element in B, join the set node to the element, and insert the element in the set that the previous outgoing edge pointed to.

Here we again need to be careful with the union-find structure because in our original description inserting a new element in a set was no elementary operation, just creating a new one-element set and merging it, and the general merge is certainly not a constant time operation. But it is easy to modify the structure as to allow constant time insert into the same set that a given element belongs to: just copy the up pointer without doing any path compression. We also need to adapt all the pointers in the opposite direction. Still, all this can be done in $O(1)$ time. The same holds, of course, for the symmetrical operation copy_item.

CREATING A COPY OF A SET NODE

The key operation is join_sets. Here we are given two set nodes. The following cases are possible for their outgoing pointers:

1. Both go to nodes in structure A: We perform a union in structure A of the sets they point to and adjust the pointer from the union set to the set node now representing the union.
2. The first set node points to a node in structure A and the second to a node in structure B: We create a new element in A and make it element of the set to which the first set node points. This new element then points to the element in B to which the second set node pointed. The first set node now represents the union and the second set node is discarded.
3. Both set nodes point to nodes in structure B or item nodes: We create two new elements in structure A and join them to a new set. The elements point to the nodes in structure B or item nodes to which the set nodes previously pointed, the set in structure A points to the set node representing the union.
4. The first set node points to a node in structure A and the second to an item node: We create a new element in A and make it element of the set to which the first node points. The new element then points to the item node.

These operations require in the worst case one set union and $O(1)$ additional work. So the complexity of join_sets and its dual join_elements is $O(\mathrm{uf}(n))$.

Then we need the insert operation to insert an item in a set that up to now does not contain it. We are given an item node and a set node, and then

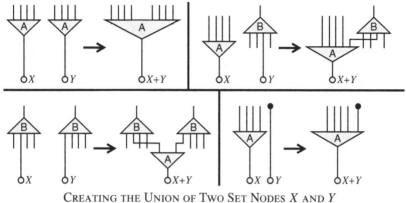

CREATING THE UNION OF TWO SET NODES X AND Y

the following cases are possible for their outgoing pointers:

1. The set node points to a node in structure A, and the item node points to a
   node in structure A or a set node: We create two new elements in structure
   B and join them to a new set. The set is then connected to the item node,
   and one of the new elements points to the element in A or the set node to
   which the item node previously pointed. Then we create a new element in
   A, join it to the set to which the set node points, and join this new
   A-element to the other new B-element.
2. The set node points to a node in structure A, and the item node points to a
   node in structure B: We create a new element in A, and join it to the set to
   which the set node points, and a new element in B, and join it to the set, to
   which the item node points. Then we point the two new elements to each
   other.
3. The set node points to a node in structure B or an item node, and the item
   node points to a node in structure A or a set node: We create two new
   elements in A and join them together to a set. This new set points to the set
   node, and one of the new A-elements points to the B node or item node that
   the set node previously pointed to. We also create two new elements in B
   and join them together to a set. This new set points to the item node, and
   one of the new B-elements points to the A-node or set node that the item
   node previously pointed to. Then we point the two new elements to each
   other.
4. The set node points to a node in structure B or an item node, and the item
   node points to a node in structure B: We create two new elements in
   structure A and join them to a new set. The set is then connected to the set
   node, and one of the new elements points to the element in B or the item

node to which the set node previously pointed. Then we create a new element in B, join it to the set to which the item node points, and join this new B-element to the other new A-element.

These operations only require to create new elements in A and B, join them to existing sets, and adjust some pointers. So the insert operation has complexity $O(1)$.

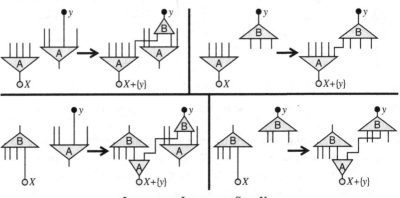

INSERTING ITEM y IN SET X

Finally, we need an operation to destroy a set. Again this needs some modification of the underlying union-find structure, and we need to be able to delete an element in it. The necessary modifications for that are nontrivial if one wants to keep the optimal complexity (Kaplan et al. 2002a) in the amortized or worst-case optimal bounds. For destroy_set, we are given a set node. The algorithm is similar to the listing of the set and also takes time depending on the size of the set to be destroyed.

0. Put the initial outgoing edge of the set node on the stack.
1. While the stack is not empty, take the next edge from the stack.
    1.1 If this edge goes to an item node, remove that edge.
    1.2 If this edge goes to union-find structure A, perform a listing query and put all outgoing edges listed in the answer on the stack.
    1.3 If this edge goes to union-find structure B and the set containing this element contains at least two further elements, just delete the element from B.
    1.4 If this edge goes to union-find structure B and the set containing this element contains only one other element, connect the node pointed to by this other element directly to the node pointed to by the set in B. If both these nodes are nodes in A, perform a union of these sets in A.

We follow here essentially the same tree we follow during the list_items operation, but have to perform some set unions along the way. If the set we destroy contains k elements, we visit $O(k)$ nodes in which we perform $O(k)$ set unions, so the complexity of destroy_set, applied to a set with k elements, is $O(k\,\mathrm{uf}(n))$.

So we can summarize the performance of this structure. If we use an underlying union-find structure that supports unions, deletions, and naming queries in $\mathrm{uf}(n)$ time, insert of a new element in a set in $O(1)$, and listing queries in output-sensitive $O(k)$ time, we have the following:

Theorem. The union-copy structure keeps track of a system of sets of total size n, supporting the operations

- create_item, create_set, insert, copy_set, copy_item in $O(1)$;
- list_sets, list_items in output-sensitive $O(k\,\mathrm{uf}(n))$ time if the output has size k;
- join_sets, join_items in $O(\mathrm{uf}(n))$ time; and
- destroy_set, destroy_item in $O(k\,\mathrm{uf}(n))$ time if the size of the destroyed object was k.

Here, union is allowed only for disjoint sets, and inserts may be performed only when the item is not already contained in the set.

The structure is easiest to implement if we do not need the deletion operations delete_set and delete_item and are satisfied with $\mathrm{uf}(n) = O(\log n)$ in the above complexity bounds. Then we can just use trees with union-by-rank for the union-find operation. We support the node listing operation of the extended union-find structure either by keeping a list of the nodes for each tree or by connecting the lower neighbors of each tree node into a list, and then traversing that tree using a stack of size $O(\log n)$. In any case, we obtain a structure that supports create_item, create_set, insert, copy_set, copy_item in $O(1)$, list_sets, list_items in output-sensitive $O(k \log n)$ time, if the output has size k, and join_sets, join_items in $O(\log n)$ time.

If we wish to realize the destroy_set and destroy_item operations, we must be able to remove nodes from the trees and still keep the trees balanced. For this, we can use a set union structure with deletions, as in Kaplan et al. (2002a), or, again slightly worse than optimal but simpler, use height-balanced trees for the sets in the union-find structure.

We now apply the structure to segment trees. The segment trees we described in Chapter 4 were a static structure: given a set of intervals, they were once constructed and then answered queries. We can use the union-copy structure to allow at least insertion of new intervals. The idea here is that in the segment trees we associated with each node a set of intervals, and in this set, no further structure was required.[5] In the segment trees, we just needed to be able to insert an interval in the set associated with a node while building the tree, and at query time to list the set associated with a node. The problem with making the structure dynamic is that we cannot change the underlying tree; if we want to insert an interval whose endpoints are not already existing, we should extend the underlying tree by these new key values, which is no problem on the leaf level, but then we need to rebalance, and the attached sets in the nodes do not transform well under rotations.

We can solve the problem with the rotations by choosing a different representation of the sets attached to the tree nodes, by using the above union-copy structure. Because we only need to keep the sets we meet along a path from the root to a leaf invariant and these sets are disjoint by their construction, we can move a set down in the tree. We remove it from its current node, create a copy, and join these two copies to the sets in the two lower neighbors of the node. Creating the copy takes $O(1)$, and the two unions take $O(\text{uf}(n))$. By this we reached that the set attached to the node is empty and thus creates no problem in a rotation. So for each rotation we need an additional $O(\text{uf}(n))$ time, but there are search trees that need only $O(1)$ rotations per insert. Because we need $O(\log n)$ anyway to perform an insert of a new key value in the tree and $\text{uf}(n)$ is $O(\log n)$, this is no problem. Then the new interval has to be inserted in the search tree, which now contains the new intervals as key values in leaves. The new interval is inserted in the $O(\log n)$ nodes corresponding to its canonical interval decomposition. In each of these nodes, we need to perform one insert in the union-copy structure, which takes $O(1)$. So the total complexity of the insert operations in this semidynamic segment tree is $O(\log n)$. We lose somewhat in the query complexity because listing a set takes $O(k\,\text{uf}(n))$ instead of $O(k)$ output-sensitive time; thus, the query time becomes $O(k\,\text{uf}(n))$ to list k intervals.

Theorem. A segment tree that uses the union-copy structure to represent the sets associated with the tree nodes supports `insert` into a tree already containing n intervals in $O(\log n)$ time and `list_intervals` for a query value contained in k intervals in $O(\log n + k\,\text{uf}(n))$ output-sensitive time.

---

[5] Different from the situation in interval trees, where the elements of the sets associated with the tree nodes were ordered so that we could list the first k of them in $O(k)$ time. This method does not generalize to interval trees.

In principle this structure is even fully dynamic. We can also delete an interval if the interval is given by a finger, because our union-copy structure supports deletion of items. The problem here is that the time of the deletion depends on the number of nodes in which the interval is represented. This is initially $O(\log n)$, the size of its canonical interval decomposition, but it increases each time we copy one of the node sets in the process of a rotation. One solution to that is to rebuild the tree sufficiently often. By this and choosing different structures for the underlying union-find structures A and B, van Kreveld and Overmars (1993) managed to support deletions and remove the $uf(n)$ factor in the query time, making the segment tree fully dynamic.

The same structure was also used to construct segment trees that allow splitting at a key value or joining if the intervals are separated, just as in search trees (van Kreveld and Overmars 1989).

6.3 List Splitting

In the model of the union-find data structure, we started with a very fine partition and continued to join classes until all elements were in one class. This suggests a dual problem: start with one class containing all elements and iteratively split it. One conceptual problem is that we do not know how to split a class: we have to specify which elements go into which part, but if we specify this by enumerating all elements, the problem becomes trivial. The problem becomes interesting only if we have a compact way to represent the split we selected.

This is achieved in the list-splitting problem by assuming the elements are linearly ordered, that is, given in a list. The items are identified by fingers to the items, and a split is specified by an item: cut immediately to the right of the given item. This way, the list is cut into smaller and smaller sublists, and we want to answer again the question whether two given items are in the same sublist. This problem was first stated in Hopcroft and Ullman (1973) as inverse of the union-find problem, and then in Gabow (1985, 1990) for a problem in combinatorial optimization and in Hoffmann et al. (1986) for sorting the intersections of two Jordan curves. In the model of Gabow (1985), the items also have key values, and the query for the maximum key value in the current list of the query item is supported.

Thus, for the list-splitting problem, our model is initially an ordered list of n items, each of them with a weight. Later this is replaced by a set of lists, which partition the items into intervals in the original ordering. The items are identified by fingers. The structure should, after some preprocessing, support the following operations:

- split: Splits into two lists the current list containing the given item directly to the left of the given item.
- same_list: Decides whether two given items are in the same list.
- max_weight: Returns a finger to the item of maximum weight in the same list as the given item.

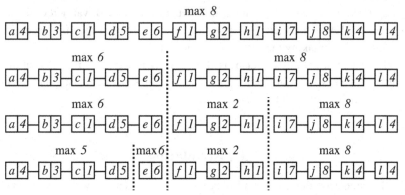

LIST-SPLITTING PROCESS, WITH SPLITS AFTER e, h, AND d

These operations can easily be supported by some balanced search trees that support splitting, for example, height-balanced trees or red-black trees. We build a single balanced tree from the list in $O(n)$ time as preprocessing and include in each node a pointer to the maximum weight item in its subtree. Then each splitting operation splits the current tree in two trees: for each same_list query we just go up to the root of the current tree and check whether both nodes arrive at the same root, and for the max_weight query we go to the root and report the pointer stored in it. Each of these operations takes just $O(\log n)$ worst-case time. This is even a dynamic data structure: we can insert new elements in a sublist as neighbor of a given element, and we can delete elements and join lists again if the tree supports this.

Theorem. Using any balanced search tree that supports split and join, we can build a dynamic structure that supports list splitting, with operations split, same_list, max_weight, join, insert, and delete, all in $O(\log n)$ worst-case time on a list of initial length n.

Several improvements in the amortized complexity have been proposed for special applications; it is important here to know what exactly we need.

An improvement that gives amortized $O(1)$ insertions, deletions, and splittings over a sequence of n operations initially starting with an empty list was used in Hoffmann et al. (1986). They observed that a level-linked (2, 4)-tree, as described in Section 3.7, has amortized insertion and deletion cost $O(1)$ in this setting, as discussed in Section 3.3. Also, the splitting is amortized faster; splitting a tree of size k into parts of size k_1 and k_2 takes $O(\log \min(k_1, k_2))$ plus an amortized $O(1)$ rebalancing time instead of the worst-case $O(\log(k_1 + k_2))$ for arbitrary splittable balanced search trees. This is a small, but useful, difference, because these $O(\log \min(k_1, k_2))$ terms can themselves be amortized over a sequence of splitting operations. This follows from a potential argument. We use as potential of the current family of lists the sum of the potentials of the individual lists, with the potential of a list of length k being $k - \log k$. Then, if we split a list of length k in two lists of length k_1, k_2, in time $O(\log \min(k_1, k_2))$, the change of potential is

$$
\begin{aligned}
pot^{\text{before}} - pot^{\text{after}} &= (k - \log k) - (k_1 - \log(k_1) + k_2 - \log(k_2)) \\
&= -\log(k) + \log(\max(k_1, k_2)) + \log(\min(k_1, k_2)) \\
&= \log\left(\frac{\max(k_1, k_2)}{k}\right) + \log(\min(k_1, k_2)) \\
&\geq \log\frac{1}{2} + \log(\min(k_1, k_2)).
\end{aligned}
$$

Performing a sequence of $n - 1$ splits on a list of initial size n, splitting off list of size $k_1, \ldots, k_{n-1}$, in time $O(\log k_1), \ldots, O(\log k_{n-1})$, we get

$$
\begin{aligned}
pot^{\text{beginning}} - pot^{\text{end}} &= (n - \log n) - n(1 - \log 1) = -\log n \\
&\geq \left(\log k_1 + \log\frac{1}{2}\right) + \cdots + \left(\log k_{n-1} + \log\frac{1}{2}\right),
\end{aligned}
$$

so

$$
\log k_1 + \cdots + \log k_{n-1} \leq n \log 2 - \log n = O(n).
$$

Thus, over a sequence of $n - 1$ splits of a list, which is initially of length n, we get an amortized time bound of $O(1)$ per split in this setting.

In this structure, it is important that the nodes for the queries are identified by fingers; otherwise we cannot avoid $\Omega(\log n)$ time just to find the node. This problem did not exist in the splittable search-tree version of the structure; there we could, for example, identify nodes by their number in the original list. For the queries, we can take some advantage of the finger search allowed by a level-linked tree, so we can answer same_list queries for two items given by fingers in time $O(\log d)$, where d is their distance in the original list, before the splitting, or the length of the list currently containing either of the items.

A different strategy of amortized improvement was followed by Hopcroft and Ullman (1973) and Gabow (1985); they increase the degree of the nodes in the tree model used to represent the lists. This decreases the height of the trees and allows by this faster same_list queries. Because we need to split all nodes along the path to the root if we split a list represented as tree, nodes of large degree are expensive in the worst case. But if we start with a list of length n and do not allow any insertions or deletions, only $n - 1$ split operations, then the amortized performance is better. Gabow (1985) used a blocking scheme related to the partitions $\mathcal{B}_i$, which we used in Section 6.1, to obtain a total complexity of $O(n\alpha(n))$ for such a sequence of operations. This gives an amortized $O(\alpha(n))$ complexity for the splitting and a worst-case complexity $O(\alpha(n))$ for the same_set queries. If we want a uniform bound on the splits and queries, la Poutré (1990b) showed that Gabow's structure has optimal amortized complexity.

If we may view the lists as subintervals of a fixed interval, it is also natural to join the intervals again so as to join sublists that were consecutive in the original list. This is the union-split–find problem; it was studied by van Emde Boas, Kaas, and Zijlstra (1977) and Mehlhorn, Näher, and Alt (1988). The algorithm from van Emde Boas et al. (1977) solves this problem with an $O(\log\log n)$ worst-case complexity for each operation, which was shown to be optimal (Mehlhorn et al. 1988). An interesting side issue is that the "separation assumption" here makes a big difference. This is a technical assumption on the algorithms in a pointer machine that was introduced by Tarjan and used as added condition in all his lower bounds for the union-find and related problems; only la Poutré (1990a, b) showed that this assumption can be removed from those lower bounds. But for the union-split-find problem, Mehlhorn et al. (1988) showed that any algorithm that satisfies the "separation assumption" needs $\Omega(\log n)$ time, whereas the optimal algorithm has complexity $\Theta(\log\log n)$.

6.4 Problems on Root-Directed Trees

The structures we used for the union-find structure were directed trees with all edges directed to the root. For the union-find structures, these were just a tool for defining the data structure, but there are also problems for which this type of tree is the underlying abstract object. The best-studied problem here concerns least common ancestor (lca) queries on such a tree: given two nodes of the tree, each node defines a path to the root, what is the first node that lies on both paths? One can interpret the underlying tree as a family tree, then this node is the first common ancestor, or one could interpret the tree as an ordered set, then this node is the meet (or join) of the given nodes. Root-directed tree can represent many kinds of things, for example, Sharir (1982) used them to represent sparse functions on a finites and their concatenation.

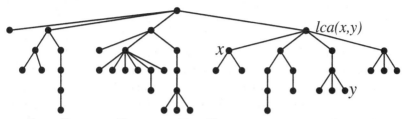

ROOT-DIRECTED TREE WITH TWO NODES x, y, AND THEIR lca(x, y)

This structure was first studied in Aho, Hopcroft, and Ullman (1976); at the same time they also studied the union-find structure. This problem has developed many variants, depending on the extent to which we may change the tree, adding only leaves or linking entire subtrees, linking subtrees anywhere or only to the root; also there are offline variants in which all the operations must be announced in advance before the queries have to be answered. Numerous possible combinations of this with the relevant literature are listed in Alstrup and Thorup (2000).

The structure keeps track of a set of root-directed trees and supports at least the following operations:

– `create_tree`: Creates a new tree with just one node, the root, and returns a pointer to that root.
– `add_leaf`: Adds a new leaf that is linked to a given node and returns a pointer to that new leaf node.
– `lca`: Returns a pointer to the least common ancestor of the two given nodes or NULL if they are not in the same tree.

Much stronger than simply adding leaves is the linking of entire subtrees, but not all structures support it.

– `link`: Takes two nodes x and y and different subtrees, of which x is root of its subtree, and links the subtrees by introducing an edge from x to y.

There are also reverse operations to `add_leaf` and `link`, but again they are more difficult to realize.

– `delete_leaf`: Removes a given node, which must be a leaf.
– `cut`: Removes the link from a given node to its upper neighbor, making the given node the root of a new tree.

There are several additional operations that might be useful and are supported by some structures:

– `find_root`: Returns a pointer to the root of a given node.
– `depth`: Returns the distance to the root of a given node.

An optimal method for create_tree, link, and lca was found by Alstrup
and Thorup (2000), in the pointer-machine model, where it matches a lower
bound by Harel and Tarjan (1984), improving earlier structures in Aho et al.
(1976), Maier (1979), Harel and Tarjan (1984), and Tsakalidis (1988). Related
problems were also studied in Gabow (1990), Gambosi, Protasi, and Talamo
(1993), Buchsbaum et al. (1998), Cole and Hariharan (2005), and Georgiadis,
Tarjan, and Werneck (2006). The method of Alstrup and Thorup (2000)
performs a sequence of n link and m lca operations on a set of n nodes in
time $O(n + m \log \log n)$, so with $O(\log \log(n))$ amortized time per operation.
We will describe here only several simpler structures, which were combined
by Alstrup and Thorup to overcome the limitations of the individual structures.

One of these structures allows lca queries in time $O(\log h)$, where h is
the height of the underlying tree. So if the tree, of height $O(\log n)$, itself is
balanced, this already gives us the $O(\log \log n)$ performance we aim for. But
the structure does not support the general link operation, only add_leaf,
and additionally find_root, depth, and delete_leaf.

The idea of this structure is binary search on the paths from the given nodes
to the root. Suppose first that both nodes are at the same depth and then they
are joined by paths of equal length to the root, and we ask for the smallest i
such that the ith node on both paths is the same. If we add for each node a
list of forward pointers up to the 2^jth node along the path to the root, we can
find that first common node by binary search. To achieve $O(\log h)$ time, the
forward pointers should be tested in the sequence from largest to smallest, so
each pointer length will be tested only once.

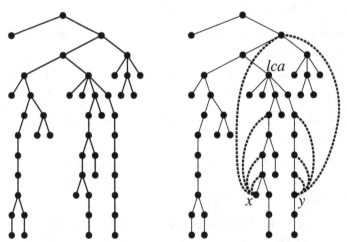

ROOT-DIRECTED TREE, WITH NODES x, y, lca(x, y),
AND FORWARD POINTERS OF LENGTH 2^j FROM x AND y

If the given nodes are not at the same depth, but one at depth k_1, k_2 with $k_1 > k_2$, then we can use the same forward pointers to replace the node at depth k_1 by the node along its path to the root $k_1 - k_2$ steps on, reducing the general case to the equal depth case. This idea of binary search on the paths was already introduced in Aho et al. (1976) and extended and adapted in Tsakalidis (1988) and Alstrup and Thorup (2000). We need in each node that list of $O(\log h)$ forward pointers. The depth of the node could be recovered again by binary search with the forward pointers, but it is as easy to store it in the node. This gives a query time of $O(\log h)$ and a space requirement of $O(n \log h)$; the space requirement can be reduced to $O(n)$ by attaching the list of forward pointers not to all nodes, but only to a fraction of $\frac{1}{\log h}$ of them: then each query starts by moving upward to the next node with forward pointers. The fundamental limitation of this structure is that there is no way to update all the lists after a link operation. Adding a new leaf and constructing its list from the available lists is easy, but for a link we would have to extend many lists. So the performance of this structure is the following:

Theorem. The lca structure based on trees with lists of exponential forward pointers attached to the nodes supports create_tree, depth in $O(1)$ and add_leaf, delete_leaf, lca, and find_root in time $O(\log h)$, where h is the maximum height of the trees in the underlying set.

This structure is easy to implement. We use an up pointer to represent the edges in the underlying tree and a next pointer to connect the list of forward pointers, with a prev pointer to make it a doubly linked list. The tree node is simultaneously also the first list node; in the later list nodes, the up pointer is used to point to the corresponding list item for the node 2^j steps ahead. A minor problem with this arrangement is that we need the existence of list nodes as target of the incoming edges even if there are no outgoing edges, and the number of list nodes needed for incoming edges depends not on the depth of the tree node itself but on the maximum depth of tree nodes below the current node. The solution used here is to add list nodes to the target list as they are required. An alternative would be to immediately create for each tree node a list with list nodes of all orders 2^j less than the depth of the node. Then all but the last one of these list nodes would have a correct target node for their up pointers; the last node would have only incoming, but no outgoing, edges.

```
typedef struct lca_n_t {
                int             depth;
                item_t          *item;
```

```
                    struct lca_n_t   *up;
                    struct lca_n_t   *next;
                    struct lca_n_t   *prev;
                         } lca_node_t;

  lca_node_t *create_tree(item_t *new_item)
  {  lca_node_t *new_node;
     new_node = get_lca_node();
     new_node->item = new_item;
     new_node->depth = 0;     new_node->prev = NULL;
     new_node->up = NULL;     new_node->next = NULL;
     return( new_node );
  }

  lca_node_t *add_leaf(lca_node_t *node,
                      item_t *new_item)
  {  lca_node_t *new_node;
     /* create tree node */
     new_node = get_lca_node();
     new_node->item = new_item;
     new_node->depth = node->depth + 1;
     new_node->up = node;   new_node->prev = NULL;
     /* now create new list of forward pointers */
     {  lca_node_t *tmp; int i;
        tmp = new_node;
        for( i = new_node->depth; i>1 ; i /=2 )
        {  /* add node to new_node list */
           tmp->next = get_lca_node();
           tmp->next->prev = tmp;
           tmp->next->depth = tmp->depth;
           if( tmp->up->up->next == NULL )
           {  /* create new target node */
              tmp->up->up->next = get_lca_node();
              tmp->up->up->next->prev =
              tmp->up->up;
              tmp->up->up->next->depth =
              tmp->up->up->depth;
              tmp->up->up->next->next = NULL;
              tmp->up->up->next->up = NULL;
```

```
      } /* now set forward pointer */
      tmp->next->up = tmp->up->up->next;
      tmp = tmp->next;
    } /* and finish list */
    tmp->next = NULL;
  }
  return( new_node );
}


int depth(lca_node_t *node)
{  return( node->depth );
}


lca_node_t *lca(lca_node_t *node1,
                lca_node_t *node2 )
{  lca_node_t *tmp; int diff;
   if( node1->depth < node2->depth )
   {  tmp = node1;  node1 = node2; node2 = tmp;
   } /* now node1 has larger depth. Move up to
   the same depth */
   { int diff;
     diff = node1->depth - node2->depth;
     while( diff > 1 )
     {  if( diff% 2 == 1 )
           node1 = node1->up->next;
        else
           node1 = node1->next;
        diff /= 2;
     }
     if( diff == 1 )
       node1 = node1->up;
     while( node1->prev != NULL )
       node1 = node1->prev; /* move
       back to beginning of list */
   } /* now both nodes at same depth */
   if( node1 == node2 )
      return( node1 );
   /* if not the same, perform exponential
   search */
```

```
{  int current_depth, step_size;
   current_depth = node1->depth;
   step_size = 1;
   while( current_depth >= 2* step_size )
   {  node1 = node1->next;
      node2 = node2->next;
      step_size *= 2;
   }  /* maximum stepsize, now go up,
   and decrease stepsize */
   while( current_depth >= 1 )
   {  if( step_size > current_depth )
      {  node1 = node1->prev;
         node2 = node2->prev;
         step_size /= 2; /* steps too large,
         halve size */
      }
      else if( node1->up != node2->up )
      {  node1 = node1->up; /* step up
         still below lca */
         node2 = node2->up;
         current_depth -= step_size;
      }
      else /* node1->up == node2->up */
      {  if( step_size > 1) /* upper bound
         for lca */
         {  node1 = node1->prev;
            node2 = node2->prev;
            step_size /= 2;
         }
         else /* immediately below lca */
            return( node1->up );
      }
   }
   return( NULL ); /* different trees */
}
}
```

We used explicit numbers for the depth in this `lca` code; we could instead just have tested the existence of pointers.

This structure also supports a different type of query, the level-ancestor query: given a node, what is the node k steps nearer to the root? This is just the same binary search on the path to the root, using the list of forward pointers, so this query can again be answered in $O(\log h)$ time. Level ancestor queries were studied in Berkman and Vishkin (1994), Alstrup and Holm (2000), and Bender and Farach-Colton (2004). Maier (1979) and Alstrup and Holm (2000) used a different scheme of forward pointers. Instead of attaching to each node n a list of pointers to the nodes 2^i steps up from n, for all possible i, they attach two groups of pointers to each node: one containing a list of pointers to the nodes j steps up for all $j \le 2^{r(n)}$ and another containing pointers to the next nodes up that have larger values of $r(n)$. Then the second group of pointers is used to reach in $O(1)$ steps a node for which the pointer to the searched-for node is in the first group of pointers. The first group of pointers is quite large for some nodes, but by the proper choice of the function $r(n)$, it is only $O(1)$ on the average. If the groups of pointers can be realized as arrays, this allows one to answer the level-ancestor queries in $O(1)$ time. In our pointer-machine model, we would have to use a tree to find the jth pointer of a group, which gives again the worst-case time of $O(\log h)$ we already had with the simple list of exponential-steps forward pointers. And supporting updates in this structure is again quite complicated. Tsakalidis (1988) uses yet another system of pointers, which gives again $O(\log h)$ query time, but supports adding leaves and deleting arbitrary nodes in amortized constant time. The structure described in Bender and Farach-Colton (2004) also supports answers to level-ancestor queries in $O(1)$, but it again needs arrays of pointers, and it is a static structure not allowing any updates.

The performance of the aforementioned structures depends on the height h of the tree being small. To reach the $O(\log \log n)$ performance instead of the $O(\log h)$, one can transform the underlying tree. This technique was introduced by Sleator and Tarjan (1983) and used in Harel and Tarjan (1984) and Alstrup and Thorup (2000). The idea is to partition the root-oriented tree into oriented paths. The compressed graph has these paths as vertices, each path represented by the node nearest to the root, which is called the apex of the path. Two vertices in the compressed tree are connected by an edge if there is some edge in the original tree between the paths, that is, going from the apex of one path to some node on the other path. If we can answer lca queries on the compressed tree, we can almost recover the lca query on the original tree.

We need slightly more information from the query in the compressed tree: to find the lca of nodes x and y, we find first the path p that contains that lca which is a usual lca query in the compressed tree. The paths from x and y to the root in the original tree enter the path p at vertices $\hat{x}$ and $\hat{y}$ and then follow

p to the apex of p. So the lca, which is the first common node of these paths, is that node of $\hat{x}$ and $\hat{y}$ which is nearer to the root, so has smaller depth.

One method to get this additional information is to use as representation of the compressed tree the following structure: an oriented tree with all the original nodes and one additional node as representative for each path; within each path, all nodes point to the representative of the path and that itself points to the node to which the apex of the path pointed. On this tree, any lca query of the original tree will give one of the path representatives as answer because all original nodes have indegree 1. But if we extend our lca query code to give back the two nodes immediately preceding the first common node on the two paths, as is easily done, then the correct lca is that of the two nodes that in the original graph has smaller depth.

The usefulness of this compression depends on whether it actually decreases the height. But this is easy. To define the partition into paths, we have to choose for each node one of its incoming edges. If a large part of the subtree below the current node, for example, more than $\frac{2}{3}$ of it, is below one of its lower neighbors, then we choose the edge to that lower neighbor; otherwise we are free to choose any edge to a lower neighbor. Then the compressed tree has height $O(\log n)$ because each edge in the compressed tree corresponds to an edge in the original tree along which the size of the subtree decreased by at least a factor of $\frac{2}{3}$.

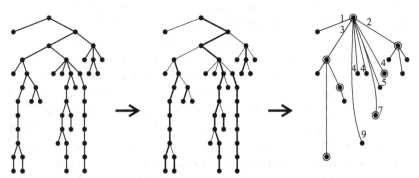

ROOT-DIRECTED TREE, PARTITIONED INTO PATHS, AND COMPRESSED TREE
EDGES ENTERING A PATH VERTEX ARE LABELED BY THE DEPTH IN THE PATH

Using only this compressed tree representation, combined with a trivial search for the lca by walking along the paths to the root and looking for the first common vertex, one obtains a structure with $O(\log n)$ query time. We have to store in each tree node the distance on the path to the apex of the path; then we can compute the depth of a node in $O(\log n)$ by following the path in the compressed tree and summing up the distances. After we have the depth of both query nodes, we can go up again this path of length $O(\log n)$ and find the first common node of both paths, which must be at the same depth. Then we know the compressed node that contains the answer to the lca query and can select the right node in original tree by going one step back in the compressed tree and comparing the depth of the upper neighbors.

When we want to use this structure to link two trees, we have the problem that we might have to change the path structure in the nodes that are linked, and possibly all paths above; and this can force us to visit all nodes of those paths to update the compressed tree. One solution is to realize the compressed nodes not only by pointers to the path representative but build a balanced search tree within each compressed node for the path nodes with their depth as key. This allows split and join of individual nodes in $O(\log n)$, but then the time to traverse a single compressed node also becomes $\Omega(\log n)$.

Theorem. The lca structure based on compressed trees, with compressed tree nodes realized as search trees, supports create_tree in $O(1)$, and lca, link, depth, find_root in worst-case time $O((\log n)^2)$ on a set with n elements.

Sleator and Tarjan (1983) outline a reduction of this complexity from worst-case $O((\log n)^2)$ to amortized $O(\log n)$ using biased search trees (Bent et al. 1985), or in Tarjan (1983b) using splay trees.

The completely static version of this problem also received some attention: given a root-directed tree of size n, preprocess it in time $O(n)$ such that lca queries, or at least comparison queries, can be answered fast. Already Harel and Tarjan (1984) gave a method for this, on a word-based RAM, which answered lca queries in $O(1)$. There it is related to the problem of preprocessing an array of numbers such that for any index range the minimum number in that range can be found in $O(1)$ (Wen 1994). Some claimed applications (Kaplan, Milo, and Shabo 2002) motivated further study in the constants involved, specifically for labeling schemes such that based on the labels alone one can decide comparison queries; labels of size $\log n + O(\sqrt{\log n})$ are sufficient for that (Alstrup and Rauhe 2002), improving Abiteboul, Kaplan, and Milo (2001). A survey of related results is given in Alstrup et al. (2002).

Asking lca queries naturally extend from root-directed tree-structured orders to more general orders. Arbitrarily directed trees were discussed in Nykänen and Ukkonen (1994); if we do not require all edges to be directed to the root, two elements might not have any common ancestor, but if they have one, it is unique, and the techniques for the root-directed trees generalize to this situation. The natural models for lca queries, in which the lca always exists and is unique, are semilattices and lattices. For these, there is no reasonable dynamic variant, there is no local change to lattices that preserves the lattice property, and especially the existence of an lca for any pair of elements. So in that setting, one can ask only for a static structure. If we allow $\Theta(n^2)$ preprocessing and storage, we can just precompute and tabulate all answers. If we may use an array to store the answers, this gives $O(1)$ queries, using a search tree we get $O(\log n)$ query time. A static structure with subquadratic space complexity supporting the lattice operations was constructed in Talamo and Vocca (1997, 1999).

Another type of query and operation on root-directed trees was discussed in Alstrup, Husfeldt, and Rauhe (1998). They considered a tree in which some nodes were marked, with these marks dynamically changing, and the queries ask for the next marked node on the path to the root. So here we have the operations as follows:

– mark: Marks a given node.
– unmark: Removes the mark from a given node.
– marked_ancestor: Returns the next node on the path from the given node to the root which is marked.

If the underlying tree is just a path, this is just the union-split-find problem mentioned in Section 6.3 again: the marked nodes are the ends of the sublists, so marking a node splits the sublist, unmarking joins it to the next, and by comparing the marked ancestor we can check whether two nodes are in the same sublist (Mehlhorn et al. 1988).

For this problem we can again use the partition of the given tree into paths as well as the compressed tree, and represent the paths by search trees with the depth of the nodes as keys. We subdivide the paths at the marked vertices, splitting the trees at these points and joining them together again when the vertices become unmarked. Then each path in the compressed tree is a union of subpaths, of which all but possibly the highest have a marked vertex as apex. So to find the nearest marked ancestor, we have to traverse at most $O(\log n)$ paths whose apex is not marked and one whose apex is marked, each time taking $O(\log n)$ in the search-tree representation of the paths to reach the apex. This gives an $O((\log n)^2)$ query time, with $O(\log n)$ time per mark or unmark operation, which is just a split or join of search trees. This structure also supports the general link of trees, as earlier, by updating the path decomposition, in $O((\log n)^2)$ time. The structure in Alstrup et al. (1998) supports mark, unmark, and marked_ancestor in time $O(\frac{\log n}{\log \log n})$, but it needs a stronger computation model; they also proved a matching lower bound.

6.5 Maintaining a Linear Order

The problem of maintaining a linear order under insertions and deletions has been discussed in a number of papers under the description of maintaing order in a list. This might be misleading because the structure we are implementing is not necessarily a linked list; the underlying abstract model is a set with a linear order, which can be visualized by a list. The operation we want to support is the comparison in the linear order: is element x smaller (to the left in the list) than element y? The set changes by insertion of new elements, and possibly also by deletion, where the position of a new element is identified by its immediate neighbor in the linear order. The elements are identified by fingers. So we want to support the following operations:

- insert (x, y) : Inserts x as immediate smaller neighbor of y and returns a finger to x.
- delete (x) : Deletes element x.
- compare (x, y) : Decides whether x is smaller than y in the current linear order.

This problem would be easy if the elements came with a key and the order was the order of the keys. Then we needed just a key comparison to check the order relation. Our problem is that we have to assign these keys based on the neighbor information at the insertion time. If the keys were real numbers, this would again be easy, assigning each element on insertion the average of the keys of its neighbors. But in a reasonable computation model, we can only assume integers here, and our integers are bounded in size. Certainly, our problem size n must be in the range of admissible integers and perhaps even n^2, but not much more. So we cannot just start with 2^n, which would allow us to insert n times in the middle of the interval of the new element's neighbors.

There is a simple solution that does not need any assignment of key values, but instead uses a balanced search tree. If the elements are the leaves of the search tree, we can compare two elements in the left-to-right order of the leaves by going the paths up to the root and checking the order in which the paths enter their first common vertex. If the nodes carry depth information, this is easily realized and takes time $O(\log n)$ for a comparison, as well as for any insertion or deletion. We can even reduce the update time to $O(1)$ using a tree that allows constant time update at a known location. So the simple search tree–based solution has the following performance:

Theorem. Using a balanced search tree that allows constant time update at a known location, we can maintain a linear order with $O(1)$ worst-case time of insert and delete and $O(\log n)$ worst-case time of compare.

If we had key values, we could perform the comparison in $O(1)$ time. Dietz (1982) used the tree to construct the key values. If we use an (a, b)-tree or any tree with all leaves at the same depth and nodes of degree at most b, we can label the outgoing edges of any interior node in their natural order by $1, \ldots, b$ (at most, perhaps fewer). Then the sequence of edge labels along the path from the root to a node gives a key value for the node, written in base b, that is compatible with the natural order of the leaves. The problem with this is that when we change a node, we need to relabel all the leaves in its subtree. Dietz used a modified $(2, 3)$-tree to obtain an amortized $O(\log n)$ bound for the time of relabeling: any sequence of n insertions on an initially empty tree takes $O(n \log n)$ time. One can use instead a weight-balanced tree; then one can reuse the property that between two rebalancings in the same node, a positive fraction of the leaves in its subtree has been changed, which allows to amortize the relabeling of that subtree over those node updates. But in the weight-balanced tree, not all leaves are at the same depth, so one needs a different labeling scheme (Tsakalidis 1984). Both solutions give an $O(\log n)$ amortized update time and an $O(1)$ worst-case comparison time.

In that first paper (Dietz 1982), this construction is then iterated; if the lower levels of the tree are grouped in copies of the structure, then any query first tests whether the elements are in the same lower-level structure and compares them there if possible, else it goes up to the next higher-level structure and compares there. For this we need as many elementary comparisons as there are levels of the structure, but most inserts need to be performed only on the low-level structures and propagate up only when the lower-level structures overflow. Using $\log^*(n)$ levels, Dietz obtained an $O(\log^*(n))$ worst-case query time and an $O(\log^*(n))$ amortized insertion time. Here $\log^*$ is the iterated logarithm function defined by the recursion $\log^*(n) = 1 + \log^*(\log n)$, which grows extremely slow, but still faster than the Ackermann function (see Appendix 10.5).

But we can avoid the multiple levels. Two are sufficient if we use a different method for the lower-level structure. This is possible if the individual sets in the lower-level structure are small, less than $\log n$. On these small sets, we can assign integer key values less than n, giving in each insertion as key the average of the neighboring keys. If we initially start with the keys 0 and 2^k, we can perform k such averaging steps before we get a difference less than 1. So for sets of size $\lfloor \log n \rfloor$, we can assign integer keys bounded by n in time $O(1)$ per insertion and $O(1)$ per key comparison. We now cut the entire set of n elements into $O(\frac{n}{\log n})$ groups of consecutive elements, each group of size at most $\lfloor \log n \rfloor$, and use the numbering scheme within each group and a structure with $O(1)$ comparisons and amortized $O(\log n)$ insertion to represent the order relation between the groups. Then each comparison takes $O(1)$: one comparison between the groups and one comparison within the group. And each insertion takes an amortized $O(1)$ time: if the insertion is possible in the group, it is performed there in $O(1)$ time; else the group overflows and has to be split into two groups, which are renumbered in $O(\log n)$ time, and the new group is inserted in the structure on the groups, in $O(\log n)$ amortized time, but it needs $\log n$ insertions to make a new group overflow. This argument with a different top-level structure was introduced by Tsakalidis (1984) and used again, with a different top-level structure that avoids explicit use of trees, in Dietz and Sleator (1987),[6] and again with yet another top-level structure in Bender et al. (2002).[7] A minor difficulty is that in the lower-level numbering we assumed n to be known in the assignment of the initial numbers; but as we have to rebuild the lists anyway, we can additionally rebuild them whenever n passes another power of two; this gives only $O(1)$ amortized additional work per insertion. Adding deletions on the lower level is trivial, and on the upper level depends on the structure we chose, but is possible.

Theorem. Using a two-level structure, we can maintain a linear order with $O(1)$ amortized time of `insert` and `delete` and $O(1)$ worst-case time of `compare`.

A special case of this problem that is of independent interest concerns maintaining dynamic dense sequential files. A sequential file is a set of items with a linear order, which have to be mapped on addresses in a way that preserves this order and that does not use too many addresses: only a small constant factor more than the number of items. If items are inserted or deleted, this might require renumbering, which corresponds to moving the item to a different memory address. We want to keep the number of data movements small or, if the addresses are grouped in disk blocks, keep the number of block changes small. An important difference to our previous problem is that here the order has to be encoded in a single integer key and the range of available keys is small. This problem was studied by Willard (1982, 1986, 1992), who gave an amortized $O((\log n)^2)$ algorithm and then a complicated deamortization of it; but his model is not quite compatible because he assumes the maximum size to be given in advance. The deamortized version was used with some further

---

[6] With a cryptic explanation of the lower-level numbering idea. It is really described only in the technical report D.D. Sleator and P.F. Dietz: Two Algorithms for Maintaining Order in a List, CMU-CS-88-113, Carnegie-Mellon University, September 1988, which dates after Dietz and Sleator (1987).

[7] Which references Dietz and Sleator (1987) for the details of the lower-level structure.

complications, running the algorithm in small steps to distribute the time of an update and adding multiple versions to the underlying structures, because queries must be answered consistently on partially performed updates in Dietz and Sleator (1987) to deamortize their structure for maintaining a linear order with $O(1)$ update and query time. Another deamortization was announced in Bender et al. (2002).[8]

---

[8] Which postpones the details to the full version.

7

Data Structure Transformations

Up to now we have described many specific data structures. There are also some general methods that add some additional capabilities or properties to a given data structure. Without any further knowledge about the structure, there is not much we can do, so in each case we need some further assumptions about the operation supported by the structure or its implementation. The two well-studied problems here are how to make a static structure dynamic and how to allow queries in old states of a dynamic data structure.

7.1 Making Structures Dynamic

Several of the structures we have discussed were static structures, like the interval trees: they are built once and then allow queries, but no changes of the underlying data. To make them dynamic, we want to allow changes in the underlying data. In this generality, there is not much we can do, but with some further assumptions, there are efficient construction methods that take the static data structure as a black box, which is used to build the new dynamic structure.

The most important such class is the *decomposable searching problems*. Here, the underlying abstract object is some set X, and in our queries we wish to evaluate some function $f(X, \text{query})$, and this function has the property that for any partition $X = X_1 \cup X_2$, the function value $f(X, \text{query})$ can be constructed from $f(X_1, \text{query})$ and $f(X_2, \text{query})$. If the function value is not a constant-size object, we also need that this construction happens in constant time. This is a property of the underlying abstract problem, and the transformation can then be applied to any structure that solves it.

The one-dimensional dual-range searching, that is, given a set of intervals, list for a query value all intervals that contain this value, is just one such problem; for that the interval trees are one static solution to which we can apply the methods developed in this section to obtain a dynamic solution. The segment trees are a different static solution to this problem, to which we could also apply this methods, but we already saw in Section 6.3 a different method to make segment trees dynamic.

There are many problems with this property. The nearest-neighbor problem, to find for a given query point the nearest point in a set, is perhaps the most interesting, but finding an element of given key (dictionary), or finding the smallest element (heap), or the sum of elements, or range searching, are all of this type. But there are also problems that do not fit in this class; the problems on root-oriented trees discussed in Section 6.4 do not even have a set as underlying object; and finding the smallest element in a set is decomposable, but finding the second-smallest element, or the median, is not. Thus it is a restricted, but important class.

The notion of decomposable search problems, and the idea of a static-to-dynamic transformation, goes back to Bentley (1979). Initially, the structures allowed only insertions and had only amortized bounds, but soon deletions were added; bounds were made worst case, and trade-offs between query time, insertion time, and deletion time were introduced (Bentley and Saxe 1980; van Leeuwen and Wood 1980a; Mehlhorn and Overmars 1981; Overmars and van Leeuwen 1981a, b; Edelsbrunner and Overmars 1985; Rao, Vaishnavi, and Iyengar 1988). The canonical reference to all methods of dynamization is the monograph by Overmars (1983).

The underlying idea is always that the current set is partitioned in a number of blocks $X = X_1 \cup \cdots \cup X_m$. Each block is stored by one static structure; queries are answered by querying each of these static structures and reconstructing the answer for the entire set, and updates are performed by rebuilding one or several blocks. The differences between the methods are the size restrictions for the blocks and the details of the rebuilding policy.

The original method in Bentley (1979) uses only blocks whose size is a power of two, and only one block of each size. So if the underlying set X has n elements, then the blocks X_i correspond to 1s in the binary expansion of n. Thus there are at most $\log n$ blocks. For each query on X we perform at most $\log n$ queries on the X_i, so the query time increases by at most the factor $\log n$. To insert a new element, a block of size 1, we create a block of size 1 and then perform binary addition on the blocks until each block size exists at most once. To add two blocks of the same size, the structures are taken apart to recover the elements and then one new structure is built.

This gives a bad worst-case complexity because we might have to rebuild everything into one structure; but the structure of size 2^i is rebuilt only when the ith bit of n changes, which is every 2^{i-1}th step. If preproc(k) is the time to build a static structure of size k, then the total time of the first n inserts is

$$\sum_{i=0}^{\lfloor \log n \rfloor} \frac{n}{2^i} \operatorname{preproc}(2^i).$$

Thus the amortized insertion time in a set of n elements is

$$\operatorname{ins}(n) = \sum_{i=0}^{\lfloor \log n \rfloor} \frac{\operatorname{preproc}(2^i)}{2^i} = \begin{cases} O(\log n) & \text{if } \operatorname{preproc}(n) = O(n) \\ O((\log n)^{c+1}) & \text{if } \operatorname{preproc}(n) = O(n(\log n)^c) \\ O(n^\varepsilon) & \text{if } \operatorname{preproc}(n) = O(n^{1+\varepsilon}). \end{cases}$$

Some further fine-tuning by using other systems of block sizes is possible, and in many instances the rebuilding of a block with an additional element, or the merging of two blocks, is slightly easier than building the static structure from scratch because one can reuse some order information. Many details were discussed in Bentley and Saxe (1980); this frequently allows to gain a $\log n$ factor. The systems of block sizes and their implications for the bounds were further analyzed in Overmars and van Leeuwen (1981a) and Mehlhorn and Overmars (1981). But we can summarize the most important special case of the basic method.

Theorem. Given a static structure for a decomposable searching problem that can be built in time $O(n(\log n)^c)$ and that answers queries in time $O(\log n)$ for an n-element set, the exponential-blocks transformation gives a structure for the same problem that supports insertion in amortized $O((\log n)^{c+1})$ time and queries in worst-case $O((\log n)^2)$ time.

If we apply this to the interval tree structure, which can be built in $O(n \log n)$ time, we get a structure that supports insertions and queries in $O((\log n)^2)$ time, where the insertion bound is only amortized.

This method is not useful for deletion; if we delete an element from the largest block, we have to rebuild everything, so we can easily construct a sequence of alternating `insert` and `delete` operations, in which each time the entire structure has to be rebuilt.

A method that also supports deletion partitions the set in $\Theta(\sqrt{n})$ blocks of size $O(\sqrt{n})$ and uses fingers or an additional search tree or other dictionary to keep track of the information about in which block each element is stored (van Leeuwen and Wood 1980a). Then for each insert or delete, we have to touch only one block, using $O(\operatorname{preproc}(\sqrt{n}))$ time, and for each query, we have to perform $O(\sqrt{n})$ queries in the blocks of size $O(\sqrt{n})$.

This is a lot worse than the previous structure: if the static structure had preprocessing time $O(n(\log n)^c)$ and query time $O(\log n)$, then the first dynamic structure has update time $O((\log n)^{c+1})$ and query time $O((\log n)^2)$, whereas the second dynamic structure has update time $O(\sqrt{n}(\log n)^c)$ and query time $O(\sqrt{n}\log n)$, but in the first structure updates were only insertions and the time was amortized, whereas in the second structure we have both insertions and deletions, and the time is worst case.

But this is about best possible if we can use our static structure only this way, by rebuilding and querying (Bentley and Saxe 1980). Because any query has to be performed on all blocks, to achieve a query time $O(\sqrt{n})$ we may have at most $O(\sqrt{n})$ blocks, so the largest of the blocks has size at least $\Omega(\sqrt{n})$. An adversary that alternatingly inserts an element and deletes an element from the currently largest block forces each delete to rebuild a block of size $\Omega(\sqrt{n})$. Thus, although there are some trade-offs between the query time and the update time, and a $\log n$ factor that can be reduced, we cannot get update and query time below $\Omega(\sqrt{n})$ in this model. We again summarize the performance in the most important special case.

Theorem. Given a static structure for a decomposable searching problem that can be built in time $O(n(\log n)^c)$ and that answers queries in time $O(\log n)$ for an n-element set, the $\sqrt{n}$-blocks transformation gives a structure for the same problem that supports insertion and deletion in $O(\sqrt{n}(\log n)^c)$ time and queries in $O(\sqrt{n}\log n)$ time, all times worst case.

If we want a better performance in a structure that supports deletion, we need more information about the structure. A useful property here is that the static structure supports "weak deletion" (Overmars and van Leeuwen 1981b; Overmars 1981b). A weak deletion deletes the element, so that the queries are answered correctly, but the time bound for subsequent queries and weak deletions does not decrease. The prototype of this situation is the deletion without rebalancing in search trees: the element is deleted, but even though the number of items in the tree decreased, the height, and by this the time for later tree operations, does not decrease. Supporting weak deletions is a property of the static structure, not of the underlying problem.

If we combine the weak deletion with the exponential-blocks idea, we get the following structure: The current set is partitioned into blocks, where each block has a nominal size and an actual size. The nominal size is a power of 2, with each power occurring at most once. The actual size of a block with nominal size 2^i is between $2^{i-1} + 1$ and 2^i. The operations then work as follows:

- To delete an element, we find its block and perform a weak deletion, decreasing the actual size. If by this the actual size of the block becomes

2^{i-1}, we check whether there is a block of nominal size 2^{i-1}; if there is none, we rebuild the block of actual size 2^{i-1} as block of nominal size 2^{i-1}. Else, we rebuild the block of actual size 2^{i-1} together with the elements of the block of nominal size 2^{i-1} as block of nominal size 2^i.

– To insert an element, we create a block of size 1 and perform the binary addition of the blocks, based on their nominal size.

– To query, we perform the query for each block.

With this method, we get again only amortized bounds. The amortized analysis is slightly more complicated. We have to keep track of two potentials. The deletion potential is the sum over all blocks of the difference between the nominal and actual size. Each time we perform a weak deletion, it increases by 1 and an insertion does not change it. If we rebuild a block of size 2^i as a result of a deletion, the deletion potential decreases by 2^{i-1}. So the decrease in potential is proportional to the size of the structure we rebuild. So if the time of this rebuilding is preproc(2^i), then we can amortize the cost over 2^i weak deletions to get an amortized deletion cost of $\frac{1}{2^i}$ preproc(2^i) $\leq \frac{\text{preproc}(n)}{n}$ plus the cost of the weak deletion.

For the analysis of the insertion, we give a block of nominal size 2^i a weight of $(\lceil \log n \rceil - i)2^{i-1}$ and use as insertion potential the sum of the weights of all blocks. Here n is an upper bound for the maximum size of the underlying set over the sequence of operations, so $i \leq \lceil \log n \rceil$ and all the weights are positive. Then during the insertion, we create a new block of size $1 = 2^0$, increasing the potential by $\lceil \log n \rceil$, and then, if there are now two blocks of size 2^0, we destroy two blocks of size 2^0 and one each of size 2^1 up to 2^{i-1}, and build a new block of size 2^i. By this, we change the potential by

$$-2\lceil \log n \rceil - \sum_{j=1}^{i-1}(\lceil \log n \rceil - j)2^{j-1} + (\lceil \log n \rceil - i)2^{i-1}$$

$$= \left(\sum_{j=1}^{i-1} j2^{j-1} \right) - i2^{i-1} = \left((i-2)2^{i-1} + 1 \right) - i2^{i-1} = -2^{i+1} + 1,$$

so the potential decreases by an amount proportional to the size of the block we build. Only insertions increase the potential by $\lceil \log n \rceil$; deletions can only decrease the nominal size of a block, and by this its weight and the potential. Thus, we get for insertions a set of size at most n and amortized complexity of $(\log n)\frac{\text{preproc}(n)}{n}$. We again summarize the performance of this structure.

Theorem. Given a static structure for a decomposable searching problem that can be built in time preproc(n) and that supports weak deletion in time weakdel(n), and answers queries in time query(n) for an n-element set, the exponential-blocks transformation with weak deletion gives a structure for the same problem that supports insertion in amortized $O((\log n)\frac{\text{preproc}(n)}{n})$ time, deletions in amortized $O(\text{weakdel}(n) + \frac{\text{preproc}(n)}{n})$ time, and queries in worst-case $O(\log n \, \text{query}(n))$ time.

Again some further refinements to this basic scheme are possible. One can remove the amortization from the deletions by concurrent rebuilding of shadow copies, but this requires further access to the internal structure of the rebuilding method, so that instead of being executed once in full during a delete operation, it is executed in small fragments over a sequence of delete operations (Overmars and van Leeuwen 1981b).

The methods discussed up to now were based on complete rebuilding of the static structure, which was just a black box, supporting some operations. With more information, we can do better. One class of problems where we get an outline for building the dynamic structure out of lower-level black boxes are the *order-decomposable problems* discussed by Overmars (1981a, 1983) as an abstraction of divide-and-conquer algorithms. A problem is order de-composable if the underlying abstract object is some set X, and we wish to evaluate some function $f(X)$ with the property that the elements of the set can be ordered $X = \{x_1, \ldots, x_n\}$ in such a way that $f(X)$ can be computed from $f(\{x_1, \ldots, x_i\})$ and $f(\{x_{i+1}, \ldots, x_n\})$. Note that, different from the de-composable searching problems, the function f does not have any additional parameters given by the query. So the static case is not a structure that answers queries, but an algorithm that once computes $f(X)$, and we want to update that function value under changes of the underlying set.

The strategy here is to maintain a balanced search tree on the underlying set, with the elements in the leaves in that order that allows decomposition. Then each interior node corresponds to the subset of all leaves in its subtree, which is an interval $\{x_i, x_{i+1}, \ldots, x_j\}$ in that order, and in each interior node we store the function value $f(\{x_i, \ldots, x_j\})$ for that set. For a query, we just read the function value stored in the root. To update, we insert or delete a leaf and then go the path up to the root, rebalancing and recomputing the function value in each node along the way.

Suppose computing $f(A \cup B)$ from $f(A)$ and $f(B)$, where A and B are consecutive intervals in the decomposition order, takes at most merge($|A \cup B|$) time. Then the time for an insert or delete is $O(\sum_{i=1}^{m} \text{merge}(n_i))$, where $(n_i)_{i=1}^{m}$ are the sizes of the subtrees below the nodes for which the function had to be recomputed. These are the nodes along the path to the root, and for each node possibly the other lower neighbor, which might have changed by a rotation. That lower neighbor has a smaller subtree, so we really need to bound only the sizes of the subtrees along the path from the leaf to the root. This is especially convenient if we choose a weight-balanced tree, as described in Section 3.2, as underlying balanced tree. In the weight-balanced tree, a node whose subtree has k leaves has lower neighbors whose subtrees contain at most $(1 - \alpha)k$ leaves. So the size of the subtrees along a path from the root to a leaf decreases at least geometrically. Thus the time for an update in a tree with n leaves is $O\left(\sum_{i=0}^{O(\log n)} \text{merge}\left((1 - \alpha)^i n\right)\right)$. We additionally need to find the correct place in the decomposition order before we can start to insert or delete, but that can usually be done by binary search in $O(\log n)$.

But there is a nonobvious problem with this nice technique in case the function we wish to compute has a value that is not of constant size. An important example, for which the technique was used in Overmars and van Leeuwen (1980) before it was stated in the more abstract setting, is the dynamic convex hull computation of a set of points in the plane with insertions and deletions. If the points are ordered according to their first coordinate, then it is, in principle, possible to merge the convex hulls of two sets with separated first coordinates in time $O(\log n)$, although this also requires a nontrivial representation of the convex hulls. But if we perform this merging, we destroy the individual structures we merge, so we cannot reuse them in the next update. The obvious alternative, copying the structure, requires time proportional to the size of the structure, so in the convex hull example it increases the complexity of merging from $O(\log n)$ to $\Theta(n)$, but in that time we could have computed the convex hull of a sorted set anyway. To make use of the technique, we need a second function, which is the inverse of the merging function: it splits the structure in the node and restores the structures in its lower neighbors. Then for any update, we perform the splits while going down from the root to the leaf where we perform the update and then after the update we go up again and merge along the way. For each rotation, we might have to perform yet another split merge pair. So the update time is

$$
\sum_{i=0}^{O(\log n)} \text{merge}\left((1 - \alpha)^i n\right) = \begin{cases} O(\log n) & \text{if merge}(n) = O(1) \\ O((\log n)^{c+1}) & \text{if merge}(n) = O((\log n)^c) \\ O(n^\varepsilon) & \text{if merge}(n) = O(n^\varepsilon), \end{cases}
$$

if either the merge is nondestructive or there is a split inverting the merge that runs with the same time bound. We summarize again the performance of this structure in its most important special case.

Theorem. Given an order-decomposable problem for which we can find the correct place of an item in the decomposition order in $O(\log n)$, and for which we have either a nondestructive merge operation or a complementary pair of merge and split operations that work in time $O((\log n)^c)$, then we can maintain the function value for that problem under insertion and deletion in the underlying set in worst-case time $O((\log n)^{c+1})$ per update.

The fundamental restrictions of this model are the order-decomposition property, and the fact that we are looking only for a single value, not for a function depending on the query. This allows us to precompute the answer in the tree nodes. It can be extended slightly if we choose the function values itself to be functions of constant description complexity, but it is inherent to the model that, to answer a query, we have to look only at the data found in the root node. Many structures we discussed were similar to this: they are built on a balanced search tree by adding some information to the nodes. But to evaluate a query in those structures, we have to follow this search tree down and combine the information in the nodes along the path to answer the query.

There is a general dynamization method for this type of data structure which is based on partial rebuilding. The canonical reference is again the monograph by Overmars (1983), where partial rebuilding methods are studied systematically. Special instances of this were already used slightly earlier, such as Lueker and Willard (1982) for the dynamization of range counting with orthogonal range trees. The model assumption here is that we have a static structure that can be built using any underlying search tree; it adds some additional information to the nodes, and queries are answered by following a path down in the tree and combining the information in the nodes. For this structure we must have an update method that keeps this additional structure correct, so queries are still answered correctly, but it changes the tree structure only by performing basic inserts and deletes, so the tree might become unbalanced. And we need a method to rebuild entire subtrees optimally balanced.

The fundamental insight here is that if we use weight-balanced trees as underlying search trees, then large subtrees will become unbalanced only after many updates. In Section 3.2, we had a theorem that there is an $\varepsilon > 0$ such that between one rebalancing of the subtree below a fixed node and the next rebalancing, at least an ε-fraction of the leaves of that subtree have been inserted or deleted. This can be used for an amortized complexity bound for the updates. Each update of a leaf node contributes unit cost to each subtree that contains it, that is, to each of the $O(\log n)$ nodes on the path from the root to that leaf node. If we rebuild a subtree with k leaves, then there are εk updates that contributed to it. If the cost of rebuilding of a subtree with

k leaves is rebuild(k), then we can amortize this cost over these updates and get an amortized cost of rebuilding per update of $O(\frac{\log n}{k}$ rebuild(k)), which is $O(\frac{\log n}{n}$ rebuild(n)). In addition to this, we of course need the time to perform the basic insert or delete and adjust the structure; this is some time basic_update(n), which is at least $\Omega(\log n)$ to perform the update of the tree, but it might be larger because the additional information in the nodes also needs to be updated. The query time does not change by these updates because we always maintain a correct weight-balanced tree. We again summarize the performance of this method.

Theorem. Given a static data structure, which consists of a balanced search tree with additional node information and that allows basic inserts and deletes without rebalancing in a tree with n leaves in time basic_update(n), and optimal rebuilds of a subtree with k leaves in time rebuild(k), we can keep this tree balanced in amortized time per insert or delete

$$O\left(\text{basic\_update}(n) + \frac{\log n}{n}\,\text{rebuild}(n)\right).$$

If the query time in this structure for a tree of height h is query(h), we maintain a worst-case query time query($\log n$).

In Section 3.8 we have already used the partial rebuilding technique for rebalancing in search trees with a different balance criterion and amortized analysis, but they can also be viewed as the simplest special case of this method.

Another class of problems allowing some dynamization are the two-variable minimization problems studied by Dobkin and Suri (1991) and Eppstein (1995). Here the underlying model is that we have a function $f(x, y)$ and want to maintain the minimum over all pairs from a cartesian product $\min\{f(x, y) \mid x \in X, y \in Y\}$ under insertions and deletions in the sets X and Y. Without additional information on f, there is no hope for a non-trivial algorithm: when we insert a new point x^{new} in X, we would have to evaluate $f(x^{\text{new}}, y)$ for all $y \in Y$. The additional structure we need is a dynamic structure that, for a set Y and a query point x^{query}, finds the $y \in Y$ for which $f(x^{\text{query}}, y)$ is minimal. Then maintaining the minimum, if only insertions are allowed, is trivial: we just need to check whether the new point generates a smaller minimum than the previous minimizing pair. But that approach does not support deletions. Eppstein (1995) found a method that maintains the two-variable minimum under insertions and deletions, with an amortized factor $\log n$ overhead on the complexity of the underlying minimum-query structure for insertions and an amortized $(\log n)^2$ overhead for deletions.

7.2 Making Structures Persistent

A dynamic data structure changes over time, and sometimes it is useful if we can access old versions of it. Besides the obvious interpretation of answering queries about the past, this is useful as a tool for geometric algorithms that perform a sweep; in such algorithms one typically has a structure that keeps track of the state on the current position of the sweepline, but sometimes we have to access regions we have already passed over. Another obvious application is revision control and the implementation of the "undo" command in editors (Myers 1984; Fraser and Myers 1987; Dannenberg 1990), multiple file versions (Burton, Huntbach, and Kollias 1985; Burton et al. 1990), and error recovery (Mullin 1981a). One can construct special-purpose structures for such applications, but the success in finding general techniques for dynamization motivated a search for similar techniques to solve this problem.

The question how to access past versions of a dynamic data structure was first studied by Dobkin and Munro[1] and Overmars.[2] The first papers (Dobkin and Munro 1985; Chazelle 1985) were motivated by the geometric applications, which allowed them to make the additional assumption that the underlying universe was known in advance, which is reasonable for sweep algorithms, where we know the entire set even if it has not been passed over by the sweepline. Indeed, the sequence in which the objects are passed by the sweepline is known in advance, so for that application it is only the question of preprocessing the set so that queries for various positions of the sweepline can be answered. For search trees, the problem of queries in the past was also discussed in Field (1987).

The main progress was the paper by Driscoll et al. (1989), in which general techniques were discussed that transform a given dynamic data structure into a dynamic data structure allowing access to earlier versions. They define several grades of access. The most natural persistence, which they called "partial persistence," allows queries to previous versions. There is a current version to which the next update will be applied to generate a new current version, but

---

[1] In a paper in FOCS 1980, whose journal version appeared only five years later (Dobkin and Munro 1985).

[2] In two preprints, M.H. Overmars: Searching in the Past I, II, Rijksuniversiteit Utrecht preprints RUU-CS-81-7 and RUU-CS-81-9, April and May 1981, which are amazingly still available online.

we can also query old versions, which could be identified by timestamps or version numbers.

They also studied a more general scheme they called "full persistence," in which past versions can also be changed, giving rise to a version tree without any special current version. Here even identifying the version one wishes to reference is nontrivial; for this they produced a numbering of the versions compatible with the partial order of the version tree. Even more general, but applicable only to structures that support a join operation, is the "confluent persistence" studied first for double-ended queues (Driscoll, Sleator, and Tarjan 1994; Buchsbaum and Tarjan 1995; Kaplan, Okasaki, and Tarjan 2000) and then in general in Fiat and Kaplan (2003); in a confluently persistent structure, one may also join different versions. But these stronger variants of persistence seem only of theoretical interest.

More important, but much less deep, is a transformation that allows backtracking, that is, setting the current version back to an old version and discarding all changes since then. The use of a stack for old versions predates all persistence considerations.

Again, as in the dynamization of data structures, we need some information on the underlying structure. Some general models similar to those discussed for the dynamization were discussed by Overmars.[3] If the structure is just a black box allowing some operations, we can copy that black box to preserve an old state or keep a list of performed update operations that we can execute again to reconstruct a state. These two methods can be mixed: if we have a structure of size at most n with query time query(n) and update time update(n), if we copy the structure after every kth update, we get an amortized update cost of $O(\frac{n}{k} + \text{update}(n))$; and for any query we first copy the nearest saved state and perform the at most $k - 1$ updates on it, before finally executing the query on the reconstructed state. This gives a query time of $O(n + k\,\text{update}(n) + \text{query}(n))$. The largest component here is the time $O(n)$ for the initial copying of the structure before we can apply the updates. This can be avoided if the update operations come in inverse pairs, like insertion and deletion. Then for any query, we take the nearest saved state, perform the at most $k - 1$ updates on it, perform the query, and then the sequence of inverse updates to recover the saved state. This gives a query time $O(k\,\text{update}(n) + \text{query}(n))$. The choice of k as a function of n allows trade-offs between update and query time, but without further knowledge of the structure, we cannot get update and query simultaneously below $O(\sqrt{n})$.

---

[3] In the preprint, M.H. Overmars: Searching in the Past II, Rijksuniversiteit Utrecht preprint RUU-CS-81-9, May 1981.

The big progress achieved in Driscoll et al. (1989) are two structures that work in the pointer-machine model, the first of which works on any structure in the pointer-machine model, but carries an $O(\log n)$ factor worst-case overhead, and the second, which has only an $O(1)$ amortized overhead, but requires that the nodes in the pointer structure have bounded indegree. The amortized $O(1)$ of the second structure was improved to $O(1)$ worst case in Dietz and Raman (1991) and Brodal (1996b), but with the same indegree condition. That indegree restriction is satisfied, for example, for all search trees, but it is not satisfied for the union-find structure. The leftist heap satisfies that restriction, while Brodal's heap does not, so the indegree property is a nontrivial restriction.

The first transformation, called the "fat nodes" method, replaces each node of the pointer-based structure by a search tree for the correct version of the node, using the query time as key. Each time the underlying structure is modified, any "fat" node whose content is modified just receives a new version entry in its search tree; and newly created nodes contain new search trees, initially with one version only. Thus, any query is executed on a simulation of the underlying structure, where finding the value of some field of a node that is correct for the query time requires a query in a search tree, so $O(\log n)$ time per elementary operation in the underlying structure, giving an $O(\log n)$ factor increase of the query time. For updates, the same argument holds – we are simulating the underlying structure, but we can do better than the $O(\log n)$ time bound per simulation step. Because in the update, all accesses and changes happen at the maximum key end of the search tree, we can use a tree that supports insert and find at the end in constant time, as does a finger tree with constant update time. By this, we get a simulation of the underlying structure with $O(1)$ time per simulated step. This gives the following performance:

Theorem. Any dynamic structure in the pointer-machine model that supports queries in time query(n) and updates in time update(n) on a set with n elements can be made persistent, allowing queries to past versions, with a query time $O(\log n \text{ query}(n))$ for past versions, $O(\text{query}(n))$ for the current version, and update time $O(\text{update}(n))$, using the "fat nodes" method combined with a search tree that allows constant-time queries and updates at the maximum end.

If we want to add backtracking to our structure, we need to be able to go back to a previous version in time and discard all updates since then. We can do this for any pointer-based structure, again using fat nodes, which this time just contain a stack of values together with their version numbers. Each time we perform an update, we push a new value on the stack of all nodes we change, and each time we perform a query, we use the top value of the stack. Both of these changes generate only a constant-factor overhead for each update or query operation. To perform a backtrack operation, we need to pop from each stack all the values of discarded versions, so we need a list of all fat nodes. The backtrack time can be very long in the worst case if we return to the beginning and have to clear all stacks. But the amortized complexity of the backtrack operation is constant, hidden by the update operations, because each item removed from a stack by the backtrack operation was previously put there by an update operation.

Theorem. Any dynamic structure in the pointer-machine model that supports queries in time query(n) and updates in time update(n) on a set with n elements can be made to support backtracking, using stacks for "fat nodes," with a query time $O(\text{query}(n))$, update time $O(\text{update}(n))$, and backtrack time amortized $O(1)$, with a sequence of a updates, b queries, and c backtracks, starting on an initially empty set, taking $O(a\,\text{update}(a) + b\,\text{query}(a) + c)$.

To make the amortized complexity of backtracking worst case, we could use splittable search trees in all fat nodes, but then an $O(\log n)$ factor overhead applies to the update and query times.

Because in each fat node we have a search tree over essentially the same object, a set of version dates, we are performing very similar searches again and again; this suggests to try to connect the search trees in such a way that the result of the search in the previous node can be reused to find the correct version in the current node. This is again a form of the fractional cascading idea, but the problem is that we do not have the same version dates in each node, and so it is not really the same search. If in the underlying structure the update time is $O(\log n)$, then in each update we add a new version date only to $O(\log n)$ of the $\Omega(n)$ nodes, so the set of all version dates is much larger than the sets we encounter in the individual nodes.

The idea of the second structure of Driscoll et al. (1989), called "node copying method," is to replace the search tree in each fat node by a list of constant-sized nodes, each holding only a few versions and linked to the nodes with the corresponding versions in the lists in neighboring fat nodes. The problem here is that if we add a new version at time t to the last list node and it overflows, so we have to create a new list node, then we have to update all the incoming pointers to this new node. In the lists of all fat nodes that point to the fat node we just updated, we have to add a new version for this time t, pointing to the new node. This can cause those lists themselves to overflow and force to create new nodes, so this creation of new nodes propagates through the structure and stops only in those places where the node still has room for a new version. By making the nodes large enough, it finally stops; in Driscoll et al. (1989) an amortized $O(1)$ bound for the number of newly created nodes was shown. Using a good strategy when to create a new node, occasionally also creating new nodes before forced to do so, this was reduced to worst-case $O(1)$ new nodes per update step by Brodal (1996b) following Dietz and Raman (1991). But all this is possible only if the indegree of each node in the underlying structure is bounded because we have to propagate the creation of new versions along all incoming edges. The necessary number of versions per list node depends on this indegree and is quite large. To summarize the performance of this transformation we have the following:

Theorem. Any dynamic structure in the pointer-machine model that has bounded indegree and that supports queries in time query(n) and updates in time update(n) on a set with n elements can be made persistent, allowing queries to past versions with a query time $O(\text{query}(n))$ and update time $O(\text{update}(n))$ using the "node copying" method combined with Brodal's node copying strategy.

A property related to persistence is the retroactivity proposed in Demaine, Iacono, and Langerman (2004); they call a structure retroactive if it allows the change of updates in the past while keeping all the updates that followed the changed update. A fully persistent structure would allow the change in the past, starting a new branch in the version tree, but would not include the later updates in the branch. The concept of retroactivity is motivated by the idea that one wants to correct an erroneous update in the past without having to perform all the later updates again; but this involves many conceptual problems because the later updates might depend on the earlier updates and queries. So, unlike persistence, there is no general technique for adding retroactivity to a data structure.

8

Data Structures for Strings

Up to now we always assumed that the data items are of constant size, and key values can be compared in constant time, so essentially that they are numbers. A very important class of objects for which these assumptions fail are strings. In real applications, text processing is more important than the processing of numbers, and text fragments have a length; they are not elementary objects that the computer can process in a single step. So we need different structures for strings than for numeric keys; especially the balanced binary search trees, our most useful previous tool, require a key comparison in each node and are quite inefficient as dictionary structure for strings. Also, for strings we will ask different questions. Even though strings can be ordered lexicographically, this order does not reflect the similarity of strings, for two strings that differ in the first character only are closer related than two strings that differ from the third to the tenth character. Thus, range searching makes little sense for strings.

The concept of strings is not entirely uniform and therefore requires some attention. We have an underlying alphabet A, for example, the ASCII codes, and strings are sequences of characters from this alphabet. But for use in the computer, we need an important further information: how to recognize where the string ends. There are two solutions for this: we can have an explicit termination character, which is added at the end of each string, but may not occur within the string, or we can store together with each string its length. The first solution is the ' \0 '-terminated strings used in the C language, and the other model is followed, for example, in the Pascal language and its descendants.[1] The use of the special termination character ' \0 ' has a

---

[1] Some languages have a different string concept in which higher-level operations such as deleting an interval from a string are considered elementary operations (Housden 1975). Current examples of this are the C++ and Java string classes. But these are not constant-time operations, so these systems are not suitable for the type of efficient operation that we study.

number of advantages in simplifying code, but it has the disadvantage of having one reserved character in the alphabet that may not occur in strings. If the strings are really fragments of text, this is no problem; there are many nonprintable ASCII codes that should never occur in a text and ' \0 ' (ASCII code 0) is just one of them. But there are also many applications in which the strings do not represent text, but, for example, machine instructions, and in such applications we cannot assume that the strings do not contain this reserved character. In the following we will use ' \0 ' -terminated strings in our code examples, but one must be aware of the limitation of this model and the possible alternative.

Strings, especially over a small alphabet, recently found much interest in the context of bioinformatics because a type of data obtained there in large amounts is DNA/RNA or protein sequence data, with alphabet sizes of 4 and 20, respectively. This presents challenges that motivate most of the newer papers on string data structures and algorithms. Books entirely dedicated to algorithmic problems on strings are the seminal books by Gusfield (1997) and Crochemore and Rytter (2003).

8.1 Tries and Compressed Tries

The basic tool for string data structures, similar in role to the balanced binary search tree, is called "trie," which is said to derive from "retrieval." This structure was invented by de la Briandais (1959); the first easily accessible reference, which also introduced this unfortunate name, is Fredkin (1961). The underlying idea is very simple – again a tree structure is used to store a set of strings. But in this tree, the nodes are not binary; instead, they contain potentially one outgoing edge for each possible character, so the degree is at most the alphabet size $|A|$. Each node in this tree structure corresponds to a prefix of some strings of the set; if the same prefix occurs several times, there is only one node to represent it. The root of the tree structure is the node corresponding to the empty prefix. The node corresponding to the prefix σ_1 contains for each character $a \in A$ a pointer to the node corresponding to the prefix $\sigma_1 a$ if such a node exists, that is, if there is a string $\sigma_1 a \sigma_2$ in the set.

To perform a find operation in this structure, we start in the node corresponding to the empty prefix and then read the query string, following for each read character the outgoing pointer corresponding to that character to the next node. After we read the query string, we arrived at a node corresponding to that string as prefix. If the query string is contained in the set of strings stored in

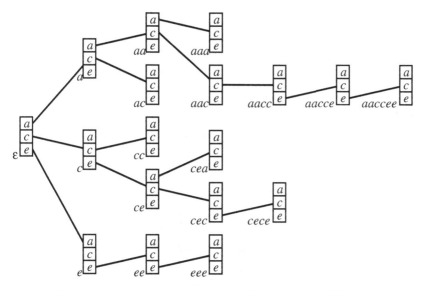

the trie, and that set is prefix-free, then this node belongs to that unique string.
And we can assume that the set of strings is prefix free if we use the model
of ' \ 0 ' -terminated strings: if the character ' \ 0 ' occurs only as termination
character in the last position of each string, then no string can be a prefix of
another string. With this assumption, we can now write the basic version of the
trie structure. Each node has the following form:

```
typedef struct trie_n_t {
                struct trie_n_t    *next[256];
          /* possibly additional information*/
                } trie_node_t;
```

We now implement the same dictionary structure that we also assumed for
the search trees: we are keeping track of a set of (key, object) pairs under
operations insert, delete, and find, but now the key is a string. We
use the next [(int) ' \ 0 '] field to hold the pointer to the object because
for ' \ 0 ' terminated strings we will never need that field to point to another
node. If we need a string model without a specific termination character, we

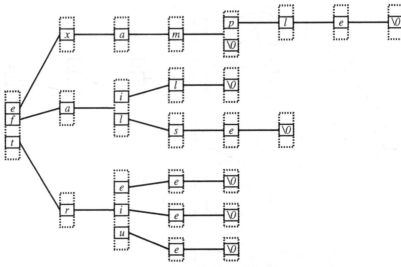

TRIE FOR THE STRINGS *exam, example, fail, false, tree, trie, true:*
IN EACH ARRAY NODE, ONLY THE USED FIELDS SHOWN

must use an extra field in the node for that. An implementation of the trie for
'\0'-terminated strings can look as follows:

```
trie_node_t *create_trie(void)
{   trie_node_t *tmp_node;
    int i;
    tmp_node = get_node();
    for( i=0; i<256; i++)
        tmp_node->next[i] = NULL;
    return( tmp_node );
}

object_t *find(trie_node_t *trie,
               char *query_string)
{   trie_node_t *tmp_node;
    char *query_next;
    tmp_node = trie; query_next = query_string;
    while(*query_next != '\0')
    {   if( tmp_node->next[(int)(*query_next)] ==
            NULL)
            return( NULL ); /* query string
            not found */
        else
        {   tmp_node =
```

```
            tmp_node->next[(int) (*query_next)];
            query_next += 1; /* move to next
            character of query */
      }
   }
   return((object_t *)
   tmp_node->next[(int)'\0']);
}

int insert(trie_node_t *trie,
           char *new_string, object_t *new_object)
{  trie_node_t *tmp_node, *new_node;
   char *query_next;
   tmp_node =  trie; query_next = new_string;
   while(*query_next != '\0')
   {   if( tmp_node->next[(int)(*query_next)] ==
          NULL)
      {   new_node = get_node();
          /* create missing node */
          for( i=0; i<256; i++)
             new_node->next[i] = NULL;
          tmp_node->next[(int)(*query_next)]
          = new_node;
      }
      /* move to next character */
      tmp_node = tmp_node->next[(int)(*query_next)];
      query_next += 1; /* move to
      next character */
   }
   if( tmp_node->next[(int)'\0'] != NULL )
      return( -1 ); /* string already exists,
      has object */
   else
      tmp_node->next[(int)'\0']
      = (trie_node_t *) new_object;
   return( 0 );
}


object_t *delete(trie_node_t *trie,
                 char *delete_string)
{  trie_node_t *tmp_node;
   object_t *tmp_object;
   char *next_char;
   int finished = 0;
```

```
create_stack();
tmp_node = trie; next_char = delete_string;
while(*next_char != '\0')
{  if( tmp_node->next[(int)(*next_char)] ==
      NULL)
      return( NULL ); /* delete_string
      does not exist */
   else
   {  tmp_node =
      tmp_node->next[(int) (*next_char)];
      next_char += 1; /* move to next
      character */
      push( tmp_node );
   }
}
tmp_object = (object_t *)
tmp_node->next[(int)'\0'];
/* remove all nodes that became unnecessary */
/* the root is not on the stack, so it is
never deleted */
while( !stack_empty() && !finished )
{  tmp_node = pop();
   tmp_node->next[(int)(*next_char)] = NULL;
   for( i=0; i<256; i++)
      finished ||= (tmp_node->next[i] != NULL );
   /* if  tmp_node is all NULL,
   it should be deleted */
   if( !finished )
   {  return_node( tmp_node );
      next_char -= 1;
   }
}
return( tmp_object );
}


void remove_trie(trie_node_t *trie)
{  trie_node_t *tmp_node;
   create_stack();
   push( trie );
   while( !stack_empty() )
   {  int i;
      tmp_node = pop();
      for( i=0; i<256; i++)
      {  if( tmp_node->next[i] != NULL
```

```
        && i != (int)'\0' )
          push( tmp_node->next[i] );
      }
      return_node( tmp_node );
    }
}
```

This structure looks very simple and extremely efficient; the one problem is the dependence on the size of the alphabet that determines the size of the nodes. In this basic implementation, each node contains 256 pointers, one for each character, and a pointer might be 4–8 bytes, so the size of each node is at least 1 kB. And, unless the strings we wish to store have very much overlap, we need approximately as many nodes as the total length of all strings together is: almost all nodes will contain only one valid pointer because almost all prefixes have only one possible continuation. So the space requirement is enormous. But even if we have unbounded space available, the alphabet size enters here in the `insert` and `delete` operations because new nodes must be initialized with NULL pointers, and when deleting nodes we must check whether they are still used. The performance of the basic trie structure given here is as follows:

Theorem. The basic trie structure stores a set of words over an alphabet A. It supports a `find` operation on a query string q in time $O(\text{length}(q))$ and `insert` and `delete` operations in time $O(|A| \text{length}(q))$. The space requirement to store n strings $w_1, \ldots, w_n$ is $O(|A| \sum_i \text{length}(w_i))$.

We can get rid of the $|A|$-dependence in the `delete` operation by using reference counts. Then all nodes that are returned to the free list are correctly filled with NULL pointers, so the `insert` operation does not need to initialize them if they are reused. But all new nodes do have to be initialized, so the $|A|$-dependence in the `insert` operation does not disappear.

There are several ways to reduce or avoid the problem of the alphabet size, and the mostly empty nodes. In each method, we trade some loss in the query time against an improvement in space and update time.

A simple method, which is most efficient exactly in those cases where the basic implementation was most wasteful, if almost all nodes are almost empty, is to replace the big nodes by linked lists of all the entries that are really used. That technique was already suggested in the first paper by de la Briandais (1959) and discussed again in Sussenguth (1963).

In the next implementation, the empty string, represented by the '\0'-character, is already contained in the empty trie when we create it. We use this as entry point to the structure because any list node must contain at least one entry, whereas in the array implementation, we could have an initial array node with only NULL pointers. Of course, we could use separate list-head nodes, but they would increase the path length.

```
typedef struct trie_n_t { char      this_char;
                struct trie_n_t   *next;
                struct trie_n_t   *list;
                /* possibly additional information*/
                        } trie_node_t;

trie_node_t *create_trie(void)
{  trie_node_t *tmp_node;
   tmp_node = get_node();
   tmp_node->next = tmp_node->list = NULL;
   tmp_node->this_char = '\0';
   return( tmp_node );
}

object_t *find(trie_node_t *trie,
                char *query_string)
{  trie_node_t *tmp_node;
   char *query_next;
   tmp_node =  trie; query_next = query_string;
   while(*query_next != '\0')
   {  while( tmp_node->this_char != *query_next )
      {  if( tmp_node->list == NULL )
            return( NULL );
            /* query string not found */
         else
            tmp_node  = tmp_node->list ;
      }
      tmp_node = tmp_node->next;
      query_next += 1;
   }
   /* reached end of query string */
   while( tmp_node->this_char != '\0' )
   {  if( tmp_node->list == NULL )
         return( NULL );
         /* query string not found */
      else
```

```
            tmp_node   = tmp_node->list ;
   }
   return( (object_t *) tmp_node->next);
}


int insert(trie_node_t *trie,
           char *new_string, object_t *new_object)
{  trie_node_t *tmp_node;
   char *query_next; int finished = 0;
   tmp_node =  trie; query_next = new_string;
   /* first go as far as possible in
   existing trie */
   while( !finished )
   {  /* follow list till matching character
      is found */
      while( tmp_node->this_char != *query_next
             &&  tmp_node->list != NULL )
         tmp_node   = tmp_node->list ;
      if( tmp_node->this_char == *query_next  )
      {  /* matching character found,
         might be last */
         if( *query_next != '\0' )
         /* not last. follow */
         {  tmp_node = tmp_node->next;
            query_next += 1;
         }
         else /* insertion not possible,
         string already exists */
            return( -1 );
      }
      else
         finished = 1;
   }
   /* left existing trie, create new branch */
   tmp_node->list = get_node();
   tmp_node = tmp_node->list;
   tmp_node->list = NULL;
   tmp_node->this_char = *query_next;
```

```
    while( *query_next != '\0')
    {   query_next += 1;
        tmp_node->next = get_node();
        tmp_node = tmp_node->next;
        tmp_node->list = NULL;
        tmp_node->this_char = *query_next;
    }
    tmp_node->next = (trie_node_t *) new_object;
    return( 0 );
}


object_t *delete(trie_node_t *trie,
                 char *delete_string)
{   trie_node_t *tmp, *tmp_prev,
                *first_del, *last_undel;
    object_t *del_object;
    char *del_next;
    if( trie->list == NULL ||
        *delete_string == '\0' )
        return( NULL ); /* delete failed:
        trie empty */
    else /* trie not empty, can start */
    {   int finished = 0; int branch = 1;
        last_undel = tmp_prev = trie;
        first_del  = tmp = trie->list;
        del_next = delete_string;
        while( !finished )
        {   while( tmp->this_char != *del_next )
            {   /* follow list to find
                matching character */
                if( tmp->list == NULL ) /* none
                found*/
                    return( NULL );
                    /* deletion failed */
                else /* branching trie node */
                {   tmp_prev = tmp; tmp = tmp->list;
                    branch = 1;
                }
```

```
      } /* tmp has matching next character */
      if( branch || (tmp->list != NULL) )
      {  /* update position where
         to start deleting */
         last_undel = tmp_prev;
         first_del  = tmp;  branch = 0;
      }
      if( *del_next == '\0' )
         finished = 1; /* found
         deletion string */
      else
      {  del_next += 1;
         tmp_prev = tmp; tmp = tmp->next;
      }
   } /* reached the end. now unlink and
     delete path */
   del_object = (object_t *) tmp->next;
   tmp->next = NULL; /* unlink del_object */
   if( first_del == last_undel->next )
      last_undel->next = first_del->list;
   else /* first_del == last_undel->list */
      last_undel->list = first_del->list;
   /* final path of nonbranching
   nodes unlinked */
   tmp = first_del;
   while( tmp != NULL ) /* follow
   path, return nodes */
   {  first_del = tmp->next;
      return_node( tmp );
      tmp  = first_del;
   }
   return( del_object );
   }
}


void remove_trie(trie_node_t *trie)
{  trie_node_t *tmp_node;
   create_stack();
```

```
push( trie );
while( !stack_empty() )
{   tmp_node = pop();
    if( tmp_node->this_char != '\0')
        push( tmp_node->next );
    if( tmp_node->list != NULL)
        push( tmp_node->list );
    return_node( tmp_node );
}
}
```

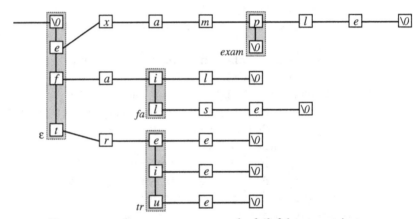

TRIE FOR THE STRINGS *exam, example, fail, false, tree, trie, true*
IMPLEMENTED WITH LIST NODES: ALL POINTERS GO RIGHT OR DOWN

The only difficult part here is the delete operation because the deletion of unused nodes requires different unlinking operations, depending on whether it is reached by a next or a list pointer. We avoid some difficulties by just traversing the structure twice: once to find the place from which we have to delete and another to actually perform the deletion. This turns out to be simpler than a stack-based implementation. The performance of this structure is as follows:

Theorem. The trie structure with nodes realized as lists stores a set of words over an alphabet A. It supports a find operation on a query string q in time $O(|A| \text{length}(q))$ and insert and delete operations in time $O(|A| \text{length}(q))$. The space requirement to store n strings $w_1, \ldots, w_n$ is $O\left(\sum_i \text{length}(w_i)\right)$.

So the main improvement is the space complexity, which stops being a problem. The dependence on $|A|$ in both query and update operations happens only in those instances when the basic trie would be efficient: when there are many prefixes that allow many different next characters. So in applications with normal text strings, the performance will be much better. If we have some information about the access probabilities of the words, we can optimize the structure by choosing the right sequence for the characters on each list (Suraweera 1986).

Another way to avoid the problem with the alphabet size $|A|$ is alphabet reduction. We can represent the alphabet A as set of k-tuples from some direct product $A_1 \times \cdots \times A_k$; by this each string gets longer by a factor of k, but the alphabet size can be reduced to $\lceil |A|^{\frac{1}{k}} \rceil$. For our standard ASCII codes, we can break each 8-bit character by two 4-bit characters, which reduces the node size from 256 pointers to 16 pointers, but doubles the length of each search path.

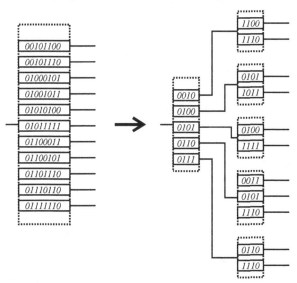

ALPHABET REDUCTION: INSTEAD OF ONE NODE WITH 256 ENTRIES, OF WHICH ONLY 11 ARE USED, WE HAVE FIVE NODES WITH 16 ENTRIES EACH

At the extreme end, we could use a 1-bit alphabet, representing the strings as sequences of single bits; this has been variously discussed in literature because it seems a natural model, but the many necessary bit operations make it a bad choice in real implementations. For more general alphabets the same technique applies, but if we do not have direct access to the bit representation of the characters, we might need to keep tables of the individual maps $A \rightarrow A_i$ to the k subalphabets of the direct product embedding. But these tables are only of total size $k|A|$ and need to be kept only once, so this is an insignificant memory overhead.

By alphabet reduction, the special role of the termination character is lost; it is mapped on a termination string, and we need additional bookkeeping to recognize it. But it is also a good structure for the string model with explicit length, without termination character. Next we give an implementation of the trie structure, for strings of 8-bit characters broken in two 4-bit characters, with no special role of the ' \ 0 ' -character but instead a given length of each string. We also use reference counts in the nodes to speed up the deletion.

```
typedef struct trie_n_t {
            struct trie_n_t    *next[16];
            object_t                *object;
            int              reference_count;
            /* possibly additional information*/
                } trie_node_t;


trie_node_t *create_trie(void)
{   trie_node_t *tmp_node;   int i;
    tmp_node = get_node();
    for( i = 0; i < 16; i++ )
       tmp_node->next[i] = NULL;
    tmp_node->object = NULL;
    tmp_node->reference_count = 1;
    /* root cannot be deleted */
    return( tmp_node );
}


object_t *find(trie_node_t *trie,
            char *query_string, int query_length)
{   trie_node_t *tmp1_node, *tmp2_node;
    int query_pos;
    tmp1_node =  trie;
    for( query_pos = 0;
    query_pos < query_length; query_pos ++)
    {  tmp2_node =
       tmp1_node->next[((((int)query_string
       [query_pos])& 0xF0)>>4)];
       if( tmp2_node != NULL )
```

```
                tmp1_node = tmp2_node;
                /* used upper four bits */
            else
                return( NULL );
                /* query string not found */
            tmp2_node =
              tmp1_node->next[((int)query_string
              [query_pos]) & 0x0F];
            if( tmp2_node != NULL )
                tmp1_node = tmp2_node;
                /*used lower four bits */
            else
                return( NULL );
                /* query string not found */
    }
    /* reached end of query string */
    return( tmp1_node->object);
    /* NULL if query string not found */
}


int insert(trie_node_t *trie,
            char *new_string, int new_length,
            object_t *new_object)
{   trie_node_t *tmp1_node, *tmp2_node;
    int current_pos; int next_sub_char;
    tmp1_node =  trie;
    for( current_pos = 0; current_pos
        < 2*new_length; current_pos++)
    {   if( current_pos % 2 == 0 )
        /* use upper four bits next */
            next_sub_char = (((int)new_string
                      [current_pos/2]) & 0xF0)>>4;
        else /* use lower four bits next */
            next_sub_char = ((int)new_string
                      [current_pos/2]) & 0x0F;
        tmp2_node =
        tmp1_node->next [ next_sub_char ];
        if( tmp2_node != NULL )
```

```
         tmp1_node = tmp2_node;
         /* used four bits */
       else /* need to create new node */
       {  int i;
          tmp2_node = get_node();
          for( i = 0; i < 16; i++ )
             tmp2_node->next[i] = NULL;
          tmp2_node->object = NULL;
          tmp2_node->reference_count = 0;
          tmp1_node->next[ next_sub_char ] =
          tmp2_node;
          tmp1_node->reference_count += 1;
          tmp1_node = tmp2_node;
       }
     }
     if( tmp1_node->object != NULL )
       return( -1 );/* string already exists,
       has associated object*/
     else
     {  tmp1_node->object = new_object;
        tmp1_node->reference_count += 1;
     }
     return( 0 );
}


object_t *delete(trie_node_t *trie,
                 char *del_string,
                 int del_length)
{  trie_node_t *tmp1_node, *tmp2_node;
   int current_pos; int next_sub_char;
   trie_node_t *del_start_node;
   int del_start_pos;
   object_t *tmp_object;
   tmp1_node =  trie;
   del_start_node = trie; del_start_pos = 0;
   for( current_pos = 0;
   current_pos < 2*del_length; current_pos++)
   {  if( current_pos % 2 == 0 )
```

```
    /* use upper four bits next */
        next_sub_char = (((int)del_string
                    [current_pos/2]) & 0xF0)>>4;
    else /* use lower four bits next */

        next_sub_char = ((int)del_string
                    [current_pos/2]) & 0x0F;
    tmp2_node =
    tmp1_node->next [ next_sub_char ];
    if( tmp2_node != NULL )
    {   if( tmp1_node->reference_count > 1 )
        {   del_start_node = tmp1_node;
            del_start_pos = current_pos;
        }  /* del_start_node is the
        last node with two pointers */
        tmp1_node = tmp2_node;
        /* used four bits */
    }
    else
        return( NULL ); /* delete_string
        did not exist */
}
if( tmp1_node->object == NULL )
    return( NULL ); /* delete_string
    did not exist */
else
{   tmp1_node->reference_count -= 1;
    tmp_object = tmp1_node->object;
    tmp1_node->object = NULL;
}
if( tmp1_node->reference_count == 0)
{   tmp1_node = del_start_node;
    for( current_pos = del_start_pos;
    current_pos < 2*del_length; current_pos++)
    {   if( current_pos % 2 == 0 )
        /* use upper four bits next */
            next_sub_char = (((int)del_string
                    [current_pos/2]) & 0xF0)>>4;
        else /* use lower four bits next */
```

```
                    next_sub_char = ((int)del_string
                            [current_pos/2]) & 0x0F;
                tmp2_node =
                tmp1_node->next[ next_sub_char ];
                tmp1_node->next[ next_sub_char ] = NULL;
                tmp1_node->reference_count -= 1;
                if( tmp1_node->reference_count == 0 )
                    return_node( tmp1_node );
                tmp1_node = tmp2_node;
            }
        return_node( tmp1_node );
        }
    return( tmp_object );
    }


    void remove_trie(trie_node_t *trie)
    {  trie_node_t *tmp_node;
       create_stack();
       push( trie );
       while( !stack_empty() )
       {  int i;
          tmp_node = pop();
          for( i=0; i<16; i++)
          {  if( tmp_node->next[i] != NULL )
                push( tmp_node->next[i] );
          }
          return_node( tmp_node );
       }
    }
```

The performance of this structure is as follows:

Theorem. The trie structure with k-fold alphabet reduction stores a set of words over an alphabet A. It supports find and delete operations on a query string q in time $O(k \operatorname{length}(q))$ and insert operations in time $O(k|A|^{\frac{1}{k}} \operatorname{length}(q))$. The space requirement to store n strings $w_1, \ldots, w_n$ is $O(k|A|^{\frac{1}{k}} \sum_i \operatorname{length}(w_i))$.

The inverse operation of alphabet reduction is level compression, which is the use of some power A^k of the original alphabet to reinterpret the string as groups of k symbols. This received some theoretical study (Andersson and Nilsson 1993, 1994; Nilsson and Tikkanen 1998, 2002) in the context of bit strings, where $A = \{0, 1\}$, and for other very small alphabets (quadtree), but for strings over an ASCII alphabet it is not feasible.

Each node of the basic trie structure is itself again a dictionary, with the character as key and the pointer to the next node as object. Thus we can realize the nodes by any dictionary structure of our choice. The trie version using lists for the nodes corresponds to a dictionary realized as list of (key, object) pairs, which is very inefficient if that list is long. The trie version using alphabet reduction can be interpreted as using a trie over the smaller alphabet as dictionary in each node of the trie over the original alphabet. Another natural choice is to use a balanced search tree in each trie node. Here we have the choice of the numerous types of search trees, but in principle we can use just any balanced tree. Because in each node the dictionary contains at most $|A|$ entries, we get at worst an $O(\log |A|)$ time overhead to find the correct entry in each node, and possibly to change it. And the space used by any search tree is linear in the number of keys it stores, so the performance of the structure is as follows:

Theorem. The trie structure with balanced search trees as nodes stores a set of words $w_1, \ldots, w_n$ over an alphabet A. It supports `find`, `delete`, and `insert` operations on a query string q in time $O(\log |A| \operatorname{length}(q))$ and requires $O\left(\sum_i \operatorname{length}(w_i)\right)$ space.

The dependence on the alphabet size is thus harmless; still the overhead of a search tree gives it an advantage over the list only if many nodes have many entries.

In the previous argument we overestimated the height of the search trees in most nodes because most nodes will not have an entry for each possible next letter. We can improve the bound a bit if we balance not each node individually, but use some global balance criterion. For a static trie structure, this was done by Bentley and Sedgewick (1997), who introduced the "ternary trie." They use as underlying search tree a tree of our model 2 (node tree), a ternary tree, where each node contains one character as key and one pointer each for query characters that are smaller, larger, or equal. To build a ternary trie, we assume that the strings are already sorted in lexicographic order. In each node, we choose as comparison key the character at the current position of that string, which is the lexicographic median of the strings that remain along that search path. Then in a query step, when we compare the current query character with the node key,

- either query character and node key are equal, then we move on to the next query character and follow the "equal" pointer of the node; this happens only length(q) times,
- or the query character and node key are not equal, then we follow the "smaller" or "larger" pointer; this reduces the number of possible strings to less than half the previous number, so this happens only $O(\log n)$ times.

The performance of this structure is as follows:

Theorem. The ternary trie structure is a static structure that stores a set of words $w_1, \ldots, w_n$ over an alphabet A. It supports find operations for a query string q in time $O(\log n + \text{length}(q))$. The space requirement is $O\left(\sum_i \text{length}(w_i)\right)$, and it can be built from a sorted set of strings in this time.

Some heuristic dynamic variants of this structure have been discussed in Badr and Oommen (2004), but a true dynamization is surprisingly difficult. The idea of subdividing tries into binary comparisons with median characters has occurred before in Breslauer (1995) and Cole and Lewenstein (2003) in the context of suffix trees.

A different type of compression of tries is path compression, which is the idea that instead of explicitly storing nodes with just one outgoing edge, we skip these nodes and keep track of the number of skipped characters. So the path compressed trie contains only nodes with at least two outgoing edges, and together with each edge it contains a number, which is the number of characters that should be skipped before the next relevant character is looked at. This reduces the required number of nodes from the total length of all strings to the number words in our structure. But, as we skip all those intermediate nodes, we need in each access a second pass over the string to check all those skipped characters of the found string against the query string. This structure is known as Patricia tree (Morrison 1968), which is an acronym for "Practical algorithm to retrieve information coded in alphanumeric." The idea of path compression can be combined with any of the aforementioned variants of tries; originally it was described for bit strings, but for a two-element alphabet the space overhead is so small that today there is no need for path compression;

this technique to reduce the number of nodes is justified only if the alphabet is large.

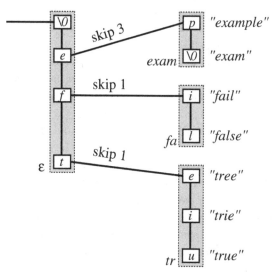

PATRICIA TREE FOR THE STRINGS *exam, example, fail, false, tree, trie, true:*
NODES IMPLEMENTED AS LISTS; EACH LEAF CONTAINS ENTIRE STRING

As a static data structure, the Patricia tree seems to be quite straightforward, but the insertion and deletion operations create significant difficulties. To insert a new string, we need to find where to insert a new branching node, but this requires that we know the skipped characters. It seems an obvious solution to attach to each node the skipped substring that led to it, but then we have to allocate and deallocate many small strings of varying sizes; even if we group them in a few standard sizes, this is a procedure with high overhead. Another solution would be a pointer to one of the strings in the subtrie reached through that node, for there we have that skipped substring already available. But we need to be careful because that string might again be deleted, in which case we would have to replace all those pointers by pointers to a different string in that same subtrie. To allow us to detect that a pointer on the path points to some place in the string we wish to delete, all those pointers would need to be represented as pointer to the beginning of the string plus offset. This is a clumsy solution, but still feasible; its performance would be the following:

Theorem. The Patricia tree structure stores a set of words over an alphabet A. It supports find operations on a query string q in time $O(\text{length}(q))$ and insert and delete operations in time $O(|A|\,\text{length}(q))$. The space requirement to store n strings $w_1, \ldots, w_n$ is $O(n|A| + \sum_i \text{length}(w_i))$.

Another obvious solution attempt would be to follow some branch just to its end to find out which the skipped characters were; they have to be the same for all branches. But this does not give any bound for the insertion time of a string q in terms of length(q), because even to insert a very short string, we might have to follow very long paths to the end.

Thus, a Patricia tree is a structure whose implementation overhead uses up its efficiency advantage over normal tries, for example, those with nodes realized as lists. The significance of Patricia trees is mainly as building block of suffix trees, where these problems do not occur.

Although it is most natural to use the string in this left-to-right fashion, there is no intrinsic reason to do so. The sequence in which we evaluate the characters of the strings does influence the size of the resulting trie structure; if, for example, all strings have a long common suffix, it might be advantageous to read them from that end. We could even, for each trie node, specify which position we next look at – there is no need for these positions to be in any particular sequence or the same sequence along all branches of the trie. But optimizing the possible sequence choices turns out to be NP-complete in any variant (Comer and Sethi 1977).

A number of additional ways to compress tries have been proposed (Heinz, Zobel, and Williams 2002). The compression methods in Maly (1978) and al-Suwaiyel and Horowitz (1984) are suitable only for static tries; the method in Aoe, Morimoto, and Sato (1992) requires very large arrays, but the method in Morimoto, Iriguchi, and Aoe (1994) works with the same nodes as the normal trie and has, in the experiments they report, a space reduction by a factor $\frac{1}{2}$. But in any of these space-saving modifications we lose the simple elegance of the trie structure. A related question is how to represent tries, or sets of strings, on external memory. Strings are variable-length keys, so they do not fall in the model of B-trees, but these are structures like string-B-trees, prefix-B-trees and O-trees (Ferragina and Grossi 1999; Orlandic and Mahmoud 1996).

8.2 Dictionaries Allowing Errors in Queries

The trie-based structures we discussed in the previous section find only exact matches; if the query string contains an error, for example, a word is misspelled or a typing or transmission error happened, the correct string will not be found. This situation is different from the numeric keys in the search trees discussed in Chapter 3, or the range trees for higher-dimensional data discussed in Chapter 4; for these, it is easy to find a neighbor of a query value even if the query value is slightly off the correct value. That does not work in a trie-based structure because the trie essentially mirrors the lexicographic order of the strings: if the first character of the query string is incorrect, we are searching at entirely the wrong place. It would be highly desirable to have a dictionary structure that keeps track of a set of strings and finds all strings that differ only in d characters from the query string. This problem has for $d = 1$ an elegant, efficient, and practicable solution (Brodal and Gąsieniec 1996), and several even more efficient solutions in computation models less relevant for our purposes (Yao and Yao 1997; Ferragina, Muthukrishnan, and de Berg 1999; Brodal and Venkatesh 2000); for $d \geq 2$, it is essentially open.

Suppose we have a set of n words $w_1, \ldots, w_n$ over an alphabet A, with total length $\Sigma_w = \sum_{i=1}^{n} \text{length}(w_i)$, and we want to preprocess this into a structure that can find all words of our set that differ in at most d places from a query string q for some fixed d. Then there are two trivial solutions:

1. We could generate for each word w_i all the words that differ in at most d places from it and store all these word variants in a trie.
   For each word w_i, we get $\Theta(|A|^d \text{length}(w_i)^d)$ variants, so if we use a standard trie, the size of the underlying structure increases from
   $O(|A|\Sigma_w) = O(|A| \sum_{i=1}^{n} \text{length}(w_i))$ to $O(|A|^{d+1} \sum_{i=1}^{n} \text{length}(w_i)^{d+1})$,
   whereas the query time stays $O(\text{length}(q))$. This size is infeasible even for $d = 1$.
2. We could use just a standard trie for the words, but generate for each query string q all the words that differ in at most d places, and perform all these queries on the trie.
   This generates $\Theta(|A|^d \text{length}(q)^d)$ queries, each of time $\Theta(\text{length}(q))$, which again is useless at least for $d \geq 2$.

There are minor improvements possible. In the first solution we could perform path compression, which would reduce the exponent for the required space from $d + 1$ to d, because there are only so many leaves; but it is not obvious how to construct the structure in that time (Brodal and Gąsieniec 1996). One could use a trie with list-based nodes, which would remove one $|A|$ factor. And one can combine both solutions, storing all variants with d_1 errors and asking all query variants with d_2 errors, to find all words with $d_1 + d_2$ errors. All this is useless, but essentially the best we have for $d \geq 2$.

The remarkable achievement of Brodal and Gąsieniec (1996) is a structure for $d = 1$, which, in our standard model, consists of just two tries on the words, so of size $O(|A|\Sigma_w)$ each, if we use the standard trie, and one balanced search tree of size $O(\Sigma_w)$. The query time is $O(\text{length}(q) \log \Sigma_w)$. It is even a dynamic structure, inserting or deleting a word w takes $O(\text{length}(w) \log \Sigma_w)$ time. It can be combined with all the trie variants, so one might use the trie with list-based nodes to decrease the space complexity. Only the path compression cannot be used if we want to have the structure as dynamic dictionary. If we leave our computational model and allow ourselves the use of a hash table instead of the search tree, even the $\log \Sigma_w$ factor disappears and both preprocessing and query are linear-time operations.

The idea of this double-trie structure is to build one trie for all words w_i and a second trie for the words written backward w_i^{reversed}. Then each node in the first trie corresponds to some prefix π of some word w_i, and each node in the second trie corresponds to some suffix σ of a word w_j. For each word w_i we look at all pairs of (prefix, suffix) that are separated by a single character, so as to have different ways to write $w_i = \pi c \sigma$, where c is a character. Each word w_i generates length(w_i) for such pairs (π, σ), which are represented by pairs of trie nodes, addresses or numbers. We generate all these pairs for a given word by first following in the first trie the path of the word to its end, pushing a pointer for each passed node on the stack, and then following in the second trie the path of the reversed word, pairing each node we reach in the second trie with the corresponding next node from the stack. So we can generate all the node pairs in time $O(\text{length}(w_i))$. Each of these node pairs, that is, pairs of pointers or node numbers, we enter in our search-tree, together with a pointer to the word w_i that generated that pair. The total number of pairs are Σ_w, so each search-tree operation costs only $O(\log \Sigma_w)$. So we build the entire structure in time $O(\Sigma_w \log \Sigma_w)$.

The query method now follows the same outline: follow the path of the query word in the first trie as far as possible, pushing a pointer to each visited node on the stack. Unless the query word is indeed correct, we will not reach the end, but there is a maximum prefix of the query word that is also prefix of some correct word. Then we follow the path of the reversed word in the second trie until we are one character before the end of that maximum prefix. From then on, while we continue to follow the path in the second trie, we pair each visited node with a prefix node from the stack and look up in the search tree whether that node pair belongs to any correct word. Thus the query time is $O(\text{length}(q) \log \Sigma_w)$.

If we use a trie with list-based nodes and any balanced search tree, the performance of this structure is as follows:

Theorem. The double-trie structure, with trie nodes realized as lists and a balanced search tree, stores a set of words of total length Σ_w over an alphabet A. It supports a find operation on a query string q to find all words that differ in at most one place from q in output-sensitive time $O(|A| \text{length}(q) \log \Sigma_w + k)$ if there are k such words. It supports insert and delete operations of a word w in time $O(|A| \text{length}(w) \log \Sigma_w)$. The space requirement is $O(\Sigma_w)$, and the time to build the structure is $O(|A| \Sigma_w \log \Sigma_w)$.

This is almost as good as possible, and if our computational model allows the use of a hash table instead of the search tree, the $\log \Sigma_w$ factor disappears, so all operations become linear time in the length of the input, which is certainly optimal. In a somewhat intermediate model, Ferragina et al. (1999) give a much more complicated structure in which the $\log \Sigma_w$ is reduced to $\log \log \Sigma_w$. Another method with worse performance was proposed in Amir et al. (2000).

The double-trie structure even supports queries for a more general model of errors; not only one character might be exchanged for a different character, but instead also one character could be inserted or deleted. This corresponds to using the edit distance instead of the Hamming distance. For the double-trie structure it just means that for each word w we need to insert another length(w) + 1 acceptable (prefix, suffix) pairs into the search tree, those decompositions $w = \pi\sigma$ without intermediate letter; then the same query algorithm will also accept all query words q with $q = \pi c\sigma$; and to accept the query words which are missing one character, we use the original set of acceptable pairs, but pair in the query the current suffix with its immediate prefix instead of the prefix one character shorter. Neither of these modifications changes the complexity.

Brodal and Gąsieniec (1996) also gave a different solution to use the two tries and obtain a linear query time, without the use of a hash table, but using a more complicated tool: sorting all the input strings in lexicographic order in $O(\Sigma_w)$ time and assigning them their rank in that order as their number. Then,

– each trie node in the first trie then corresponds to an interval in that order, the words w_i that start with that prefix;
– each trie node in the second set corresponds to some subset: the words that end with that suffix.

Instead of testing whether a pair of nodes from the first and second trie represent a (prefix, suffix) pair from a word w_i by looking up that pair of nodes in our search tree, they test whether the interval of the first node intersects the subset of the second node. This is a situation in which fractional cascading can be applied: when we follow a path in the second trie, the subsets get sparser, so we represent the subsets by sorted lists and sublists, with pointers from any node in the list to its next neighbors in the sublists. Going the corresponding path backward in the first trie, we get a sequence of increasing intervals. So, when we follow the path in second trie and compare with the corresponding node from the stack in the first trie, we get a sequence of increasing intervals and a sequence of decreasing sorted sublists, and we want to test whether there is at any stage an intersection between the interval and the sublist. For this, we just have to find the position of the interval in the first list, for which we need a search tree, then we can follow in each step in $O(1)$ time the pointers to the neighbors in the sublist to obtain the position of the previous interval in the new sublist, and then extend the interval and check whether it now contains one of the neighbors in the sublist. The complexity of this query-processing algorithm is $O(\text{length}(q))$ to follow the first trie as far as possible and put the nodes on the stack, the same time to reach the corresponding position in the second trie, $O(\log n)$ to determine the initial position position of the interval in the list, and $O(1)$ for each step to the next sublist and interval, giving a total query time of $O(\text{length}(q) + \log n)$.

All this assumed that the characters of the string were approximately of the same size as the elementary units of the computer memory, so the time necessary to read a string is essentially its length, and we have an $\Omega(\text{length}(w))$ lower bound for any operation on a word w. The situation changes when we may read the entire word in constant time, which is the model considered in Yao and Yao (1997) and Brodal and Venkatesh (2000); there they consider sets of n bit strings of length m in machine model of word length at least m. Then we can read the entire query word in time $O(1)$, and for an exact match query we could just use it directly in a hash table and find the corresponding entry in $O(1)$. Here the question again is how fast we can extend this to words that differ in a single position. A first solution was given in Yao and Yao (1997) that used $O(n \log m)$ words of length m space and a query time of $O(\log \log n)$; this was improved in Brodal and Venkatesh (2000) to $O(1)$ query time.[2]

For queries for distance $d \geq 2$, essentially nothing is known, although some aspects were discussed in Dolev et al. (1994) and Greene, Parnas, and Yao (1994), neither of them leading to an algorithm.

8.3 Suffix Trees

The suffix tree is a static structure that preprocesses a long string s and answers for a query string q, if and where it occurs in the long string. Thus, it solves the substring matching problem, as do the classical string-matching algorithms. The difference is that the time to answer a substring query is not dependent on the length of the long string, but only on the length of the query string. The query time is $O(\text{length}(q))$ for a query string q. The idea is very simple at least on the query side: each substring of s is prefix of a suffix of s, and

---

[2] They used a bitwise computation model, but if we would reinterpret those bounds just as strings over the binary alphabet, the performance would be worse than the double-trie structure combined with a hash table. The strength of the results is that the operations on the words of length m are performed in $O(1)$ time.

the nodes of any trie correspond to the prefixes of the strings stored in the trie, so if we construct a trie that stores all suffixes of the long string s, then its nodes correspond to the substrings of s, and we can decide for any query q in $O(\text{length}(q))$ whether it is a substring of s.

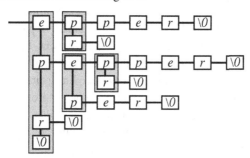

TRIE OF THE SUFFIXES OF *pepper*

As it is, this structure would use $O(\text{length}(s)^2)$ nodes and take the same time to build; but if we now apply path compression, we see that there are only length(s) branching nodes and, different from Patricia trees, we do not need to store all those strings explicitly, but can encode each by a beginning and end address in the long string s. Thus we get an $O(\text{length}(s))$ representation for the Patricia tree of the suffixes of s, which allows us to answer substring queries q in $O(\text{length}(q))$ time.

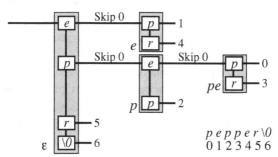

PATRICIA TREE OF THE SUFFIXES OF *pepper:*
THE LEAF NUMBERS GIVE THE STARTING POSITIONS OF THE SUFFIXES

This idea was introduced by Weiner (1973).[3] The major problem is to build that linear-sized representation in linear time. Several algorithms have been proposed, all of which require some thought. The classical methods are by Weiner (1973), who builds the structure backward, starting from the end of

---

[3] But the name was given by McCreight (1976). In Weiner (1973), the structure was called a prefix bitree and a very similar structure was called position tree (Aho, Hopcroft, and Ullman 1974).

the string and adding the suffixes in order of increasing length; by McCreight (1976), who builds the structure by adding suffixes in order of decreasing length; and by Ukkonen (1995), who builds the structure incrementally from front while maintaining a suffix tree of the already-processed prefix. Before Ukkonen's solution, the problem of constructing the suffix tree incrementally, while reading the string, had been studied in a number of papers; the algorithm in Majster and Reiser (1980) does not work in linear time, but the algorithms in Kempf, Bayer, and Güntzer (1987) for the related position trees and Kosaraju's "quasi-real-time" algorithm (Kosaraju 1994) are linear-time constructions. An incremental method that allows addition at either end of the string was developed by Inenaga (2003); a "lazy" version that builds the tree only during the queries was described in Giegerich, Kurtz, and Stoye (2003), and an attempt at a common model for these algorithms was made in Giegerich and Kurtz (1997). In Tian et al. (2005), a quadratic-time algorithm is proposed for a memory-restricted setting and various experimental results are reported in Hunt, Atkinson, and Irving (2002).

Because any realization of the suffix tree has a trie as underlying structure, the space requirements of tries, especially for large alphabets, are also a problem for suffix trees. This problem has been considered in Andersson and Nilsson (1995), Farach (1997), Kurtz (1999), Munro et al. (2001), and Kim and Park (2005). We can combine the suffix tree idea with any of the trie representations discussed in the previous section. Some applications of the structure already have a small alphabet, for example, for substring search in a genetic sequence; but for a long text over the normal alphabet, the representation of the trie nodes as lists is probably most convenient.

The algorithms are easiest to understand if first described without the path compression, so the underlying abstract structure is a trie that stores a set of suffixes of the input string and the trie nodes correspond to prefixes of those suffixes, that is, the substrings. Each node has some outgoing pointers that are the normal trie edges, corresponding to possible extensions of the current prefix of a suffix, that is, a longer substring with some additional character at the end. In addition to these pointers, both McCreight (1976) and Ukkonen (1995) use a further pointer in each node – the suffix link – which points from a node representing a string $a_0 \ldots a_k$ to the node representing the string $a_1 \ldots a_k$, that is, its suffix after deleting the first character.

We describe here Ukkonen's method. Suppose we have already built the structure for the string $c_0 \ldots c_{n-1}$ and want to add one further character c_n in the end. We need to change only those nodes that correspond to strings $c_i \ldots c_{n-1}$; a node whose string does not occur as suffix of $c_0 \ldots c_{n-1}$ cannot change by the extension to $c_0 \ldots c_{n-1}c_n$. Those nodes that potentially might

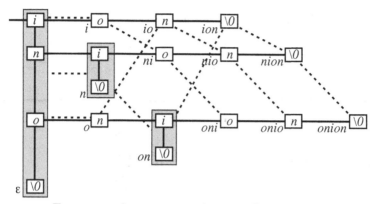

TRIE OF THE SUFFIXES OF *onion* WITH SUFFIX LINKS

change are reached from the node corresponding to $c_0 \ldots c_{n-1}$ by following suffix pointers; this path is known as the boundary path. Each node on the boundary path is in one of the following situations:

- type 1: The node has no outgoing edge.
- type 2: The node has an outgoing edge, but none that corresponds to the next character c_n.
- type 3: The node has an outgoing edge corresponding to the next character c_n.

If we follow the boundary path from $c_0 \ldots c_{n-1}$ to c_{n-1}, these three types form consecutive, possibly empty, intervals. If the node corresponding to $c_i \ldots c_{n-1}$ is of type 1, this substring occurs only at the end, so the longer substring $c_{i-1}c_i \ldots c_{n-1}$ also occurs only at the end and its corresponding node is also of type 1. In the same way, if the node corresponding to $c_i \ldots c_{n-1}$ is of type 3, the substring $c_i \ldots c_{n-1}c_n$ has already occurred somewhere before and so the shorter substring $c_{i+1} \ldots c_{n-1}c_n$ also has occurred somewhere before and its corresponding node is also of type 3. Thus, all type 1 nodes are in the beginning of the boundary path, all type 3 nodes in the end, and type 2 nodes possibly between them.

We do not need to make any change in a type 3 node because the node we need for the new last character c_n already exists. In a type 2 node, we need to create a new branch, a new node for the string $c_i \ldots c_{n-1}c_n$, which did not occur before. This is a new branch off a node that already had at least one outgoing edge, because the total number of leaves of the trie structure is n, we meet type 2 nodes only a total of $n - 1$ times while inductively building the trie structure for a string of length n. So the main work is the type 1 nodes, where we have to just add another node to a node that previously had no outgoing

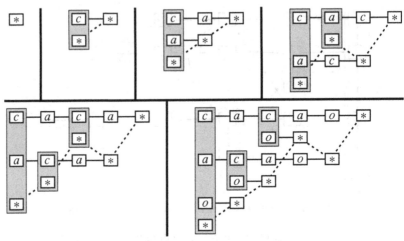

INCREMENTAL CONSTRUCTION OF TRIE OF THE SUFFIXES OF *cacao:*
THE *-NODES MARK THE CURRENT END; THEY FORM THE BOUNDARY PATH

pointer. There we just make a long path at the end one node longer, exactly
the structure we wanted to avoid by path compression. To represent such a
path, which has no branches and extends to a leaf, we need just the first node,
together with the position in the long string where the substring represented by
that first node occurs, and the information to accept all continuations of that
substring up to the end of the long string. Such an "open-ended" node does not
need to be updated at all, when the long string grows at its end, unless the path
represented by this node develops a new branch. For the open-ended nodes, the
suffix link stays undefined.

So all the update work that needs to be done on the boundary path is among
the type 2 nodes, starting at the first node that corresponds to a substring
$c_i \ldots c_{n-1}$ that has already occurred before as $c_j \ldots c_{j-i+n-1}$, and ending at the
first node that already has an entry for c_n, so even the substring $c_i \ldots c_{n-1}c_n$
has already occurred before. The starting node in each step of the inductive
construction is easy to find: the end node of one round is predecessor of the
starting node of the next round. If, in the step of adding c_n, we found $c_i \ldots c_{n-1}$
as the end node, and that the first node already had an entry for c_n (type 3),
then in the step of adding c_{n+1}, we will find $c_i \ldots c_n$ as the first node that
already has an outgoing pointer (type 2 or 3). The only exception to this is
that if we did not find any node that already had an entry for c_n, we walked
down the boundary path to the root node representing the empty string and
added there a new entry for c_n, then the root node is the starting node of the
next round.

So the outline of this algorithm to construct the suffix tree of a given string $s = c_0 \ldots c_{n-1}$ is as follows:

0. Create the root node, representing the trie of the empty string. Set the active node to that node, and $i = 0$.
1. While $i < n$
    1.1 While the active node has no entry for c_i
        1.1.1 Create a new node, reached from the active node by the entry for c_i. This new node is a leaf.
        1.1.2 Move the active node down its suffix link if it is not already the root.
    1.2 Move the active node up the link for c_i unless it is the root and we just created that link. Increment i.

In this outline, we see two types of steps: in 1.1 the active node follows a suffix link, so it moves to a node representing a string shorter by one character, and in 1.2 it follows a regular link, so it moves to a node representing a string longer by one character. There are only n iterations of step 1.2, so the step 1.1 is also taken only n times. This suggests an $O(n)$ complexity. There are, however, several problems because the nodes we want to use may be missing due to the path compression, especially in the nodes represented by the open-ended paths. And for those nodes the suffix links will also not exist.

So we have to find implicit nodes when we need them and make them explicit. We can represent each implicit node by an explicit node, followed by a substring: if the explicit node represents string α and the substring is $c_i \ldots c_j$, they together represent $\alpha c_i \ldots c_j$. This is a constant-sized representation if we use (i, j) to describe $c_i \ldots c_j$. Each implicit node has many such representations, one for each explicit node on the path to that implicit node. Given such a representation of an implicit node, we make it explicit by first following the path in the compressed trie, as far as possible, and in the last explicit node we insert a newly created explicit node in the correct link. This also solves the problem of missing suffix links for implicit nodes: if the implicit node is represented by an explicit node followed by $c_i \ldots c_j$, then the node reached by the suffix link from the implicit node is represented by the node reached by the suffix link from the explicit node, followed by the same substring $c_i \ldots c_j$.

We still need to bound the time we need to make the missing nodes explicit. We make an implicit node explicit in step 1.1.1 only when it becomes a branching node; there are only at most $n - 1$ branching nodes, so this happens only $O(n)$ times. There is no $O(1)$ bound for the individual operation because we might have to go through many explicit nodes to finally find the link in which the implicit node has to be inserted. But a similar accounting argument as before works, applied to the current representation of the active node instead of the active node itself. The representation of the active node consists of an explicit node and a substring. The substring gets longer only in step 1.2; each time we follow a suffix link, the length of the string does not change, and each time we follow a link to another explicit node, in the process of making an implicit node explicit, the string gets shorter. So the total number of explicit nodes traversed while making implicit nodes explicit is only $O(n)$. This gives a total $O(n)$ bound for the complexity of the construction of the suffix tree of a string of length n.

The performance of this structure is as follows:

Theorem. The suffix tree structure is a static structure that preprocesses a string s and supports substring queries. If the trie nodes are realized as linked lists, the operation make_suffix_tree preprocesses a string of length n over an alphabet A in time $O(|A|n)$ into a structure of size $O(n)$, which supports find_string queries for a string q in time $O(|A| \operatorname{length}(q))$.

The suffix tree structure turned out to be very useful for various string pattern processing tasks (Apostolico 1985; Gusfield 1997). Some applications motivated variants of the underlying structure, like parametrized strings introduced in Baker (1993) and further discussed in Kosaraju (1995) and Cole and Hariharan (2003); a parametrized string consists of characters of the underlying alphabet and variables, where all occurrences of the same variable have to be replaced by the same string. This can be viewed as an equivalence class of strings, for example, a program under renaming of variables.

Another variant are the two-dimensional strings, rectangular arrays of symbols from an alphabet, which can be viewed as abstraction of images, where a two-dimensional substring corresponds to a match of a translate of a small image in the big image. Two-dimensional suffix trees were introduced in Giancarlo (1995) and further developed in Choi and Lam (1997) and Cole and Hariharan (2003); higher-dimensional versions are discussed in Kim, Kim, and Park (2003).

Suffix trees can also be used to find repetitions in text, which is an important subtask of dictionary-based compression methods like Lempel-Ziv. A closely related structure is the directed acyclic word graph (DAWG), which is the smallest automaton that accepts the subwords of a given word (Blumer et al. 1985; Blumer 1987; Holub and Crochemore 2002); it can also be constructed by the same algorithms as suffix trees (Chen and Seiferas 1987; Ukkonen 1995). Yet another variant is the affix tree studied in Maass (2003).

Because the suffix tree structure is so useful, it would be desirable to have a dynamic variant of it, in which we can change the underlying string. This question has already been considered by McCreight (1976), but there are words of length n for which a change of $O(1)$ places in the word forces $\Omega(n)$ changes in the suffix tree structure (Ayala-Rincón and Conejo 2003).

Suffix trees can also be built for multiple strings if we want to decide whether a query string q occurs as substring of any of k strings $s_1, \ldots, s_k$. The construction is exactly the same; indeed, we can just concatenate the strings to $s_1 s_2, \cdots, s_k$ and build a normal suffix tree for this combined string.

8.4 Suffix Arrays

The suffix array is an alternative structure to the suffix tree that was developed by Manber and Myers (1993).[4] It supports the same operations as the suffix tree: it preprocesses a long string and then answers for a query string whether it occurs as substring in the preprocessed string. The possible advantage of the suffix array structure is that its size does not depend on the size of the alphabet and that it offers a quite different tool to attack the same type of string problems. It is said to be smaller than suffix trees, but that somewhat depends on various compact encoding tricks; in its most straightforward implementation, it requires three integers per character of the long string, whereas an implementation of the suffix tree with list nodes requires five pointers per node, and the number of nodes is at most the length of the string, but possibly smaller. In any case the query structure is significantly larger than the underlying string – our suffix tree by a factor of 20,[5] the basic suffix array by a factor of 12 – both factors can be reduced by some encoding tricks; a study of this was made by Kurtz (1999), and many further papers have been aimed at this topic. Especially for the suffix array, we need to consider not only the space of the structure itself, but also the additional space used during the construction (Itoh and Tanaka 1999; Burkhardt and Kärkkäinen 2003; Manzini and Ferragina 2004; Kim, Jo, and Park 2004b; Na 2005). Some structures intermediate between suffix array, and suffix tree have also been proposed (Kärkkäinen 1995; Colussi and De Col 1996; Kim, Jeon, and Park 2004a).

In the previous chapters we frequently claimed that space is no longer a problem, but for structures on strings, it is a legitimate problem because the overhead is so large. The main reason for this is that standard ASCII characters

---

[4] The same structure was developed at the same time under the name PAT array by Gonnet (1992) for the application of an Index to the *Oxford English Dictionary*.

[5] Frequently, a factor of 28 is cited for suffix trees.

are so small compared to integers or pointers. If we used an even smaller alphabet, the ratio would be even worse. In the same way, the word width influences the ratio: if we use 64-bit pointers, the overhead of the straightforward implementation doubles, and if we have only text of length at most 2^{16}, we could fit all our pointers and integers in 16 bit and halve the overhead. So the various numbers stated in literature have to be taken with care; they assume the text length to be less than 2^{32}, and especially for the variants of the suffix tree, whose size depends on the given text, they frequently are experimental values obtained for some specific set of text samples. A clean way to compare the various methods in models like our pointer machine would be to count integers and pointers per text character in the worst case. Or one can start to count the bits of additional space needed for the structure (Hon, Sadakane, and Sung 2003).

The underlying idea of the suffix array structure is to consider all suffixes of the preprocessed string s in lexicographic order and perform binary search on them to find a given query string. This already shows one disadvantage of the structure: the query time to find a string q in the long string s also depends on length(s); to find the right one among the length(s) possible suffixes, we need $O(\log \text{length}(s))$ lexicographic comparisons between q and some suffix of s. Without additional information, each comparison takes $O(\text{length}(q))$ time for a total of $O(\text{length}(q) \log \text{length}(s))$; if some additional information on the length of common prefixes of the suffixes of s is available, this reduces to $O(\text{length}(q) + \log \text{length}(s))$. The suffix tree needs only $O(\text{length}(q))$ query time, independent of s.

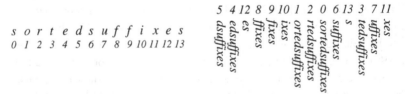

```
s   o   r   t   e   d   s   u   f   f   i   x   e   s
0   1   2   3   4   5   6   7   8   9  10  11  12  13
```

5 4 12 8 9 10 1 2 0 6 13 3 7 11

THE SUFFIXES OF *sortedsuffixes* IN LEXICOGRAPHIC ORDER
WITH THEIR STARTING INDICES IN THE STRING

We need to represent the suffixes of the string s in a way that they are sorted in lexicographic order and we can perform binary search on them. The most natural way is to have one big array in which the starting indices of the lexicographically sorted suffixes are stored. So we need an integer array of the same length of the string. This is another disadvantage. There might be a problem of allocating an array of length(s) integers if length(s) is very large. And for the common prefix information, we need another two such arrays. The structure does not fit into our pointer-machine model, which allows only fixed-size arrays.

A final problem is how to build the structure. Manber and Myers (1993) originally gave an algorithm that built the suffix array of a string of length n in time $O(n \log n)$, compared to $O(n)$ for the suffix tree. One can construct the suffix array from the suffix tree in $O(n)$ time, but if one already has the suffix tree, there is no point in building a suffix array. Ten years later, many different methods to construct the structure directly in $O(n)$ time were found simultaneously by Kärkkäinen and Sanders (2003), Kärkkäinen, Sanders, and Burkhardt (2006), Kim et al. (2003, 2005), Ko and Aluru (2003, 2005), and Hon et al. (2003); of these, the method of Kärkkäinen and Sanders (2003) is probably the simplest[6] and we will describe it later. By now, many different construction methods have been found; a survey and comparison is given in Puglisi, Smyth, and Turpin (2007). It appears that some algorithms with a worst-case complexity as bad as $O(n^2)$ outperform the $O(n)$ algorithms on real test data.

In all those papers, as well as in Manber and Myers (1993) and Itoh and Tanaka (1999), constructing the array of sorted suffixes is viewed as the main problem, which is a special instance of the classical string sorting problem. But there are really two steps in building the structure: sorting the suffixes and finding the common prefix information. For that second step, a nice method was presented in Kasai et al. (2001), which constructs in $O(n)$ time the common prefix information from the sorted suffixes.

We will now describe the query algorithm for suffix arrays, as developed in Manber and Myers (1993). We are basically performing binary search on an array that contains the starting indices of the suffixes of our string s in lexicographic order. In addition, we have two additional arrays that contain longest common prefix information for questions asked during the binary search. Suppose we already know that the query string q is lexicographically between the strings *left* and *right* and we want to compare now with the string *middle*. If we know that *left* and *middle* share the first k characters, then any other string between them in the lexicographic order also shares these first characters. So if *left* and q share the first l characters, with $l < k$, then the query string cannot be between *left* and *middle*. And by the same argument, if $l > k$, then *middle* cannot be between *left* and q.

So if we have the numbers k and l, we can decide the outcome of the comparison in that step of binary search without looking at the string q unless $l = k$. If $l = k$, we have to compare the strings q and *middle* in time proportional to the length of the common prefix of q and *middle*. If, as a result of this comparison, we find that q is to the right of *middle*, then in the binary

---

[6] They even give explicit code for it in their paper, but they allocate four auxiliary arrays of the same length, per recursion, which destroys the main virtue of the suffix array structure.

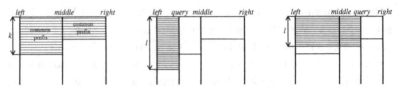

COMMON PREFIX LENGTHS IN THE BINARY SEARCH
AND THE POSITION OF *query* RELATIVE TO *middle*

search *middle* becomes the new *left*, and we have spent the possibly large comparison time usefully, for we updated l, the length of the common prefix of q, with *left*. But if q is to the left of *middle*, that information does not help us avoid future comparison. If we search for $q = b^{50}a$ in the string ab^{100}, using the left common prefix information only, we will in each step compare $b^{50}a$ from the beginning to the *middle* string $b^{\geq 50}$ because the length of the common prefix with the *left* string a stays 0. We avoid this by maintaining both the information about the common prefix length to the left and to the right. In each step in which a string comparison between q and *middle* is necessary, either the left or the right common prefix length increases by the number of additional common characters we found, which is at most length(q) in total, over all steps. If we can decide the binary search step without comparing characters, on base of the length of common prefix information only, then this information also gives the new common prefix length of the query string q to the new *left* or *right* string.

Of these numbers, the length of the common prefix of *left* and *middle* can be precomputed, whereas the other number needs to be maintained during the query. We have one array `left_middle_cp`, which gives the length of the common prefix of *left* and *middle*, and another array `right_middle_cp`, which gives the length of the common prefix of *middle* and *right*, for each interval that can occur in the binary search. Each of these arrays is only as long as the original sorted list of strings because in a binary search each item occurs for at most one interval as subdivision point. So we can use the number of the middle item as the address in the array for the interval of the binary search.

During the query, we maintain two numbers – `left_query_cp` and `right_query_cp` – that are the length of the common prefixes of the query string with the left and right endpoints of the current interval in the binary search. And we need the array `sorted_str`, which contains pointers to the strings sorted in lexicographic sequence. In the suffix array application, these strings are the suffixes of the preprocessed string, but the query algorithm works on any array of lexicographically sorted strings and is also useful outside suffix array application.

To analyze this algorithm for binary search on a set of sorted strings, we observe that the main loop of the binary search is executed only log(n) times, and everything in it but the common prefix computations takes constant time. Whenever we compute a common prefix of length i, it takes $O(1 + i)$, and we add that length either to left_query_cp or to right_query_cp, either of which is bounded by the length of the query string. We summarize the performance of this structure as follows:

Theorem. An array of pointers to n lexicographically sorted strings, together with two arrays of n integers each, containing the common prefix length information, allows to find for a query string q whether it is prefix of any of these strings in time $O(\text{length}(q) + \log n)$.

To use this query algorithm for suffix arrays, we need to construct the array of the sorted suffixes. We now describe the construction by Kärkkäinen and Sanders (2003). The idea of the algorithm is to construct the suffix array for a shorter string over a larger alphabet recursively and then recover the suffix arrays for parts of the original string and merge them. This general outline is also used in Kim et al. (2003), and it was already present in the suffix-tree algorithm of Farach (1997); indeed the principle of interpreting pairs of consecutive characters as characters of a new alphabet, and perform string matching for the shorter string over the larger alphabet, already occurs in Karp, Miller, and Rosenberg (1972). The problem is in the details.

Kärkkäinen and Sanders consider the triples of consecutive characters s $[i]$ s $[i + 1]$ s $[i + 2]$ for $i \not\equiv 0 \bmod 3$. These are $\frac{2}{3}n$ triples, which are ordered by the lexicographic order for triples, and by radixsort we can assign each triple its rank in that set of triples as its canonical name. We use radixsort because the triples we sort are triples of numbers less than n, and so of numbers less than n^3, which can be sorted by radixsort in time $O(n)$. We now construct a new string of length $\frac{2}{3}n$ that consists of the sequence of canonical names of the triples s $[3i + 1]$ s $[3i + 2]$ s $[3i + 3]$ for $i = 0, \ldots, \frac{1}{3}n - 1$ followed by the sequence of names of the triples s $[3i + 2]$ s $[3i + 3]$ s $[3i + 4]$ for $i = 0, \ldots, \frac{1}{3}n - 1$. This is a string over an alphabet of integers at most n. The suffix of this new string starting in position i of the first group corresponds to the string that is the suffix of the original string starting in position $3i + 1$ followed by the end mark and the original string starting in position 2. And the suffix of this new string starting in position i of the second group corresponds to the string that is the suffix of the original string starting in position $3i + 2$ followed by the end mark. For the lexicographic order of these string, the part after the end mark is irrelevant, so the lexicographic order of the suffixes of the new string allows us to read off the lexicographic order of those suffixes of the original string that started in positions $3i + 1$ or $3i + 2$.

As next step, we have to find the order of the suffixes starting in positions $3i + 0$ and merge these orders to obtain the lexicographic order of all suffixes. But the order of the suffixes starting in positions $3i + 0$ is determined by the first character of that suffix, and among those with the same first character, by the order of the remaining suffix, which we know because it starts at position $3i + 1$. So we can construct in $O(n)$ time the lexicographic order of the remaining suffixes. We finally have to merge these two orders for which we need to compare the lexicographic order between a suffix starting in a position of form $3i + 0$ and a suffix starting in a position of form $3i + 1$ or $3i + 2$. This comparison can be done in constant time, using again the first character or the first two characters:

- If we are comparing the suffix starting in position $3i$ with the suffix starting in position $3j + 1$, then this is determined either by their first characters, or, if those agree, by the comparison of the rest, which are the suffixes starting in $3i + 1$ and $3j + 2$, so they occur both in the same sorted sequence and can be compared in $O(1)$ time.
- If we are comparing the suffix starting in position $3i$ with the suffix starting in position $3j + 2$, then this is determined either by their first two characters, or, if those agree, by the comparison of the rest, which are the suffixes starting in $3i + 2$ and $3j + 4$, so they occur both in the same sorted sequence and can be compared in $O(1)$ time.

Thus, the time to sort all suffixes of a string of length n is $O(n)$, plus the time to sort the suffixes of a string of length $\frac{2}{3}n$, which gives an $O(n)$ bound in total. It should be noted that although the size of the alphabet increases, it never becomes larger than n because each character corresponds to a k-character subsequence that occurs in the string for some fixed k.

It remains to compute the arrays `left_middle_cp` and `right_middle_cp`. We follow here the method proposed in Kasai et al. (2001) to construct first the array `cp`, where `cp[i]` is the length of the common prefix of the suffixes starting in `sorted_suffix[i − 1]` and `sorted_suffix[i]`. We use an additional array `rank` that contains the inverse of the `sorted_suffix` array: `rank[i] = j` if `sorted_suffix[j] = i`. The key observation here is that when we already know that the suffix starting in position i and its adjacent suffix in the lexicographic order, which starts in position `sorted_suffix[rank[i] + 1]`, have a common prefix of length l, then the suffix starting in position $i + 1$

and its adjacent suffix in the lexicographic order, which starts in position sorted_suffix[rank[$i + 1$] $+ 1$], have a common prefix of length at least $l - 1$. So if we determine the lengths of common prefixes of lexicographically consecutive suffixes in the sequence given by the rank array, then there are two types of steps: those in which that length decreases by 1, which takes a constant time, and those in which the length stays the same or increases, which takes a time proportional to the increase. But the length cannot be larger than n and the total decrease is at most n, so the total increase is less than $2n$ and the time to determine all these lengths is $O(n)$.

Finally, we derive the arrays left_middle_cp and right_middle_cp from cp. For this we use that the length of the common prefix of any two suffixes is the minimum of the lengths of the common prefix of two lexicographically consecutive suffixes between them. The entries in the arrays left_middle_cp and right_middle_cp are thus maxima over those intervals that can occur in a binary search between middle and left and between middle and right endpoint. But each such interval is the union of two intervals that can occur one step further down in the binary search. So if we construct them bottom-up, starting with the smallest, we can construct each entry in $O(1)$ time from previous entries, giving a complexity of $O(n)$ in total.

We summarize the performance of this structure as follows:

Theorem. The suffix array structure is a static structure that preprocesses a string s and supports substring queries. This structure can be built in time $O(\text{length}(s))$, requires space $O(\text{length}(s))$, and supports find_string queries for a string q in time $O(\text{length}(q) + \log(\text{length}(s)))$.

So the suffix array can be constructed in the same time as the suffix tree and gives almost the same query performance. Suffix arrays and suffix trees can be used in many applications interchangeably (Abouelhoda, Kurtz, and Ohlebusch 2004). But if space is not an issue, suffix trees seem conceptually more elegant.

9

Hash Tables

Hash tables are a dictionary structure of great practical importance and can be very efficient. The underlying idea is quite simple: we have a universe $\mathcal{U}$ and want to store a set of objects with keys from $\mathcal{U}$. We also have s buckets and a function h from $\mathcal{U}$ to $S = \{0, \ldots, s - 1\}$. Then we store the object with key u in the $h(u)$th bucket. If several objects that we want to store are mapped to the same bucket, we have a collision between these objects. If there are no collisions, then we can realize the buckets just as an array, each array entry having space for one object. The theory of hash tables mainly deals with the questions of what to do about the collisions and how to choose the function h in such a way that the number of collisions is small.

The idea of hash tables is quite old, apparently starting in several groups at IBM in 1953 (Knott 1972). For a long time the main reason for the popularity of hash tables was the simple implementation; the hash functions h were chosen ad hoc as some unintelligible way to map the large universe to the small array allocated for the table. It was the practical programmer's dictionary structure of choice, easily written and conceptually understood, with no performance guarantees, and it still exists in this style in many texts aimed at that group. The development and analysis of hash table methods that are provably good in some sense started only in the 1980s, and now a well-designed hash table can indeed be a very efficient structure.

9.1 Basic Hash Tables and Collision Resolution

If we map the keys of a big universe $\mathcal{U}$ to a small set $S = \{0, \ldots, s - 1\}$, then it is unavoidable that many universe elements are mapped to the same element of S. In a dictionary structure, we do not have to store the entire universe, but only some set $X \subset \mathcal{U}$ of n keys for the objects currently in the dictionary. But if we do not know the set X when we choose the hash function $h : \mathcal{U} \to S$, as it is unavoidable if the set X is dynamic, changing by insertions and deletions, then we can choose a set X all of whose elements are mapped to the same $s \in S$. So something must be done about colliding elements in X.

There are two classical solutions to this problem:

1. Having for each $s \in S$, a secondary structure that stores all the elements $x \in X$ with $h(x) = s$. So each of the s buckets contains another dictionary, but because the buckets should contain only few elements, this secondary dictionary can be very simple. The simplest method is just a linked list of the elements; this is called "chaining."[1] This is the recommended method.
2. Having for each $u \in \mathcal{U}$ a sequence of alternative addresses in S: if $h(u) = h_1(u)$ is already used by a colliding element, we try $h_2(u)$, $h_3(u)$, ... until we find an empty bucket. This is called "open addressing," and it has been much studied, but its use is *strongly discouraged*.[2]

In the first solution, we partition the universe $\mathcal{U}$ by $h^{-1}(S)$ and store those $x \in X \subset \mathcal{U}$ that are in the same partition class in the same secondary structure. We can insert and delete in the structure if we can insert and delete in the secondary structure; the function h just directs us to the right secondary structure. If the partition induced on X is fine, with only at most a few elements in each bucket, this is especially good, but if there are many elements in the same bucket, it degrades no worse than the secondary structure we are using. We could use a balanced search tree as secondary structure and get a worst-time $O(\log n)$ bound in addition to an $O(1)$ time for all those elements whose bucket contains few elements. But we will show that with proper choice of the hash function and a not-too-small set S, most buckets are expected to be almost empty. So the choice of a linked list as secondary search structure is enough.

The second solution was very popular because we do not need linked lists, so no kind of dynamic memory allocation. It was, thus, considered especially easy to implement and space efficient, because it is an implicit structure without need for pointers. These minor advantages, which seem irrelevant on today's computers, are countered by a fundamental disadvantage: this structure does not support deletions. To insert an element x, we look at sequence of buckets $h_1(x), h_2(x), \ldots, h_k(x)$ to find an empty bucket. So in a find operation, we

---

[1] The literature calls this "indirect" or "separate" chaining because we allocate the nodes of the lists outside the hash table; "direct chaining" uses hash table entries as nodes and suffers from the same defects as method 2. Some variant chaining methods are described in Bays (1973a).

[2] Writing further papers on variants of open addressing should also be discouraged.

need to look again at the same sequence of buckets till we have found either the element or an empty bucket. If we delete an element along this sequence, its bucket becomes empty, so a later find operation for x will be unsuccessful because we broke the search path.

We could avoid this by marking the deleted element as invalid, but the bucket still as full; in that case we will accumulate many invalid buckets, which may be reused in insert operations, but will contribute to the search path length even though invalid. Or, if we delete an element in bucket i, we could try to move up along its search path any other element that had i in its search path and found that bucket full. But this is possible only if we know where that potential other element is; so all elements that have i occurring in their search path must have the same bucket j as the next element of their search path. This is very bad, because it leads to clustering, blocks of full buckets growing together; and any method that allows deletions will necessarily lead to that clustering.

The most obvious choice $h_i(x) = h_0(x) + i$ is for this reason a bad choice. If we do not use deletions, many different sequences of functions $(h_i(x))_{i=1}^s$ are possible as search paths, and they have been studied under the aspect of the expected length of the longest search path. A large number of papers have been written on the optimal choice of the sequence $(h_i(x))_{i=1}^s$, called probe sequences (Král 1971; Ullman 1972; Ecker 1974; Knuth 1974; Ajtai, Komlós, and Szemerédi 1978; Guibas and Szemerédi 1978; Gonnet 1981; Larson 1982, 1983; Yao 1985a,b; Lueker and Molodowitch 1988; Ramakrishna 1989a). But the small space advantage of avoiding pointers does never outweigh the fundamental disadvantage of losing deletions.

Next we give code for the basic hash table structure with chaining

```
typedef struct l_node {  key_t      key;
                         object_t   *obj;
                         struct l_node  *next;
                       } list_node_t;


typedef struct { int            size;
                 list_node_t **table;
                 int (*hash_function)
                 (key_t, hf_param_t);
                 /* the hash function might
                 need some parameters */
                 hf_param_t hf_param;
               } hashtable_t;
```

```
hashtable_t *create_hashtable(int size)
{  hashtable_t *tmp; int i;
   tmp = (hashtable_t *)
   malloc( sizeof(hashtable_t) );
   tmp->size = size;
   tmp->table = (list_node_t **)
   malloc(size*sizeof(list_node_t *));
   for( i=0; i<size; i++ )
      (tmp->table)[i] = NULL;
   /* fill in the hash function: needs to
      be added */
   /* and choose necessary parameters */
   return( tmp );
}


object_t *find(hashtable_t *ht, key_t query_key)
{  int i; list_node_t *tmp_node;
   i = ht->hash_function(query_key,
                         ht->hf_param );
   tmp_node = (ht->table)[i];
   while( tmp_node != NULL &&
          tmp_node->key != query_key )
     tmp_node = tmp_node->next;
   if( tmp_node == NULL )
      return( NULL ); /* not found */
   else
      return( tmp_node->obj ); /* key found */
}


void insert(hashtable_t *ht, key_t new_key,
            object_t *new_obj)
{  int i; list_node_t *tmp_node;
   i = ht->hash_function(new_key, ht->hf_param );
   tmp_node = (ht->table)[i];
   /* insert in front */
   (ht->table)[i] = get_node();
   ((ht->table)[i])->next = tmp_node;
   ((ht->table)[i])->key  = new_key;
```

```
    ((ht->table)[i])->obj   = new_obj;
}


object_t *delete(hashtable_t *ht, key_t del_key)
{   int i; list_node_t *tmp_node;
    object_t *tmp_obj;
    i = ht->hash_function(del_key, ht->hf_param );
    tmp_node = (ht->table)[i];
    if( tmp_node == NULL )
        return( NULL ); /* list empty,
        delete failed */
    if( tmp_node->key == del_key ) /* if first
    in list */
    {   tmp_obj = tmp_node->obj;
        (ht->table)[i] = tmp_node->next;
        return_node( tmp_node );
        return( tmp_obj );
    }
    /* list not empty, delete not first in list */
    while( tmp_node->next != NULL &&
            tmp_node->next->key != del_key )
        tmp_node = tmp_node->next;
    if( tmp_node->next == NULL )
        return( NULL ); /* not found,
        delete failed */
    else
    {   list_node_t *tmp_node2; /* unlink node */
        tmp_node2 = tmp_node->next;
        tmp_node->next = tmp_node2->next;
        tmp_obj = tmp_node2->obj;
        return_node( tmp_node2 );
        return( tmp_obj );
    }
}
```

Both methods have generated many variants. Because we are examining consecutive objects until we find the right key, walking down the list in the correct bucket in the chaining method, we want frequently accessed objects to be found early in each list. So within each bucket we have an instance of the much-studied list accessing problem for which the move-to-front strategy is known to be 2-competitive, that is, accessing at most twice as many list items as the strategy with the optimum sequence of list items. So it is an easy modification that brings some advantages for very skewed access patterns to move in each find operation the found object to the front within its list. This was proposed as self-adjusting hash tables (Pagli 1985; Wogulis 1989); it can also be combined with the open addressing strategy, but there it gets much more complicated. Next is the find function combined with the move-to-front strategy.

```
object_t *find(hashtable_t *ht, key_t query_key)
{   int i; list_node_t *front_node,
    *tmp_node1, *tmp_node2;
    i = ht->hash_function(query_key,
                          ht->hf_param );
    front_node = tmp_node1 = (ht->table)[i];
    tmp_node2 = NULL;
    while( tmp_node1 != NULL &&
           tmp_node1->key != query_key )
    { tmp_node2 = tmp_node1;
      tmp_node1 = tmp_node1->next;
    }
    if( tmp_node1 == NULL )
        return( NULL ); /* not found */
    else /* key found */
    {   if( tmp_node1 != front_node )
        /* move to front */
        {   tmp_node2->next = tmp_node1->next;
            /* unlink */
            tmp_node1->next = front_node;
            (ht->table)[i] = tmp_node1;
        }
        return( tmp_node1->obj );
    }
}
```

Many further variants have been studied for open addressing schemes. One key observation is that in a collision the situation of the two colliding elements is entirely symmetrical; we have to choose one of them to move further down along its search path, while the other stays in the bucket. In the basic open addressing scheme, we always move the new element, but there is no necessity for that. So there is some freedom to rearrange the table during an insert. This was first studied in Brent (1973) and then analyzed in many different strategies in Amble and Knuth (1974), Mallach (1977), Gonnet and Munro (1979), Maddison (1980), Rivest (1978), and Lyon (1985); Robin-Hood hashing (Celis, Larson, and Munro 1985; Devroye, Morin, and Viola 2004), last-come-first-served hashing (Poblete and Munro 1989), and Cuckoo hashing (Pagh and Rodler 2004; Devroye and Morin 2003) all belong to this category. Another type or open addressing variant is split sequence hashing (Lodi and Luccio 1985; Wogulis 1989), where the next step in the probe sequence depends on the key of the element occupying the current bucket, which makes it similar to using a search tree as secondary structure in chaining.

By its conceptual simplicity and lack of intrinsic problems, chaining generated much less variants and continues to be the recommended solution. One interesting variant is two-way chaining, in which each element of the universe is assigned to two possible buckets; on insertion, it is added to the bucket that contains fewer elements. This was introduced in Azar et al. (1999) and further analyzed in Berenbrink et al. (2000).

There are several variants that avoid the use of pointers up to a maximum capacity, and only then resort to chaining. The trivial solution is to have a hash table as array, in which each bucket has space for a fixed number of items, and to use chaining only when that bucket is full. Another method is the use of a sequence of hash tables; if the entry is already used in the first table, we look in the second table, with a different hash function, and so on, up to a fixed maximal number of tables; at the end we still have to resort to chaining. This has been proposed as especially convenient for parallelization because the lookup in the different tables is independent (Larson 1980; Broder and Karlin 1990; Mairson 1992).

9.2 Universal Families of Hash Functions

Up to the end of the 1970s, any theoretical analysis of hashing assumed that the hash values of the elements were independent random values, uniformly distributed on the available addresses; this is known as the uniform hashing model. And in actual use of a hash function, the implicit assumption was that any function that is complicated enough that the programmer does not really understand its effects will behave like a random assignment, mixing the values of the input set sufficiently well (Pearson 1990). This situation was very unsatisfactory, because in each use of a hash table, we are dealing with a concrete set, and the sets that are used are certainly not uniformly distributed in the universe $\mathcal{U}$.

The breakthrough was the introduction of the concept of universal families of hash functions by Carter and Wegman (1979). The idea here is that instead of keeping the hash function fixed and making an unjustified assumption on the random distribution of the input, we make a random choice of the hash function from a family of hash functions and show that for any input set the values of the hash functions are well distributed with high probability.

Let $\mathcal{F}$ be a family of functions that map $\mathcal{U}$ to S. The crucial property of the family $\mathcal{F}$, which is sufficient to distribute any set $X \subset \mathcal{U}$ well over S, is the following: We choose a function $f \in \mathcal{F}$ uniformly at random. Then we need for some c,

$$\text{for all distinct } u_1, u_2 \in \mathcal{U} \text{ holds} \qquad \text{Prob}(f(u_1) = f(u_2)) \leq \frac{c}{|S|}.$$

So the probability of a collision of any two elements under the randomly chosen hash function is only slightly larger than the probability if the values were chosen independently and uniformly from S, which is $\frac{1}{|S|}$. Any family $\mathcal{F}$ with this property is called a universal family of hash functions.[3] Sometimes this property is denoted as 2-universal because it is a restriction on pairs, and k-universal then denotes a similar property for k-tuples: any k-tuple $u_1 \ldots u_k$ of distinct elements of the universe will collide with probability at most $\frac{c}{|S|^{k-1}}$.

It is an immediate consequence of this definition that for any set X, stored in the hash table S by a randomly chosen function $h \in \mathcal{F}$, any y will have in expectation less than $c\frac{|X|}{|S|}$ collisions; this follows just by linearity of expectation, applied to all possible colliding pairs. This is, up to that factor of c, the same as for a completely random assignment. If the hash table is at least large enough to store all elements of X in distinct buckets, so $|S| \geq |X|$, then for any element $y \in \mathcal{U}$, the expected number of elements of X colliding with y is $O(1)$, so at least if we use chaining, the expected time of any find, insert, or delete is $O(1)$.

The property of the hash values we get by choice from a universal family of hash functions is very similar to pairwise independence of the hash values. This is much weaker than the complete independence assumed in the old uniform hashing model, but for the expected number of collisions with a single element, it is sufficient to also give an $O(1)$ bound. For distribution properties, it is much weaker: n random variables, each with an $O(1)$ expectation, can still have a

---

[3] Some literature demands this property with $c = 1$, but this slightly weaker property is easier to obtain and still sufficient for the results. Several further variants of the property are discussed in Stinson (1994) and Krovetz and Rogaway (2006).

large maximum. For the expected maximum size of a bucket, when hashing an
n-element set into a hash table of size s, we get only an $O(1 + \sqrt{\frac{n^2}{s}})$ bound,
because

$$\max_{i=1,\dots,s} bucketsize(i) \leq 1 + \sqrt{\sum_{i=1}^{s} (\max(0, bucketsize(i) - 1))^2}$$

$$< 1 + \sqrt{\sum_{i=1}^{s} 2\binom{bucketsize(i)}{2}},$$

and $\sum_{i=1}^{s} \binom{bucketsize(i)}{2}$ is the total number of colliding pairs, which is in expectation less than $\binom{n}{2}\frac{c}{s}$, so

$$E\left[\max_{i=1,\dots,s} bucketsize(i)\right] < 1 + E\left[\sqrt{\sum_{i=1}^{s} 2\binom{bucketsize(i)}{2}}\right]$$

$$\leq 1 + \sqrt{2E\left[\sum_{i=1}^{s} \binom{bucketsize(i)}{2}\right]}$$

$$\leq 1 + \sqrt{2\binom{n}{2}\frac{c}{s}} \quad \leq \quad 1 + \sqrt{c\frac{n^2}{s}}.$$

We summarize these properties of universal families of hash functions as follows:

Theorem. When we distribute a set $X \subset \mathcal{U}$ of n items over a hash table S of size s, using a randomly chosen hash function from a universal family of hash functions,

- the expected number of collisions of any element $y \in \mathcal{U}$ is $\leq c\frac{n}{s}$; and
- the expected maximum bucket size is $\leq 1 + \sqrt{c\frac{n^2}{s}}$.

This is, of course, only an upper bound for the expected maximum bucket size, but Alon et al. (1999) showed that this is the best we can get out of the universality assumption, by giving a specific universal family of hash functions for a hash table of size n, and n-element set, so that for any function in that family there is a bucket that received $\Theta(\sqrt{n})$ elements. So for the maximum bucket size, the universality assumption is much weaker than the complete independence of the uniform hashing model, which gives an expected maximum bucket size of $\Theta(\frac{\log n}{\log \log n})$ for hashing an n-element set into a table of size n (Gomet 1981). Some specific universal families of hash functions behave much better than this $O(\sqrt{n})$ bound (Alon et al. 1999).

Up to now we did not give an example of a universal family of hash functions. The trivial example is the family of all functions from $\mathcal{U}$ to S; this is the same as assigning independently to each universe element its image, so it is just a different way to express the uniform hashing model. This family of hash functions is useless because it is too large; just to specify a function, we would need a table with $|\mathcal{U}|$ entries. So we need two further properties of a family of universal hash functions:

- it must be small and have a convenient parametrization, so we can easily select the random function from this family, and
- it must be easy to evaluate.

To give such a family, we need more structure on the universe $\mathcal{U}$.

The classical theory assumes that $\mathcal{U} = \{0, \dots, p - 1\}$ for some prime p. This is reasonable if our universe is a set of numbers. Then we choose some sufficiently large prime, slightly less than the square root of maximum integer our machine arithmetic can handle, because we will need products of two such numbers, and larger than all the numbers that can occur in our application.[4] But it is important that we can really perform the arithmetic operations without numerical overflow and reduction modulo 2^{wordsize}; otherwise the families might stop being universal and may behave quite badly (Mullin 1991). We assume that $S = \{0, \dots, s - 1\}$ with $s \leq p$.

The simplest universal family of hash functions is the family

$$\mathcal{F}_{ps} = \{h_a : \mathcal{U} \to S \mid h_a(x) = (ax \bmod p) \bmod s, 1 \leq a \leq p - 1\}.$$

This family consists of $p - 1$ functions; to show that it is a universal family, we need to bound the number of a for which $h_a(x) = h_a(y)$ for any fixed pair x, y of distinct elements of $\mathcal{U}$. But if $x \neq y$ and

$$(ax \bmod p) \bmod s = (ay \bmod p) \bmod s,$$

then there is a $q \neq 0$ with $-(p - 1) \leq qs \leq (p - 1)$ such that

$$ax \bmod p = ay \bmod p + qs.$$

---

[4] On a machine with 32-bit integers, so INT_MAX $= 2147483647$, choose $p = 46337$. On a machine with 64-bit integers, choose $p = 3037000493$.

There are at most $\frac{2(p-1)}{s}$ possible choices for q. For each q, the congruence

$$ax \equiv ay + qs \bmod p$$

has a unique solution a. So there are at most $\frac{2(p-1)}{s}$ functions h_a for which x and y will collide. With uniform random choice from the $p-1$ functions of the family, this gives a collision probability at most $\frac{2}{s}$, as required by the definition of a universal family.

The classical universal family of hash functions given already by Carter and Wegman (1979) is the two-parameter family

$$\mathcal{G}_{ps} = \{h_{ab}\colon \mathcal{U} \to S \mid h_{ab}(x) = ((ax+b) \bmod p) \bmod s, 0 \le a,b \le p-1\}.$$

Note that this is not just a cyclic permutation of the previous functions by b steps: $h_{ab}(x) = h_{ab}(y)$ does not imply $h_{a(b+1)}(x) = h_{a(b+1)}(y)$. Like the previous class, it is very convenient class: for the initial random choice, we just need to select two integers, and to evaluate the function, we need only four arithmetic operations. To show that this family is universal, we have to show that for each pair $x, y \in \mathcal{U}$, $x \ne y$, at most a fraction of $\frac{c}{s}$ of the p^2 possible parameter pairs a, b generates a collision. But if $h_{ab}(x) = h_{ab}(y)$, then there is an $r \in \{0, \ldots, s-1\}$ with $h_{ab}(x) = r$ and $h_{ab}(y) = r$ or

$$((ax+b) \bmod p) - r \equiv 0 \bmod s,$$
$$((ay+b) \bmod p) - r \equiv 0 \bmod s.$$

So there are integers q_x, q_y with

$$((ax+b) \bmod p) - r = q_x s,$$
$$((ay+b) \bmod p) - r = q_y s,$$

and because the left-hand side is a number between $-(s-1)$ and $p-1$, we find $q_x, q_y \in \{0, \ldots, \left\lfloor \frac{p-1}{s} \right\rfloor\}$. But for each choice of r, q_x, q_y, there is a unique pair a, b that solves the system of linear equations $\bmod\, p$

$$ax + b \equiv r + q_x s \bmod p,$$
$$ay + b \equiv r + q_y s \bmod p,$$

viewed as linear equations for a, b. This system is nondegenerate because $x \ne y$ and the coefficient of b is 1. Thus, there are as many pairs (a, b) that lead to a collision as there are choices for r, q_x, q_y, which is $s \lceil \frac{p}{s} \rceil \lceil \frac{p}{s} \rceil$. This is a $\frac{c}{s}$ fraction of all pairs (a, b) for $c = \left(\frac{\lceil \frac{p}{s} \rceil}{\frac{p}{s}}\right)^2$, which is very near 1 for p much larger than s. Thus, the family $\mathcal{G}_{ps}$ is a universal family of hash functions, with a slightly better constant c.

Frequently we want to have a universe that is not just a set of numbers, but something that can be encoded as a k-tuple of numbers for some fixed k, for example, a set of board positions in a game. The family of hash functions easily extends to that situation: if $\mathcal{U} = \{0, \ldots, p - 1\}^k$ for some prime p, we use the family of functions

$$h_{a_1 \ldots a_k b}(x_1, \ldots, x_k) = ((a_1 x_1 + \cdots + a_k x_k + b) \bmod p) \bmod s.$$

The proof is completely analogous to the special case $k = 1$: given $(x_1, \ldots, x_k)$ and $(y_1, \ldots, y_k)$, there are $r \in \{0, \ldots, s - 1\}$ and $q_x, q_y \in \{0, \ldots, \left\lfloor \frac{p-1}{s} \right\rfloor \}$ with

$$(a_1 x_1 + \cdots + a_k x_k + b) \bmod p = r + q_x s,$$
$$(a_1 y_1 + \cdots + a_k y_k + b) \bmod p = r + q_y s,$$

and for given r, q_x, q_y the system of linear equations

$$a_1 x_1 + \cdots + a_k x_k + b \equiv r + q_x s \bmod p,$$
$$a_1 y_1 + \cdots + a_k y_k + b \equiv r + q_y s \bmod p$$

has p^{k-1} solutions $(a_1, \ldots, a_k, b) \in \{0, \ldots, p - 1\}^{k+1}$.

For strings, we have the problem that they are not of fixed length. We can implicitly extend them by 0 in all later positions up to some maximum length k. This will not change the hash value, so for short strings we do not have to compute those implicit extended positions. We need, however, as many coefficients as the maximum length of any string requires, but these random coefficients can be selected when they become necessary.

Another universal family of hash functions that is both easy to implement and good in performance is the family of all linear maps of bit strings of length t to bit strings of length r, both viewed as linear spaces over Z_2. So in that situation we have $\mathcal{U} = \{0, 1\}^t$ and $S = \{0, 1\}^r$, which is very natural for computer applications. To specify a linear map, we need the images of a basis, so t numbers of r bits each. To evaluate the linear map for a given element of the universe, that is, a t-bit number x, we perform addition $\bmod 2$, that is, xor, on those numbers of the basis that correspond to 1 bit in x. It is obvious from linear algebra that the family of all linear maps is indeed a universal family of hash functions; this family was studied in Markowsky, Carter, and Wegman (1978) and Alon et al. (1999), where it was shown that it is in some ways nearer to the behavior of uniform hashing and thus preferable to the families $\mathcal{F}_{ps}$ or $\mathcal{G}_{ps}$. The price of this is that the family is larger, so needs more bits of specification; where the previous family needed only two numbers of size $\log |\mathcal{U}|$, this family needs $\log |\mathcal{U}|$ numbers of size $\log |S|$. It might be still preferable, especially in view of the simple bit operations it uses.

Next we give code for the universal hash functions of the family $\mathcal{G}_{ps}$, for a universe $\mathcal{U} = \{0, \ldots, \text{MAXP} - 1\}$, with MAXP prime.

```c
#define MAXP 46337   /* prime,
and 46337*46337 < 2147483647 */

typedef struct l_node {  key_t      key;
                         object_t  *obj;
                 struct l_node  *next;
               } list_node_t;

typedef struct { int a; int b; int size;
               } hf_param_t;

typedef struct { int          size;
        list_node_t **table;
        int (*hash_function)(key_t, hf_param_t);
        hf_param_t hf_param;
               } hashtable_t;

hashtable_t *create_hashtable(int size)
{  hashtable_t *tmp; int i;
   int a, b;
   int universalhashfunction(key_t,
   hf_param_t);
   if( size >= MAXP )
      exit(-1); /* should not be called with
      that large size */
   /* possibly initialize random number
   generator here */
   tmp = (hashtable_t *)
         malloc( sizeof(hashtable_t) );
   tmp->size = size;
   tmp->table = (list_node_t **)
           malloc(size*sizeof(list_node_t *));
   for(i=0; i<size; i++)
      (tmp->table)[i] = NULL;
   tmp->hf_param.a = rand()%MAXP;
   tmp->hf_param.b = rand()%MAXP;
```

```
        tmp->hf_param.size = size;
        tmp->hashfunction = universalhashfunction;
        return( tmp );
}


int universalhashfunction(key_t key,
                          hf_param_t hfp)
{  return( ((hfp.a*key + hfp.b)%MAXP)%hfp.size );
}
```

Next is another version of the same functions for the universe of strings;
here we organize the parameters of the universal hash function as a list of the
coefficients, which gets extended whenever the maximum length of the strings
increases. Here the find, insert, and delete functions also need to be
changed, because we need to compare the entire string to check whether we
found the right key.

```
#define MAXP 46337   /* prime,
and 46337*46337 < 2147483647 */


typedef struct l_node {  char       *key;
                         object_t   *obj;
                      struct l_node  *next;
                         } list_node_t;

typedef struct htp_l_node { int a;
                      struct htp_l_node *next;
                         } htp_l_node_t;

typedef struct { int b;   int size;
                 struct htp_l_node *a_list;
                 } hf_param_t;

typedef struct { int            size;
        list_node_t **table;
        int (*hash_function)(char *, hf_param_t);
        hf_param_t hf_param;
                } hashtable_t;
```

```
hashtable_t *create_hashtable(int size)
{  hashtable_t *tmp; int i;
   int universalhashfunction(char *, hf_param_t);
   if( size >= MAXP )
      exit(-1); /* should not be called with that
      large size */
   tmp = (hashtable_t *)
         malloc( sizeof(hashtable_t) );
   tmp->size = size;
   tmp->table = (list_node_t **)
            malloc(size*sizeof(list_node_t *));
   for(i=0; i<size; i++)
      (tmp->table)[i] = NULL;
   tmp->hf_param.b = rand()%MAXP;
   tmp->hf_param.size = size;
   tmp->hf_param.a_list =
   (htp_l_node_t *) get_node();
   tmp->hf_param.a_list->next = NULL;
   tmp->hash_function = universalhashfunction;
   return( tmp );
}


int universalhashfunction(char *key,
                          hf_param_t hfp)
{  int sum;
   htp_l_node_t *al;
   sum = hfp.b;
   al = hfp.a_list;
   while( *key != '\0' )
   { if( al->next == NULL )
      {  al->next = (htp_l_node_t *) get_node();
         al->next->next = NULL;
         al->a = rand()%MAXP;
      }
      sum += ( (al->a)*((int) *key))%MAXP;
      key += 1;
      al = al->next;
   }
   return( sum%hfp.size );
}
```

```
object_t *find(hashtable_t *ht, char *query_key)
{  int i; list_node_t *tmp_node;
   char *tmp1, *tmp2;
   i = ht->hash_function(query_key,
                         ht->hf_param );
   tmp_node = (ht->table)[i];
   while( tmp_node != NULL )
   { tmp1 = tmp_node->key; tmp2 = query_key;
     while( *tmp1 != '\0' && *tmp2 != '\0' &&
            *tmp1 == *tmp2 )
     {  tmp1++; tmp2++; }
     if( *tmp1 != *tmp2 ) /*strings not equal */
       tmp_node = tmp_node->next;
     else /* strings equal: correct entry
     found */
       break;
   }
   if( tmp_node == NULL )
     return( NULL ); /* not found */
   else
     return( tmp_node->obj ); /* key found */
}

void insert(hashtable_t *ht, char *new_key,
            object_t *new_obj)
{  int i; list_node_t *tmp_node;
   i = ht->hash_function(new_key, ht->hf_param );
   tmp_node = (ht->table)[i];
   /* insert in front */
   (ht->table)[i] = get_node();
   ((ht->table)[i])->next = tmp_node;
   ((ht->table)[i])->key  = new_key;
   ((ht->table)[i])->obj  = new_obj;
}

object_t *delete(hashtable_t *ht, char * del_key)
{  int i; list_node_t *tmp_node;
   object_t *tmp_obj;
   char *tmp1, *tmp2;
```

```
i = ht->hash_function(del_key, ht->hf_param );
tmp_node = (ht->table)[i];
if( tmp_node == NULL )
   return( NULL ); /* list empty,
   delete failed */
/* test first item in list */
tmp1 = tmp_node->key; tmp2 = del_key;
while( *tmp1 != '\0' && *tmp2 != '\0' &&
       *tmp1 == *tmp2 )
{  tmp1++; tmp2++; }
if( *tmp1 == *tmp2 )/* strings equal:
correct entry found */
{  tmp_obj = tmp_node->obj; /* delete first
   entry in list */
   (ht->table)[i] = tmp_node->next;
   return_node( tmp_node );
   return( tmp_obj );
}
/* list not empty, delete not first in list */
while( tmp_node->next != NULL )
{ tmp1 = tmp_node->next->key; tmp2 = del_key;
  while( *tmp1 != '\0' && *tmp2 != '\0' &&
         *tmp1 == *tmp2 )
  {  tmp1++; tmp2++; }
  if( *tmp1 != *tmp2 ) /* strings not equal */
     tmp_node = tmp_node->next;
  else /* strings equal: correct entry
  found */
     break;
}
if( tmp_node->next == NULL )
   return( NULL ); /* not found, delete
   failed */
else
{  list_node_t *tmp_node2; /* unlink node */
   tmp_node2 = tmp_node->next;
   tmp_node->next = tmp_node->next->next;
   tmp_obj = tmp_node2->obj;
   return_node( tmp_node2 );
```

```
        return( tmp_obj );
    }
}
```

We summarize the performance of the hash table structure as follows:

Theorem. The hash table with chaining, using a universal family of hash functions, stores a set of n elements in a table of size s, supporting the operations find, insert, and delete, in expected time $O(1 + n/s)$ for each operation and requires space $O(n + s)$.

Universal families of hash functions are a very useful tool both in theory and in practice. Further families with stronger independence properties were studied in Siegel (1989, 2004) and Mansour et al. (1993).

9.3 Perfect Hash Functions

A hash function is perfect if it does not cause any collisions for the set it stores. This sounds like a great advantage, but it should be noted that this is a definition relative to the set, so we need to know the set in advance and keep it fixed. If we are given a set $X \in \mathcal{U}$ and a hash table $S = \{0, \ldots, s - 1\}$, we can ask for a function that maps $\mathcal{U}$ to S and is injective on X.

If $|X| \leq |S|$, there are always such functions: if $\mathcal{U}$ is linearly ordered, we can build a search tree for X and store in each leaf its address in S. This is, of course, quite useless, so there is an important additional restriction: we must be able to evaluate the function fast, in constant time. This is first mentioned in Knuth (1973) as an exercise for the ingenuity of the function constructor, to be done by hand. As an algorithmic problem, to find a perfect hash function for a given set X, this was first studied in Sprugnoli (1977), where some methods were given, which always construct a perfect hash function, but might require a very large table S and might take very long to find that function. Many further construction methods were proposed, for example, Cichelli (1980),[5] Jaeschke (1981), Bell and Floyd (1983), Chang (1984), Cormack, Horspool, and Kaiserswerth (1985), Sager (1985), Yang and Du (1985), Chang and Lee (1986), Chang, Chen, and Jan (1991), Czech et al. (1992), Fox et al. (1992), Czech and Majewski (1993), Majewski et al. (1996), and Czech (1998) (see

---

[5] Which, in spite of the fact that it obviously in general does not work and looks only at the first and the last letter of a string and its length, is still recommended by various "practical" authors.

Czech, Havas, and Majewski (1993) for a survey). All these methods are just heuristics and do not work for arbitrary sets X; at best, they have a high success probability if the set X is chosen uniformly at random from $\mathcal{U}$. Methods that in principle always give a perfect hash function, but are not practically realizable, were given by Tarjan and Yao (1979) and Yao (1981). But the method of Fredman, Komlós, and Szemerédi (1984) is really the ultimate solution: it works always, is elegant, and simple enough to be practical. The only disadvantage is the general disadvantage of perfect hash functions, that they do not support changes in the underlying set.

The idea underlying Fredman et al. (1984) is to use a two-level scheme, first distributing the set X over a table of size $|X|$, using a function from a universal family of hash functions. This partitions the set X into the classes that are assigned the same hash value $X = X_1 \cup \cdots \cup X_k$. All elements of each class X_i are in collision, but the use of a universal family of hash functions bounds the expected total number of colliding pairs.

$$E[\text{total number of colliding pairs}] = E\left[\sum_{i=1}^{k} \binom{|X_i|}{2}\right]$$

$$\leq c \binom{|X|}{2} \frac{1}{\text{table size}} < \frac{c}{2}|X|$$

Now for each set X_i, we choose again a universal hash function to distribute X_i over a table of size $|X_i|^2$. We showed in the previous section that the expected maximum bucket size, when distributing n elements over a hash table of size s, is $O(1 + \sqrt{\binom{n}{2}\frac{c}{s}})$, so for each of these second-level hash tables the expected maximum bucket size is $O(1)$. Thus, we have a method that gives us access to the correct element in $O(1)$ time: evaluate the first hash function, look up in the first hash table what the correct second hash function is, evaluate that second hash function, and go through the at most $O(1)$ candidates. And the total size of the structure is only $O(|X|)$ because $\sum_{i=1}^{k} \binom{|X_i|}{2} = O(|X|)$. By choosing the secondary hash tables a bit larger and by a constant factor that depends on the c of the universal family of hash functions, we can even achieve that there are no collisions at all in the secondary hash tables.

Fredman, et al. (1984) used this idea with the first universal family of hash functions $h_a(x) = ((ax) \bmod p) \bmod s$ we gave in the previous section. Using some further tricks, they managed to reduce the size of the structure representing a set of n numbers from $O(n)$ to $n + o(n)$, with $O(1)$ time to access an item. Here we assume that our arithmetic operations, as well as the table access, are constant-time operations. The problem has also been studied in other models of computation, but these do not appear relevant for practical implementation.

Indeed, the practical importance of perfect hash functions remains, in spite of numerous papers, dubious. If we need to store a static set of integers, the method of Fredman et al. is, at least in the version without space optimization, indeed easily realized and very efficient. But there are not many situations in which we need to store a static dictionary of integers. The frequently cited application is a static set of strings; the early literature always gives the set of keywords of a programming language as motivation. But for strings, we get the same performance with tries, and they support insertion and deletion.

Next we give an implementation of the method of Fredman et al. (1984) without the size optimization. The hash functions are chosen randomly and then we check whether they have the required properties, that is, the bound on the sum of squared bucket sizes for the primary hash function and injectivity for each of the secondary hash functions; we repeat the choice until the conditions are satisfied, which needs $O(1)$ attempts. We do not move the items to separate bucket structures after the primary hashing, because that would require additional space, instead we select for all buckets a secondary hash function and start to distribute the items with these hash functions. If the secondary hash function of a bucket causes a collision, we mark that bucket as defect. If there were any defect buckets, we choose a new secondary hash function for each of them, clear all defect buckets, and again distribute all items with these hash functions. After $O(1)$ repetitions, there will be no defect buckets left. This method has the additional overhead that in each round, we distribute all items, even those whose buckets were already collision-free; but we avoid the need for an intermediate structure to store the contents of the buckets for redistribution, and the time overhead is only a constant factor. To check for collisions, we need a value that is different from all keys occurring in the data. We use MAXP, which is assumed to be larger than all keys in the universe.

```
#define MAXP 46337   /* prime,
and 46337*46337 < 2147483647 */

typedef struct { int          size;
                 int       primary_a;
                 int     *secondary_a;
                 int     *secondary_s;
                 int     *secondary_o;
                 int          *keys;
                 object_t      *objs;
               } perf_hash_t;
```

```
perf_hash_t *create_perf_hash(int size,
                  int keys[], object_t objs[])
{  perf_hash_t *tmp;
   int *table1, *table2, *table3, *table4;
   int i, j, k, collision, sq_bucket_sum,
       sq_sum_limit, a;
   object_t *objects;
   tmp = (perf_hash_t *)
         malloc( sizeof(perf_hash_t) );
   table1 = (int *) malloc( size * sizeof(int) );
   table2 = (int *) malloc( size * sizeof(int) );
   table3 = (int *) malloc( size * sizeof(int) );
   sq_sum_limit  =   5*size;
   sq_bucket_sum = 100*size;
   while(sq_bucket_sum > sq_sum_limit)
   /* find primary factor */
   {  a = rand()%MAXP;
      for(i=0; i<size; i++)
         table1[i] = 0;
      for(i=0; i<size; i++)
         table1[ (((a*keys[i])%MAXP)% size) ]
         +=1;
      sq_bucket_sum = 0;
      for(i=0; i<size; i++)
         sq_bucket_sum += table1[i]*table1[i];
   }
   /* compute secondary table sizes and
   their offset */
   for(i=0; i< size; i++ )
   {  table1[i] = 2*table1[i]*table1[i];
      table2[i] = (i>0) ? table2[i-1] +
      table1[i-1] : 0;
   }
   table4 = (int *)
   malloc( 2*sq_bucket_sum * sizeof(int) );
   for( i=0; i< 2*sq_bucket_sum; i++ )
      table4[i] = MAXP; /* different from
      all keys */
   collision = 1;
```

```
for( i=0; i< size; i++ )
   table3[i] = rand()%MAXP; /* secondary
   hash factor */
while( collision )
{  collision = 0;
   for( i=0; i< size; i++ )
   {  j = ((keys[i]*a)% MAXP) % size;
      k = ((keys[i]*table3[j])% MAXP)
         % table1[j] + table2[j];
      if( table4[k] == MAXP ||
         table4[k] == keys[i] )
         table4[k] = keys[i]; /* entry up
         to now empty */
      else /* collision */
      {  collision = 1;
         table3[i] = 0; /* mark bucket
         as defect */
      }
   }
   if( collision )
   {  for( i=0; i< size; i++)
      {  if( table3[i] == 0 )
         /* defect bucket */
         {  table3[i] = rand()%MAXP;
            /* choose new factor */
            for( k= table2[i];
               k< table2[i]+table1[i]; k++)
              table4[k] = MAXP;
              /* clear i-th secondary table */
         }
      }
   }
} /* now the hash table is collision-free */
/* keys are in the right places, now put
objects there */
objects =(object_t *)
   malloc(2*sq_bucket_sum*sizeof(object_t) );
for( i=0; i< size; i++ )
{  j = ((keys[i]*a)% MAXP) % size;
   k = ((keys[i]*table3[j])% MAXP)
```

```
                    % table1[j] + table2[j];
               objects[k] = objs[i];
          }
          tmp->size = size;
          tmp->primary_a = a;
          /* primary hash table factor */
          tmp->secondary_a = table3;
          /* secondary hash table factors */
          tmp->secondary_s = table1;
          /* secondary hash table sizes */
          tmp->secondary_o = table2;
          /* secondary hash table offsets */
          tmp->keys = table4;
          /* secondary hash tables */
          tmp->objs = objects;
          return( tmp );
     }


     object_t *find(perf_hash_t *ht, int query_key)
     {   int i, j;
         i = ((ht->primary_a*query_key)% MAXP)
             %ht->size;
         if( ht->secondary_s[i] == 0 )
            return( NULL ); /* secondary bucket empty */
         else
         {   j = ((ht->secondary_a[i]*query_key)% MAXP)
                 %ht->secondary_s[i] + ht->secondary_o[i];
             if( ht->keys[j] == query_key )
                 return( (ht->objs)+j ); /* right
                 key found */
             else
                 return( NULL ); /* query_key does not
                 exist. */
         }
     }
```

We summarize the performance of this structure.

Theorem. The perfect hash table structure of Fredman et al. is a static dictionary that keeps track of a set of n elements identified by integer keys. It can be created in $O(n)$ time, requires $O(n)$ space, and supports find operations in $O(1)$ time.

Perfect hash functions have also been studied in other computation models, especially counting the bit complexity of the program size of a family of functions that contains a perfect hash function for every n-element set of the universe, for example, in Mehlhorn (1982), Fredman and Komlós (1984), Schmidt and Siegel (1990), Mairson (1992), Dietzfelbinger and Hagerup (2001), and Hagerup and Tholey (2001).

9.4 Hash Trees

Up to now we always assumed that the hash function maps the universe $\mathcal{U}$ into a set of integers $S = \{0, \ldots, s - 1\}$, which are then used as the addresses in an array. An alternative model was introduced by Coffman and Eve (1970). They considered hash functions that map the universe $\mathcal{U}$ into a potentially infinite bit string, of which one can take as much as necessary to distinguish each element in the current set from all other elements. They then proposed to break this bit string into pieces of k bits and interpret this as key to a trie structure over the alphabet $\{0, 1\}^k$. The object is then stored in the trie under that key. This is a structure that does not require any arrays, but instead has fixed-size trie nodes as the basic unit.

This key string of potential infinite length can be viewed as another method to avoid collisions: if two elements $u_1, u_2 \in \mathcal{U}$ collide in the current structure, we just take a longer prefix of their key until they are separated. But if the key string is not a constant, this forces some changes on the trie structure, depending on the way we resolve these collisions. There are two methods proposed in Coffman and Eve (1970). If we insert a new element u_2 and there is already an element u_1 whose hash key string agrees with that of u_2 up to the point that is used in the current structure, then

– Either we take a longer prefix of its hash key string for u_2 and leave u_1 in the node where it is already stored: This method was called sequence trees; it has the advantage of the simpler insertion, but to find the object with hash key $b_0 b_1 b_2 \ldots$, we have to look in the nodes b_0, $b_0 b_1$, $b_0 b_1 b_2$, $\ldots$; each of these nodes contains an object, and for each of these objects, we have to check whether its original key in $\mathcal{U}$ agrees with the query key;

– Or we take longer prefixes of the hash key strings of both u_1 and u_2, long enough to distinguish u_1 and u_2, and store u_1 and u_2 in those nodes: This method was called prefix trees; it stores objects only in the leaf nodes of the trie structure. On insertion we might have to move both colliding elements to a new node, but in a find operation, we need to make a key comparison of the original key in $\mathcal{U}$ only for one node.

If a key comparison of the original keys in $\mathcal{U}$ is expensive, for example, because we hashed long strings into short strings, the second method is clearly preferable. But it has the disadvantage that there might be many trie nodes with a single outgoing edge if there are hash keys with a long common prefix. So we trade key comparisons in the original universe against hash key comparisons and space.

Because each trie node has at most 2^k outgoing edges and we have at least n nodes, there is a leaf at distance at least $\log_{2^k}(n) = \frac{1}{k} \log n$ from the root. So even with the best hash function, we cannot get a complexity better than $O(\frac{1}{k} \log n)$. For small k that is the performance, we could as well achieve by a balanced search tree if key comparisons in $\mathcal{U}$ are constant time. For larger k the nodes get larger, because the size of a single node is $O(2^k)$, but we can, assuming an optimal hash function, reach the correct leaf faster, until for $k = \log n$ we just need the root node, which becomes a normal hash table. So the hash trees are in their behavior between hash tables and balanced search trees, and are interesting especially if key comparisons of the original keys are expensive.

As in all hash table structures, we hope that the mapping performed by the hash function improves the distribution properties of our set; if the hash function is bad, because there are hash keys with long common prefixes, the sequence tree variant can degenerate into a simple unordered list and the prefix trees can be arbitrary bad. The assumption in Coffman and Eve (1970) was, as in all papers of that period, that the hash values would be independent and uniformly distributed. The infinite bit strings can then be interpreted as real numbers in the interval $[0, 1[$. The expected maximum length of the path we have to follow in the trie to find a given key is then $O(\frac{1}{k} \log n)$, with nodes of size $O(2^k)$.

9.5 Extendible Hashing

The classical hash table structure has a fixed maximum size. For the open addressing-related methods of collision resolution, this is really a hard limit, and performance degrades so badly near the maximum capacity that one has to stay well below it. For the chaining methods, which we recommended, the situation is not as bad, and they can be used beyond their nominal capacity, but lose the expected constant-time operations. So, to make hash tables a truly dynamic structure, the maximum size limitations should be avoided, while retaining the advantages of constant-time find, insert, and delete operations.

This can easily be achieved by the standard technique of building shadow copies, as described in Section 1.5, by building a copy of the hash table in a larger array, doubling the size, and copying in each step several elements from the smaller to the larger hash table, so that the copy is complete before the smaller hash table overflows. This generates only a constant factor of overhead for each operation, so all operations still retain their expected constant time performance, if we use a universal family of hash functions.

This is now only an obvious combination of the tools we have developed before, but it appeared in literature only rather late in Brassard and Kannan (1988). Total rebuilding of the hash table on reaching a capacity limit has been used already early (Bays 1973b); but then we give up on worst-case performance bounds, interrupt everything else, and build the new hash table. This is much less demanding on the memory requirement because the two tables coexist only during this rebuilding phase, whereas if we rebuild the table concurrent with its use, we permanently block an additional piece of memory that is larger than the hash table actually used.

Earlier work on extendible hash tables focused on a different type of structure that typically was interpreted as an external-memory structure, frequently compared to B-trees. We see here again the influence of memory limitations in the earlier work on data structures.

The classical structures known as extendible hashing were first proposed in papers by Larson (1978) as "dynamic hashing," by Litwin (1978) as "virtual hashing" and Litwin (1980) "linear hashing," and by Fagin et al. (1979) as "extendible hashing." Many related methods have since been proposed (see Enbody and Du (1988) for a survey). All these methods are based on the idea of splitting buckets when they are overfull, while maintaining some bookkeeping system to keep track of the buckets. They all assume that the hash function really gives an arbitrary long bit string, as in the hash tree model; so if the hash table gets larger, they can just take more bits of the hash function. All analysis was done under the uniform hashing assumption that the hash values are arriving independent, uniformly distributed. They all lack any worst-case performance guarantee.[6]

---

[6] In spite of frequently repeated claims like "... guaranteed no more than two page faults to locate the data ..." (Fagin et al. 1979), similar claims for many other structures are repeated in many well-known textbooks. These structures are interpreted as external-memory structures, counting only external block accesses, but unlike true external-memory structures, they do not keep the amount of internal memory constant.

These structures are two-level structures: with a primary structure converting the hash value into a bucket number and a secondary structure for each
bucket. The bucket itself has a finite maximum capacity B, and it is frequently
identified with an external memory page; but in a main-memory application, it
can be realized in many ways, for example, as array, linked list, or as another
hash table. The measure analyzed in many papers is the memory utilization
expressed in the number of buckets used to store n elements; the primary
structure is assumed to be small and fit in the main memory, whereas the
buckets are in external memory.

In the first of these methods, the "dynamic hashing" method by Larson
(1978) is related to the prefix hash trees described in the previous section.
The only difference is that each leaf can hold several items. Thus, the primary
structure is a binary trie, where the buckets are associated with the leaves of
the trie. To find an element, we interpret the hash value as bit string and use
a prefix of it that is so long as to lead to a leaf in the trie; then, we use the
rest of the hash value to find the required element in the bucket associated
with the leaf. To insert a new element, we follow the same path and try to
insert the new element in the bucket associated with the leaf; if the bucket
overflows, we split the leaf, taking the next bit of the hash value, and distribute
the contents of the previous leaf bucket over the two buckets associated with the
new leaves. Under the uniform hashing assumption, this trie will be balanced,
having height $O(\log \frac{n}{B})$, and the number of buckets used to store the n elements
will be $O(\frac{n}{B})$, indeed about $1.44\frac{n}{B}$, giving a 70% storage utilization, and some
further refinements were analyzed (Larson 1978). If the hashing is not uniform,
it is easy to make this structure arbitrary bad, always forcing the same bucket
to be split.

The "virtual hashing" method of Litwin (1978) makes the primary structure
implicit and uses sequence hash trees instead of prefix hash trees, following
a search path through multiple buckets. If the hash value is $b_1b_2b_3\ldots$, the
method first looks in bucket b_1, then in bucket b_1b_2, then in bucket $b_1b_2b_3$, and
so on. For an insertion, we follow this sequence of buckets until we find one
that has still room for a new element. We need to keep track of the longest
prefix length of buckets that are in use, and increase that when necessary. A
simple method to translate these bit strings of increasing length in integer array
addresses is to map $b_1b_2\ldots b_k$ to $2^k - 1 + |b_1b_2\ldots b_k|$, where $|\cdots|$ denotes
the number represented by the bit string. Again, if the hash values are uniformly
distributed, the behavior of this is reasonable, using $O(\frac{n}{B})$ buckets to store n
items; to look up an item, we need to check $O(\log \frac{n}{B})$ buckets, instead of the
one bucket checked by the previous method; the advantage here is that upon a
bucket overflowing, we do not have to redistribute the elements of that bucket,

but just continue with the new elements in the next bucket along that prefix path. Again the structure can become arbitrary bad if the hash values are not uniformly distributed. And there is an additional problem that if we want to avoid the primary structure in this way, we assume that we can allocate an arbitrary number of consecutive buckets. Otherwise, we still need a primary structure to translate the bucket number into the address where the bucket is really stored. Litwin assumed this to be just an array, but indeed it would have to be an extendible array, as described in Section 1.5, with all the problems that this structure causes. If the array has fixed maximum size, we are back at our original problem.

The "linear hashing" method by Litwin (1980), the "extendible hashing" by Fagin et al. (1979), and the "spiral storage" by Martin[7] also assume the availability of an extendible array as primary structure and use a prefix of the hash value as index to that array, which then gives the address of the bucket containing the element. If buckets get overfull, the array size is doubled and a longer prefix of the hash value is used. Linear hashing and extendible hashing differ in the policy of splitting buckets.

Linear hashing just splits in a fixed cyclic order, so not the overflowing bucket is split, but that bucket whose turn is next. The overflow problem is then handled by attaching an overflow bucket to the intended bucket. When it finally becomes its turn to be split, all items from the bucket and all overflow buckets it might have acquired are redistributed according to their next bit in the hash value. If the hash values are assumed to be independent and uniformly distributed, this simple policy is sufficient to keep the expected number of overflow buckets small. But many buckets might be split although they do not yet require it. Spiral storage follows the same idea of splitting in a cyclic order, but differs in the numbering scheme for the buckets. In linear hashing, one part of a split bucket retains the old number and the other gets the next number above the currently existing bucket numbers, so the array grows only at its end, but begins always with index 0. In spiral storage, both parts of the split bucket get new numbers and the old entry is deleted. Many variants of these methods have been proposed (Litwin 1981; Mullin 1981b; Scholl 1981; Tamminen 1981; Ramamohanarao and Lloyd 1982; Tamminen 1982; Larson 1985; Mullin 1985; Larson 1988; Ouksel and Scheuermann 1988; Ou and Tharp 1991; Chu and Knott 1994; Baeza-Yates and Soza-Pollman 1998).

Extendible hashing differs from the previous methods in that it splits only overflowing buckets and allows several entries in the primary structure to refer

---

[7] Introduced in the technical report, G.N. Martin: Spiral Storage: Incrementally Augmentable Hash Addressed Storage, Technical Report 27, University of Warwick, USA, 1978; appears in a paper published first in Mullin (1985).

to the same bucket. When a bucket overflows, it is first checked whether we can split the bucket within the framework of the current primary structure, because the items corresponding to several different entries are stored in that bucket. If that is the case, we just create the new bucket and separate the items. Else we have to increase the depth of the primary structure; for that we double the array, copying all previous entries into two consecutive array entries, so now every bucket is referred by at least two array entries corresponding to two hash value prefixes differing in the last bit. Then we can split the overflowing bucket and distribute the items on two buckets according to that last bit. It is easy to check whether there are multiple array entries referring to the same bucket, because they share a prefix in their hash value, so the array entries are consecutive. This property needs to be preserved when we split a bucket; the entries referring to the old and the new bucket must again be consecutive array entries. Variants of the extendible hashing method were proposed in Lomet (1983) and Chung (1992).

A higher-dimensional analog of this extensible hashing structure is the "grid file" (Nievergelt, Hinterberger, and Sevcik 1984; Hinrichs 1985; Regnier 1985); here our data items have as key not only one sequence of bits, but d such sequences. Then we take in each sequence a prefix and interpret that as number, and use these d numbers as index to a d-dimensional array, which gives us the number of the bucket containing that data item. Again we have potentially many array positions pointing to the same bucket, but they form a d-dimensional interval among the index positions, so we can split an overflowing bucket as long as there are several array positions pointing to it. Higher-dimensional index structures for points have some similarity to the other structures discussed in this section and have again developed many variants.

A totally different class of structures that combine hash tables with variable size are the methods of dynamic perfect hashing introduced by Dietzfelbinger and Mayer auf der Heide (1992) and Dietzfelbinger et al. (1994). That is a dynamization of the perfect hash method by Fredman et al. (1984), where parts of the two-level structure are occasionally rebuilt. That is a randomized structure that supports worst-case constant find operations and amortized expected constant time insertions and deletions.

9.6 Membership Testers and Bloom Filters

The dictionary structures we discussed in the earlier chapters, search trees, tries, and hash tables, all were keeping track of a set of keys, associating with each key an object. A membership tester does slightly less, he just answers membership queries for the set: is the query key contained in the set? This weaker structure is interesting in a number of applications related to external memory and network applications. If we are looking for some data that might be in any of a number of buckets, we can avoid looking in each bucket if we have a membership tester for its content. If the buckets are external memory pages or other computers in a distributed system, we can perhaps keep a membership tester for each bucket in our main memory, but not the content of the bucket itself. So membership testers are mainly interesting if their size is small compared to the size of the entire set, which would be the size of a classical dictionary structure.

For membership testers, it is possible to relax the requirements and accept false positives, that is, query keys incorrectly accepted as members of the set, as long as they are few. This significantly reduces the size of the structure, without significantly degrading its usefulness: at worst we look in a bucket too much. Another application, which was the main motivation of the first study, is a spelling checker: we just need a decision whether the word is correct, and incorrectly accepting a few misspelled words is not harmful. It has also been proposed for some textual index applications (Mullin 1987; Ramakrishna 1989b; Shepherd, Phillips, and Chu 1989). This structure was invented by Bloom (1970), and an approximate membership tester is called a Bloom filter. Exact and approximate membership testers were then studied in Carter et al. (1978), and recently became the object of many further studies, especially motivated by network applications (Little, Shrivastava, and Speirs 2002; Broder and Mitzenmacher 2004). Classical dictionaries, unlike membership testers, have an approximate version only if we can approximate the associated object in a meaningful way (Chazelle et al. 2004), which is usually not the case: there are no approximate pointers.

For the construction and analysis of membership testers, it is necessary to make further assumptions on the nature of the universe $\mathcal{U}$ from which the sets are selected, and the computational model. In all structures proposed in this context, the universe is assumed to be a finite set with u elements. This makes the structure similar to hash tables and different from search trees, where the assumption was only that we could compare two universe elements in constant time.

If we have to represent all 2^u possible subsets of the universe, we cannot do better than using a bitmap, u bits, each representing one universe element that may be in the current set or not. We cannot encode the 2^u possible subsets by less than $u = \log(2^u)$ bits. If we restrict ourselves to subsets of a fixed size, n elements of the u possible universe elements, we get a lower bound of $\log \binom{u}{n}$, which is approximately $n \log u$ for n much smaller than u. Already in Carter et al. (1978), several exact membership testers of almost that size were proposed, but the query times that can be achieved depend on the computational model: in some models, almost minimal space and constant query time are possible (Brodnik and Munro 1999).

For approximate membership testers, the situation is more difficult. The original method proposed by Bloom is that we have a bit string of length b, and k hash functions $h_i : \mathcal{U} \to \{1, \ldots, b\}$. For each element x that belongs to the set X we wish to represent, the structure sets the bits $h_1(x), \ldots, h_k(x)$ to 1. The same bit might be set to 1 for many different elements of the represented set. To query whether $y \in \mathcal{U}$ is in that set X, we compute $h_1(y), \ldots, h_k(y)$ and check whether all these bits are 1; then we claim that y belongs to X, else we know that it does not belong to X. This allows false positives, but no false negatives. This was studied in Bloom (1970), Carter et al. (1978), and Mullin (1983) under the uniform hashing assumption; if the $h_i(x)$ are independent and uniformly distributed, and we use $b = (\log_2 e)kn$ bits and k hash functions to represent an n-element set, we get an upper bound of 2^{-k} for the error rate, independent of the size of the universe.

Another method, which requires less assumption on the independence of the hash values, is just to map the large universe $\mathcal{U}$ by a hash function h chosen from a universal family to a smaller universe $\mathcal{V}$ and use an exact membership tester there. This was also already proposed in Bloom (1970), where a normal hash table was used for that smaller universe; in Carter et al. (1978) it was then combined with exact membership testers. Given a query element y, we claim y belongs to X if $h(y)$ belongs to $h(X)$, otherwise we know it does not belong to X. A false positive results if there is an $x \in X$, $x \neq y$, with $h(x) = h(y)$. Using a smaller universe of size $n2^k$, we get a probability of a collision under the universal hash function, corresponding to a false positive, of $c2^{-k}$. The space required by this structure is the space for an exact membership tester of an n-element set in a universe of size $n2^k$. Again the space requirement is independent of the size of the original universe $\mathcal{U}$ and depends only on n and the error rate.

Further structures for membership testers, of almost optimal size and query time, were developed in Brodnik and Munro (1999), Buhrman et al. (2000), and Pagh, Pagh, and Rao (2005); related structures were also proposed in Kirsch and Mitzenmacher (2006), Mitzenmacher (2001), a version also allowing false negatives in Pagh and Rodler (2001) and a version for multisets answering approximate multiplicity queries in Cohen and Matias (2003). All these structures are just static structures, not allowing any insertions or deletions of the underlying set. A trivial way to make the structure dynamic is to replace the bits in the first structure above by counters, incrementing each counter on insertions and decrementing on deletions, with the test criterion in a query becoming that all counters are positive. This is known as counting Bloom filter

(Fan et al. 2006; Buhrman et al. 2000), but the structure is not fully dynamic in the same way that hash tables had a maximum size, because the number of counters, as well as their size, is not changed during insertions. That would require techniques like the shadow copies, extendible arrays, or extendible hash tables, as discussed in the previous section. But the main motivation for the apparent practical interest in approximate membership testers is their small size.

10
Appendix

In the following, I collected some comments on relevant concepts, useful techniques, and the subject choices and restrictions of this book.

10.1 The Pointer Machine and Alternative Computation Models

In this book we restricted ourselves as far as possible to structures that can be represented in the model of the pointer machine and excluded structures that require stronger models of computation.

In the pointer machine,[1] the memory consists of nodes that are of size $O(1)$, each node containing possibly some values and some pointers to other nodes. The only thing we can do with these pointers is to follow them and create a pointer to a given node, or create a node and a pointer to it. All operations on pointers, as well as the creation and deletion of nodes, take constant time.

Almost all our structures fall into this model, the main exception being the hash tables, which were included for their great practical importance. In hash tables we compute a pointer out of some input data; there is no "pointer arithmetic" in the pointer machine. The other exceptions are our frequent use of arrays for stacks and the array-based heaps, which both again require address computations and non-constant-sized memory objects. We include these structures for their efficiency, but could have avoided them: the linked-list implementation of a stack is an obvious example of a pointer-machine structure, and we gave many heaps that fall into this model. The Fibonacci

---

[1] There are a number of concepts in literature that go under the popular name of "pointer machine" and that differ in details. Ben-Amram (1995) tried to systematize them. According to his classification, we are using "pointer algorithms."

heap is not a pointer-machine structure; we included it as a moderately simple heap with an amortized fast decrease-key operation.

An important alternative, and more powerful, model of computation is the word-based RAM with word length $\Theta(\log n)$. In the pointer-machine model, we do not worry about the size of the values in the various fields of the nodes; in this book we never discussed any problem of numerical range overflow. If we want to allow computation with addresses in our model, we have to be more specific in what the addresses are. The pointer-machine model was based exactly on the abstraction from that detail. If we model our computer memory as a big array of memory words, each memory word having a fixed width, w bits, and a pointer to a memory address fitting in a memory word, we need a word size $w \geq \Omega(\log n)$ to be able at least to address the n parts of the input. If we assume that our program needs only space polynomial in n, which is a very weak upper bound for a reasonable program, $O(\log n)$ bits are sufficient to address all those memory cells used by the program. For this reason, word-based RAMs normally assume a word length of $\Theta(\log n)$.

Having the word length of your machine that depends on the size of the input appears strange and unrealistic, but if we keep the word length fixed, then even following a pointer needs $\Omega(\log n)$ time just to read the entire pointer. And if the input data consist of n items, each of which fits in a single word of constant size w, there are only $2^w = O(1)$ possible values for each input item, so a large input will consist only of repeated items. This changes the problems very much, making, for example, counting sort a reasonable algorithm for sorting.

Allowing direct access to the addresses and computations with these addresses allows some operations to be much faster than it is possible in the pointer machine. Because that asymptotic speed does not translate into a fast implementation, we excluded these types of structures in this book.

Another model choice is the question what numbers the machine supports. For word-based RAMs it is natural to use only integers that fit into a word; but especially in geometric structures, it is very convenient to allow real numbers as elementary objects, with which one can do arbitrary arithmetic operations in constant time. For the pointer machine, this fits especially well; then the number components of a node, like the pointer components, are just elementary objects with which some constant-time operations are possible. With the RAM it depends on whether we keep real numbers and integers separate; then we get the standard real RAM; or whether we allow in our model operations like rounding, thus converting a real number into an integer, which makes serious differences in the complexity of some problems and adds another model question, whether the derived integer then fits into a word or can be used as address.

Being specific about the underlying computation model is especially important for lower bounds, which do depend strongly on the choice of the computation model. In this book we focused on algorithms and excluded lower bounds.

In principle, we could claim that our computational model is the set of correct C programs. Any programming language does not have a stated restriction on the word length of the integers and pointers used in your program, although it is possible to access them on bit level. But these restrictions are present in the computer, making asymptotic runtimes for $n \to \infty$ a theoretical concept anyway.

10.2 External Memory Models and Cache-Oblivious Algorithms

We described the basic external memory model, in which blocks of fixed (large) size are accessed on the external memory, in our discussion of B-trees and (a, b)-trees. The same questions can be asked not only for search trees but also for all other structures discussed here: how many blocks of size B have to be accessed to solve the given problem. This is a different complexity measure for the same problem; instead of counting operations, we count block transfers and want to minimize that number by the design of our algorithms.

These questions have been discussed in many papers and for many different underlying data structure problems. A recent survey is given in Vitter (2001). Especially the database community, in which the assumption that the data will not fit into the main memory is standard, is interested in these external memory structures. In many cases, a suitable modification of some B-tree variant turns out to be the solution, other cases, especially with geometric underlying problems, are more difficult.

In this book we mostly excluded that external memory setting, with the exception of (a, b)-trees that were also useful as main memory data structure; but any of our problems could also be studied in that setting, and many have been. Both computers and problems get larger; the problems of five years ago now fit into main memory, but new problems become feasible. The big majority of problems, however, does fit into main memory, and the normal main-memory model is both simpler and basic to other models, so its study has priority. Ultimately, we believe it possible that the external memory models disappear to specialized application niches, like the sequential access memory (tape) structures that were an important model variant 30 years ago.

A currently much-studied memory variant is the cache-oblivious structures, introduced in Frigo et al. (1999); they are like external memory structures, but without knowledge of the block size. They are based on the insight that the main memory of a modern computer is not as homogeneous as we assume in our standard model; there is a hierarchy of various levels of faster cache memory between the actual processor and the main memory. Each of these cache memories is structured in blocks; an access to a cached block is fast, whereas a cache miss forces an access to the next slower level of cache, from which not only the requested address, but an entire (small) block, the "cache line" is read and stored. The cache-oblivious structure should behave well with respect to the number of block transfers for any block size. This is again a modification that can be combined with any data structure problem; we get a set of different complexity measures, the numbers of block transfers for the different block sizes, all of which should simultaneously be near optimal. Like the B-tree for external memory problems, there is a canonical tool, the van-Emde-Boas tree layout, which can be frequently adapted to make a given main memory structure cache-oblivious. Again, we excluded this topic from this book.

10.3 Naming of Data Structures

In general, a structure or concept with a name is easier to reference than one that is just identified by its author. This is noticeable in many places; indeed a named structure is more probable to get cited. But in our subject, it is frequently not clear what a name applies to, whether it is the abstract structure or the method to realize that structure. A typical example is heaps: a large part of the literature holds that the abstract structure is named "priority queue," and heaps are just the original implementation, the array-based heaps. But the names given to later implementations are clearly always "heaps," as in binomial heaps, Fibonacci heaps, relaxed heaps, pairing heaps, and so on. Only the leftist heaps fail to follow that scheme; in literature they are referred to as leftist trees. For this reason, we used "heap" as the name of the abstract structure. Some authors use "meld" instead of "merge" for the merging of heaps, but we preferred the better-known word "merge."

The word "queue" has been used for so many unrelated concepts, as "catenable queues" for search trees supporting split and join, that it should be avoided for anything that is not really a queue. In the same way, "list" is a word that gives very little explanation, having been used in many structures whose only common aspect is a linear order occuring somewhere. We use "list" only for linked lists.

Good naming continues to be a problem, and we tried to be at least consistent with the names used in this book.

10.4 Solving Linear Recurrences

Linear recurrences with constant coefficients occured in the analysis of height-balanced trees and, in principle, at many other places that have an exponential or logarithmic growth rate. Because there is a simple technique to solve any such recursion, we present it here.

Suppose you have a function defined by a recursion of the form

$$f(n + k) = a_{k-1}f(n + k - 1) + a_{k-2}f(n + k - 2) + \cdots + a_1 f(n + 1)$$
$$+ a_0 f(n),$$

as well as some initial conditions for the small values $(f(1), \ldots, f(k))$. The set of all solutions of this recursion is closed under taking constant multiples and sums, so it forms a linear space. The dimension of this linear space is k: we can choose $f(1), \ldots, f(k)$ arbitrarily and then define the function for $n > k$ by the recursion. This always gives a solution of that recursion, and any two solutions that agree on the first k values are identical. So we just need to find k linearly independent solutions to this recursion and then we can form their linear combination to satisfy the k given initial conditions.

Define a polynomial of degree k by $p(x) = x^k - a_{k-1}x^{k-1} - a_{k-2}x^{k-2} - \cdots - a_1 x - a_0$. This is called the characteristic polynomial of the recursion. A polynomial of degree k has exactly k zeros, at least if we count them with multiplicities (and allow complex numbers). Let c be one of these zeros, so

$$c^k = a_{k-1}c^{k-1} + a_{k-2}c^{k-2} + \cdots + a_1 c + a_0,$$

then $f_c(n) = c^n$ is a solution of the recursion:

$$f_c(n + k) = c^{n+k} = c^n \cdot c^k$$
$$= c^n(a_{k-1}c^{k-1} + a_{k-2}c^{k-2} + \cdots + a_1 c + a_0)$$
$$= a_{k-1}c^{n+k-1} + a_{k-2}c^{n+k-2} + \cdots + a_1 c^{n+1} + a_0 c^n$$
$$= a_{k-1}f_c(n + k - 1) + a_{k-2}f_c(n + k - 2) + \cdots$$
$$+ a_1 f_c(n + 1) + a_0 f_c(n).$$

If c is a multiple zero of the polynomial p, so that $p(x) = (x - c)^i r(x)$ for some $i \geq 2$, and some polynomial r, then c is also a zero of the derivatives

$p', \ldots, p^{(i-1)}$. So we have

$$c^k - a_{k-1}c^{k-1} - a_{k-2}c^{k-2} - \cdots - a_1 c - a_0 = 0,$$
$$kc^{k-1} - a_{k-1}(k-1)c^{k-2} - a_{k-2}(k-2)c^{k-3} - \cdots - a_1 = 0,$$

$$\vdots$$

$$k(k-1)\cdots(k-i+2)c^{k-i+1} - a_{k-1}(k-1)(k-2)\cdots(k-i+1)c^{k-i}$$
$$-a_{k-2}(k-3)(k-4)\cdots(k-i)c^{k-i-1} - \cdots - (i-1)(i-2)\cdots 1 a_{i-1} = 0.$$

Thus, there are polynomials $q_0, \ldots, q_{i-1}$ of degree $0, \ldots, i-1$
$(q_j(x) = x(x-1)(x-2)\cdots(x-j+1))$ with

$$q_0(k)c^k - q_0(k-1)a_{k-1}c^{k-1} - q_0(k-2)a_{k-2}c^{k-2} - \cdots - q_0(1)c - q_0(0) = 0,$$
$$q_1(k)c^k - q_1(k-1)a_{k-1}c^{k-1} - q_1(k-2)a_{k-2}c^{k-2} - \cdots - q_1(1)c - q_1(0) = 0,$$

$$\vdots$$

$$q_{i-1}(k)c^k - q_{i-1}(k-1)a_{k-1}c^{k-1} - q_{i-1}(k-2)a_{k-2}c^{k-2}$$
$$- \cdots - q_{i-1}(1)c - q_{i-1}(0) = 0.$$

These polynomials are linearly independent and form a basis of the space of polynomials of degree at most $i - 1$. So we can express any polynomial q of degree at most $i - 1$ as linear combination of the q_j, and obtain by the corresponding linear combination of the above equations that

$$q(k)c^k - q(k-1)a_{k-1}c^{k-1} - q(k-2)a_{k-2}c^{k-2} - \cdots - q(1)c - q(0) = 0.$$

Therefore, if c is an i-fold zero of the characteristic polynomial p, then any polynomial q with degree at most $i - 1$ also generates a solution $f_{c,q}(n) = q(n)c^n$ of our recurrence. We just have to use that $q(n+k)$ is a polynomial in k.

$$f_{c,q}(n+k) = q(n+k)c^{n+k} = c^n \cdot q(n+k)c^k$$
$$= c^n \Big(q(n+(k-1))a_{k-1}c^{k-1} + q(n+(k-2))a_{k-2}c^{k-2} + \cdots$$
$$+ q(n+1)a_1 c + q(n+0)a_0 \Big)$$
$$= a_{k-1}q(n+k-1)c^{n+k-1} + a_{k-2}q(n+k-2)c^{n+k-2} + \cdots$$
$$+ a_1 q(n+1)c^{n+1} + a_0 q(n+0)c^n$$
$$= a_{k-1}f_{c,q}(n+k-1) + a_{k-2}f_{c,q}(n+k-2) + \cdots$$
$$+ a_1 f_{c,q}(n+1) + a_0 f_{c,q}(n).$$

Thus we have found a system of linearly independent solutions of the given recursion whose cardinality is the dimension of the space of solutions. So they form a basis for the space.

In summary to solve a given recursion of this type, we just write down the characteristic polynomial p, find its zeros with their multiplicities, write down the basis, and find the linear combination that satisfies the given initial conditions. The only potential problem in this method is to find the zeros of a given polynomial.

10.5 Very Slowly Growing Functions

We frequently used the logarithm function that is already quite slow growing for all normal purposes. After all, problem sizes of $n > 2^{100}$ are irrelevant, so we could assume for practical purposes that $\log n \leq 100$. Indeed, we did this when choosing the array size for array-based stacks in the implementation of several tree structures.

Still, there are many functions that grow slower than $\log n$, and some of them do occur in the analysis of data structures and algorithms. Of course $\log \log n$ grows slower than $\log n$ and that occured in the worst-case optimal structure for the set union problem in Section 6.1. To get a feeling for very slow-growing functions, it is easier to look at their inverses, which are very fast-growing functions. The inverse of $\log n$ is 2^n, and the inverse of $\log \log n$ is 2^{2^n}. An occasionally useful function that grows much slower is the "iterated logarithm" function $\log^* n$, which is usually defined as the number of times we have to apply the logarithm to make the result less than 1. An equivalent, but better understandable, version is

$$\log^* n = k \qquad \text{if} \qquad \left. 2^{2^{2^{\cdot^{\cdot^{2}}}}} \right\}k \ \leq n < \left. 2^{2^{2^{\cdot^{\cdot^{2}}}}} \right\}k+1 \,.$$

So the inverse function of $\log^*(n)$ is an exponential tower of height n. The Ackermann function grows even faster than the exponential tower. This was defined in Chapter 6 by

$$A(m, 0) = 0 \quad \text{for } m \geq 1,$$
$$A(m, 1) = A(m - 1, 2) \quad \text{for } m \geq 1,$$
$$A(0, n) = 2n \quad \text{for } n \geq 0,$$
$$A(m, n) = A(m - 1, A(m, n - 1)) \quad \text{for } m \geq 1, n \geq 2.$$

Ackermann[2] (1928) then took the diagonal function $A(n, n)$ as his example of a function that grows so fast that it cannot be expressed as primitive recursive function. To get a feeling for the growth rate, we observe that

$A(0, n) = 2n$ (by definition),

$A(1, n) = A(0, A(1, n - 1)) = 2A(1, n - 1) = \cdots = 2^{n-1}A(1, 1) = 2^{n+1}$,

$A(2, n) = A(1, A(2, n - 1)) = 2^{A(2,n-1)+1} > 2^{A(2,n-1)}$, so

$$A(2, n) > \left. 2^{2^{2^{\cdot^{\cdot^{\cdot^{2}}}}}} \right\} n+2 \text{ times.}$$

In general, $A(k, n)$ is the result of n-fold application of $A(k - 1, \cdot)$.

Some simple properties of $A(m, n)$ are that it is increasing in both variables (increasing very fast), and $A(m, 1) > m$. With this, we note that

$A(i, 1) = A(i - 1, 2) = A(i - 2, A(i - 1, 1)) > A(i - 2, i - 2) > A(i - 2, 1)$,

so the value of the diagonal Ackermann function $A(n, n)$ lies between the first-column values $A(n, 1)$ and $A(n + 2, 1)$. So the inverse Ackermann function defined in Section 6.1 as

$$\alpha(n) = \min\{i \mid A(i, 1) > n\}$$

differs from the inverse of the diagonal Ackermann function $\alpha^{\mathrm{diag}}(n) = \min\{i \mid A(i, i) > n\}$ by at most two. This function $\alpha(n)$ is the slowest-growing function that occurs in this book.

---

[2] Actually this is not quite what Ackermann defined. Since 1928, the idea has been simplified and several variants for the initial conditions of the recursion exist, of which we choose one suitable especially for our application. But the behavior of the function is always the same.

11

References

Whenever a paper exists in a conference and a journal version, I cite the journal version. I do not cite technical reports and other inaccessible references.

S. Abiteboul, H. Kaplan, T. Milo: Compact Labeling Schemes for Ancestor Queries, in: SODA 2001 (Proceedings 12th ACM-SIAM Symposium on Discrete Algorithms), 547–556.

M.I. Abouelhoda, S. Kurtz, E. Ohlebusch: Replacing Suffix Trees with Enhanced Suffix Arrays, *Journal of Discrete Algorithms* **2** (2004) 53–86.

W. Ackermann: Zum Hilbertschen Aufbau der reellen Zahlen, *Mathematische Annalen* **99** (1928) 118–133.

G.M. Adel'son-Vel'skiĭ, E.M. Landis: An Algorithm for the Organization of Information, *Dokl. Akad. Nauk. SSSR* **146**(2) (1962) 1259–1262; English translation in *Soviet Mathematics Doklady* **3** (1962) 1259–1263.

P.K. Agarwal, L. Arge, K. Yi: An Optimal Dynamic Interval Stabbing-Max Data Structure, in: SODA 2005 (Proceedings 16th ACM-SIAM Symposium on Discrete Algorithms), 803–812.

P.K. Agarwal, M. de Berg, J. Gudmundsson, M. Hammar, H.J. Haverkort: Box-Trees and R-Trees with Near-Optimal Query Time, *Discrete & Computational Geometry* **28** (2002) 291–312.

A.V. Aho, J.E. Hopcroft, J.D. Ullman: *The Design and Analysis of Computer Algorithms*, Addison-Wesley 1974.

A.V. Aho, J.E. Hopcroft, J.D. Ullman: On Finding Lowest Common Ancestors in Trees, *SIAM Journal on Computing* **5** (1976) 115–132.

M. Ajtai, J. Komlós, E. Szemerédi: There Is No Fast Single Hashing Algorithm, *Information Processing Letters* **7** (1978) 270–273.

S. Albers, M. Karpinski: Randomized Splay Trees: Theoretical and Experimental Results, *Information Processing Letters* **81** (2002) 213–221.

B. Allen, J.I. Munro: Self-Organizing Binary Search Trees, *Journal of the ACM* **25** (1978) 526–535.

N. Alon, M. Dietzfelbinger, P.B. Miltersen, E. Petrank, G. Tardos: Linear Hash Functions, *Journal of the ACM* **46** (1999) 667–683.

S. Alstrup, A.M. Ben-Amram, T. Rauhe: Worst-Case and Amortized Optimality in Union-Find, in: STOC 1999 (Proceedings 31st Annual ACM Symposium on Theory of Computing), 499–506.

S. Alstrup, C. Gavoille, H. Kaplan, T. Rauhe: Nearest Common Ancestors: A Survey and a New Distributes Algorithm, in: SPAA 2002 (Proceedings 14th ACM Symposium on Parallel Algorithms and Architectures), 258–264.

S. Alstrup, J. Holm: Improved Algorithms for Finding Level-Ancestors in Dynamic Trees, in: ICALP 2000 (Proceedings 27th International Colloquium on Automata, Languages, and Programming), Springer. *LNCS* **1853**, 73–84.

S. Alstrup, T. Husfeldt, T. Rauhe: Marked Ancestor Queries, in: FOCS 1998 (Proceedings 39th Annual IEEE Symposium on Foundations of Computer Science), 534–543.

S. Alstrup, T. Husfeldt, T. Rauhe, M. Thorup: Black Box for Constant Time Insertion in Priority Queues, *ACM Transactions on Algorithms* **1** (2005) 102–106.

S. Alstrup, T. Rauhe: Improved Labeling Schemes for Ancestor Queries, in: SODA 2002 (Proceedings 13th ACM-SIAM Symposium on Discrete Algorithms), 947–953.

S. Alstrup, M. Thorup: Optimal Pointer Algorithms for Finding Nearest Common Ancestors in Dynamic Trees, *Journal of Algorithms* **35** (2000) 169–188.

O. Amble, D.E. Knuth: Ordered Hash Tables, *The Computer Journal* **17** (1974) 135–142.

A. Amir, D. Keselman, G.M. Landau, M. Lewenstein, N. Lewenstein, M. Rodeh: Text Indexing and Dictionary Matching with One Error, *Journal of Algorithms* **37** (2000) 309–325.

A. Andersson: Optimal Bounds on the Dictionary Problem, in: Proc. Symposium on Optimal Algorithms 1989a, Varna, Springer. *LNCS* **401**, 106–114.

A. Andersson: Improving Partial Rebuilding by Using Simple Balance Criteria, in: WADS 1989b (Proceedings 1st Workshop on Algorithms and Data Structures), Springer. *LNCS* **382**, 393–402.

A. Andersson: Maintaining α-Balanced Trees by Partial Rebuilding, *International Journal of Computer Mathematics* **38** (1990) 37–48.

A. Andersson: Balanced Search Trees Made Simple, in: WADS 1993 (Proceedings 3rd Workshop on Algorithms and Data Structures), Springer. *LNCS* **709**, 60–71.

A. Andersson: General Balanced Trees, *Journal of Algorithms* **30** (1999) 1–28.

A. Andersson, C. Icking, R. Klein, T. Ottmann: Binary Search Trees of Almost Optimal Height, *Acta Informatica* **28** (1990) 165–178.

A. Andersson, S. Nilsson: Improved Behavior of Tries by Adaptive Branching, *Information Processing Letters* **46** (1993) 295–300.

A. Andersson, S. Nilsson: Faster Searching in Tries and Quadtrees, in: ESA 1994 (Proceedings of the 2nd Annual European Symposium on Algorithms), Springer. *LNCS* **855**, 82–93.

A. Andersson, S. Nilsson: Efficient Implementation of Suffix Trees, *Software – Practice and Experience* **25** (1995) 129–141.

C.-H. Ang, K.-P. Tan: The Interval B-Tree, *Information Processing Letters* **53** (1995) 85–89.

J.-I. Aoe, K. Morimoto, T. Sato: An Efficient Implementation of Trie Structures, *Software — Practice and Experience* **22** (1992) 685–721.

A. Apostolico: The Myriad Virtues of Subword Trees, in: *Combinatorial Algorithms on Words, Proceedings of the NATO ASI*, A. Apostolico, Z. Galil, eds., Springer 1985, 85–96.

A. Apostolico, G.F. Italiano, G. Gambosi, M. Talamo: The Set Union Problem with Unlimited Backtracking, *SIAM Journal on Computing* **23** (1994) 50–70.

B.W. Arden, B.A. Galler, R.M. Graham: An Algorithm for Equivalence Declarations, *Communications ACM* **4** (1961) 310–314.

L. Arge, M. de Berg, H.J. Haverkort, K. Yi: The Priority R-Tree: A Practically Efficient and Worst-Case Optimal R-Tree, in: SIGMOD 2004 (Proceedings 2004 ACM SIGMOD Conference on Management of Data), 347–358.

L. Arge, J.S. Vitter: Optimal External Memory Interval Management, *SIAM Journal on Computing* **32** (2003) 1488–1508.

A. Arvind, C.P. Rangan: Symmetric Min-Max Heap: A Simpler Data Structure for Double-Ended Priority Queue, *Information Processing Letters* **69** (1999) 197–199.

M.D. Atkinson, J.-R. Sack, N. Santoro, T. Strothotte: Min-Max Heaps and Generalized Priority Queues, *Communications ACM* **29** (1986) 996–1000.

M. Ayala-Rincón, P.D. Conejo: A Linear Time Lower Bound on McCreight and General Updating Algorithms for Suffix Trees, *Algorithmica* **37** (2003) 233–241.

Y. Azar, A.Z. Broder, A.R. Karlin, E. Upfal: Balanced Allocations, *SIAM Journal on Computing* **29** (1999) 180–200.

G.H. Badr, B.J. Oommen: Self-Adjusting of Ternary Search Tries Using Conditional Rotations and Randomized Heuristics, *The Computer Journal* **48** (2004) 200–219.

J.-L. Baer: Weight-Balanced Trees, in: NCC 1975 (Proceedings National Computer Conference) AFIPS Conference Proceedings **44**, 467–472.

R.A. Baeza-Yates, H.J. Soza-Pollman: Analysis of Linear Hashing Revisited, *Nordic Journal of Computing* **5** (1998) 70–85.

A. Bagchi, A.L. Buchsbaum, M.T. Goodrich: Biased Skip Lists, in: ISAAC 2002 (Proceedings 13th International Symposium on Algorithms and Computation), Springer. *LNCS* **2518**, 1–13.

B.S. Baker: A Theory of Parametrized Pattern Matching: Algorithms and Applications, in: STOC 93 (Proceedings 25th Annual ACM Symposium on Theory of Computing), 71–80.

L. Banachowski: A Complement to Tarjan's Result About the Lower Bound on the Complexity of the Set Union Problem, *Information Processing Letters* **11** (1980) 59–65.

S. Bansil, S. Sreekanth, P. Gupta: M-Heap: A Modified Heap Data Structure, *International Journal Foundations of Computer Science* **14** (2003) 491–502.

R. Bayer: Binary B-Trees for Virtual Memory, in: Proc. ACM SIGFIDET Workshop on Data Description, Access and Control 1971, 219–235.

R. Bayer: Symmetric Binary B-Trees: Data Structure and Maintenance Algorithms, *Acta Informatica* **1** (1972a) 290–306.

R. Bayer: Oriented Balanced Trees and Equivalence Relations, *Information Processing Letters* **1** (1972b) 226–228.

R. Bayer, E. McCreight: Organization and Maintenance of Large Ordered Indexes, *Acta Informatica* **1** (1972) 173–189.

C. Bays: Some Techniques for Structuring Chained Hash Tables, *The Computer Journal* **16** (1973a) 126–131.

C. Bays: The Reallocation of Hash-Coded Tables, *Communications ACM* **16** (1973b) 11–14.

N. Beckmann, H.-P. Kriegel, R. Schneider, B. Seeger: The R*-Tree: An Efficient and Robust Access Method for Points and Rectangles, in: SIGMOD 1990 (Proceedings 1990 ACM SIGMOD Conference on Management of Data), 322–331.

R.C. Bell, B. Floyd: A Monte-Carlo Study of Cichelli Hash-Function Solvability, *Communications ACM* **26** (1983) 924–925.

A.M. Ben-Amram: What Is a "Pointer Machine"?, *ACM SIGACT News* **26**(2) (1995) 88–95.

M.A. Bender, R. Cole, E.D. Demaine, M. Farach-Colton, J. Zito: Two Simplified Algorithms for Maintaining Order in a List, in: ESA 2002 (Proceedings of the 10th Annual European Symposium on Algorithms), Springer. *LNCS* **2461**, 152–164.

M.A. Bender, M. Farach-Colton: The Level Ancestor Problem Simplified, *Theoretical Computer Science* **321** (2004) 5–12.

M. Ben-Or: Lower Bounds for Algebraic Computation Trees, in: STOC 1983 (Proceedings of the 15th ACM Symposium on Theory of Computing), 80–86.

S.W. Bent, D.D. Sleator, R.E. Tarjan: Biased Search Trees, *SIAM Journal on Computing* **14** (1985) 545–568.

J.L. Bentley: Multidimendional Binary Search Used for Associative Searching, *Communications ACM* **18** (1975) 509–517.

J.L. Bentley: Decomposable Searching Problems, *Information Processing Letters* **8** (1979) 244–251.

J.L. Bentley: kd-Trees for Semidynamic Point Sets, in: SCG 1990 (Proceedings 6th ACM Symposium on Computational Geometry), 360–369.

J.L. Bentley, J.H. Friedman: Data Structures for Range Searching, *ACM Computing Surveys* **11** (1979) 397–409.

J.L. Bentley, H.A. Maurer: Efficient Worst-Case Data Structures for Range Searching, *Acta Informatica* **13** (1980) 155–168.

J.L. Bentley, J.B. Saxe: Decomposable Searching Problems I. Static-to-Dynamic Transformations, *Journal of Algorithms* **1** (1980) 301–358.

J.L. Bentley, R. Sedgewick: Fast Algorithms for Sorting and Searching Strings, in: SODA 1997 (Proceedings 8th ACM-SIAM Symposium on Discrete Algorithms), 360–369.

P. Berenbrink, A. Czumaj, A. Steger, B. Vöcking: Balanced Allocations: The Heavily Loaded Case, in: STOC 2000 (Proceedings 32nd Annual ACM Symposium on Theory of Computing), 745–754.

O. Berkman, U. Vishkin: Finding Level Ancestors in Trees, *Journal of Computer and System Sciences* **48** (1994) 214–230.

J.R. Bitner: Heuristics That Dynamically Organize Data Structures, *SIAM Journal on Computing* **8** (1979) 82–110.

G. Blankenagel, H. Güting: External Segment Trees, *Algorithmica* **12** (1994) 498–532.

G.E. Blelloch, B.M. Maggs, S.L.M. Woo: Space-Efficient Finger Search on Degree-Balanced Search Trees, in: SODA 2003 (Proceedings 14th Annual ACM-SIAM Symposium on Discrete Algorithms), 374–383.

B.H. Bloom: Space/Time Trade-offs in Hash Coding with Allowable Errors, *Communications ACM* **13** (1970) 422–426.

N. Blum: On the Single-Operation Worst-Case Time Complexity of the Disjoint Set Union Problem, *SIAM Journal Computing* **15** (1986) 1021–1024.

N. Blum, K. Mehlhorn: On the Average Number of Rebalancing Operations in Weight-Balanced Trees, *Theoretical Computer Science* **11** (1980) 303–320.

J.A. Blumer: How Much Is That DAWG in the Window? A Moving Window Algorithm for the Directed Acyclic Word Graph, *Journal of Algorithms* **8** (1987) 451–469.

A. Blumer, J.A. Blumer, A. Ehrenfeucht, D. Haussler, M.T. Chen, J. Seiferas: The Smallest Automaton Recognizing the Subwords of a Text, *Theoretical Computer Science* **40** (1985) 31–55.

F. Bonomi, M. Mitzenmacher, R. Panigrahy, S. Singh, G. Varghese: An Improved Construction for Counting Bloom Filters, in: ESA 2006 (Proceedings 14th Annual European Symposium on Algorithms), Springer. *LNCS* **4168**, 684–695.

P. Bose, M. van Kreveld, A. Maheshwari, P. Morin, J. Morrison: Translating a Regular Grid over a Point Set, *Computational Geometry Theory Applications* **25** (2003) 21–34.

P. Bozanis, A. Nanopoulos, Y. Manolopoulos: LR-Tree: A Logarithmic Decomposable Spatial Index Method, *The Computer Journal* **46** (2003) 319–331.

P. Brass: Multidimensional Heaps and Complementary Range Searching, *Information Processing Letters* **102** (2007) 152–155.

G. Brassard, S. Kannan: The Generation of Random Permutations on the Fly, *Information Processing Letters* **28** (1988) 207–212.

R.P. Brent: Reducing the Retrieval Time in Scatter Storage Techniques, *Communications ACM* **16** (1973) 105–109.

D. Breslauer: Dictionary Matching on Unbounded Alphabets: Uniform Length Dictionaries, *Journal of Algorithms* **18** (1995) 278–295.

R. de la Briandais: File Searching Using Variable Length Keys, in: Proceedings of the Western Joint Computer Conference 1959, 295–298.

G.S. Brodal: Fast Meldable Priority Queues, in: WADS 1995 (Proceedings 4th Workshop on Algorithms and Data Structures), Springer. *LNCS* **955**, 282–290.

G.S. Brodal: Worst-Case Efficient Priority Queues, in: SODA 1996a (Proceedings 7th ACM-SIAM Symposium on Discrete Algorithms), 52–58.

G.S. Brodal: Partially Persistent Data Structures of Bounded Degree with Constant Update Time, *Nordic Journal of Computing* **3** (1996b) 238–255.

G.S. Brodal: Finger Search Trees with Constant Insertion Time, in: SODA 1998 (Proceedings 9th ACM-SIAM Symposium on Discrete Algorithms), 540–549.

G.S. Brodal, L. Gąsieniec: Approximate Dictionary Queries, in: CPM 1996 (Proceedings 7th Annual Symposium on Combinatorial Pattern Matching), Springer. *LNCS* **1075**, 65–74.

G.S. Brodal, G. Lagogiannis, C. Makris, A.K. Tsakalidis, K. Tsichlas: Optimal Finger Search Trees in the Pointer Machine, in: STOC 2002 (Proceedings 34th Annual ACM Symposium on Theory of Computing), 583–591.

G.S. Brodal, S. Venkatesh: Improved Bounds for Dictionary Look-Up with One Error, *Information Processing Letters* **75** (2000) 57–59.

A.Z. Broder, A.R. Karlin: Multilevel Adaptive Hashing, in: SODA 1990 (Proceedings 1st ACM-SIAM Symposium on Discrete Algorithms), 43–53.

A.Z. Broder, M. Mitzenmacher: Network Applications of Bloom Filters: A Survey, *Internet Mathematics* **1** (2004) 485–509.

A. Brodnik, J.I. Munro: Membership in Constant Time and Almost-Minimum Space, *SIAM Journal on Computing* **28** (1999) 1627–1640.

H. Brönnimann, F. Cazals, M. Durand: Randomized Jumplists: A Jump-and-Walk Dictionary Data Structure, in: STACS 2003 (Proceedings of the 20th Annual Symposium on Theoretical Aspects of Computer Science), Springer. *LNCS* **2607**, 283–294.

M.R. Brown: Implementation and Analysis of Binomial Queue Algorithms, *SIAM Journal on Computing* **7** (1978) 298–319.

M.R. Brown, R.E. Tarjan: Design and Analysis of a Data Structure for Representing Sorted Lists, *SIAM Journal on Computing* **9** (1980) 594–614.

A.L. Buchsbaum, H. Kaplan, A. Rogers, J.R. Westbrook: Linear-Time Pointer-Machine Algorithms for Least Common Ancestors, MST Verification, and Dominators, in: STOC 1998 (Proceedings 30th Annual ACM Symposium on Theory of Computing), 279–288.

A.L. Buchsbaum, R. Sundar, R.E. Tarjan: Data Structural Bootstrapping, Linear Path Compression, and Catenable Heap Ordered Double Ended Queues, in: FOCS 1992 (Proceedings 33rd IEEE Symposium Foundations of Computer Science), 40–49.

A.L. Buchsbaum, R.E. Tarjan: Confluently Persistent Dequeues via Data Structural Bootstrapping, *Journal of Algorithms* **18** (1995) 513–547.

H. Buhrman, P.B. Miltersen, J. Radhakrishnan, S. Venkatesh: Are Bitvectors Optimal?, in: STOC 2000 (Proceedings 32nd Annual ACM Symposium on Theory of Computing), 449–458.

J. Burghardt: Maintaining Partial Sums in Logarithmic Time, *Nordic Journal of Computing* **8** (2001) 473–474.

W.A. Burkhard: Nonrecursive Traversals of Trees, *The Computer Journal* **18** (1975) 227–230.

S. Burkhardt, J. Kärkkäinen: Fast Lightweight Suffix Array Construction and Checking, in: CPM 2003 (Proceedings 14th Annual Symposium on Combinatorial Pattern Matching), Springer. *LNCS* **2676**, 55–69.

F.W. Burton, M.M. Huntbach, J.G. Kollias: Multiple Generation Text Files Using Overlapping Tree Structures, *The Computer Journal* **28** (1985) 414–416.

F.W. Burton, J.G. Kollias, V.G. Kollias, D.G. Matsakis: Implementation of Overlapping B-Trees for Time and Space Efficient Representation of Collections of Similar Files, *The Computer Journal* **33** (1990) 279–280.

H. Cameron, D. Wood: A Note on the Path Length of Red-Black Trees, *Information Processing Letters* **42** (1992) 287–292.

S. Carlsson: Improving Worst-Case Behavior of Heaps, *BIT* **24** (1984) 14–18.

S. Carlsson: A Variant of Heapsort with Almost Optimal Number of Comparisons, *Information Processing Letters* **24** (1987) 247–250.

S. Carlsson: The Deap – A Double-Ended Heap to Implement Double-Ended Priority Queues, *Information Processing Letters* **26** (1987/88) 33–36.

S. Carlsson: An Optimal Algorithm for Deleting the Root of a Heap, *Information Processing Letters* **37** (1991) 117–120.

S. Carlsson, J. Chen: The Complexity of Heaps, in: SODA 1992 (Proceedings 3rd ACM-SIAM Symposium on Discrete Algorithms), 393–402.

S. Carlsson, J. Chen, T. Strothotte: A Note on the Construction of the Data Structure "DEAP," *Information Processing Letters* **31** (1989) 315–317.

S. Carlsson, J.I. Munro, P.V. Poblete: An Implicit Binomial Queue with Constant Insertion Time, in: SWAT 1988 (Proceedings 1st Scandinavian Workshop on Algorithm Theory), Springer. *LNCS* **318**, 1–13.

J.L. Carter, R. Floyd, J. Gill, G. Markowsky, M.N. Wegman: Exact and Approximate Membership Testers, in: STOC 1978 (Proceedings 10th Annual ACM Symposium on Theory of Computing), 59–65.

J.L. Carter, M.N. Wegman: Universal Classes of Hash Functions, *Journal Computer System Sciences* **18** (1979) 143–154.

P. Celis, P.- A. Larson, J.I. Munro: Robin Hood Hashing, in: FOCS 1985 (Proceedings 26th Annual IEEE Symposium on Foundations of Computer Science), 281–288.

D.J. Challab: Implementation of Flexible Arrays Using Balanced Trees, *The Computer Journal* **34** (1991) 386–396.

C.-C. Chang: The Study of an Ordered Minimal Perfect Hashing Scheme, *Communications ACM* **27** (1984) 384–387.

C.-C. Chang, C.Y. Chen, J.-K. Jan: On the Design of a Machine-Independent Perfect Hashing Scheme, *The Computer Journal* **34** (1991) 469–474.

S.C. Chang, M.W. Du: Diamond Deque: A Simple Data Structure for Prioririty Deques, *Information Processing Letters* **46** (1993) 231–237.

H. Chang, S.S. Iyengar: Efficient Algorithms to Globally Balance a Binary Search Tree, *Communications ACM* **27** (1984) 695–702.

C.-C. Chang, R.C.T. Lee: A Letter-Oriented Minimal Perfect Hashing Scheme, *The Computer Journal* **29** (1986) 277–281.

P. Chanzy, L. Devroye, C. Zamora-Cura: Analysis of Range Search for Random kd-Trees, *Acta Informatica* **37** (2001) 355–383.

B. Chazelle: How to Search in History, *Information and Control* **64** (1985) 77–99.

B. Chazelle: Lower Bounds for Orthogonal Range Searching: I. The Reporting Case, *Journal of the ACM* **37** (1990a) 200–212.

B. Chazelle: Lower Bounds for Orthogonal Range Searching: II. The Arithmetic Model, *Journal of the ACM* **37** (1990b) 439–463.

B. Chazelle, L.J. Guibas: Fractional Cascading I: A Data Structuring Technique, *Algorithmica* **1** (1986a) 133–162.

B. Chazelle, L.J. Guibas: Fractional Cascading II: Applications, *Algorithmica* **1** (1986b) 163–191.

B. Chazelle, J. Killian, R. Rubinfeld, A. Tal: The Bloomier Filter: An Efficient Data Structure for Static Support Lookup Tables, in: SODA 2004 (Proceedings 15th Annual ACM-SIAM Symposium on Discrete Algorithms), 30–39.

J. Chen: An Efficient Construction Algorithm for a Class of Implicit Double-Ended Priority Queues, *The Computer Journal* **38** (1995) 818–821.

L. Chen: O(1) Space Complexity Deletion in AVL Trees, *Information Processing Letters* **22** (1986) 147–149.

L. Chen, R. Schott: Optimal Operations on Red-Black Trees, *International Journal Foundations of Computer Science* **7** (1996) 227–239.

M.T. Chen, J. Seiferas: Efficient and Elegant Subword-Tree Construction, in: Combinatorial Algorithms on Words, Proceedings of the NATO ASI (A. Apostolico, Z. Galil, eds.) Springer 1985, 97–107.

S.-W. Cheng, R. Janardan: Efficient Maintenance of the Union of Intervals on a Line, with Applications, *Journal of Algorithms* **12** (1991) 57–74.

S. Cho, S. Sahni: Weight-Biased Leftist Trees and Modified Skip Lists, *ACM Journal on Experimental Algorithmics* **3** (1998) Article 2.

S. Cho, S. Sahni: Mergeable Double-Ended Priority Queues, *International Journal Foundations of Computer Science* **10** (1999) 1–17.

S. Cho, S. Sahni: A New Weight Balanced Binary Search Tree, *International Journal Foundations of Computer Science* **11** (2000) 485–513.

Y. Choi, T.-W. Lam: Dynamic Suffix Trees and Two-Dimensional Texts Management, *Information Processing Letters* **61** (1997) 213–220.

K.-R. Chong, S. Sahni: Correspondence-Based Data Structures for Double-Ended Priority Queues, *ACM Journal on Experimental Algorithmics* **5** (2000) Article 2.

J.-H. Chu, G.D. Knott: An Analysis of Spiral Hashing, *The Computer Journal* **37** (1994) 715–719.

S.M. Chung: Indexed Extendible Hashing, *Information Processing Letters* **44** (1992) 1–6.

R.J. Cichelli: Minimal Perfect Hash Functions Made Simple, *Communications ACM* **23** (1980) 17–19.

D.W. Clark: A Fast Algorithm for Copying Binary Trees, *Information Processing Letters* **4** (1975) 62–63.

E.G. Coffman, Jr., J. Eve: File Structures Using Hashing Functions, *Communications of the ACM* **13** (1970) 427–436.

S. Cohen, Y. Matias: Spectral Bloom Filters, in: SIGMOD 2003 (Proceedings 2003 ACM SIGMOD Conference on Management of Data), 241–252.

R. Cole, R. Hariharan: Faster Suffix Tree Construction with Missing Suffix Links, *SIAM Journal on Computing* **33** (2003) 26–42.

R. Cole, R. Hariharan: Dynamic LCA Queries on Trees, *SIAM Journal on Computing* **34** (2005) 894–923.

R. Cole, M. Lewenstein: Multidimensional Matching and Fast Search in Suffix Trees, in: SODA 2003 (Proceedings 14th Annual ACM-SIAM Symposium on Discrete Algorithms), 851–852.

L. Colussi, A. De Col: A Time and Space Efficient Data Structure for String Searching on Large Texts, *Information Processing Letters* **58** (1996) 217–222.

D. Comer, R. Sethi: The Complexity of Trie Index Construction, *Journal of the ACM* **24** (1977) 428–440.

G.V. Cormack, R.N.S. Horspool, M. Kaiserswerth: Practical Perfect Hashing, *The Computer Journal* **28** (1985) 54–58.

M. Crochemore, W. Rytter: *Jewels of Stringology*, World Scientific 2003.

K. Culik, II, T. Ottmann, D. Wood: Dense Multiway Trees, *ACM Transactions on Database Systems* **6** (1981) 486–512.

K. Culik, II, D. Wood: A Note on Some Tree Similarity Measures, *Information Processing Letters* **15** (1982) 39–42.

W. Cunto, G. Lau, P. Flajolet: Analysis of kdt-Trees: kd-Trees Improved by Local Reorganization, in: WADS 1989 (Proceedings 1st Workshop on Algorithms and Data Structures), Springer. *LNCS* **382**, 24–38.

Z.J. Czech: Quasi-Perfect Hashing, *The Computer Journal* **41** (1998) 416–421.

Z.J. Czech, G. Havas, B.S. Majewski: An Optimal Algorithm for Generating Minimal Perfect Hash Functions, *Information Processing Letters* **43** (1992) 257–264.

Z.J. Czech, G. Havas, B.S. Majewski: Perfect Hashing, *Theoretical Computer Science* **182** (1997) 1–143.

Z.J. Czech, B.S. Majewski: A Linear-Time Algorithm for Finding Minimal Perfect Hash Functions, *The Computer Journal* **36** (1993) 579–587.

R.B. Dannenberg: A Structure for Efficient Update, Incremental Redisplay, and Undo in Graphical Editors, *Software – Practice and Experience* **20** (1990) 109–132.

A.C. Day: Balancing a Binary Tree, *The Computer Journal* **19** (1976) 360–361.

E.D. Demaine, J. Iacono, S. Langerman: Retroactive Data Structures, in: SODA 2004 (Proceedings 15th Annual ACM-SIAM Symposium on Discrete Algorithms), 281–290.

L. Devroye: A Limit Theory for Random Skip Lists, *Annals of Applied Probability* **2** (1992) 597–609.

L. Devroye, P. Morin: Cuckoo Hashing: Further Analysis, *Information Processing Letters* **86** (2003) 215–219.

L. Devroye, P. Morin, A. Viola: On Worst-Case Robin Hood Hashing, *SIAM Journal on Computing* **33** (2004) 923–936.

G. Diehr, B. Faaland: Optimal Pagination of B-Trees with Variable-Length Items, *Communications ACM* **27** (1984) 241–247.

P.F. Dietz: Maintaining Order in a Linked List, in: STOC 1982 (Proceedings 14th Annual ACM Symposium on Theory of Computing), 122–127.

P.F. Dietz, R. Raman: Persistence, Amortization, and Randomization, in: SODA 1991 (Proceedings 2nd Annual ACM-SIAM Symposium on Discrete Algorithms), 78–88.

P.F. Dietz, D.D. Sleator: Two Algorithms for Maintaining Order in a List, in: STOC 1987 (Proceedings 19th Annual ACM Symposium on Theory of Computing), 365–372.

M. Dietzfelbinger, T. Hagerup: Simple Minimal Perfect Hashing in Less Space, in: ESA 2001 (Proceedings 9th Annual European Symposium on Algorithms), Springer. *LNCS* **2161**, 109–120.

M. Dietzfelbinger, A. Karlin, K. Mehlhorn, F. Meyer auf der Heide, H. Rohnert, R.E. Tarjan: Dynamic Perfect Hashing: Upper and Lower Bounds, *SIAM Journal on Computing* **23** (1994) 738–761.

M. Dietzfelbinger, F. Meyer auf der Heide: Dynamic Hashing in Real Time, in: *Informatik-Festschrift zum 60*, Geburtstag von Günter Hotz, J. Buchmann et al., eds., Teubner 1992, 95–115.

Y. Ding, M.A. Weiss: The Relaxed Min-Max Heap, *Acta Informatica* **30** (1993) 215–231.

Y. Ding, M.A. Weiss: On the Complexity of Building an Interval Heap, *Information Processing Letters* **50** (1994) 143–144.

A.A. Diwan, S. Rane, S. Seshadri, S. Sudarshan: Clustering Techniques for Minimizing External Path Length, in: VLDB 1996 (Proceedings 22nd International Conference on Very Large Data Bases), 342–353.

D.P. Dobkin, J.I. Munro: Efficient Uses of the Past, *Journal of Algorithms* **6** (1985) 455–465.

D.P. Dobkin, S. Suri: Maintenance of Geometric Extrema, *Journal of the ACM* **38** (1991) 275–298.

D. Dolev, Y. Harari, N. Linial, N. Nisan, M. Parnas: Neighborhood Preserving Hashing and Approximate Queries, in: SODA 1994 (Proceedings 5th ACM-SIAM Symposium on Discrete Algorithms), 251–259.

J.R. Driscoll, H.N. Gabow, R. Shrairman, R.E. Tarjan: Relaxed Heaps: An Alternative to Fibonacci Heaps with Applications to Parallel Computation, *Communications ACM* **31** (1988) 1343–1354.

J.R. Driscoll, N. Sarnak, D.D. Sleator, R.E. Tarjan: Making Data Structures Persistent, *Journal of Computer and System Sciences* **38** (1989) 86–124.

J.R. Driscoll, D.D. Sleator, R.E. Tarjan: Fully Persistent Lists with Catenation, *Journal of the ACM* **41** (1994) 943–959.

A. Duch, V. Estivill-Castro, C. Martinez: Randomized k-Dimensional Binary Search Trees, in: ISAAC 1998 (Proceedings 9th International Symposium on Algorithms and Computation), Springer. *LNCS* **1533**, 199–209.

A. Duch, C. Martinez: On the Average Performance of Orthogonal Range Search in Multidimensional Data Structures, *Journal of Algorithms* **44** (2002) 226–245.

B. Dwyer: Simple Algorithms for Traversing a Tree without Additional Stack, *Information Processing Letters* **2** (1974) 143–145.

A. Ecker: The Period of Search for the Quadratic and Related Hash Methods, *The Computer Journal* **17** (1974) 340–343.

H. Edelsbrunner: A Note on Dynamic Range Searching, *Bulletin of the EATCS* **15** (1981) 34–40.

H. Edelsbrunner, H.A. Maurer: On the Intersection of Orthogonal Objects, *Information Processing Letters* **13** (1981) 177–181.

H. Edelsbrunner, M.H. Overmars: Batched Dynamic Solutions to Decomposable Searching Problems, *Journal of Algorithms* **6** (1985) 515–542.

A. Elmasry: Parametrized Self-Adjusting Heaps, *Journal of Algorithms* **52** (2004) 103–119.

P. van Emde Boas, R. Kaas, E. Zijlstra: Design and Implementation of an Efficient Priority Queue, *Mathematical Systems Theory* **10** (1977) 99–127.

R.J. Enbody, H.-C. Du: Dynamic Hashing Schemes, *ACM Computing Surveys* **20** (1988) 85–113.

D. Eppstein: Dynamic Euclidean Minimum Spanning Trees and Extrema of Binary Functions, *Discrete & Computational Geometry* **13** (1995) 111–122.

F. Ergun, S.C. Sahinalp, J. Sharp, R.K. Sinha: Biased Skip Lists for Highly Skewed Access Patterns, in: ALENEX 2001 (Proceedings 3rd Workshop on Algorithms Engineering and Experimentation), Springer. *LNCS* **2153**, 216–229.

J.B. Evans: Experiments with Trees for the Storage and Retrieval of Future Events, *Information Processing Letters* **22** (1986) 237–242.

R. Fagerberg: Binary Search Trees: How Low Can You Go?, in: SWAT 1996a (Proceedings 5th Scandinavian Workshop on Algorithm Theory), Springer. *LNCS* **1097**, 428–439.

R. Fagerberg: A Generalization of Binomial Queues, *Information Processing Letters* **57** (1996b) 109–114.

R. Fagin, J. Nievergelt, N. Pippenger, H.R. Strong: Extendible Hashing – A Fast Access Method for Dynamic Files, *ACM Transactions on Database Systems* **4** (1979) 315–344.

S.M. Falconer, B.G. Nickerson: On Multilevel k-Ranges for Range Search, *International Journal Computational Geometry Applications* **15** (2005) 565–573.

L. Fan, P. Cao, J. Almeida, A.Z. Broder: Summary Cache: A Scaleable Wide-Area Web Cache Sharing Protocol, *ACM Transactions on Networking* **8** (2000) 281–293.

M. Farach: Optimal Suffix Tree Construction with Large Alphabets, in: FOCS 1997 (Proceedings 38th Annual IEEE Symposium on Foundations of Computer Science), 137–143.

S. Felsner: *Geometric Graphs and Arrangements*, Vieweg Verlag, 2004.

P. Ferragina, R. Grossi: The String B-Tree: A New Data Structure for String Search in External Memory and Its Applications, *Journal of the ACM* **46** (1999) 236–280.

P. Ferragina, S. Muthukrishnan, M. de Berg: Multi-Method Dispatching: A Geometric Approach with Applications to String Matching Problems, in STOC 1999 (Proceedings 30th Annual ACM Symposium on Theory of Computing), 483–491.

A. Fiat, H. Kaplan: Making Data Structures Confluently Persistent, *Journal of Algorithms* **48** (2003) 16–58.

D. Field: A Note on a New Data Structure for In-The-Past Queries, *Information Processing Letters* **24** (1987) 95–96.

M.J. Fischer: Efficiency of Equivalence Algorithms, in: *Complexity of Computer Computations*, R.E. Miller, J.W. Thatcher, eds., Plenum Press 1972, 153–168.

M.J. Fischer, M.S. Paterson: Fishspear: A Priority Queue Algorithm, *Journal ACM* **41** (1994) 3–30.

R. Fleischer: A Tight Lower Bound for the Worst Case of Bottom-Up Heapsort, *Algorithmica* **11** (1994) 104–115.

R. Fleischer: A Simple Balanced Search Tree with $O(1)$ Worst-Case Update Time, *International Journal Foundations of Computer Science* **7** (1996) 137–149.

R.W. Floyd: Algorithm 113: Treesort, *Communications ACM* **5** (1962) p. 434.

R.W. Floyd: Algorithm 245: Treesort 3, *Communications ACM* **7** (1964) p. 701.

C.C. Foster: A Generalization of AVL-Trees, *Communications ACM* **16** (1973) 513–517.

E.A. Fox, L.S. Heath, Q.F. Chen, A.M. Daoud: Practical Minimal Perfect Hash Functions for Large Databases, *Communications ACM* **35** (1992) 105–121.

C.W. Fraser, E.W. Myers: An Editor for Revision Control, *ACM Transactions on Programming Languages and Systems* **9** (1987) 277–295.

E. Fredkin: Trie Memory, *Communications ACM* **4** (1961) 490–499.

M.L. Fredman: A Near Optimal Structure for a Type of Range Query Problems, in: STOC 1979 (Proceedings 11th Annual ACM Symposium on Theory of Computing), 62–66.

M.L. Fredman: A Lower Bound on the Complexity of Orthogonal Range Queries, *Journal ACM* **28** (1981a) 696–705.

M.L. Fredman: Lower Bounds on the Complexity of Some Optimal Data Structures, *SIAM Journal on Computing* **10** (1981b) 1–10.

M.L. Fredman: The Complexity of Maintaining an Array and Computing Its Partial Sums, *Journal ACM* **29** (1982) 250–260.

M.L. Fredman: Information Theoretic Implications for Pairing Heaps, in: STOC 1998 (Proceedings 30th Annual ACM Symposium on Theory of Computing), 319–326.

M.L. Fredman: On the Efficiency of Pairing Heaps and Related Data Structures, *Journal ACM* **46** (1999a) 473–501.

M.L. Fredman: A Priority Queue Transform, in: WAE 1999b (Proceedings 3rd Workshop on Algorithms Engineering), Springer. *LNCS* **1668**, 243–257.

M.L. Fredman, J. Komlós: On the Size of Separating Systems and Families of Perfect Hash Functions, *SIAM Journal Algebraic Discrete Methods* **5** (1984) 61–68.

M.L. Fredman, J. Komlós, E. Szemerédi: Storing a Sparse Table with $O(1)$ Worst Case Access Time, *Journal ACM* **31** (1984) 538–544.

M.L. Fredman, M.E. Saks: The Cell Probe Complexity of Dynamic Data Structures, in: STOC 1989 (Proceedings 21st Annual ACM Symposium on Theory of Computing), 345–354.

M.L. Fredman, R. Sedgewick, D.D. Sleator, R.E. Tarjan: The Pairing Heap: A New Form of Self-Adjusting Heap, *Algorithmica* **1** (1986) 111–129.

M.L. Fredman, R.E. Tarjan: Fibonacci Heaps and Their Uses in Improved Network Optimization Algorithms, *Journal ACM* **34** (1987) 596–615.

M.L. Fredman, B. Weide: On the Complexity of Computing the Measure of $\bigcup[a_i, b_i]$, *Communications of the ACM* **21** (1978) 540–544.

M. Freeston: A General Solution of the n-Dimensional B-Tree Problem, in: SIGMOD 1995 (Proceedings 1995 ACM SIGMOD Conference on Management of Data), 80–91.

M. Frigo, C.E. Leiserson, H. Prokop, S. Ramachandran: Cache Oblivious Algorithms, in: FOCS 1999 (Proceedings 40th Annual IEEE Symposium on Foundations of Computer Science), 285–298.

M. Fürer: Randomized Splay Trees, in: SODA 1999 (Proceedings 10th ACM-SIAM Symposium on Discrete Algorithms), 903–904.

H.N. Gabow: A Scaling Algorithm for Weighted Matching on General Graphs, in: FOCS 1985 (Proceedings 26th Annual IEEE Symposium on Foundations of Computer Science), 90–100.

H.N. Gabow: Data Structures for Weighted Matching and Nearest Common Ancestors with Linking, in: SODA 1990 (Proceedings 1st ACM-SIAM Symposium on Discrete Algorithms), 434–443.

H.N. Gabow, R.E. Tarjan: A Linear Time Algorithm for a Special Case of Disjoint Set Union, *Journal of Computer and System Sciences* **30** (1985) 209–221.

V. Gaede, O. Günther: Multidimensional Access Methods, *ACM Computing Surveys* **30** (1998) 170–231.

H. Gajewska, R.E. Tarjan: Deques with Heap Order, *Information Processing Letters* **22** (1986) 197–200.

B.A. Galler, M.J. Fisher: An Improved Equivalence Algorithm, *Communications ACM* **7** (1964) 301–303.

Z. Galil, G.F. Italiano: Data Structures and Algorithms for Disjoint Set Union Problems, *ACM Computing Surveys* **23** (1991) 319–344.

I. Galperin, R.L. Rivest: Scapegoat Trees, in: SODA 1993 (Proceedings 4th ACM-SIAM Symposium on Discrete Algorithms), 165–174.

G. Gambosi, G.F. Italiano, M. Talamo: Getting Back to the Past in the Union-Find Problem, in: STACS 1988 (Proceedings of the 5th Annual Symposium on Theoretical Aspects of Computer Science), Springer. *LNCS* **294**, 8–17.

G. Gambosi, G.F. Italiano, M. Talamo: The Set Union Problem with Dynamic Weighted Backtracking, *BIT* **31** (1991) 382–393.

G. Gambosi, M. Protasi, M. Talamo: An Efficient Implicit Data Structure for Relation Testing and Searching in Partially Ordered Sets, *BIT* **33** (1993) 29–45.

D. Gardy, P. Flajolet, C. Puech: Average Cost of Orthogonal Range Queries in Multiattribute Trees, *Information Systems* **14** (1989) 341–350.

T.E. Gerasch: An Insertion Algorithm for a Minimal Internal Pathlength Binary Search Tree, *Communications ACM* **31** (1988) 579–585.

G.F. Georgakopoulos, D.J. McClurkin: Generalized Template Splay: A Basic Theory and Calculus, *The Computer Journal* **47** (2004) 10–19.

L. Georgiadis, R.E. Tarjan, R.F. Werneck: Design of a Data Structure for Mergeable Trees, in: SODA 2006 (Proceedings 17th ACM-SIAM Symposium on Discrete Algorithms), 394–403.

R. Giancarlo: A Generalization of the Suffix Tree to Square Matrix, with Applications, *SIAM Journal on Computing* **24** (1995) 520–562.

R. Giegerich, S. Kurtz: From Ukkonen to McCreight and Weiner: A Unifying View of Linear-Time Suffix Tree Construction, *Algorithmica* **19** (1997) 331–353.

R. Giegerich, S. Kurtz, J. Stoye: Efficient Implementation of Lazy Suffix Trees, *Software – Practice and Experience* **33** (2003) 1035–1049.

J. Gil, A. Itai: How to Pack Trees, *Journal of Algorithms* **32** (1999) 108–132.

G.H. Gonnet: Expected Length of the Longest Probe Sequence in Hash Code Searching, *Journal of the ACM* **28** (1981) 289–304.

G.H. Gonnet, R.A. Baeza-Yates, T. Snider: New Indices for Texts: PAT Trees and PAT Arrays, in: *Information Retrieval: Data Structures and Algorithms*, W.B. Frakes, R.A. Baeza-Yates, eds., Prentice Hall 1992, 66–82.

G.H. Gonnet, J.I. Munro: Efficient Ordering of Hash Tables, *SIAM Journal on Computing* **8** (1979) 463–478.

G.H. Gonnet, J.I. Munro: Heaps on Heaps, *SIAM Journal on Computing* **15** (1986) 964–971.

G.H. Gonnet, J.I. Munro, D. Wood: Direct Dynamic Structures for Some Line-Segment Problems, *Computer Vision, Graphics, and Image Processing* **23** (1983) 178–186.

G.H. Gonnet, H. Olivié, D. Wood: Height-Ratio Balanced Trees, *The Computer Journal* **26** (1983) 106–108.

D. Greene, M. Parnas, F. Yao: Multi-Index Hashing for Information Retrieval, in: FOCS 1994 (Proceedings 34th Annual IEEE Symposium on Foundations of Computer Science), 722–731.

R. Grossi, G.F. Italiano: Efficient Splitting and Merging Algorithms for Order Decomposable Problems, in: ICALP 1997 (Proceedings 24th International Colloquium on Automata, Languages, and Programming), Springer. *LNCS* **1256**, 605–615.

L.J. Guibas, E.M. McCreight, M.F. Plass, J.R. Roberts: A New Representation for Linear Lists, in: STOC 1977 (Proceedings 9th Annual ACM Symposium on Theory of Computing), 49–60.

L.J. Guibas, R. Sedgewick: A Dichromatic Framework for Balanced Trees, in: FOCS 1978 (Proceedings 19th Annual IEEE Symposium on Foundations of Computer Science), 8–21.

L.J. Guibas, E. Szemerédi: Analysis of Double Hashing, *Journal Computer System Sciences* **16** (1978) 226–274.

D. Gusfield: *Algorithms on Strings, Trees, and Sequences*, Cambridge University Press 1997.

A. Guttman: R-Trees: A Dynamic Index Structure for Spatial Searching, in: SIGMOD 1984 (Proceedings 1984 ACM SIGMOD Conference on Management of Data), 47–57.

T. Hagerup, T. Tholey: Efficient Minimal Perfect Hashing in Nearly Minimal Space, in: STACS 2001 (Proceedings of the 18th Annual Symposium on Theoretical Aspects of Computer Science), Springer. *LNCS* **2010**, 317–326.

S.E. Hambrusch, C.-M. Liu: Data Replication in Static Tree Structures, *Information Processing Letters* **86** (2003) 197–202.

H. Hampapuram, M.L. Fredman: Optimal Biweighted Binary Trees and the Complexity of Maintaining Partial Sums, *SIAM Journal on Computing* **28** (1998) 1–9.

D. Harel, R.E. Tarjan: Fast Algorithms for Finding Nearest Common Ancestors, *SIAM Journal on Computing* **13** (1984) 338–355.

G.C. Harfst, E.M. Reingold: A Potential-Based Amortized Analysis of the Union-Find Structure, *ACM SIGACT News* **31** (2000) 86–95.

A. Hasham, J.-R. Sack: Bounds for Min-Max Heaps, *BIT* **27** (1987) 315–323.

S. Heinz, J. Zobel, H.E. Williams: Burst Tries: A Fast, Efficient Data Structure for String Keys, *ACM Transactions on Information Systems* **20** (2002) 192–223.

J.M. Hellerstein, E. Koutsoupias, C.H. Papadimitriou: On the Analysis of Indexing Schemes, in: PODS 1997 (Proceedings 16th ACM Symposium on Principles of Database Systems), 249–256.

T. Herman, T. Masuzawa: Available Stabilizing Heaps, *Information Processing Letters* **77** (2001) 115–121.

K. Hinrichs: Implementation of the Grid File: Design Concepts and Experience, *BIT* **25** (1985) 569–592.

D.S. Hirschberg: An Insertion Technique for One-Sided Height-Balanced Trees, *Communications ACM* **19** (1976) 471–473.

K. Hoffmann, K. Mehlhorn, P. Rosenstiehl, R.E. Tarjan: Sorting Jordan Sequences in Linear Time Using Level-Linked Search Trees, *Information and Control* **68** (1986) 170–184.

J. Holub, M. Crochemore: On the Implementation of Compact DAWGs, in: CIAA 2002 (Proceedings 7th Conference on Implementation and Applications of Automata) Springer. *LNCS* **2608** (2003) 289–294.

W.-K. Hon, K. Sadakane, W.-K. Sung: Breaking a Time-and-Space Barrier in Constructing Full-Text Indices, in: FOCS 2003 (Proceedings 44th IEEE Symposium Foundations of Computer Science), 251–260.

J.E. Hopcroft, J.D. Ullman: Set Merging Algorithms, *SIAM Journal on Computing* **2** (1973) 294–303.

M. Hoshi, T. Yuba: A Counterexample to a Monotonicity Property of kd-Trees, *Information Processing Letters* **15** (1982) 169–173.

R.J.W. Housden: On String Concepts and Their Implementation, *The Computer Journal* **18** (1975) 150–156.

P. Høyer: A General Technique for Implementing Efficient Priority Queues, in: ISTCS 1995 (Proceedings 3rd Israel Symposium on Theory of Computing and Systems), IEEE 1995, 57–66.

S. Huddleston, K. Mehlhorn: A New Data Structure for Representing Sorted Lists, *Acta Informatica* **17** (1982) 157–184.

L.C.K. Hui, C. Martel: Unsuccessful Search in Self-Adjusting Data Structures, *Journal Algorithms* **15** (1993) 447–481.

E. Hunt, M.P. Atkinson, R.W. Irving: Database Indexing for Large DNA and Protein Sequence Collections, *The VLDB Journal* **11** (2002) 256–271.

J. Iacono: Improved Upper Bounds for Pairing Heaps, in: SWAT 2000 (Proceedings 7th Scandinavian Workshop on Algorithm Theory), Springer. *LNCS* **1851**, 32–45.

J. Iacono: Alternatives to Splay Trees with $O(\log n)$ Worst-Case Access Time, in: SODA 2001 (Proceedings 12th ACM-SIAM Symposium on Discrete Algorithms), 516–522.

J. Iacono, S. Langerman: Queaps, in: ISAAC 2002 (Proceedings 13th International Symposium on Algorithms and Computation), Springer. *LNCS* **2518**, 211–218.

S. Inenaga: Bidirectional Construction of Suffix Trees, *Nordic Journal of Computing* **10** (2003) 52–67.

H. Itoh, H. Tanaka: An Efficient Method for in Memory Construction of Suffix Arrays, in: SPIRE 1999 (Proceedings 6th IEEE Symposium String Processing Information Retrieval), 81–88.

G. Jaeschke: Reciprocal Hashing: A Method for Generating Minimal Perfect Hashing Functions, *Communications ACM* **24** (1981) 829–831.

D.B. Johnson: Priority Queues with Update and Finding Minimum Spanning Trees, *Information Processing Letters* **4** (1975) 53–57.

A. Jonassen, O.-J. Dahl: Analysis of an Algorithm for Priority Queue Administration, *BIT* **15** (1975) 409–422.

D.W. Jones: A Note on Bottom-Up Skew Heaps, *SIAM Journal on Computing* **16** (1987) 108–110.

H. Jung: The d-Deap: A Simple and Cache-Aligned d-ary Deap, *Information Processing Letters* **93** (2005) 63–67.

H. Jung, S. Sahni: Supernode Binary Search Trees, *International Journal Foundations of Computer Science*, **14** (2003) 465–490.

A. Kaldewaij, B. Schoenmakers: The Derivation of a Tighter Bound for Top-Down Skew Heaps, *Information Processing Letters* **37** (1991) 265–271.

H. Kaplan, C. Okasaki, R.E. Tarjan: Simple Confluently Persistent Catenable Lists, *SIAM Journal on Computing* **30** (2000) 965–977.

H. Kaplan, T. Milo, R. Shabo: A Comparison of Labeling Schemes for Ancestor Queries, in: SODA 2002 (Proceedings 13th ACM-SIAM Symposium on Discrete Algorithms), 954–963.

H. Kaplan, E. Molad, R.E. Tarjan: Dynamic Rectangular Intersection with Priorities, in: STOC 2003 (Proceedings 35th Annual ACM Symposium on Theory of Computing), 639–648.

H. Kaplan, N. Shafrir, R.E. Tarjan: Union-Find with Deletions, in: SODA 2002a (Proceedings 13th ACM-SIAM Symposium on Discrete Algorithms), 19–28.

H. Kaplan, N. Shafrir, R.E. Tarjan: Meldable Heaps and Boolean Union-Find, in: STOC 2002b (Proceedings 34th Annual ACM Symposium on Theory of Computing), 573–582.

J. Kärkkäinen: Suffix Cactus: A Cross between Suffix Tree and Suffix Array, in CPM 1995 (Proceedings 6th Annual Symposium on Combinatorial Pattern Matching), Springer. *LNCS* **937**, 191–204.

J. Kärkkäinen, P. Sanders: Simple Linear Work Suffix Array Construction, in: ICALP 2003 (Proceedings 30th International Colloquium on Automata, Languages, and Programming), Springer. *LNCS* **2719**, 943–955.

J. Kärkkäinen, P. Sanders, S. Burkhardt: Linear Work Suffix Array Construction, *Journal of the ACM* **53** (2006) 918–936.

P.L. Karlton, S.H. Fuller, R.E. Scroggs, E.B. Kaehler: Performance of Height-Balanced Trees, *Communications ACM* **19** (1976) 23–28.

R.M. Karp, R.E. Miller, A.L. Rosenberg: Rapid Identification of Repeated Patterns in Strings, Trees, and Arrays, in: STOC 1972 (Proceedings 4th Annual ACM Symposium on Theory of Computing), 125–136.

T. Kasai, G. Lee, H. Arimura, S. Arikawa, K. Park: Linear-Time Longest-Common-Prefix Computation in Suffix Arrays and Its Applications, in CPM 2001 (Proceedings 12th Annual Symposium on Combinatorial Pattern Matching), Springer. *LNCS* **2089**, 181–192.

A.F. Kaupe, Jr.: Algorithm 143: Treesort 1, Algorithm 144: Treesort 2, *Communications ACM* **5** (1962) p. 604.

M. Kempf, R. Bayer, U. Güntzer: Time Optimal Left to Right Construction of Position Trees, *Acta Informatica* **24** (1987) 461–474.

J.L.W. Kessels: On-the-Fly Optimization of Data Structures, *Communications ACM* **26** (1983) 895–901.

C.M. Khoong, H.W. Leong: Double-Ended Binomial Queues, in: ISAAC 1993 (Proceedings 4th International Symposium on Algorithms and Computation), Springer. *LNCS* **762**, 128–137.

C.M. Khoong, H.W. Leong: Relaxed Inorder Heaps, *International Journal Foundations of Computer Science*, **5** (1994) 111–128.

D.K. Kim, J.E. Jeon, H. Park: An Efficient Index Data Structure with the Capabilities of Suffix Trees and Suffix Arrays for Alphabets of Non-Negligible Size, in: SPIRE 2004a (Proceedings 11th Symposium String Processing Information Retrieval), Springer. *LNCS* **3246**, 138–149.

D.K. Kim, J. Jo, H. Park: A Fast Algorithm for Constructing Suffix Arrays for Fixed-Size Alphabet, in: WEA 2004b (Proceedings 3rd Workshop on Experimental and Efficient Algorithms), Springer. *LNCS* **3059**, 301–314.

D.K. Kim, Y.A. Kim, K. Park: Generalization of Suffix Arrays to Multi-Dimensional Matrices, *Theoretical Computer Science* **302** (2003) 223–238.

D.K. Kim, H. Park: The Linearized Suffix Tree and Its Succinct Representation, in: Proceedings 2005 Korea-Japan Joint Workshop on Algorithms and Computation 51–58.

D.K. Kim, J.S. Sim, H. Park, K. Park: Linear-Time Construction of Suffix Arrays, in: CPM 2003 (Proceedings 14th Annual Symposium on Combinatorial Pattern Matching), Springer. *LNCS* **2676**, 186–199.

D.K. Kim, J.S. Sim, H. Park, K. Park: Constructing Suffix Arrays in Linear Time, *Journal of Discrete Algorithms* **3** (2005) 126–142.

A. Kirsch, M. Mitzenmacher: Less Hashing, Same Performance: Building a Better Bloom Filter, in: ESA 2006 (Proceedings 14th Annual European Symposium on Algorithms), Springer. *LNCS* **4168**, 456–467.

P. Kirschenhofer, H. Prodinger: The Path Length of Random Skip Lists, *Acta Informatica* **31** (1994) 775–792.

V. Klee: Can the Measure of $\bigcup_{i-1}^{n}[a_i, b_i]$ Be Computed in Less Than $O(n \log n)$ Steps?, *American Mathematical Monthly* **84** (1977) 284–285.

R. Klein, D. Wood: A Tight Upper Bound for the Path Length of AVL Trees, *Theoretical Computer Science* **72** (1990) 251–264.

G.D. Knott: Hashing Fuctions, *The Computer Journal* **18** (1972) 265–278.

D.E. Knuth: *The Art of Computer Programming, Vol 3: Sorting and Searching*, Addison-Wesley 1973.

D.E. Knuth: Computer Science and Its Relation to Mathematics, *American Mathematical Monthly* **81** (1974) 323–343.

P. Ko, S. Aluru: Space-Efficient Linear-Time Construction of Suffix Arrays, in: CPM 2003 (Proceedings 14th Annual Symposium on Combinatorial Pattern Matching), Springer. *LNCS* **2676**, 200–210.

P. Ko, S. Aluru: Space-Efficient Linear-Time Construction of Suffix Arrays, *Journal of Discrete Algorithms* **3** (2005) 143–156.

A.P. Korah, M.R. Kaimal: Dynamic Optimal Binary Search Tree, *International Journal Foundations of Computer Science* **1** (1990) 449–464.

A.P. Korah, M.R. Kaimal: A Short Note on Perfectly Balanced Binary Search Trees, *The Computer Journal* **35** (1992) 660–662.

S.R. Kosaraju: Insertion and Deletion in One-Sided Height-Balanced Trees, *Communications ACM* **21** (1978) 226–227.

S.R. Kosaraju: Localized Search in Sorted Lists, in: STOC 1981 (Proceedings 13th Annual ACM Symposium on Theory of Computing), 62–69.

S.R. Kosaraju: Real-Time Pattern Matching and Quasi-Real-Time Construction of Suffix Arrays in: STOC 1994 (Proceedings 26th Annual ACM Symposium on Theory of Computing), 310–316.

S.R. Kosaraju: Faster Algorithms for the Construction of Parametrized Suffix Trees, in: FOCS 1995 (Proceedings 36th IEEE Symposium Foundations of Computer Science), 631–637.

E. Koutsoupias, D.S. Taylor: Tight Bounds for 2-Dimensional Indexing Schemes, in: PODS 1998 (Proceedings 17th ACM Symposium on Principles of Database Systems), 44–51.

J. Král: Some Properties of the Scatter Storage Technique with Linear Probing, *The Computer Journal* **14** (1971) 145–149.

M.J. van Kreveld, M.H. Overmars: Concatenable Segment Trees, in: STACS 1989 (Proceedings of the 6th Annual Symposium on Theoretical Aspects of Computer Science), Springer. *LNCS* **349**, 493–504.

M.J. van Kreveld, M.H. Overmars: Divided kd-Trees, *Algorithmica* **6** (1991) 840–858.

M.J. van Kreveld, M.H. Overmars: Union-Copy Structures and Dynamic Segment Trees, *Journal ACM* **40** (1993) 635–652.

T. Krovetz, P. Rogaway: Variationally Universal Hashing, *Information Processing Letters* **100** (2006) 36–39.

S. Kurtz: Reducing the Space Requirement of Suffix Trees, *Software – Practice and Experience* **29** (1999) 1149–1171.

T.W. Lai, D. Wood: Updating Almost Complete Trees or One Level Makes All the Difference, in: STACS 1990 (Proceedings of the 7th Annual Symposium on Theoretical Aspects of Computer Science), Springer. *LNCS* **415**, 188–194.

T.W. Lai, D. Wood: A Top-Down Updating Algorithm for Weight-Balanced Trees, *International Journal Foundations of Computer Science* **4** (1993) 309–324.

E. Langetepe, G. Zachmann: *Geometric Data Structures for Computer Graphics*, A K Peters 2006.

M.J. Lao: A New Data Structure for the Union-Find Problem, *Information Processing Letters* **9** (1979) 39–45.

K.S. Larsen: Amortized Constant Relaxed Rebalancing Using Standard Rotations, *Acta Informatica* **35** (1998) 859–874.

K.S. Larsen: AVL Trees with Relaxed Balance, *Journal of Computer and System Sciences* **61** (2000) 508–522.

K.S. Larsen: Relaxed Red-Black Trees with Group Updates, *Acta Informatica* **38** (2002) 565–586.

K.S. Larsen: Relaxed Multi-Way Trees with Group Updates, *Journal of Computer and System Sciences* **66** (2003) 657–670.

K.S. Larsen, R. Fagerberg: Efficient Rebalancing of B-Trees with Relaxed Balance, *International Journal Foundations of Computer Science* **7** (1996) 169–186.

P.-Å. Larson: Dynamic Hashing, *BIT* **18** (1978) 184–201.

P.-Å. Larson: Analysis of Repeated Hashing, *BIT* **20** (1980) 25–32.

P.-Å. Larson: Expected Worst-Case Performance of Hash Files, *The Computer Journal* **25** (1982) 347–352.

P.-Å. Larson: Analysis of Uniform Hashing, *Journal of the ACM* **30** (1983) 805–819.

P.- Å. Larson: Performance Analysis of a Single-File Version of Linear Hashing, *The Computer Journal* **28** (1985) 319–329.

P.- Å. Larson: Dynamic Hash Tables, *Communications of the ACM* **31** (1988) 448–457.

D.-T. Lee, C.-K. Wong: Worst-Case Analysis for Region and Partial Region Searches in Multidimensional Binary Search Trees and Balanced Quad Trees, *Acta Informatica* **9** (1977) 23–29.

D.-T. Lee, C.-K. Wong: Quintary Trees: A File Structure for Multidimensional Database Systems, *ACM Transactions Database Systems* **5** (1980) 339–353.

J. van Leeuwen, D. Wood: Dynamization of Decomposable Searching Problems, *Information Processing Letters* **10** (1980a) 51–56; for a minor correction, see **11** (1980) p. 57.

J. van Leeuwen, D. Wood: The Measure Problem for Rectangular Ranges in d-Space, *Journal of Algorithms* **2** (1980b) 282–300.

J. van Leeuwen, D. Wood: Interval Heaps, *The Computer Journal* **36** (1993) 209–216.

C. Levcopoulos, M. Overmars: A Balanced Search Tree with $O(1)$ Worst-Case Update Time, *Acta Informatica* **26** (1988) 269–277.

A.M. Liao: Three Priority Queue Applications Revisited, *Algorithmica* **7** (1992) 415–427.

G. Lindstrom: Scanning List Structures without Stacks and Tag Bits, *Information Processing Letters* **2** (1973) 47–51.

R.J. Lipton, P.J. Martino, A. Neitzke: On the Complexity of a Set-Union Problem, in: FOCS 1997 (Proceedings 38th IEEE Symposium Foundations of Computer Science), 110–115.

M.C. Little, S.K. Shrivastava, N.A. Speirs: Using Bloom Filters to Speed-Up Name Lookup in Distributed Systems, *The Computer Journal* **45** (2002) 645–652.

W. Litwin: Virtual Hashing: A Dynamically Changing Hashing, in: VLDB 1978 (Proceedings 4th IEEE Conference on Very Large Databases), 517–523.

W. Litwin: Linear Hashing: A New Tool for File and Table Addressing, in: VLDB 1980 (Proceedings 6th IEEE Conference on Very Large Databases), 212–223.

W. Litwin: Trie Hashing, in: SIGMOD 1981 (Proceedings ACM SIGMOD Conference on Management of Data), 19–29.

E. Lodi, F. Luccio: Split Sequence Hash Tables, *Information Processing Letters* **20** (1985) 131–136.

M. Loebl, J. Nešetřil: Linearity and Unprovability of Set Union Strategies, *Journal of Algorithms* **23** (1997) 207–220.

D.B. Lomet: Bounded Index Exponential Hashing, *ACM Transactions on Database Systems* **8** (1983) 136–165.

D.B. Lomet, B. Salzberg: The hB-Tree: A Multiattribute Indexing Method with Good Guaranteed Performance, *ACM Transactions on Database Systems* **15** (1990) 625–658.

F. Luccio, L. Pagli: On the Upper Bound for the Rotation Distance of Binary Trees, *Information Processing Letters* **31** (1989) 57–60.

G.S. Lueker: A Data Structure for Orthogonal Range Queries, in: FOCS 1978 (Proceedings 19th IEEE Symposium Foundations of Computer Science), 28–34.

G.S. Lueker, M. Molodowitch: More Analysis of Double Hashing, in: STOC 1988 (Proceedings 20th Annual ACM Symposium on Theory of Computing), 354–359.

G.S. Lueker, D.E. Willard: A Data Structure for Dynamic Range Queries, *Information Processing Letters* **15** (1982) 209–213.

R.W.P. Luk: Near Optimal β-Heap, *The Computer Journal* **42** (1999) 391–399.

G. Lyon: Achieving Hash Table Searches in One or Two Bucket Probes, *The Computer Journal* **28** (1985) 313–318.

M.G. Maaß: Linear Bidirectional On-Line Construction of Affix Trees, *Algorithmica* **37** (2003) 43–74.

J.A.T. Maddison: Fast Lookup in Hash Tables with Direct Rehashing, *The Computer Journal* **23** (1980) 188–189.

R. Maelbráncke, H. Olivié: Dynamic Tree Rebalancing Using Recurrent Rotations, *International Journal Foundations of Computer Science* **5** (1994) 247–260.

D. Maier: An Efficient Method for Storing Ancestor Information in Trees, *SIAM Journal on Computing* **8** (1979) 599–618.

D. Maier, S.C. Salveter: Hysterical B-Trees, *Information Processing Letters* **12** (1981) 199–202.

H.G. Mairson: The Effect of Table Expansion on the Program Complexity of Perfect Hash Functions, *BIT* **32** (1992) 430–440.

B.S. Majewski, N.C. Wormald, G. Havas, Z.J. Czech: A Family of Perfect Hashing Methods, *The Computer Journal* **39** (1996) 547–554.

M.E. Majster, A. Reiser: Efficient Online Construction and Correction of Position Trees, *SIAM Journal on Computing* **9** (1980) 785–807.

E. Mäkinen: On Top-Down Splaying, *BIT* **27** (1987) 330–339.

E. Mäkinen: On the Rotation Distance of Binary Trees, *Information Processing Letters* **26** (1988) 271–272.

C. Makris, A. Tsakalidis, K. Tsichlas: Reflected Min-Max Heaps, *Information Processing Letters* **86** (2003) 209–214.

E.G. Mallach: Scatter Storage Techniques: A Unifying Viewpoint and a Method for Reducing Retrieval Times, *The Computer Journal* **20** (1977) 137–140.

K. Maly: Compressed Tries, *Communications ACM* **19** (1978) 409–415.

U. Manber, G. Myers: Suffix Arrays: A New Method for On-Line String Searching, *SIAM Journal on Computing* **22** (1993) 935–948.

H. Mannila, E. Ukkonen: The Set Union Problem with Backtracking, in: ICALP 1986 (Proceedings 13th International Colloquium on Automata, Languages, and Programming), Springer. *LNCS* **226**, 236–243.

Y. Mansour, N. Nisan, P. Tiwari: The Computational Complexity of Universal Hashing, *Theoretical Computer Science* **107** (1993) 121–133.

G. Manzini, P. Ferragina: Engineering a Lightweight Suffix Array Construction Algorithm, *Algorithmica* **40** (2004) 33–50.

G. Markowsky, J.L. Carter, M.N. Wegman: Analysis of a Universal Class of Hash Functions, in: MFCS 1978 (Proceedings Conference on Mathematical Foundations of Computer Science), Springer. *LNCS* **64**, 345–354.

C. Martel: Self-Adjusting Multi-Way Search Trees, *Information Processing Letters* **38** (1991) 135–141.

W.A. Martin, D.N. Ness: Optimal Binary Trees Grown with a Sorting Algorithm, *Communications ACM* **15** (1972) 88–93.

C. Martinez, S. Roura: Randomized Binary Search Trees, *Journal of the ACM* **4** (1998) 288–323.

H.A. Maurer, T. Ottmann, H.-W. Six: Implementing Dictionaries Using Binary Trees of Very Small Height, *Information Processing Letters* **5** (1976) 11–14.

E.M. McCreight: A Space Economical Suffix Tree Construction Algorithm, *Journal of the ACM* **23** (1976) 262–272.

E.M. McCreight: Pagination of B*-Trees with Variable-Length Records, *Communications ACM* **20** (1977) 670–674.

C.J.H. McDiarmid, B.A. Reed: Building Heaps Fast, *Journal of Algorithms* **10** (1989) 352–365.

K. Mehlhorn: Dynamic Binary Search, *SIAM Journal on Computing* **8** (1979) 175–198.

K. Mehlhorn: On the Program Size of Perfect and Universal Hash Functions, in: FOCS 1982 (Proceedings 23rd Annual IEEE Symposium on Foundations of Computer Science), 170–175.

K. Mehlhorn, S. Näher, H. Alt: A Lower Bound on the Complexity of the Union-Split-Find Problem, *SIAM Journal on Computing* **17** (1988) 1093–1102.

K. Mehlhorn, M.H. Overmars: Optimal Dynamization of Decomposable Searching Problems, *Information Processing Letters* **12** (1981) 93–98.

D.P. Mehta, S. Sahni (eds.): *Handbook of Data Structures*, CRC Press/Chapman & Hall 2005.

M. Mitzenmacher: Compressed Bloom Filters, in: PODC 2001 (Proceedings 20th ACM Symposium on Principles of Distributed Computing), 144–150.

K. Morimoto, H. Iriguchi, J.-I. Aoe: A Method for Compressing Trie Structures, *Software – Practice and Experience* **24** (1994) 265–288.

J.M. Morris: Traversing Binary Trees Simply and Cheaply, *Information Processing Letters* **9** (1979) 197–200.

D.R. Morrison: PATRICIA – Practical Algorithm to Retrieve Information Coded in Alphanumeric, *Journal of the ACM* **15** (1968) 514–534.

J.K. Mullin: Change Area B-Trees: A Technique to Aid Error Recovery, *The Computer Journal* **24** (1981a) 367–373.

J.K. Mullin: Tightly Controlled Linear Hashing Without Separate Overflow Storage, *BIT* **21** (1981b) 390–400.

J.K. Mullin: A Second Look at Bloom Filters, *Communications ACM* **26** (1983) 570–571.

J.K. Mullin: Spiral Storage: Efficient Dynamic Hashing with Constant Performance, *The Computer Journal* **28** (1985) 330–334.

J.K. Mullin: Accessing Textual Documents Using Compressed Indexes of Small Bloom Filters, *The Computer Journal* **30** (1987) 343–348.

J.K. Mullin: A Caution on Universal Classes of Hash Functions, *Information Processing Letters* **37** (1991) 247–256.

J.I. Munro, T. Papadakis, R. Sedgewick: Deterministic Skip Lists, in: SODA 1992 (Proceedings 3rd ACM-SIAM Symposium on Discrete Algorithms), 367–375.

J.I. Munro, V. Raman, S.S. Rao: Space Efficient Suffix Trees, *Journal of Algorithms* **39** (2001) 205–222.

E.W. Myers: Efficient Applicative Data Types, in: POPL 1984 (Proceedings 11th ACM Symposium on Principles of Programming Languages), 66–75.

J.C. Na: Linear-Time Construction of Compressed Suffix Arrays Using $o(n \log n)$-Bit Working Space for Large Alphabets, in: CPM 1995 (Proceedings 16th Annual Symposium on Combinatorial Pattern Matching), Springer. *LNCS* **3537** (2005) 57–67.

J. Nievergelt: Binary Search Trees and File Organization, *ACM Computing Surveys* **6** (1974) 195–207.

J. Nievergelt, H. Hinterberger, K.C. Sevcik: The Grid File: An Adaptable, Symmetric Multikey File Structure, *ACM Transactions on Database Systems* **9** (1984) 38–71.

J. Nievergelt, E.M. Reingold: Binary Trees of Bounded Balance, *SIAM Journal on Computing* **2** (1973) 33–43.

J. Nievergelt, P. Widmayer: Spatial Data Structures: Concepts and Design Choices, in: Handbook of Computational Geometry, J.-R. Sack, J. Urrutia, eds., Elsevier 1999, 723–764.

J. Nievergelt, C.-K. Wong: Upper Bounds for the Total Path Length of Binary Trees, *Journal ACM* **20** (1973) 1–6.

S. Nilsson, M. Tikkanen: Implementing a Dynamic Compressed Trie, in: WAE 1998 (Proceedings 2nd Workshop on Algorithms Engineering), Max-Planck-Institut für Informatik, Saarbrücken 1998, 25–36.

S. Nilsson, M. Tikkanen: An Experimental Study of Compression Methods for Dynamic Tries, *Algorithmica* **33** (2002) 19–33.

H. Noltemeier: On a Generalization of Heaps, in: WG 1980 (Proceedings Workshop on Graph-Theoretic Concepts in Computer Science), Springer. *LNCS* **100** (1981) 127–136.

O. Nurmi, E. Soisalon-Soininen: Chromatic Binary Search Trees – A Structure for Concurrent Rebalancing, *Acta Informatica* **33** (1996) 547–557.

O. Nurmi, E. Soisalon-Soininen, D. Wood: Concurrency Control in Database Structures with Relaxed Balance, in: PODS 1987 (Proceedings 6th ACM Symposium on Principles of Database Systems), 170–176.

M. Nykänen, E. Ukkonen: Finding Lowest Common Ancestors in Arbitrarily Directed Trees, *Information Processing Letters* **50** (1994) 307–310.

S. Olariu, C. Overstreet, Z. Wen: A Mergeable Double-Ended Priority Queue, *The Computer Journal* **34** (1991) 423–427.

H.J. Olivié: On the Relationship between Son-Trees and Symmetric Binary B-Trees, *Information Processing Letter* **10** (1980) 4–8.

H.J. Olivié: A New Class of Balanced Search Trees: Half-Balanced Binary Search Trees, *RAIRO Informatique Théorique* **16** (1982) 51–71.

R. Orlandic, H.M. Mahmoud: Storage Overhead of O-Trees, B-Trees and Prefix B-Trees: A Comparative Analysis, *International Journal Foundations of Computer Science* **7** (1996) 209–226.

T. Ottmann, D.S. Parker, A.L. Rosenberg, H.-W. Six, D. Wood: Minimal-Cost Brother Trees, *SIAM Journal on Computing* **13** (1984) 197–217.

T. Ottmann, H.-W. Six: Eine neue Klasse von ausgeglichenen Binärbäumen, *Angewandte Informatik* **9** (1976) 395–400.

T. Ottmann, H.-W. Six, D. Wood: Right Brother Trees, *Communications ACM* **21** (1978) 769–776.

T. Ottmann, D. Wood: Deletion in One-Sided Height-Balanced Search Trees, *International Journal Computational Mathematics* **6** (1978) 265–271.

S.F. Ou, A.L. Tharp: Hash Storage Utilization for Single-Probe Retrieval Linear Hashing, *The Computer Journal* **34** (1991) 455–468.

M. Ouksel, P. Scheuermann: Implicit Data Structures for Linear Hashing Schemes, *Information Processing Letters* **29** (1988) 183–189.

M. Overmars: Dynamization of Order Decomposable Set Problems, *Journal of Algorithms* **2** (1981a) 245–260.

M. Overmars: General Methods for "All Elements" and "All Pairs" Problems, *Information Processing Letters* **12** (1981b) 99–102.

M. Overmars: An $O(1)$ Average Time Update Scheme for Balanced Search Trees, *Bulletin of the EATCS* **18** (1982) 27–29.

M. Overmars: *The Design of Dynamic Data Structures*, Springer. *LNCS* **156**, 1983.

M. Overmars, J. van Leeuwen: Dynamically Maintaining Configurations in the Plane, in STOC 1980 (Proceedings 12th Annual ACM Symposium on Theory of Computing), 135–145.

M. Overmars, J. van Leeuwen: Some Principles for Dynamizing Decomposable Searching Problems, *Information Processing Letters* **12** (1981a) 49–53.

M. Overmars, J. van Leeuwen: Worst-Case Optimal Insertion and Deletion Methods for Decomposable Searching Problems, *Information Processing Letters* **12** (1981b) 168–173.

M. Overmars, C.-K. Yap: New Upper Bounds in Klee's Measure Problem, *SIAM Journal on Computing* **20** (1991) 1034–1045.

A. Pagh, R. Pagh, S.S. Rao: An Optimal Bloom Filter Replacement, in: SODA 2005 (Proceedings 16th ACM-SIAM Symposium on Discrete Algorithms), 823–829.

R. Pagh, F.F. Rodler: Lossy Dictionaries, in: ESA 2001 (Proceedings of the 9th Annual European Symposium on Algorithms), Springer. *LNCS* **2161**, 300–311.

R. Pagh, F.F. Rodler: Cuckoo Hashing, *Journal of Algorithms* **51** (2004) 122–144.

L. Pagli: Self-Adjusting Hash Tables, *Information Processing Letters* **21** (1985) 23–25.

T. Papadakis, J.I. Munro, P.V. Poblete: Average Search and Update Costs in Skip Lists, *BIT* **32** (1992) 316–332.

M. Pătraşcu: Lower Bounds for 2-Dimensional Range Counting, in: STOC 2007 (Proceedings 39th Annual ACM Symposium on Theory of Computing), 40–46.

M. Pătraşcu, E.D. Demaine: Tight Bounds for the Partial-Sums Problem, in: SODA 2004 (Proceedings 15th ACM-SIAM Symposium on Discrete Algorithms), 20–29.

P.K. Pearson: Fast Hashing of Variable-Length Text Strings, *Communications ACM* **33** (1990) 677–680.

S. Pettie: Towards a Final Analysis of Pairing Heaps, in: FOCS 2005 (Proceedings 46th Annual IEEE Symposium on Foundations of Computer Science), 174–183.

P.V. Poblete, J.I. Munro: Last-Come-First-Served Hashing, *Journal of Algorithms* **10** (1989) 228–248.

J.A. La Poutré: New Techniques for the Union-Find Problem, in: SODA 1990a (Proceedings 1st ACM-SIAM Symposium on Discrete Algorithms), 54–63.

J.A. La Poutré: Lower Bounds for the Union-Find and the Split-Find Problem on Pointer Machines, in: STOC 1990b (Proceedings 22nd Annual ACM Symposium on Theory of Computing), 583–591.

O. Procopiuc, P.K. Agarwal, L. Arge, J.S. Vitter: Bkd-Tree: A Dynamic Scalable kd-Tree, in: SSTD 2003 (Proceedings 8th International Symposium on Spatial and Temporal Databases) Springer. *LNCS* **2750**, 46–65.

W. Pugh: Skip Lists: A Probabilistic Alternative to Balanced Trees, *Communications ACM* **33** (1990) 437–449.

S.J. Puglisi, W.F. Smyth, A.H. Turpin: A Taxonomy of Suffix Array Construction Algorithms, *Computing Surveys* **39** (2007) Article 4, 31 pages.

K.-J. Räihä, S.H. Zweben: An Optimal Insertion Algorithm for One-Sided Height-Balanced Binary Search Trees, *Communications ACM* **22** (1979) 508–512.

M.V. Ramakrishna: Analysis of Random Probing Hashing, *Information Processing Letters* **31** (1989a) 83–90.

M.V. Ramakrishna: Practical Performance of Bloom Filters and Parallel Free-Text Searching, *Communications ACM* **32** (1989b) 1237–1239.

K. Ramamohanarao, J.W. Lloyd: Dynamic Hashing Schemes, *The Computer Journal* **25** (1982) 478–485.

N.S.V. Rao, V.K. Vaishnavi, S.S. Iyengar: On the Dynamization of Data Structures, *BIT* **28** (1988) 37–53.

K.V. Ravi Kanth, A. Singh: Optimal Dynamic Range Searching in Non-Replicating Index Structures, in: ICDT 1999 (Proceedings 7th International Conference on Database Theory) Springer. *LNCS* **1540**, 257–276.

M. Regnier: Analysis of Grid File Algorithms, *BIT* **25** (1985) 335–357.

R.L. Rivest: Optimal Arrangement of Keys in a Hash Table, *Journal of the ACM* **25** (1978) 200–209.

J.T. Robinson: The kdB-Tree: A Search Structure for Large Multidimensional Indexes, in: SIGMOD 1981 (Proceedings 1981 ACM SIGMOD Conference on Management of Data), 10–18.

J.M. Robson: An Improved Algorithm for Traversing Binary Trees without Auxiliary Stack, *Information Processing Letters* **2** (1973) 12–14.

J.-R. Sack, T. Strothotte: An Algorithm for Merging Heaps, *Acta Informatica* **22** (1985) 171–186.

T.J. Sager: A Polynomial-Time Generator for Minimal Perfect Hash Functions, *Communications ACM* **28** (1985) 522–532.

H. Samet: *The Design and Analysis of Spatial Data Structures*, Addison-Wesley 1990.

H. Samet: *Foundations of Multidimensional and Metric Data Structures*, Morgan Kaufmann 2006.

V. Samoladas, D.P. Miranker: A Lower Bound Theorem for Indexing Schemes and Its Application to Multidimensional Range Queries, in: PODS 1998 (Proceedings 17th ACM Symposium on Principles of Database Systems), 44–51.

J.B. Saxe: On the Number of Range Queries in k-Space, *Discrete Applied Mathematics* **1** (1979) 217–225.

J.P. Schmidt, A. Siegel: The Spatial Complexity of Oblivious k-Probe Hash Functions, *SIAM Journal on Computing* **19** (1990) 775–786.

B. Schoenmakers: A Systematic Analysis of Splaying, *Information Processing Letter* **45** (1993) 41–50.

B. Schoenmakers: A Tight Lower Bound for Top-Down Skew Heaps, *Information Processing Letter* **61** (1997) 279–284.

M. Scholl: New File Organizations Based on Dynamic Hashing, *ACM Transactions on Database Systems* **6** (1981) 194–211.

R. Seidel, C.R. Aragon: Randomized Search Trees, *Algorithmica* **16** (1996) 464–497.

R. Seidel, M. Sharir: Top-Down Analysis of Path Compression, *SIAM Journal on Computing* **34** (2005) 515–525.

S. Sen: Some Observations on Skip-Lists, *Information Processing Letter* **39** (1991) 173–176.

S. Sen: Fractional Cascading Revisited, *Journal of Algorithms* **19** (1995) 161–172.

M. Sharir: Fast Composition of Sparse Maps, *Information Processing Letters* **15** (1982) 183–185.

M.A. Shepherd, W.J. Phillips, C.-K. Chu: A Fixed-Size Bloom Filter for Searching Textual Documents, *The Computer Journal* **89** (1989) 212–219.

M. Sherk: Self-Adjusting k-ary Search Trees, *Journal of Algorithms* **19** (1995) 25–44.

A. Siegel: On Universal Classes of Fast High-Performance Hash Functions, Their Time-Space Tradeoff, and Their Applications, in: FOCS 1989 (Proceedings 30th IEEE Symposium Foundations of Computer Science), 20–25.

A. Siegel: On Universal Classes of Extremely Random Constant-Time Hash Functions, *SIAM Journal on Computing* **33** (2004) 505–543.

Y.V. Silva-Filho: Average Case Analysis of Region Search in Balanced k-d-Trees, *Information Processing Letters* **8** (1979) 219–223.

Y.V. Silva-Filho: Optimal Choice of Discriminators in a Balanced k-d-Trees, *Information Processing Letters* **13** (1981) 67–70.

D.D. Sleator, R.E. Tarjan: A Data Structure for Dynamic Trees, *Journal of Computer and System Sciences* **26** (1983) 362–391.

D.D. Sleator, R.E. Tarjan: Self-Adjusting Binary Search Trees, *Journal ACM* **32** (1985) 652–686.

D.D. Sleator, R.E. Tarjan: Self-Adjusting Heaps, *SIAM Journal on Computing* **15** (1986) 52–69.

D.D. Sleator, R.E. Tarjan, W.P. Thurston: Rotation Distance, Triangulations, and Hyperbolic Geometry, *Journal AMS* **1** (1988) 647–682.

M.H.M. Smid: A Data Structure for the Union-Find Problem Having Good Single-Operation Complexity, *Algorithms Review* **1** (1990) 1–11 (Newsletter of the ESPRIT II Basic Research Actions Program, Project 3075 ALCOM).

E. Soisalon-Soininen, P. Widmayer: Relaxed Balancing in Search Trees, in: *Advances in Algorithms, Languages, and Complexity*, Kluwer 1997, 267–283.

S. Soule: A Note on the Nonrecursive Traversal of Binary Trees, *The Computer Journal* **20** (1977) 350–352.

R. Sprugnoli: Perfect Hashing Functions: A Single Probe Retrieving Method for Static Sets, *Communications ACM* **20** (1977) 841–850.

R. Sprugnoli: On the Allocation of Binary Trees to Secondary Storage, *BIT* **21** (1981) 305–316.

J.T. Stasko, J.S. Vitter: Pairing Heaps: Experiments and Analysis, *Communications ACM* **30** (1987) 234–249.

D. Stinson: Universal Hashing and Authentification Codes, *Designs, Codes and Cryptography* **4** (1994) 369–380.

Q.F. Stout, B.L. Warren: Tree Rebalancing in Optimal Time and Space, *Communications ACM* **29** (1986) 902–908.

T. Strothotte, P. Eriksson, S. Vallner: A Note on Constructing Min-Max-Heaps, *BIT* **29** (1989) 251–256.

T. Strothotte, J.-R. Sack: Heaps in Heaps, *Congressus Numerantium* **49** (1985) 223–235.

A. Subramanian: An Explanation of Splaying, *Journal of Algorithms* **20** (1996) 512–525.

R. Sundar: Worst-Case Data Structures for the Priority Queue with Attrition, *Information Processing Letters* **31** (1989) 69–75.

F. Suraweera: Use of Doubly Chained Tree Structures in File Organization for Optimal Searching, *The Computer Journal* **29** (1986) 52–59.

E.H. Sussenguth: Use of Tree Structures for Processing Files, *Communications of the ACM* **6** (1963) 272–279.

M. al-Suwaiyel, E. Horowitz: Algorithms for Trie Compaction, *ACM Transactions on Database Systems* **9** (1984) 243–263.

H. Suzuki, A. Ishiguro, T. Nishizeki: Variable-Priority Queue and Doughnut Rooting, *Journal of Algorithms* **13** (1992) 606–635.

T. Takaoka: Theory of Trinomial Heaps, in: COCOON 2000 (Proceedings 6th International Symposium on Computing and Combinatorics), Springer. *LNCS* **1858**, 362–372.

T. Takaoka: Theory of 2-3 Heaps, *Discrete Applied Mathematics* **126** (2003) 115–128.

M. Talamo, P. Vocca: A Data Structure for Lattices Representation, *Theoretical Computer Science* **175** (1997) 373–392.

M. Talamo, P. Vocca: An Efficient Data Structure for Lattice Operations, *SIAM Journal on Computing* **28** (1999) 1783–1805.

M. Tamminen: Order Preserving Extendible Hashing and Bucket Tries, *BIT* **21** (1981) 419–435.

M. Tamminen: Extensible Hashing with Overflow, *Information Processing Letters* **15** (1982) 227–232.

R.E. Tarjan: Efficiency of a Good But Not Linear Set Union Algorithm, *Journal of the ACM* **22** (1975) 215–225.

R.E. Tarjan: Applications of Path Compression on Balanced Trees, *Journal of the ACM* **26** (1979a) 690–715.

R.E. Tarjan: A Class of Algorithms which Require Nonlinear Time to Maintain Disjoint Sets, *Journal of Computer and System Sciences* **18** (1979b) 110–127.

R.E. Tarjan: Updating a Balanced Search Tree in $O(1)$ Rotations, *Information Processing Letters* **16** (1983a) 253–257.

R.E. Tarjan: *Data Structures and Network Algorithms*, CBMS Lecture Note Series **44**, SIAM 1983b.

R.E. Tarjan, J. van Leeuwen: Worst-Case Analysis of Set Union Algorithms, *Journal of the ACM* **31** (1984) 245–281.

R.E. Tarjan, A.C.-C. Yao: Storing a Sparse Table, *Communications ACM* **22** (1979) 606–611.

M. Thorup: Equivalence Between Priority Queues and Sorting, in: FOCS 2002 (Proceedings 43rd Annual IEEE Symposium on Foundations of Computer Science), 125–134.

Y. Tian, S. Tata, R.A. Hankins, J.M. Patel: Practical Methods for Constructing Suffix Trees, *The VLDB Journal* **14** (2005) 281–299.

A.K. Tsakalidis: Maintaining Order in a Generalized Linked List, *Acta Informatica* **21** (1984) 101–112.

A.K. Tsakalidis: AVL-Trees for Localized Search, *Information and Computation* **67** (1985) 173–194.

A.K. Tsakalidis: The Nearest Common Ancestor in a Dynamic Tree, *Acta Informatica* **25** (1988) 37–54.

E. Ukkonen: On-Line Construction of Suffix Trees, *Algorithmica* **14** (1995) 249–260.

J.D. Ullman: A Note on the Efficiency of Hashing Functions, *Journal of the ACM* **19** (1972) 569–575.

P.M. Vaidya: Space-Time Trade-Offs for Orthogonal Range Queries, *SIAM Journal on Computing* **18** (1989) 748–758.

V.K. Vaishnavi: Computing Point Enclosures, *IEEE Transactions on Computers* **31** (1982) 22–29.

V.K. Vaishnavi: Weighted Leaf AVL-Trees, *SIAM Journal on Computing* **16** (1987) 503–537, also Erratum **19** (1990) p. 591.

J.S. Vitter: External Memory Algorithms and Data Structures, *ACM Computing Surveys* **33** (2001) 209–271.

J. Vuillemin: A Data Structure for Manipulating Priority Queues, *Communications of the ACM* **21** (1978) 309–315.

J. Vuillemin: A Unifying Look at Data Structures, *Communications of the ACM* **23** (1980) 229–239.

I. Wegener: Bottom-Up Heapsort, A New Variant of Heapsort Beating an Average Quicksort (If *n* Is Not Very Small), *Theoretical Computer Science* **118** (1993) 81–98.

P. Weiner: Linear Pattern Matching Algorithms, in: Proceedings of the 14th Annual IEEE Symposium on Switching and Automata Theory, 1973, 1–11.

M.A. Weiss: Linear-Time Construction of Treaps and Cartesian Trees, *Information Processing Letters* **52** (1994) 253–257; see also note in next volume **53** (1995) p. 127.

Z. Wen: New Algorithms for the LCA Problem and the Binary Tree Reconstruction Problem, *Information Processing Letters* **51** (1994) 11–16.

J. Westbrook, R.E. Tarjan: Amortized Analysis of Algorithms for Set Union with Backtracking, *SIAM Journal on Computing* **18** (1989) 1–11.

D.E. Willard: Maintaining Dense Sequential Files in a Dynamic Environment, in: STOC 1982 (Proceedings 14th Annual ACM Symposium on Theory of Computing), 114–121.

D.E. Willard: New Data Structures for Orthogonal Range Queries, *SIAM Journal on Computing* **14** (1985) 232–253.

D.E. Willard: Good Worst-Case Algorithms for Inserting and Deleting Records in Dense Sequential Files, in: ACM SIGMOD Newsletter **15** (June 1986) 251–260.

D.E. Willard: A Density Control Algorithm for Doing Insertions and Deletions in a Sequentially Ordered File in Good Worst-Case Time, *Information and Computation* **97** (1992) 150–204.

D.E. Willard, G.S. Lueker: Adding Range Restriction Capability to Dynamic Data Structures, *Journal of the ACM* **32** (1985) 597–617.

J.W.J. Williams: Algorithm 232: Heapsort, *Communications of the ACM* **7** (1964) 347–348.

J. Wogulis: Self-Adjusting and Split Sequence Hash Tables, *Information Processing Letters* **30** (1989) 185–188.

G. Xunrang, Z. Yuzhang: A New Heapsort Algorithm and the Analysis of Its Complexity, *The Computer Journal* **33** (1990) p. 281.

W.-P. Yang, M.W. Du: A Backtracking Method for Constructing Perfect Hash Functions from a Set of Mapping Functions, *BIT* **25** (1985) 148–164.

A.C.-C. Yao: Should Tables Be Sorted?, *Journal of the ACM* **28** (1981) 615–628.

A.C.-C. Yao: Space-Time Tradeoff for Answering Range Queries, in: STOC 1982 (Proceedings 14th Annual ACM Symposium on Theory of Computing) 128–136.

A.C.-C. Yao: Uniform Hashing Is Optimal, *Journal of the ACM* **32** (1985a) 687–693.

A.C.-C. Yao: On Optimal Arrangements of Keys with Double Hashing, *Journal of Algorithms* **6** (1985b) 253–264.

A.C.-C. Yao: On the Complexity of Maintaining Partial Sums, *SIAM Journal on Computing* **14** (1985c) 277–288.

A.C.-C. Yao, F.F. Yao: Dictionary Look-Up with One Error, *Journal of Algorithms* **25** (1997) 194–202.

N. Zivani, H.J. Olivié, G.H. Gonnet: The Analysis of an Improved Symmetric Binary B-Tree Algorithm, *The Computer Journal* **28** (1985) 417–425.

S.H. Zweben, M.A. McDonald: An Optimal Method for Deletion in One-Sided Height-Balanced Trees, *Communications of the ACM* **21** (1978) 441–445.

Author Index

This is a list of authors of papers cited in this book, together with their current affiliation, where I could find it. This shows the wide geographic distribution of the subject, as well as some centers.

WILLIAM A. MARTIN: [Martin and Ness 1972] (died 1981)

CONRADO MARTINEZ: [Duch et al. 1998; Martinez and Roura 1998; Duch and Martinez 2002] Technical University of Catalonia at Barcelona, Spain

PAUL J. MARTINO: [Lipton et al. 1997] Ahpah.com, USA

TOSHIMITSU MASUZAWA: [Herman and Masuzawa 2001] University of Osaka, Japan

YOSSI MATIAS: [Cohen and Matias 2003] Tel Aviv University, Israel

D.G. MATSAKIS: [Burton et al. 1990]

HERMANN A. MAURER: [Maurer et al. 1976; Bentley and Maurer 1980; Edelsbrunner and Maurer 1981] Technical University of Graz, Austria

DAVID J. MCCLURKIN: [Georgakopoulos and McClurkin 2004] University of Crete, Greece

EDWARD M. MCCREIGHT: [Bayer and McCreight 1972; McCreight 1976, 1977; Guibas et al. 1977]

COLIN J.H. MCDIARMID: [McDiarmid and Reed 1989] Oxford University, Great Britain

M.A. MCDONALD: [Zweben and McDonald 1978]

KURT MEHLHORN: [Mehlhorn 1979, 1982; Blum and Mehlhorn 1980; Mehlhorn and Overmars 1981; Huddleston and Mehlhorn 1982; Hoffmann et al. 1986; Mehlhorn et al. 1988; Dietzfelbinger et al. 1994] Max-Planck-Institut für Informatik, Saarbrücken, Germany

DINESH P. MEHTA: [Mehta and Sahni 2005] Colorado School of Mines, USA

FRIEDHELM MEYER AUF DER HEIDE: [Dietzfelbinger et al. 1992, 1994] University of Paderborn, Germany

RAYMOND E. MILLER: [Karp et al. 1972] University of Maryland, USA

TOVA MILO: [Abiteboul et al. 2001; Kaplan et al. 2002] Tel Aviv University, Israel

PETER BRO MILTERSEN: [Alon et al. 1999; Buhrman et al. 2000] University of Aarhus, Denmark

DANIEL P. MIRANKER: [Samoladas and Miranker 1998] University of Texas at Austin, USA

MICHAEL MITZENMACHER: [Mitzenmacher 2001; Broder and Mitzenmacher 2004;

Bonomi et al. 2006] Harvard University, USA

EYAL MOLAD: [Kaplan et al. 2003]

MARIKO MOLODOVITCH: [Lueker and Molodowitch 1988] California State University at Fullerton, USA

KATSUSHI MORIMOTO: [Aoe et al. 1992; Morimoto et al. 1994]

PAT MORIN: [Bose et al. 2003; Devroye and Morin 2003; Devroye et al. 2004] Carleton University, Canada

JOSEPH M. MORRIS: [Morris 1979] Dublin City University, Ireland

DONALD R. MORRISON: [Morrison 1968]

JASON MORRISON: [Bose et al. 2003] Carleton University, Canada

JAMES K. MULLIN: [Mullin 1981a, b; 1983, 1985, 1987, 1991] University of Western Ontario, Canada

JAMES IAN MUNRO: [Allen and Munro 1978; Gonnet and Munro 1979, 1986; Gonnet et al. 1983; Celis et al. 1985; Dobkin and Munro 1985; Carlsson et al. 1988; Poblete and Munro 1989; Munro et al. 1992, 2001; Papadakis et al. 1992; Brodnik and Munro 1999] University of Waterloo, Canada

SHANMUGAVELAYUTHAM MUTHUKRISHNAN: [Ferragina et al. 1999] AT&T Labs–Research, USA

EUGENE W. MYERS: [Myers 1984; Fraser and Myers 1987; Manber and Myers 1993] (E.W. Myers identical with G. Myers) University of California at Berkeley, USA

JOONG CHAE NA: [Na 2005] Konkook University, Korea

STEFAN NÄHER: [Mehlhorn et al. 1988] University of Trier, Germany

ALEXANDROS NANOPOULOS: [Bozanis et al. 2003] Aristotle University of Thessaloniki, Greece

ANDY NEITZKE: [Lipton et al. 1997]

JAROSLAV NEŠETŘIL: [Loebl and Nešetřil 1997] Charles University Prague, Czech Republic

D.N. NESS: [Martin and Ness 1972]

BRADFOR G. NICKERSON: [Falconer and Nickerson 2005] University of New Brunswick, Canada

JÜRG NIEVERGELT: [Nievergelt and Reingold 1973; Nievergelt and Wong 1973; Nievergelt 1974; Fagin et al. 1979; Nievergelt et al. 1984; Nievergelt and

Subject Index

A problem of this subject index is that many structures or useful ideas are not named, so this index is comparatively short.

Printed in the United States
By Bookmasters